REASON AND CHARACTER

REASON & CHARACTER

The Moral Foundations of Aristotelian Political Philosophy

⊙ ⊙

LORRAINE SMITH PANGLE

⊙ ⊙ ⊙ ⊙ ⊙ ⊙ ⊙ ⊙ ⊙ ⊙ ⊙ ⊙ ⊙ ⊙ ⊙ ⊙ ⊙ ⊙

The University of Chicago Press
CHICAGO AND LONDON

The University of Chicago Press, Chicago 60637
The University of Chicago Press, Ltd., London

Published 2020
Printed in the United States of America

29 28 27 26 25 24 23 22 21 20 1 2 3 4 5

ISBN-13: 978-0-226-68816-9 (cloth)
ISBN-13: 978-0-226-68833-6 (e-book)
DOI: https://doi.org/10.7208/chicago/9780226688336.001.0001

Library of Congress Cataloging-in-Publication Data

Names: Pangle, Lorraine Smith, author.
Title: Reason and character : the moral foundations of Aristotelian political philosophy / Lorraine Smith Pangle.
Description: Chicago : University of Chicago Press, 2020. | Includes bibliographical references and index.
Identifiers: LCCN 2019039051 | ISBN 9780226688169 (cloth) | ISBN 9780226688336 (e-book)
Subjects: LCSH: Aristotle. Nicomachean ethics. | Ethics, Ancient.
Classification: LCC B430.P255 2020 | DDC 171/.3—dc23
LC record available at https://lccn.loc.gov/2019039051

♾ This paper meets the requirements of ANSI/NISO Z39.48-1992 (Permanence of Paper).

for Sophie

CONTENTS

INTRODUCTION

What does it mean to live a good life? What does it mean to live a happy life? Can reason guide us to an answer to these questions? To what extent is reason sufficient to ensure that we live by the insights that it grasps? About these questions Aristotle's *Nicomachean Ethics* has a great deal to say, much that we still can learn from, and, despite all the trees that have been felled and ink spilled in discussing them, more than a little that we still scarcely understand.

This book is a fresh examination of Aristotle's teaching on the relation between reason and moral virtue in the *Nicomachean Ethics*, taking as its point of departure the oft-noted but still perhaps not sufficiently appreciated fact that this treatise is the first half of a two-volume work on political science.[1] As such, it lays the foundation for Aristotelian political science and in significant ways for the field of political science altogether. The proper aim of the political community according to Aristotle is to promote the human good; it is the task of the *Nicomachean Ethics* to elaborate what this good is. The *Ethics* lays the groundwork for this project with its searching analysis of human nature, including the passions and aspirations that make us political and that make our political relations so fraught. The *Ethics* likewise contains Aristotle's fullest treatment of justice. It explores the deepest presuppositions that underlie our sense of justice—the way we hold one another responsible for good and bad actions and good and bad character. It provides Aristotle's fullest answer to the most radical question about justice, the question of why we should be just or moral at all, in its teaching on the essential relation of virtue to happiness. Filling out this answer, it gives a rich, psychologically subtle, and compelling account of eleven moral virtues, culminating in Aristotle's treatment of the highest standard of justice, natural right. And it contains Aristotle's fullest account of *phronēsis* or active wisdom, the intellectual virtue that guides the moral and political life.[2] In his account of all these things, Aristotle has a descriptive but also a constructive project. Indeed, in a certain way we can say he is the discoverer or even the inventor of moral virtue.[3]

Of course as long as there have been human beings they have had ideas of virtue and vice. From the earliest times those ideas centered on qualities essential for the defense and orderly functioning of the community. It is apt and revealing that, for example, the Greek term *aretē* means both virtue generally and the one quality that simple communities naturally need most urgently and honor most highly, courage. Virtue thus comes to sight originally and most fundamentally as civic virtue. Virtue so understood is open to the charge Glaucon famously makes in book 2 of Plato's *Republic*: why should I serve what is after all the good of everyone else, at a loss to myself? Plato's best answer to this question is the alternative model of virtue he presents through his unforgettable depiction of his teacher and chief interlocutor, Socrates, the philosopher par excellence. Virtue so understood is the thoughtful quest for wisdom by one who seeks ever stronger assurance that wisdom is indeed possible and is the greatest human good; virtue is, moreover, the active exercise of such provisional wisdom as the philosopher has, good for himself and often for others as well. For such a man courage is chiefly courage of thought, moderation is the austerity that comes of treating the body as a mere instrument of the mind, piety means respectful but dogged questioning of the traditional accounts of the gods, and justice means prudential law-abidingness but above all the good order of one's own soul.

It is in this context that we can best understand the Platonic Socrates' radical claim that virtue is knowledge. Especially if the best life is the philosophic life, if the greatest good is wisdom, might it not be that all virtue worthy of the name really reduces to wisdom? And is not real wisdom—thorough, well digested knowledge of what is good and why, and what is bad and why, and how we are prone to deceiving ourselves and why it is so terribly foolish to do so—powerful enough to make itself efficacious in action? Indeed, is there not in wrongdoing of every sort a defective grasp of what is really good? Thus emerge the Socratic paradoxes in all their uncompromising strangeness—the claims that all who know the good will do the good; that vice is ignorance; that vice is involuntary; that virtue guarantees happiness; that tyrants have no power and do virtually nothing of what they wish; and that the proper remedy for crime is education, not punishment. Those claims I examine in *Virtue Is Knowledge: The Moral Foundations of Socratic Political Philosophy*, to which the present work is intended as a companion volume.

To all of these radical Socratic claims Aristotle's ethical theory comes to sight as an eminently sober response. In the *Nicomachean Ethics* Aristotle acknowledges the importance of fortune as well as virtue for human happiness, and likewise the central place not only of understanding but of discipline, practice, and habituation in the cultivation of virtue. He repeatedly condemns the folly of people who take refuge in speeches instead of training themselves in virtue. Wisdom, he insists, is itself dependent on experience. To claim as Socrates does that virtue is knowledge is to ignore the critical part that healthy passions and good habituation play in shaping character; to claim that vice is ignorance and hence involuntary is to say what is neither true nor socially responsible. Aristotle insists that both virtue and vice are voluntary and that individuals are responsible for their characters. And he insists on the existence of *akrasia*, the failure of self-control in which one acts against one's better judgment, offering an extended and nuanced explanation of what it is and how it occurs.

As he thus parries the various thrusts of radical Socratic thought, Aristotle is engaged in the constructive project of forging traditional civic virtue and Socratic wisdom together into a new synthesis. In this account the individual's moral excellence is good for the political community but not chiefly aimed at the community's good. Instead, the implicit priorities of civic virtue are largely reversed: it is the highest task of politics to promote the happiness of individuals, now understood to consist in activity in accordance with virtue. As moral virtue is not subordinate to politics, neither is it to philosophy, although Aristotle's account of the moral life accords to reason a high place. Moral virtue is rather the perfection of a *kalos kagathos*, a serious individual who is both noble and good, a citizen but more than a citizen, a cultivated man of reason but less than a philosopher: a gentleman who will be most at home as a leading citizen of a free republic, but whose essential qualities and self-understanding and satisfactions are largely accessible to serious men and women in all times and places. Aristotle's account of moral virtue reflects his judgment that human beings are by nature political but not wholly so,[4] rational but not wholly so, beings who reach their fullest but rare perfection in a philosophic realm beyond politics, but who can also reach substantial fulfillment in political activity and considerable fulfillment likewise in the serious activities of private life. If the opportunity for the fullest and most challenging exercise of active wisdom in ruling or taking a leading part in republican self-government is available to few even in the best of times, it was already waning in Aristotle's own time with the rise of Philip and Alexander of Macedon. Perhaps making a virtue of necessity, in the *Ethics* Aristotle is working to foster a new, independent-minded, gentlemanly ethos that goes beyond traditional civic virtue and points toward philosophic virtue. The individual who takes his sights by Aristotle's account will be moderate though not ascetic, disinclined to moral indignation yet serious about justice, politically responsible while also self-reliant. He will place his happiness not in external honors and offices but in his own virtuous activity; hence he will not be dependent on a good political order for the seriousness and dignity of his life. At the same time, he will be rational and respectful of philosophy, though rather more inclined to view it from afar as something sublime and even divine than to give himself over to it.

In producing this account of moral virtue, Aristotle has as his project to clarify but also to refine and reform the standards of virtue that he found around him in classical Greece of the fourth century BCE. We shall see that he is respectful toward but not an uncritical follower of the conventional moral opinion of his time, as is evidenced by his introduction of several still nameless virtues, his silent omission of piety, his silent demotion of moral indignation, and his explicit exclusion of pious reverence or shame (*aidōs*) from the ranks of the virtues. Still less, however, is Aristotle a follower of conventionalism, the view, popular among philosophers and sophists, that nature teaches what is true everywhere and always and that morality and law are mere products of convention, although he acknowledges the variability of human laws and customs that has led others to that conclusion. But rather than offering a direct refutation of it, he engages throughout the *Ethics* in the both descriptive and constructive project of listening with extraordinary care to what ordinary people around him say about moral virtue, distinguishing what is more essential from what is less, highlighting the former and setting aside the latter to produce a depiction of virtue that is surprising in some of its contours but also deeply compelling. The result of this dialectical process of discovery and refinement he offers with an implicit challenge to all of his readers, near and far, highborn and commoner, to consider whether it does not, after all, do justice to what the better angels of their own natures tell them is the substance of good character and of a life worth living.[5]

One of the central features of this account is its sustained insistence on the autonomy of the moral life. Thus the *Ethics* carves out a distinct realm of human excellence, subordinate neither to the needs of the body nor to the needs of the political community nor to the demands and rule of philosophy, a realm constituted by action in accordance with moral virtue, noble action that is chosen just because it is right, just "for itself" or "for the sake of the noble," and that promises to constitute a happy life. This independent realm of action or *praxis* Aristotle distinguishes sharply from the realm of theoretical wisdom on one hand and from the productive work of the arts on the other. Theoretical wisdom is concerned with the unchanging truths of philosophy and science; the arts are directed to making products that are themselves in the service of something further; but *praxis*, the activity of moral virtue, is splendidly independent as a noble and choiceworthy end in itself. This idea of the autonomy of the moral realm is lent considerable support by the thesis Aristotle propounds that moral virtue is the perfection of a distinct part of the soul, neither theoretical nor simply subrational but capable of listening to and following the voice of reason. Its excellence is defined not by its possession of truth but by the correct constellation of the passions, correct habits, and the love of the noble. The autonomy of the moral realm is lent further support by Aristotle's teaching that, to the extent that morality does need reason to guide it, it has its own intellectual virtue, *phronēsis* or active wisdom, a virtue that he presents not as the mere application of *sophia* or theoretical wisdom but as independent and valuable as an end in its own right.

Taking as its point of departure Aristotle's responses to Plato's Socrates, then, this book proceeds to explore the place of reason and intellectual virtue in Aristotle's moral thought, by means of a close and thematically focused commentary on those extensive portions of the *Nicomachean Ethics* in which he illuminates the role of reason in guiding the moral life, 1.1–7.10. How exactly do knowledge and opinion work in determining moral choice? Are we free to choose other than we do, given who we are and how things appear to us? Does anyone in fact ever choose vice? In what sense are we each responsible for our good or bad character? How does reason determine the mean in each of the virtues? What end or standard does active wisdom look to in guiding moral choice? And how coherent will Aristotle's new presentation of moral virtue prove to be on close examination, this new synthesis of civic and philosophic virtue that in important ways claims to be independent of both? Can acts of moral virtue truly be chosen and performed simply for their own sakes, in a way that will vindicate the purported completeness and autonomy of the moral life? Does active wisdom hold up to scrutiny as the perfection of a separate part of the soul, quite independent of theoretical wisdom and both complete and sovereign within its own sphere? This book will explore the possibility that Plato and Aristotle are in fact closer than they seem in their fundamental thought on these matters, even as Aristotle develops on the basis of Socratic insights a new moral theory that is uniquely supportive both of thriving active lives and of philosophical reflection.

Aristotle registers an important agreement with Plato in book 1 of the *Nicomachean Ethics* with his contention that the activity of virtue is the core and substance of happiness. As he does at the opening of the *Eudemian Ethics*, Aristotle marks his departure from conventional opinion by directly challenging the inscription in the temple of Delos that reads, "Noblest is what is most just, and best is to be healthy, but most pleasant by nature is to attain what one loves" (1099a27–28; cf. *EE* 1214a5–6).[6] Aristotle makes it a major goal to refute this common opinion, divinely sanctioned though it may claim to be, and to show that at the deepest level there is a unity in what we most want and need and admire. Yet this agreement never leads him to say that mere knowledge of what happiness is suffices to attain it.

Aristotle most directly challenges the Socratic thesis that virtue is knowledge in his discussion of voluntary and involuntary action, choice, and responsibility for character in the first five chapters of book 3. Here he develops a socially responsible theory of choice and character in which he makes a strong case for holding adults fully accountable for their actions, and he engages with unusual directness Socrates' most radical challenges to conventional moral opinion. To be sure, Aristotle does not here refer to Socrates by name. But four times in the course of these five short chapters, he finds his discussion somehow interrupted by a critic—a familiar, dogged, buttonholing sort of critic, whom he tries repeatedly but unsuccessfully to set aside. In the end Aristotle in fact makes major concessions to this strange interlocutor, who briefly succeeds in turning the *Ethics* into something of a Socratic dialogue and perhaps even wins the argument. The explicitly dialectical character of these chapters reflects the unusual frankness with which they explore some of the deepest moral problems. What is the theoretical basis for Aristotle's rejection of the Socratic position on the voluntariness of wrongdoing and the responsibility for character? Does his criticism amount to a significant disagreement in principle, or are the differences largely or even entirely due to a different rhetorical strategy?

Aristotle's treatment of the separate moral and intellectual virtues in books 3–6 of the *Nicomachean Ethics* in large part seems designed precisely to counter the Socratic claims that virtue is one and that all virtues reduce to wisdom. Indeed, especially in its middle books, the *Ethics* is in no small degree a project in testing these Socratic theses by assuming the opposite and exploring what follows. Thus, unlike Plato's Socrates, who treats the various virtues as different applications of a single unified wisdom about the human good and who hence tends to define the virtues in broad and overlapping ways,[7] Aristotle defines the virtues narrowly, giving each its own carefully delineated sphere and characterizing it not by the knowledge that guides it but by its own, properly habituated passions. Likewise, Aristotle is most careful not to present the exercise of moral virtue as calculating or in any way instrumental: he insists that virtuous action is chosen just for itself or for the sake of the noble, which is not reducible to the advantageous. If the noble is the goal of virtuous action, it seems especially plausible that one might know what is noble and yet not choose it.

An important task, then, will be to determine exactly what Aristotle means by the noble. Another will be to determine where active wisdom gets its ultimate principles or starting points, whether the idea of the noble gives sufficient clarity about the target reason needs to look to in each case to hit the proper mean, and how active wisdom harmonizes the noble as a standard with the individual's concerns for his own happiness and for the common good. Still another will be to assess the relation of active wisdom to theoretical wisdom and to assess the ultimate cogency of the division of intellectual faculties and parts of the soul Aristotle draws in book 6. Aristotle seems to depart sharply from the Socratic view of intellectual virtue and its relation to moral virtue through most of book 6, but he will make important concessions to Socrates on the unity of the virtues at the end.

Finally, in the first ten chapters of book 7 of the *Nicomachean Ethics* Aristotle undertakes a prolonged discussion of self-control and failures of self-control (*enkrateia* and *akrasia*) that again seems to depart radically from the Socratic claim that reason is sovereign and is never dragged about like a slave,[8] a discussion that seems, by contrast, to do full justice to the ordinary experience of lapses of self-control. Yet as Aristotle digs down into this experience and analyzes its causes, he will again qualify his claims about the possibility of *akrasia* in ways that grant considerable ground to the Socratic arguments about the sovereignty of knowledge of the good.

How far apart are Aristotle and Plato in the end, then, on the questions of reason's place in choice and character and our ultimate responsibility for our own characters? To some considerable extent the difference does seem to be one of rhetoric, following the two authors' very different rhetorical projects. Where Plato loves to bewilder, bedazzle, and inspire his readers, especially his young and most promising readers, with unsettling challenges to ordinary moral and political life and intimations of the divine madness that is philosophy, Aristotle with his sober good sense appeals first and foremost to mature gentlemen and statesmen, supporting and ennobling their self-understanding, their sense of independence from the vicissitudes of fortune, and their respect for reason. Where Plato is swift to challenge ordinary assumptions about moral responsibility, Aristotle prefers to foreground the effectual truth of the matter, the truth that how we think and talk about responsibility affects the character of the decisions we in fact make and the actions of which we are in fact capable, and that certain ways of thinking are better able than others to promote individual happiness and a healthy political society.

One possibility is that these differences reflect a division of labor, whereby each of the two philosophers appeals to a different audience and makes a different contribution to the good of society in a way that the other would fully approve. A second is that Aristotle, with the advantage of hindsight, is correcting Plato's rhetoric in ways that Plato himself would have done had he lived to see the odd assortment of cranks and fanatics his writings would prove to attract and encourage. Against this possibility is the fact that Socrates himself had already drawn an extremely odd collection of followers before Plato began to write, as Plato himself attests. So a third possibility is that behind Aristotle's different rhetorical strategy lies a real disagreement with Plato's understanding of the human soul. In particular, we may wonder whether Aristotle does not see more of a possibility for ordinary, nonphilosophic human beings to live lives that are in some important degree liberated from the authoritative myths that Plato presents as essential constituents of life in the cave. One sign that he might is the very different treatment of piety in Plato and Aristotle. Plato, in maintaining that virtue is knowledge, tends to make extravagant claims for virtue's power to produce everything good, as if men could love it only if they believed this, and both the myths with which he ends several dialogues and his practical political teaching in the *Laws* suggest that moral decency requires that one be either philosophic or seriously pious. Aristotle, by contrast, openly denies that virtue alone can guarantee happiness and not only omits piety from his catalogue of virtues but scarcely mentions the gods in his rich depiction of the moral life. Does Aristotle perhaps think that Plato underestimated the capacity of strong, subphilosophic individuals to face the vicissitudes of fortune and the necessity of death without flinching and without abandoning their dedication to living nobly, even if no otherworldly rewards are forthcoming? Against this thought are two observations that may require us to narrow again the gap I have just sketched: Plato's interlocutor Kleinias in the *Laws* does in fact seem to a considerably degree capable of liberation from traditional piety while retaining his moral seriousness;[9] and Aristotle in the *Ethics*, for all his demotion of piety, does treat respectfully and perhaps even quietly encourages the hope that death may not be utterly final. Might Aristotle in fact judge that the faintest, haziest, and least articulate of hopes for an afterlife will in healthy subphilosophic souls support the moral life most effectively? Then the difference with Plato might be as small as this: what Plato considered possible in unusual individuals and perhaps especially in statesmen or founders like Kleinias might be in Aristotle's judgment possible in considerable numbers of sturdy, well-educated citizens.

Further narrowing the gap between Plato and Aristotle on these question is the fact that if Aristotle engages more seriously in a practical educational project aimed at ordinary citizens, he is as deeply interested as Plato in all the same theoretical questions. Beyond but also by means of his practical project of clarifying and refining ordinary moral intuitions, I will argue, Aristotle is engaged in another ambitious project in the *Ethics* that lays a foundation for political science in a different sense. Precisely by listening so carefully and sympathetically to the claims made for moral virtue and making what is arguably the best case for them, Aristotle is bringing to light certain intractable tensions within morality, even when informed by philosophy, which cannot be overcome on the plane of moral and political life as such but only in the philosophic life. The wisest statesmanship requires an understanding of this problem, but it may not be helpful to political life to foreground it. For example, if even the best people tend to be self-deceiving about the purity of their motives in subtle and complex ways, and if attempts to bring this phenomenon into the clear, harsh light of public discourse have the almost invariable effect of simplifying, flattening, and hence distorting the phenomena, the reductionist accounts of morality that result are likely to make citizens less decent and less happy. To carry out his complex and sensitive political project, then, Aristotle employs a careful, political mode of writing, which in turn requires from us a careful, political mode of reading. While describing and making the case for virtue as a whole and for each virtue individually, and even while steering readers to a better version of the principles they believe in, Aristotle highlights puzzling things about the virtues and gives quiet indications of deep tensions within them. These indicators lead to another level of analysis on which the virtues are reassessed again, established on different foundations, and prove ultimately coherent in a way that they do not in the more conventional understanding of them. In this way, Aristotle demonstrates a very high form of moderation, giving ample evidence but not all of the inferences that lead to his conclusion in book 10 of the *Ethics* that the philosophic life is best. No one has fully addressed the question of the present book, the relation of reason to virtue in the *Nicomachean Ethics*, with a reading that is politically informed in the way I am proposing.

It is the thesis of this book that such an interpretive approach alone can resolve two major conundrums, one that has bedeviled interpreters since at least the nineteenth century, and another that has raged for the past half-century among Aristotle scholars. The first is the question of the ultimate source of guidance in the virtuous life. Does reason directly grasp the ends of moral action, or does it merely follow virtue, understood as properly cultivated subrational desire? Does reason weigh different ends in the process of deliberation, or merely determine in each case the best fulfillment of a single predetermined end? Does it truly give guidance to life, in other words, or is it merely the servant of desire?[10] The second is the question of what the end is that Aristotle is arguing reason can discover and use to guide the life of virtue. That end for Aristotle is agreed on all sides to be happiness, but how inclusive or exclusive a meaning is he giving to it, and can his different statements on it be made to cohere?[11] The debate on these questions has raged so long and in each case each side has shown so thoroughly the limits of the other that it has become clear that neither can satisfactorily account for all that the *Nicomachean Ethics* says on the subject. It is time, then, to consider a fresh approach that subsumes all the arguments into a new synthesis.

This study will propose that there are two forms of virtue, habit-bred and reason-guided; there are two forms of active wisdom, one of which follows well-habituated desires and conventional opinion and the other a deep knowledge of human nature and the human good; and there are two importantly different ways of viewing the soul, one divided into parts, and the other unitary. In order to do full justice to the active civic and moral form of virtue that is bred by habituation and guided by conventional opinion, I will argue that Aristotle in his dialectical ascent from common opinion is giving more weight than is usually granted by his commentators to the most inclusive understanding of happiness as consisting in goods of every kind. In doing so he is evoking all that we hope for from happiness; he is launching the simultaneously constructive and exploratory project of educating these hopes and guiding the reader to place his happiness almost entirely in the activity of moral virtue; he is then for many books testing that understanding to show its great strength and also, more quietly, certain weaknesses, preparing for his claims in book 10 that the life of philosophy satisfies better the standard of serious and intrinsically fulfilling activity that has guided the examination of moral virtue. The claim that Aristotle is simultaneously developing and exploring all these contrasting arguments is unusual, but I propose that such a politically informed, dialectical reading of the *Nicomachean Ethics* can resolve long-standing perplexities in Aristotle scholarship in ways that nonpolitical approaches have not been able to do, while also opening up unexpected riches in the book.

While this volume will explore thoroughly the relation between reason and the passions in guiding morally virtuous action and will show how Aristotle both makes the case for morally virtuous action as the sole end in life and reveals its limitations, it will not attempt a full exploration of Aristotle's final teaching on the human good. That would require an equally detailed study of the final three and one-half books of the *Ethics*, which leave the moral life behind to discuss pleasure, friendship, and (I would submit in seriously incomplete form) the life of philosophic contemplation. My previous study *Aristotle and the Philosophy of Friendship* explores the rich discussion of love and friendship in books 8 and 9, while Aristotle's treatments of pleasure in books 7 and 10 and of philosophy in book 10 venture beyond the scope of political philosophy proper and present an altogether different set of interpretive problems. His discussions of the virtues and of the quasi-virtue of self-control in the first and longest part of the *Ethics* establish that the central and highest aim of the political art is the education of citizens to live active lives that are imbued with considerable pleasures and appreciative of philosophy, but that are dedicated neither to pleasure nor to philosophy but to morally virtuous activity. By examining Aristotle's rich and compelling case for such a life, this book seeks to elucidate the foundations of his political philosophy.

Chapter 1

THE TASK AND THE PUZZLE OF REASON IN THE *NICOMACHEAN ETHICS*

THE STUDY OF POLITICS (1.1–2)

"Every art and every inquiry, and likewise action and choice, seems to aim at some good; therefore it has been nobly said that the good is that at which all things aim" (*NE* 1094a1–3). Thus Aristotle begins his magisterial two-volume treatise on politics, taking his point of departure just as Socrates did from such mundane, practical arts as medicine, shipbuilding, and bridle making. The real theme of this first volume is not politics per se or even ethics per se but rather the human good, the end for which we do what we do, the purpose of life. But *is* anything simply, intrinsically good? *Does* life have a purpose? Aristotle's use of the words "seems" and "nobly" shows that he does not assume an affirmative answer to our questions: what seems so may prove false; what is nobly said may be truly said or just beautifully said. He begins with human opinions about the way we experience things fitting together and making sense, not with facts directly perceived. And he observes that whatever may be said of the cosmos as a whole, of inanimate things, and even of impulsive human acts and idle speculations, every important activity that we engage in is purposeful, which is to say, directed to something presumed to be good. We cannot talk about anything that matters without talking about what is good and bad. And in the practical arts, at least, we have clarity about these things: a bridle maker knows that a good bridle must be snug, flexible, and sturdy; a doctor knows that cancer is bad and that the drug that can cure it with minimal side effects is good.

Moreover, Aristotle observes, the ends for which we act and think fall into ordered classes. Some activities we pursue for themselves and others for their products, and the actions directed to making products are "by nature" (1094a6) subordinate to the products. Thus Aristotle begins his great project of looking to nature for guidance for human life in a simple, even pedestrian way, by observing the inescapable structure and meaning of the things that we do. It is in the nature of action that it is directed to some end—if only to the satisfaction of engaging in that activity itself. It is in the nature of action that the end is superior to any means used to reach it, for the means have their value and find their standard in the end to which they are directed. And it is in the nature of action that some ends, such as the bridles and medical instruments produced by craftsmen and manufacturers, are subordinate to higher activities and ends, such as the arts of horsemanship and medicine. Aristotle assigns such rankings not by judging from outside but by observing the meaning the human actors give their own activity. Thus human activities fall into natural hierarchies, guided by arts or sciences that are ruling or architectonic, even if the purpose of the whole of life is difficult to discern.

At the beginning of 1.2, Aristotle acknowledges the possibility that life indeed has no purpose and that each desire is for the sake of some further desideratum in a pointless, endless regression. But, he says,

> If there is one end of actions which we want for itself . . . it is clear that this would be the good—that is, the best. And then would not the knowledge [*gnōsis*] of it carry great weight, and, like archers in possession of a target, would we not better hit on what is needed? If this is so, it is necessary to try to grasp in outline, at least, whatever this is and to what science or capacity it belongs. (1094a18–26)

Aristotle raises but immediately drops the possibility that life has no true end or ends—nothing sought or worth seeking just for itself—that knowledge can grasp and guide us by. Not addressed at all at this point is the more plausible and almost equally troubling possibility that life has multiple ends, all naturally good, that do not fit into any overarching order and are potentially in tension with one another.[1] Instead, Aristotle will start by building the best case he can that life does have a single ultimate end but that it is not well understood. Even the bare possibility that such a goal exists is enough to prove his conclusion here that the knowledge of it is something that we need if possible to find. Thus political science is required for this curious reason: life is full of activities that are purposeful in the short run and on a small scale, and we sense there should be a point to life as a whole, yet we do not know what it is. We do not even know whether that knowledge is the subject of a science or of some other kind of capacity altogether, such as inspiration. But this means we have no reasonable choice but to investigate.

Aristotle's next step is more controversial. He identifies the ultimate architectonic art or science, at least provisionally, as the art of politics.[2] Reading closely, we see that Aristotle is doing this in four different ways. The first is simply to observe the formative power that political authorities in fact have over all aspects of life, including the sciences themselves: it is the political art that "ordains what sciences there ought to be in the cities and what kind each person ought to learn and up to what point" (1094a28–b2). This is the great classical insight into the power of the regime. For better or for worse, through encouraging some pursuits and forbidding others, and through honoring certain human types and virtues and dishonoring others, each regime gives shape to the lives and the souls of its citizens.[3] Ours, for example, makes us respect liberty, economic success, scientific and technological progress, and hard work, while frowning on lives of unemployed leisure and regarding as quaint curiosities those of monastic seclusion. Ancient legislators tended to be more fully aware of the regime's all-pervasive formative power than are modern ones, the more restrained of whom often imagine that government can be merely ministerial to the great life of society that goes on almost without them, and the more active of whom are frequently surprised by the unintended social consequences of their legislation.

Aristotle's second point lends weight to the thought that the political art's claim to be architectonic rests not only on the sheer power of government but also on something inherently dignified about it. The arts that are especially honored everywhere, including generalship, economics, and rhetoric, compose and are governed by the political art.

Third and most controversially, Aristotle says that because it belongs to the political art to legislate regarding every aspect of life, its end is the human good altogether. Is this inference justified? Might one not say with equal reason that because the heavy hand of government so often does harm, the true political art is one of wielding power carefully for a few rudimentary purposes and leaving individuals as free as possible to work out their own highest ends for themselves? Aristotle's deepest thought here would seem to be that securing the general welfare and, to that end, taking on the challenge of getting clear what human well-being consists in is a task that the political art simply cannot abdicate. If we know that the greatest human happiness consists in choosing for oneself the direction of one's life and living it with the greatest possible autonomy, government's highest responsibility is to ensure that citizens are equipped and otherwise left free to do this. To the extent that it is not clear that maximum autonomy is best for everyone, government is irresponsible in not determining the limits of beneficial autonomy and the ways in which the citizens should be guided. And if we think such knowledge is unavailable, Aristotle would ask whether we can prove that or are merely assuming it.

Fourth and finally, Aristotle adds that even if the individual good and the collective good are the same—even if the good of the community is not qualitatively different from but merely an aggregate of the good enjoyed by the members individually—"still it seems to be something greater and more complete [*teleioteros*] to secure and preserve it for the city: it is desirable to do it for one alone, but nobler and more divine for a nation or a city" (1094b7–10). Again, though hedging with the word "seems," Aristotle is making the highest possible claim for the art of politics. Politics seems noble and even divine inasmuch as it operates on a grand scale, involves dedication to others, benefits a whole that can be more self-sufficient than any individual, and promises to achieve something more lasting than any of us can attain individually in our personal lives—all most impressive things. But Aristotle also invites us to consider the possibility that the collective good only appears higher in a way not justified by its greater magnitude and duration, and the further possibility that the highest end is *not* the same for the political community and for the individual. This would mean either that all or most are capable of attaining the highest good but only separately as individuals, so that the art of politics, though of critical importance, would be merely ancillary to this activity, or that the highest good attainable by most citizens with the help of the political art is still distinct from and perhaps in tension with an even higher good individually attainable by some. In the latter case, there would be no overarching end to all of human life and no single architectonic art of the human good. Aristotle reminds us of this possibility even as he proceeds with his more politically ambitious project of elaborating a single architectonic art. It is a project that the political philosopher would be irresponsible not at least to explore the feasibility of.

But, we may wonder, bringing Aristotle himself back into the picture, is the architectonic art or science he will elaborate the same as the science he himself knows and is exercising in writing this book? If the political regime determines what may be studied and up to what point, is Aristotle not pointing to a competition between its authority and his own as a philosopher? If so, how does he understand that competition?[4] And to the extent that a political art already exists and is being practiced by political men, will Aristotle simply be clarifying what that knowledge is, or developing a new and perhaps rival version of it?

METHOD AND AUDIENCE (1.3)

Immediately after raising the question of who it is that possesses the true art of the human good and alluding to the belief that this art is noble and even divine, Aristotle launches into one of four digressions on method in books 1–2, all of which stress the limits of the precision that can be expected in any inquiry into political and ethical matters.[5] Indeed, Aristotle acknowledges now, so much does human reasoning about what is noble and just seem to vary and shift that some have concluded that the noble and just "exist only by convention and not by nature" (1094b16). These people are, of course, the pre-Socratic philosophers and the sophists who followed them, who extolled nature, the study of it, and a life lived in accord with it, liberated from the pious moralism that political communities allegedly employ to keep individuals' natural, healthy desires in check for the benefit of others. Aristotle's response is two-pronged. He points out that the difficulty in attaining precision about the good is similar to that in attaining precision about the noble and just—including, therefore, whatever anyone might claim is good by nature. "For some have been destroyed by wealth, and others by courage" (1094b18–19).[6] Is there nothing simply and always good, the objector may well wonder—not even wisdom? And are the just and noble subject to "disagreement and variability" for the same reason the good is subject to "variability" (1094b15–17), or in some further way? But these questions Aristotle does not pursue. Second, he insists that knowledge is in each of these cases attainable but that we must not expect more precision than "the nature of the subject allows" (1094b25). The noble, the just, and the good do, then, exist somehow by nature and as such are knowable. But for some reason, we should expect from them only such precision as we would expect from craftsmen or rhetoricians and not from physicists or mathematicians. Why? Is Aristotle signaling that he is proceeding in this work not as a careful investigator of one part of nature—human nature—but only as a kind of craftsman or rhetorician? But if so, this omnivorously curious naturalist has left the most important part of nature unexplored, for there is no other Aristotelian treatise on human nature. Thus it seems best to keep exploring the possibility that Aristotle in fact has more than one kind of project in hand here, and that the *Nicomachean Ethics* does in some way convey his deepest reflections on human nature.

Rather than explain what prevents the political art from resting on perfectly clear and precise principles, Aristotle actually rebukes us for wanting to know. An educated person simply understands what to expect from each field of knowledge, he says, and when it comes to politics, a young person lacks the requisite experience and "is not even an appropriate student" (1095a2–3). For the young live impulsively by their passions, so that "to them knowledge [*gnōsis*] is useless, just as to those who lack self-control" (1095a8–9). This judgment about suitable students must have sounded as strange to Aristotle's immediate audience as it does to us, for by all accounts the *Nicomachean Ethics* developed out of one of the "open" courses he taught in the Lyceum that were directed both to young students and to mature auditors.[7] If these remarks are serious, why would Aristotle have taught this course in the Lyceum at all? And, on the other hand, how exactly would his mature gentlemanly listeners have stood to benefit from the course if they were already both morally virtuous and well acquainted with practical affairs? Thus we have the famous puzzle of the *Nicomachean Ethics'* audience, for one part of which the treatise would seem to have been unprofitable and for the other superfluous. But perhaps we are taking Aristotle's blame and praise of the two parts of his audience too literally.

Let us for a moment imagine the almost ill-tempered digression on method that composes 1.3 being provoked by an imaginary, peremptory interruption of Aristotle's discourse at the end of 1.2, coming perhaps from a student who is young, impressed by natural science, and skeptical as to whether any solid knowledge in moral and political matters is possible, let alone whether the art of politics is a noble and even divine art as Aristotle has just suggested. Aristotle's response could not be more gratifying to the other sector of his audience. Mature gentlemen understand the complexity of practical affairs; they take the difficulty of reducing morality to simple rules as evidence for the need for experience, prudence, and good judgment in order to live well and, even more, to rule well. They are easily annoyed by people who demand of them great precision, which seems to them petty but perhaps also threatening: consider the typical reactions to Socratic interrogation. They also believe strongly in moral responsibility and are unpersuaded by the Socratic claim that virtue is knowledge. Aristotle begins his political investigations by emphatically taking their side against young, scientifically inclined students, joining them in disparaging the demand for precision in moral and political discourse, and likewise in disparaging the power of bare knowledge to prevail against unruly passion.[8]

On the other hand, Aristotle attributes the problem with his unsuitable listeners not to chronological age but to immaturity: are all of the young necessarily immature? He speaks of the "nature" of the subject matter: are not bright young students in fact uniquely suited to raising and pressing the questions that lead into the deepest nature of things? Is it really futile to talk with the young about "the noble and the just things, which the political art investigates" (1094b14–15), as Aristotle seems to have been doing in his school and as Plato and Socrates did so extensively before him? Why is direct experience with public affairs necessary to make progress in understanding these things rather than just careful observation? Might Aristotle not be flattering the old a bit in his dismissal of the young? Finally, what are we to make of his concluding comment in 1.3 that knowledge can be "of immense benefit" to those who "form their desires in accordance with reason and act accordingly" (1095a10–11)? Do Aristotle's mature listeners already have this reason in complete form, or might there be important elements of it that even the most respectable gentleman-statesman lacks? How does the soul do such self-forming under the guidance of reason, and what is it in the soul that is acting when it does? No doubt the brightest of Aristotle's young students are alive to all of these questions, yet there is something else in them—some inclination to rush too quickly and too dismissively past something really critical in the gentlemen and perhaps even in their own souls—that prompts Aristotle to tell them to be quiet and sit down and listen more respectfully to what he has to say to their elders.

HAPPINESS: FIRST IMPRESSIONS (1.4)

Aristotle begins 1.4 by picking up the thread again after his digression, although he will soon be drawn back into the twin problems of method and audience.

> To resume, since all knowledge and choice aims at some good, let us state what is it at which we say the political art aims, and what is the highest of all the goods related to action. As for its name, it is pretty much agreed on by most people: for both the many and the cultivated call it happiness [*eudaimonia*], supposing that to live well [*eu zein*] and to do well [*eu prattein*] are the same as to be happy. But about what happiness is they disagree, and the many do not answer in the same way as the wise. (1095a14–22)

Echoing his original claim that every art, inquiry, action, and choice seems to aim at some good, Aristotle now drops the "seems" in his first formulation, thereby implicitly but unequivocally denying the existence of radical evil, or the choice of evil as such: what we choose we choose in an attempt, however benighted, to achieve something good. But what is this good toward which we are all groping? Is it a single, supreme, overarching good in which all the others culminate, the same as the end of the political art, the same in turn as the highest of all goods related to action, which consists in living well and doing well and which all human beings including the wise call happiness? And what about the Greek terms Aristotle uses here for living and doing well, terms as closely related and as distinct as "living the good life" and "living a good life" are in English: will they prove to be the same? Or might the political art even at its best aim at something that is neither highest nor comprehensive but merely the foundation for such good as most people are able to reach, a good that most people, both common and cultivated, take to be attainable through action, identify with both living well and doing well, and call happiness, but the wise do not—perhaps because they understand happiness in a way that transcends the practical realm entirely or even because they consider it unattainable? Aristotle gives every impression that he is speaking of a single, overarching, attainable human good that wisdom can grasp and set up as the target for lawgivers and private citizens alike, yet that is not precisely what he says.

What he unquestionably does, however, is to invite us all to consider what it is we are after in everything that we do, and whether we do not at least conceive of it as a single good. Here as in book 10 he calls this sought-for end *eudaimonia*. Since we are a step removed from Aristotle's Greek-speaking audience we must add that about the translation of *eudaimonia* as "happiness" there is general but not universal agreement. Concerned that "happiness" in English implies mere contentment, John Cooper has proposed the translation "flourishing." Objecting that trees can flourish, Gabriel Lear tentatively proposes "success" but concedes that it is probably too narrow. J. L. Ackrill suggests "the best possible life," to which Robert Bartlett objects that Aristotle leaves open the question of whether happiness is in fact possible. David Ross suggests "well-being" and W. F. R. Hardie "well-doing," which both have the merit of being close to Aristotle's "living well and doing well" but are perhaps too mundane in failing to capture the overtone of being blessed by fortune that *eudaimonia* carries (meaning literally "having a good guardian spirit") and that "happiness" still at least echoes. Richard Kraut persuasively argues that in "happiness" we do at least intermittently include not only contentment but the fullness of activity and self-awareness that Aristotle will go on to attribute to *eudaimonia*. Thus I agree with John Burnet that the term is good enough, so long as we do not import into it a theory of *eudaimonism*, as if Aristotle is contending for happiness as one candidate among multiple possible candidates for the proper standard and goal of human choice and action. Just as Aristotle forecloses the idea of radical evil, evidently finding for it no evidence and seeing in it nothing comprehensible, so he forecloses the possibility that human life has any *other* end than the human good that we all seek, that we most deeply want, and that we call happiness. This human good is not one of the things we care about, as if others, such as justice, could fall outside of it: Aristotle will call justice the common good (1129b11–19). It is not our own good as opposed to the good of others: Aristotle in beginning with the political art is foregrounding the statesman's concern for the well-being of his whole people. Aristotle will go on to argue that happiness consists in activity, full, flourishing activity of that which is uniquely human and indeed best in us, and to call that happiness makes good sense in English just as it does in Greek.[9]

Aristotle begins, however, with the disagreements. How many of them do we have? First distinguishing the many from the cultivated, he then introduces the wise as apparently synonymous or overlapping with the cultivated, but they in fact form a third group. For he goes on to attribute to "the many" the identification of happiness with such obvious things as pleasure, wealth, and honor; yet refined pleasures and wealth and especially honor are among the chief concerns of traditional gentlemen. From the perspective of the wise, perhaps even the cultivated are *hoi polloi*. The many, Aristotle continues, wander in their opinions of what is most important, and "when they become aware of their own ignorance they wonder at those who say grand things and speak over their heads" (1095a25–26).

Immediately he mentions the belief in a "good in itself" that is the cause of all other good things. Are those who hold this belief the wise, or are they the cultivated among the many in moments of being impressed by fancy talk? And whatever do the wise themselves think happiness is?

Without elaborating, Aristotle launches into a second digression on method, arguing that it would be pointless to seek out *all* the views on happiness, that we must be content to investigate the most "prevalent"[10] and "plausible" of them, and that we must distinguish arguments leading up to first principles from those leading from them—or inductive from deductive arguments (1095a28–b1). The study of the human good, it seems, is an inductive science, its imprecision consisting in the fact that we have no direct access to axioms as in mathematics from which to derive rules, but only to specific "facts" that we must somehow weave together to articulate general principles. "For we must begin with what is known, and this has two meanings: what is known to us and what is known simply" (1095b2–4). "Known simply" is a strange expression, but evidently Aristotle means by it the most fundamental as opposed to the most accessible facts—the "simple and intelligible" as opposed to the "composite and sensible," as Saint Thomas puts it.[11] But in moral and political matters the things that are "known to us" that the art of politics must take as its starting points (*archai*) are not the things we directly observe but those that come from one's education when one has been "nobly brought up by means of habituation" (1095b4). For, Aristotle continues, "the 'that' is a starting point, and if this is sufficiently apparent, there is no need in addition for the 'why'" (1095b6–7). The relevant "that" would seem to be a particular moral judgment, such as the judgment that stealing your classmate's pocket knife is bad. The assimilation of this and many such judgments gives sufficient or almost sufficient guidance, Aristotle maintains, for "a person of such a sort has or can easily get the starting points" (1095b7–8). Are the real starting points in the science of the human good the specific moral judgments that such a person already has, then, or the more comprehensive moral principles that he may not have but can "easily" derive from them? Aristotle here says both, though it is the former that he stresses and will reaffirm at 1098b2–3. But is it indeed so easy to form the right generalizations if we are not in possession of the "why"? Do we have any chance of ascending from the parochial moral strictures of our own time and place to anything more universal and solid without such an inquiry? What is most reassuring here to the decently brought-up gentleman can only be dismaying to the radically inquisitive young student, in whom Aristotle almost encourages these questions without encouraging hope for answers that will meet his standards.

But Aristotle takes a new direction as he concludes 1.4 by quoting at 1095b10–13 the first, third, fourth, and fifth lines of the following passage from Hesiod:

> This one is altogether best who himself understands all things
> Considering what will be better later, and in the end.
> Good in turn is he who listens well to another and is persuaded.
> But he who neither himself understands nor, listening to another,
> Takes this to heart, this one is a worthless man.[12]

The question this leaves us with is how any of these three types will benefit from Aristotle's course or treatise on ethics, if the best are capable of thinking everything through for themselves, the second best have been well educated already by their fathers, and the worst will not listen to anyone anyway. Without the second line which Aristotle omits, one might understand Hesiod and Aristotle to be suggesting that for all practical purposes it is as good to have been well taught as to be wise oneself, and that the practically important wisdom consists in judgments that one can grasp without knowing all the reasons behind them. But if wisdom especially involves being able to manage one's affairs with foresight and even more being able to govern or legislate with foresight for a whole people, then the second-best type here who knows only how to heed good advice will be defective even on his own terms. Is the *Ethics*, then, written to give fuller guidance to this second group, leaving aside the students of philosophy that make up the first, as Richard Bodéüs suggests?[13] This seems correct as to the primary audience to whom Aristotle offers his front-row seats, as it were, although Bodéüs does not do sufficient justice to the complexity of Aristotle's project even with them. In part he will offer persuasive reminders and endorsements of what they already think; in part he will articulate principles that they implicitly believe in but have never brought clearly into focus, thereby strengthening their moral commitments and giving them defenses against corrosive conventionalist challenges, but in part he will also work to redirect their admirations and aspirations into rather new channels, as his demotion of righteous indignation and his elevation of philosophy will show. But the most penetrating part of his audience will be the students who seek to know not only what is true but also why it is true, those who, if they are not perfectly autonomous learners—and who, after all, is simply capable of self-education?—will need only light spurs to think deeply.[14] Precisely by making these students listen more respectfully to his dialogue with their elders, Aristotle is directing them to the "facts" that they themselves need most to begin by examining: the powerful, deep-seated, but perhaps already disowned moral commitments of their own hearts. Something in these "facts," we shall discover, is strikingly subject to corrosion and to neglect, but something else in them is surreptitiously, almost uncannily tenacious.

It is this complex character of the audience of the *Nicomachean Ethics*, I would submit, that chiefly accounts for the book's complex structure and teaching.

CANDIDATES FOR HAPPINESS INTERROGATED (1.5)

Launching his quest for firm knowledge about the end of human life or the true substance of happiness in 1.5, Aristotle now demonstrates his method. This is, in a nutshell, a dialectical ascent from common opinion. As in 1.1, Aristotle makes preliminary advances from superficial to deeper answers simply by listening carefully to different people's own reasons for choosing what they do and making explicit the implicit hierarchies of ends that their choices reveal. But the picture is complicated. In 1.4 he distinguished the perspectives of the vulgar, the refined, and, more indirectly, the wise. He ended that chapter by citing Hesiod's division of human beings into three groups on the basis of whether they are able to understand for themselves, are willing to listen to those who speak well, or are unable to do either. Now at the start of 1.5 he identifies the three most prominent ways of life worth investigating as the pleasure-seeking, the political, and the contemplative. These three tripartite divisions would seem to track well against one another. But his investigation of the ends implied in these three ways of life is overlaid in 1.5 with another trio of ends, the ones that he said in 1.4 that the many desire: pleasure, wealth, and honor. These are in fact the things that are not only most desired by the common run of people but most pursued and enjoyed by the majority of those who pass as cultivated. As long as these three together constitute the ultimate concerns of a life, that life remains a vulgar one. But to the extent that one gives honor pride of place and becomes reflective on the limitations of each of one's ends and the ways they point to still deeper concerns, one becomes not yet wise, but cultivated. Thus, in moving honor to the center, in giving it his most serious and sustained attention, and in showing how pleasure, honor, and wealth all come up short or point beyond themselves from the perspective even or especially of their more reflective adherents, Aristotle unfolds a series of judgments and intuitions about happiness that characterize the most cultivated and that lay the groundwork for the further dialectical ascent he will make in 1.7.

Aristotle begins with pleasure. As people struggle to transcend a life of mere necessity, what first comes to sight as a happy life is the enjoyment of everything good in abundance. This is "not unreasonable," Aristotle says (1095b15), for people see even men in authority enjoying such a life. But it is scarcely an ascent from a mere animal existence; even slaves are led by pleasure and pain; surely a happy life is something more dignified and distinctively human than this. In fact the gentleman's view of pleasure is rather complicated, as we shall see in book 3, and Aristotle's is even more so, as he shows in books 7 and 10, but for now Aristotle uses this judgment about bodily pleasures to dismiss pleasure altogether from contention and to turn to higher things.

And what could be more dignified than honor? "The cultivated and active choose honor, for this is pretty much the end of the political life" (1095b22–23). Yet Aristotle shows how honor, considered as an end, fails to live up to the honor lovers' own "divination" (95b26) that the greatest good must be something truly one's own and hard to take away, and likewise to the implicit logic of their own desire for it, inasmuch as they especially value honor when it comes from those who possess active wisdom and know them well and when it is given for their virtue. Thus the honor lovers' own judgments suggest that honor is good chiefly as a sign of something else and not for itself.

Following this logic, Aristotle takes up the question of whether virtue can be the substance of happiness. Again on the basis of the cultivated person's own implicit judgments, he concludes that at least the bare possession of virtue does not measure up either. For the happy life, we sense, must be something complete and active, something that by its very nature excludes misery, whereas virtuous people can suffer terrible pain and misfortune, and "no one would deem happy someone living in this way, except to defend a thesis" (1096a1–2). Aristotle, ever the realist, refuses to impose on the phenomena doctrines that fly in the face of common sense, as Antisthenes the Cynic and later the Stoics would do in setting up virtue as the guarantor of happiness. It is better to listen most carefully to the intuitions that the logic of our own lives shows to be deepest.

These intuitions do not lead by any direct path to the thought that the substance of happiness is contemplation, which Aristotle gives only a bare mention before taking up the third of the obvious ends mentioned in the previous chapter, wealth. Again on his subject's own terms, he argues that moneymaking is too constrained a life to be the end, and money itself is merely a means to other things, and thus the chapter ends in *aporia*. But it has demonstrated well Aristotle's dialectical method, clarifying what we all sense or divine happiness must be: something that would be choiceworthy to those most blessed by fortune; something dignified as bodily pleasure is not; something that is our own and hard to take away and completely end-like as honor is not; something characteristic of a wakeful and active life, complete and completely satisfying in itself, as the simple presence of virtue is not. What relation happiness might have to thinking or to intellect, which Aristotle does not mention in this chapter (cf. 1096b16–19 and 1097b2–5), or to reason, which curiously he mentions only in connection with positions that he ostensibly rejects, especially the defense of pleasure (1095b15, 1095b21, and 1096a9–10), Aristotle does not say. By contrast, this chapter has an extraordinarily dense frequency of words for seeming, appearance, opinion, and even divination.

THE GOOD IN ITSELF (1.6)

It is perhaps little wonder, then, that Aristotle makes another sharp turn at the start of chapter 6. We can imagine that he has just been interrupted again, this time by a different, more high-minded student, impatient to cut through so much appearance and opinion, impatient to break free of this realm in which even the noblest of things, human virtue, seems incomplete, to focus on a good that is utterly perfect and invulnerable. Why might not Plato's idea of the good be our answer to the question of life's highest end? As if turning to address such a protestor, in a chapter suddenly filled with references to intellect, knowledge, philosophy, and the divine, Aristotle begins in a spirit of reluctance.

> As for the universal, perhaps it is better to examine it and look into the problem of what is meant by it, although such an inquiry is odious, because those who introduced the forms are friends. But perhaps it would seem better and indeed necessary, for the sake of securing the truth, to give up even one's own, especially for those who are philosophers. Both are beloved, but it is a pious thing to give first honor to the truth. (1096a11–17)

To our question about the character of Aristotle's inquiry, he here gives a complex answer. These sentences now suggest that his inquiry is governed not by any practical aim or moral purpose but by an uncompromising search for knowledge for its own sake, despite what social harm may come of it; yet he also presents it as a pious quest. His quarrel is with an unnamed group of people (oddly in the plural) who introduced or "brought in" the forms—the word *eisagō* being the same word used in the indictment of Socrates when he was charged with introducing new divine things.[15] Just as Socrates professed to be grieved by the offense he gave his fellow Athenians yet impelled by his duty to Apollo to persist in questioning them, Aristotle claims to be grieved by the offense he is giving, not quite to his teacher Plato but perhaps to the circle of Platonists who are his friends, yet impelled by a sacred duty to the truth to persist. How pious Aristotle's love of truth truly is, how indifferent he is to the social consequences of his teachings, and how far his genuine disagreement may reach with Socrates who claimed possession of a divine voice and with Plato who proclaimed the idea of the good, all remain obscure.[16] Even if Aristotle has no substantive disagreement with Plato, he evidently thinks that a more sober rhetorical approach is needed. Yet in attacking the idea of the good, he deploys a complex rhetoric himself.[17]

Aristotle gives a battery of distinct and subtle rebuttals to the Platonic idea of the good. They all point in different ways to one fact, that the word "good" as we use it refers not to a thing, or to a single quality with common elements or features present in every manifestation, but to a judgment we apply across all kinds of categories—human beings, things, times, places, qualities, quantities, actions, and manners of acting. Aristotle notes that in all other cases the Platonists are careful to class under a single idea objects of the same order of being and confined to a single category; only in the case of the good do they abandon this careful procedure. He observes that there is a science pertaining to every other class of beings, but not a single science of the good. He goes on to challenge not only the notion that there is a single self-subsisting idea of the good but the notion that any idea is a separate being in the way that individuals are. "Human being," for example, is a universal class comprising many individual members; to try to make it both that and a distinct entity existing alongside all the individual members within it is confused.

Finally Aristotle identifies an especially important divide even between good things that fall into a single category: they can be good either as ends or as means. This thought prompts what would seem to be a most promising step for his project of identifying the overarching human good. Granted that some things in human life are good as mere instruments, what about those sought as ends? "What sorts of things might someone set down as good in themselves? Is it so many things as are in fact pursued for themselves alone—for example, thinking and seeing, as well as certain pleasures and honors? For even if we pursue these things on account of something else as well, nonetheless one might place them among the things that are good in themselves" (1096b16–19). Is this not precisely the class of things that needs our chief attention?

But no sooner has Aristotle opened this line of inquiry than he retreats from it. "The definitions of honor, active wisdom, and pleasure are distinct and differ in the very respect in which they are goods. It is not the case, therefore, that the good is something common in reference to a single idea" (1096b23–26). Do they really differ entirely in the way in which they are good? Do they not all belong to the important class of things that human beings want just for themselves, if also for other good things that they conduce to? This retreat is so strange that Aristotle immediately feels compelled to face another objection: surely there is something these good things have in common; the word "good" as applied to them is not just a homonym. So, Aristotle asks, do they all arise from one thing, or do they contribute to a single overarching end, or are they all good by analogy as sight is good in eyes and intelligence in the soul? This is in fact a key question for Aristotle's study and the very question from which he began the *Ethics*: do all the particular ends that human beings pursue, so easily identified in the case of the arts and many quotidian activities, contribute to a single, unified end that the science of politics can identify and secure, or does the human good consist of so many disparate and competing elements that no one science can reduce them to order? Yet no sooner does Aristotle raise this key question than he retreats again. "For perhaps to be very precise about this would be more germane to another philosophy" (1096b30–31). Getting greater precision about the sense in which something can be good in itself, he suggests, would leave us no better informed about the good that is attainable for human beings. Even if this is true of the purported class of things that are good in themselves without being good for us, what about the particular things that are good for us, such as thought and honor, that he mentioned just above? Is clearer knowledge of such things not of utmost relevance for us, and is it not to be found in a deeper understanding of the way each of these desired things is related to the others and to our natures? And what shall we make of the suggestion now that great precision about the good is perhaps not unavailable after all but only extraneous to politics, the science of the human good? What other science could he have in mind as the proper place to study this, since he has no philosophic work on the good as such?

At this point Aristotle is interrupted, as it were, by a final protest—coming perhaps again from our second young student, sobered by Aristotle's gentle insistence on thinking about the good that *we* seek and seek just for itself. Surely, the protester says, knowing what is good in itself would be useful in giving us a model by which we might better know what is good for us and so better hit what we are aiming at (1097a1–3). This rejoinder echoes Aristotle's own exhortation in 1.2 to seek out the highest good so that, "like archers in possession of a target, we might better hit on what is needed" (94a23–24). We might expect Aristotle to say: "My point exactly. The good that we care about is the human good, the complete human good, insofar as it can serve for us as a target." But astonishingly, he rejects this whole line of inquiry as "inconsistent with the sciences," which do not pursue the good itself but, "aiming at some particular good, seek out what is needed" (1097a4–6).[18] Why, Aristotle asks, would all the sciences or arts neglect the good itself if it were useful? Of course it is not needed by any of them singly; Aristotle began the *Ethics* with the observation that each art or science is limited in looking only to a particular good, and that the art of politics is needed to descry the overarching human good and to bring the other arts into order in pursuit of that final end. Why does he now ignore just this practical, human, architectonic meaning of the good that he there limned and that the protester at least comes close to describing in speaking of "the good itself"?

Having entered the chapter as a philosopher in uncompromising pursuit of the truth and broached a line of questioning that seemed both susceptible of precision and most promising for answering his basic question, Aristotle thus veers away. In doing so, he indicates while declining to pursue the following path. Seeing the genuine confusions in the Platonists' notion of the good as either a self-subsisting being or a single class of beings, and provoked to wonder what all our usages of the term "good" share, we recognize the fundamentally relational character of the good. What a good dog, a good joke, a good ratio of calcium to magnesium, and a good time to attack the enemy all have in common is that they are well suited to their purpose, to bringing about a desired result. The good is precisely not self-subsisting: it is and can only be that which fills some need or want. And of course the good of chief concern to us is what is good for human beings. But seeing this, we also see that the things we consider good for us fall into two important classes: things good as a means and things good as ends. If each of the arts seeks to provide what is lacking or wanted for a particular purpose, in what way are the ends that are for no further purpose good? It can only be that they fill a basic, irreducible want or felt need of human nature. Bringing these insights together, we can identify the subject we most need to get clarity on as that which we might call "good in itself for us." And to understand that better, we would seem to need a deep investigation of human nature. While Aristotle will pose the essential question about human nature and what humans are naturally directed toward in 1.7, his investigation of these questions will soon be overtaken by a different agenda.

THE HINGE OF THE *ETHICS* (1.7)

The Final End

Returning from the digression that was 1.6, Aristotle opens the next chapter by again identifying the good in the ruling sense with the end of each action, and again, more explicitly than before, contemplating the possibility that all the meaningful human activities do not contribute to any single end: "If there is some one end of all actions, this would be the good attainable through action, and if more than one, these would be" (1097a22–24). The latter possibility raises a challenge for the prospect of guiding life by reason. If our ultimate ends are in conflict or even just good in very different ways, how can we choose meaningfully between them? Could we say we "ought" to prefer one end over another, and if so, on what basis?

Evidently to try to find unity among our ends, Aristotle proceeds to distinguish them into different kinds.

> Since the ends [*telē*] appear to be more than one, and of these we choose some on account of something else—such as money, an aulos, and instruments in general—it is clear that they are not all complete [*teleios*]; but the best appears to be something complete. So that if some one thing alone is complete, this would be what we are seeking, and if more than one, the most complete [*teleiotatos*] of these. (1097a25–30)

What meets this standard, Aristotle will argue, is happiness and happiness alone. But what precisely is the standard? The word *teleios* is tantalizingly ambiguous, and the question of how it and its superlative form *teleiotatos* should be understood here has sparked considerable controversy. As an adjectival form of the word *telos*, *teleios* describes what has reached its end or fulfilled its purpose; thus it can be translated not only as complete but as ultimate, final, perfect, full-grown, or accomplished. Is Aristotle picking out happiness and calling it the one end that is most strictly *ultimate*, leaving aside all others and thus correcting the statement he made a little before that if more than one end appear ultimate, these together would be the end of action and the good we are seeking (1097a22–24)? Or is he looking for the good that is most *comprehensive* inasmuch as it comprises all other ends? This is the debate that has raged between what have been styled the "dominant" and the "inclusive" interpretations of the meaning of the human good or happiness in 1.7 in particular and in the *Nicomachean Ethics* as a whole. The terms "dominant" and "inclusive" are both ambiguous as well: a dominant end might merely take precedence, might exclude all other ends except insofar as they serve as means to it, or might indeed be monolithic; an inclusive end might be more or less broad and more or less ordered. Given what Aristotle says here and elsewhere, the serious possibilities in fact come down to three. First, taking our sights by what Aristotle says about happiness in the *Rhetoric* (1360b14 ff.), we might understand the end in a *broadly inclusive* way, comprising all the important external and bodily goods and goods of soul that people seek—wealth, honor, good family, friends, intelligence, virtue, satisfying activity, and pleasures of every kind. Second, taking our sights from much of what Aristotle says about the life of virtue in the *Nicomachean Ethics*, we might understand the end and the substance of happiness in a *narrowly inclusive* way to comprise solely the activity of the moral and intellectual virtues. And third, taking most seriously the last book of the *Ethics*, we might understand the true end as only the activity of intellectual virtue, interpreting even the moral virtues to be ultimately good only as a means to contemplation. It seems it should at least not be hard to settle the question of how Aristotle intends the test here, for he proceeds to offer a threefold elaboration of what he means by "most *teleios*" as that which is always chosen for itself, that which is self-sufficient, and that which leaves nothing out, arguing that happiness alone meets each of these tests (1097a30–b21). Yet to our surprise and dismay, all three of these elaborations turn out to be open to multiple interpretations. No party can claim a clear victory; almost every interpreter makes strained arguments in an effort to make Aristotle as consistent as possible even in 1.7 (and much more so in the whole of the *Ethics*) but is ultimately forced to charge him with at least some degree of hesitation, equivocation, or ambivalence.[19] Is Aristotle simply confused? I would submit that his project in this chapter is instead far more deliberate and far more complex than any interpreter has yet proposed. Aristotle with each of these three elaborations is at once evoking our hopes for happiness as something that will answer *all* of our yearnings in a splendidly comprehensive way;[20] he is evoking our hopes for happiness as a single thing so pure, high, and perfect as to need nothing else; he is beginning to indicate some of the tensions within these hopes for happiness, so understood; and he is laying the groundwork for a twofold project that will follow throughout the rest of the *Ethics*: the exploration of a life first of morally virtuous activity and afterward of contemplation as possible candidates for the life that would fully answer our yearnings. The project unfolds in stages because the education of the reader must unfold in stages.[21]

Aristotle's first elaboration of the meaning of *teleiotatos* is based on a distinction between three different ways in which we choose things.

> We call what is sought for itself more complete than what is sought for something else [*di' heteron*], and what is never chosen for something else more complete than the things chosen both for themselves and for this, and simply complete what is chosen always for itself and never for something else. And happiness above all seems to be of such a kind. For we choose it always for itself and never for anything else, while honor and pleasure and intellect and all virtue we choose for themselves (for even if nothing resulted from them we would still choose each of them) but we also choose them for the sake of happiness, supposing that through them we will be happy. But happiness no one chooses for these, nor for anything further at all. (1097a30–b6)

This passage is taken by defenders of a narrowly inclusive or exclusive reading, such as Kraut (1999) and Lear (2009), to be arguing that happiness is better, higher, and more purely ultimate than all other goods because it alone is never a means and always only an end. Read in this way, Aristotle is drawing the same threefold distinction between kinds of goods as Glaucon is at the start of book 2 of Plato's *Republic* but, curiously, making a different judgment from Socrates about which of the three classes is best. For Socrates says he considers best the class of things we love both for themselves and for what comes from them. Evidently Socrates considers humans to be such needy and limited beings that we cannot afford to give ourselves over to pure but useless delights; he loves knowledge both for itself and for the practical guidance it gives; he loves the virtues in the same way. When Glaucon goes on to ignore this judgment and to demand that Socrates prove that justice is the best of things taken solely in itself apart from all its consequences, Socrates says that it is beyond his power to do what Glaucon asks but that piety demands that he try his best to defend justice somehow. Is Aristotle, then, taking the side of the fanatical Glaucon and preparing to insist that the activity of virtue alone and even contemplation alone, each undertaken just for itself, *is* happiness whole and complete—at least so long as one is not tormented by pain or overwhelming misfortune? That is an extreme argument to attribute to the sober Aristotle. It is at odds with the plurality of serious ends he here attributes to "us" and with the balanced picture of the happy life he will paint in book 1 and in many ways throughout the *Ethics*, although it is in keeping with the curious exhortation that we "try so far as possible to immortalize ourselves" in 10.7 (1177b33), for which we must try to account. According to this interpretation, Aristotle is excluding from the domain of happiness itself everything else that we hope will contribute to happiness, including many things that we love just for themselves, such as pleasure and honor and even intellect and virtue understood as possessions, relegating these to the status of mere instruments or ornaments for the happiness that consists solely in the active exercise of virtue, whether moral, intellectual, or both. Even love and friendship are on this reading no part of happiness properly understood, but only an assistance in the activity that alone matters, or a kind of dispensable grace note.

The extreme austerity of this conclusion has prompted some scholars to propose a different interpretation of the present passage. They suggest that the key distinction Aristotle is drawing here is not one between lesser goods that are chosen both for themselves and as *means* to happiness on one hand and happiness itself, chosen solely as an end, on the other. Rather, it is between lesser goods that are chosen both for themselves and as *components* of happiness, and the happiness that is chosen solely for itself. Thus Ackrill interprets the statement "if some one thing alone is complete, this would be what we are seeking, and if more than one, the most complete of these" (1097a27–30) to mean not that Aristotle is singling out one end to the exclusion of the others, but that he is identifying the one that is most complete inasmuch as it comprises all the others.[22] The Greek expression *di' heteron* can certainly mean "for something else" in the sense of a component as well as a means, and the thought is certainly attractive. But then we would have Aristotle saying that we choose each of the lesser goods not for two reasons, for itself and for a further end, but rather for the single reason that, being one of the good things that we want, it belongs to the collection of all good things that we want which we call happiness. This strains the meaning of the passage at 1097a30–b6 quoted above, and it does not seem to do justice to the importance of the psychological point Aristotle is making here.

Instead, I propose that Aristotle is arguing for something more subtle and complex than is captured by either the means-end or part-whole dichotomy. In examining our love for all the particular things we want just for themselves, we find something hypothetical and hopeful, yet in at least some cases we also find something nonnegotiable. We want our bodies and souls to be in fine condition, and likewise want the pleasures and honors that appear to be parts of a good life, both because we just want them whether they turn out to make us happy or not and because we hope that they will result in the happiness that we want most of all. But this is an expectation that could be proved wrong, and it could happen in either of two ways. Aristotle suggests that a serious person would rather be intelligent than foolish and brave than cowardly even if the net contribution to one's happiness were zero and evidently even if it were negative—if, for example, one's intelligence brought awareness of devastatingly painful truths or one's courage resulted in being tortured in a prisoner of war camp. Granted, as Ackrill points out, Aristotle would deny that we precisely choose *between* virtue and happiness, for what would be available once we gave up virtue would not amount to happiness. But Aristotle does allow, with common sense, that what is good in itself may sometimes bring great evil. Thus he points out that people have been destroyed not only by wealth but by courage (1094b18–19), that the courageous man in facing death is "deprived of the greatest goods knowingly" (1117b12–13), and that while suffering injustice is intrinsically less bad than doing injustice, "nothing prevents it from being incidentally more bad," in the same way that tripping is in itself less bad than a serious disease but may on occasion prove fatal (1138b1). Thus the serious person's concern for virtue comes to sight, at least, as bound up with a deep but uncertain hope in virtue's power to support his quest for happiness. On the other hand, at least some of the things that we initially want both as ends and for the sake of happiness, including certain bodily pleasures and external goods such as honor, we may be persuaded are not after all essential to happiness and perhaps not worth the cost they exact in terms of other goods. These reflections point to the way in which Aristotle is engaged not only in helping us discover what we think happiness is but in preparing the way for an active reassessment of what it is or might be. We must look for indications as to how far Aristotle judges it possible to decide what to place our happiness in, and, to the extent that he does, what standard he will suggest reason should look to in guiding the process.

For now, however, Aristotle is uncovering what we do in fact care about, in a way that *combines* part-whole and means-end reasoning. The important things we want as ends we expect will both directly constitute parts of our happiness and contribute as foundations or supports or means to other parts of it: we are glad to have a sound mind; we enjoy thinking; we need our intellect in many practical ways. But both as expected parts and as expected means, each of the particular things we value most may disappoint us, for each needs the support of others, and without that support it may well turn out to bring more suffering than happiness. Happiness, by contrast, as the fulfillment of all that we want, is the interlocking whole that alone appears unconditionally good and hence is wanted in a wholly unconditional way.

The problematic vulnerability of all the parts of happiness we have so far identified brings us to Aristotle's second elaboration of the meaning of completeness: "the complete good seems to be self-sufficient [*autarkes*]" (1097b7–8). This thought too is ambiguous and complex. To want a good that is self-sufficient is to want something that by its very existence would be sure to satisfy us, quite apart from anything else that might accompany it or might result from it. Happiness as the most complete good would seem to meet the test of self-sufficiency in the highest degree if it consisted in activity so pure and all-engrossing and intrinsically fulfilling at each moment that we could wish for nothing else. Indeed, to the extent that we can imagine attaining such a self-sufficient happiness, it would seem to make us self-sufficient as well. From Socrates to the Stoics to the Buddha, many sages have held out the goal of needing as little as possible from outside by carrying within oneself the grounds of one's own happiness, and much of what Aristotle will say in the *Ethics* encourages a spirit of self-sufficiency in just this sense.

Yet by nature, at least, we find ourselves threatened on many sides, desiring various things that we lack, and attached to others besides ourselves. Considered from this perspective, the complete good appears as a different kind of self-sufficiency, one that would render us least vulnerable to fortune and least in need of assistance because best equipped to provide everything good for ourselves and those we care about. And this concern for others Aristotle immediately acknowledges: "by self-sufficient we mean not just for oneself alone, living a solitary life, but also for parents and children and a wife and altogether for friends and fellow-citizens, since by nature a human being is political" (1097b8–11). Our concerns reach out beyond ourselves, creating a tension between the desire for an invulnerable autonomy and the desire for meaningful connections with others and for the well-being of those with whom we are so connected. We could not conceive ourselves fully happy if our loved ones were miserable or our country destroyed; we hope but cannot be certain that their well-being will conduce to our own happiness, just as we hope but cannot be certain that our own good qualities will; yet our hope for our personal happiness does not exhaust our concern for others, for we hope that they will still prosper when we are no longer here to see it. Since everything we want is at least a hoped-for part of the individual and collective happiness that we want most of all, it is reasonable for Aristotle to say that we do everything for the sake of happiness, but this formulation will be misleading if we forget how extensive a meaning he here gives it.

Aristotle concludes this elaboration of completeness as self-sufficiency by saying, "we set down as self-sufficient that which by itself makes life choiceworthy and in need of nothing, and such is what we suppose happiness to be" (1097b14–16). This thought of needing nothing brings the spotlight onto the concern that he specifies with his third standard: what is most complete must leave nothing out. "Further, it is of all things most choiceworthy not as something counted together [*mē sunarithmoumenēn*], for being counted together it would clearly be more choiceworthy in conjunction with the least of the good things . . . for of good things, more is always more choiceworthy" (1097b16–20). The phrase "not as something counted together" seems most obviously to mean and is generally taken to mean "not as just one good among others." As such, this statement gives the strongest support to the understanding of *teleios* as comprehensive and of happiness as broadly inclusive of *all* the goods we naturally desire. The problem is how this can ever make sense as a standard. No life can include every possible good; every choice of anything good excludes others.[23] Perhaps worse, the image of happiness as a basket into which we try somehow to fit as much as possible of as many different kinds of good things as possible fails to satisfy our intuition that true happiness cannot be just a disordered aggregate but must be a harmonious whole—a whole, we hope, so meaningful and sublime and precious that with the possession of it even such a finite life as humans are allotted can answer our deepest yearnings. This thought lends credence to an alternative way we might take the phrase "not as something counted together," and that is, "not just as an aggregate." On this reading, Aristotle is saying that happiness is complete not by containing as many goods as possible, since to any aggregate more could be added, but rather, by being a complete whole so perfect that nothing could be added to it or subtracted from it without making the whole less perfect. Its completeness is like that of a perfect string quartet, which could not be improved by the addition of horns or by the omission of a single measure: it is perfect and perfectly satisfying just as it is (cf. 1106b9–11).

In sum, if Aristotle is trying to present a tidy doctrine on what happiness is and in just what sense it is the "most *teleios*" of all ends, he is not succeeding. But if he is trying to lay a more complex foundation for a more complex project, he is doing it admirably. In the first half of 1.7 he is capturing from multiple perspectives the disparate hopes we bring to happiness, laying before us the tangle of different good things we want even as ends, the ambivalences about what is for the sake of what and in just what sense, the yearnings for self-sufficient independence from others and from the turbulence of fortune that puts every good we care about at risk, the yearnings at the same time for deep connection with others, the hunger for a capacious richness of goods, and the hope for a single-minded purity of purpose. He invites his most philosophic students to ponder how much of what we want is neither coherent nor possible; he invites all of his readers to sense it. We want a plan for life that reason can grasp and that may guide us to the wholeness we crave, but that plan is not yet in evidence.

The Function Argument

At this junction, a sober philosophic teaching on happiness that took its sights from nature and that followed the hints of the previous chapter might pursue the problem of wholeness in the following way. We want what is good, but good things come to sight as good for many people and for many purposes in many ways. Yet at the bottom of all our concerns is the simple fact that they are the concerns of the one being we each happen to be. Our ends, if in tension, are not incommensurable because there is a single standard quietly implicit in the whole analysis, and that is nothing more or less than what we in fact most deeply want. Through analysis and experience we can become clearer on what this is, how much of it is possible and how much not, which of its parts are compatible and which not, and how well the different strands of it prove in fact to answer our yearnings. Examining human nature in general and our own natures in particular, reason should be able to guide us toward the life that has the best chance of giving us the greatest satisfaction available of the deepest yearnings in us. Yet this is not what Aristotle proceeds to do, at least not in any direct way.

Instead, in elaborating so fully the tangled mass of all that we hope for in hoping for completeness, Aristotle evokes a profound, lurking frustration. Is there not, above all the disparate things that human beings in fact want, a standard to tell us what we *should* want and should pursue? If it is impossible to achieve completeness by literally leaving nothing out, or self-sufficiency by becoming equal to every contingency, might we not find in the depths of all our yearnings, even as the very best thing in us, some inkling of a single high purpose, which if clearly grasped and earnestly pursued will bring harmony and meaning to the whole of life, however long or short and however graced by fortune it may be? If this is the sense Aristotle means to evoke, he could not do it better than by adumbrating both the inclusive and the exclusive strands of our hopes for happiness, and by evoking this sense he could not prepare the ground in a finer way for the step he next takes, the launching of his famous function argument. If life itself gives us a purpose, if nature or a divine being has put us on earth to do some work that only we can do, this would seem to provide a far more solid, serious, and dignified standard than our own contingent and shifting wants. "For everything that has a work and a proper action, the good and the doing well seem to reside in the work" (1097b26–27). And through a series of rhetorical questions and conditional statements (consider the repeated "ifs" at 1097b28, 1098a7, 1098a12, 1098a16, and 1098a17), Aristotle suggests without quite affirming it that humans do have such a work. In a breathtaking series of leaps, he then suggests that nature has given us not just any purpose but a purpose that is unique to us (or perhaps to us and the gods), intimately bound up with what sets us apart from other living organisms, and good not for anything beyond us but for us ourselves, so good that fulfilling this purpose is indeed *the* comprehensive human good that the science of politics seeks to identify and secure, or happiness itself. Nature could scarcely appear more benevolent.[24]

But as Aristotle does all this, his formulations shift. His first statement on the function of human beings is that the processes of nutrition and growth that constitute mere life are shared even with plants, and sense perception is shared even with cattle, so that in seeking what is uniquely human, "there remains a certain active life of that which possesses reason" (1098a3–4). Aristotle then expands what "possesses reason" to include both "what is obedient to reason," which he will later identify as the seat of the passions whose proper orderings constitute the moral virtues, and "what possesses it and thinks" (1098a4–5; cf. 1.13). Does the first element truly possess it? But then, instead of giving priority to that in us which fully possesses and exercises reason rather than merely obeying it, Aristotle makes a different cut, between the mere possession and the full activity of a faculty: certainly the active use of something marks the possession of it "in the sovereign sense" (1098a5–7).[25] On that basis, he emphasizes activity and allows reason itself to begin receding, defining the work of a human being not quite as an activity of reason but as "an activity of soul in accord with reason, or not without reason" (1098a7–8). Next, observing that the function of a person—say, a cithara player—is the same as the function of such a person who is serious (*spoudaios*) or excellent at his work, Aristotle allows the focus to shift again to excellence or virtue, and from the question of what the work of a human is to the idea of doing that work, whatever it is, *well*. He then gives two more formulations for the work of a human being, one almost a restatement, the other subtly but momentously different:

> But if this is so—and we posit the work of a human being as a certain life, and this is *an activity of soul and actions accompanied by reason*, and it is the work of a serious man to do these things well and nobly, and each thing is brought to completion well in accord with its proper virtue—if this is so, then the human good becomes *an activity of soul in accord with virtue*, and if there is more than one virtue, in accord with the best and most complete one. But, in addition, in a complete life. For one swallow does not make a summer, or one day. And neither does one day or a short time make one blessed and happy. (1098a12–20, emphasis added)

With a gracefully sober reminder that the human good is still subject to fortune and circumscribed by death, and with a nod forward to the thought of book 10 that the human good in the full sense is the activity of contemplation alone, Aristotle puts before us the task of grasping what it means to conduct oneself well or virtuously, whatever it is that one is doing, which now takes on a life of its own that will carry the *Ethics* all the way through book 6. But Aristotle just reminded us in the previous chapter that the thing is prior to the activity and the activity prior to the mode of activity. There is a plausibility but also a limitation to the suggestion that a thing's function is best grasped when it is functioning well. A well-functioning eye does illustrate especially clearly what it is that an eye needs to do, but can we really tell what the eye is for without seeing how the organism uses it, or identify the purpose of music merely by determining how a virtuoso performer differs from an amateur?

Thus it is important and troubling that as virtue becomes the focus, in the passage just quoted, reason begins to recede from view. Indeed, Aristotle has no sooner advanced his revised claim about the work of a human being than he launches into a third digression on method, reiterating his claim that precision must not be demanded of the art of politics. He argues that we seek knowledge of "the right" (or right angle) only as a carpenter does, with a view to "use in his work," and not as a geometer does, with a view to knowing "what it is" (1098a29–31). Is there, after all, precise knowledge of the human good available, as precise as the geometer's knowledge of the Pythagorean theorem, but we do not need to study it? Aristotle reiterates that it is sufficient for our work to identify the "that"—the knowledge of specifics that a well brought up gentleman already has—and not the "cause," or the deeper knowledge of human nature that might justify particular moral rules (1098a33–b2). But can we even get true knowledge of the "that" if we neglect to ask the "what it is" question, and if, as Aristotle suggests, we are open to seeking our starting points not only through induction and perception but through habituation (1098b3–4)?

What does all of this mean for our basic questions, the function of reason within the ethical life as Aristotle presents it, and the character of the reasoned investigation that Aristotle himself is carrying out in the *Ethics*? Indicating the need for but not pursuing a radical investigation into the natural needs and natural thriving of human beings, Aristotle instead begins from respectable human opinion. Asking what is the work or function of a human being, he turns aside to consider what it means to do whatever that work is well or nobly. Hypothesizing that the human good is an activity of soul in accord with reason, he reframes it as an activity of soul in accord with virtue, bringing not the philosopher's but the gentleman's priorities to the fore. He insists nonetheless that his is the right approach, the one "natural" to the subject matter (1098b5). Somehow ethics is best investigated by building not from the ground up but, through gentle probing, from respectable opinion down. And respectable opinion tells us that what matters most is not our own needs or wants but what is noble; it tells us that what matters even more than the results we achieve is how well we perform our part; it tells us that the highest purpose of the best life is to act nobly in all that one does. Reason will prove important for the ethical life, so understood, but its place will be that of an attentive assistant rather than an autonomous guide. Although the *Ethics* will ultimately prove a profound study in human nature and a model of how philosophic reason can give guidance for life, the illumination is indirect and the best model will be found at least as much in how Aristotle proceeds as in what he explicitly says. On this most important and most difficult philosophic subject of our own souls, there is somehow no more direct path to understanding than the long, winding detour that begins at 1.7 and continues into book 6 and in a sense up to book 10.

HAPPINESS AND THE DIVINE (1.8–9)

In the next five chapters Aristotle elaborates and defends his proposal that the end of human life according to nature is happiness, understood as activity of the soul in accord with virtue. Even while insisting on beginning from decent men's intuitions into what is right and eschewing radical investigations into the "why," he supports his thesis with a survey of respectable opinion that includes the opinions of the ancients and even philosophers. Wholeness becomes the theme of 1.8 as Aristotle advances the audacious claim that he can combine what is strongest in all prior accounts of happiness to fill out an account of happiness as the activity of virtue that also unites everything that we most want. He makes a compelling case that happiness, most fundamentally, is not a possession or a state but a fullness of meaningful, excellent activity. He facilitates his task of bringing together common intuition with eminent opinion by leaving open whether the happiness he is defending is the activity of one virtue or many (1098b30–31, 1099a29–31). Yet as he proceeds he also continues to point quietly to tensions among our yearnings and hopes, and he will exclude one important alternative understanding of the human good altogether.

Aristotle begins in 1.8 by reminding us of the distinction, which he says is "ancient and agreed to by those who philosophize," between external goods, goods of the body, and goods of the soul, the last being "most authoritatively and in the greatest degree good" (1098b12–18).[26] His account accords with this ranking in putting the soul's actions and activities at the center of happiness; it does so also in acknowledging a subordinate but necessary role for external goods. Curiously, however, Aristotle is almost silent on goods of the body. After speaking of "action and activities of the soul" as the substance of happiness, he suggests a little incongruously that "actions and activities" belong altogether to the goods of the soul and not external ones (1098b15–20), and pleasures too belong to the soul (1099a7–8), leaving out the body. He also includes beauty among "external" goods (1099a31, 1099b3), while referencing strength and health only obliquely and saying nothing about bodily pleasures. Will happiness as he presents it provide wholeness in the form of full, balanced satisfaction of all our natural desires, or will some important activities and pleasures—for example, those of athletics, hunting, music, eating, drinking, and erotic love—be in fact sharply subordinated or omitted in his account? This chapter, at least, gives the impression of doing the former, while its strict logic does the latter. Perhaps something about moral virtue requires us to scorn bodily pleasures and pains, just as something about philosophizing causes one to forget them: both lives draw us in a sense to rise above our nature, and when we do not do so we tend to fall below it.[27]

Indeed, Aristotle speaks almost as if placing our happiness in the activity of virtue solves the problem of virtue's vulnerability to fortune: "It is possible for the characteristic, though present, to accomplish nothing good, as in the case of one who is asleep or otherwise idle, but this is not possible with the activity. For one will act of necessity, and will act well" (1098b33–99a3).[28] But is even virtuous activity self-sufficient? As if he has gone too far in promising this, Aristotle now allows two or three cracks of daylight to appear between virtuous activity and the happiness we desire. Drawing an analogy with the Olympic games (and thus reminding us of one realm of activity he is relegating to the shadows), he argues that just as the prize there does not go to those who are most beautiful or strongest, but the winners are found among the competitors, so "those who act correctly are winners of the noble and good things in life" (1099a3–7). Are the noble and good things they win something else beyond their virtuous actions? Do they necessarily all win it? The example of athletic contests also points in a different way to the problem of completeness by raising the question of desert: if even the athlete demands a prize for his stellar performance, virtuous action might seem to call out for a reward as much or more.

But Aristotle insists that it does not. "Their life is pleasant in itself." For, he says, "the pleasures of most people do battle with one another on account of their not being such by nature; but to the lover of the noble, the things are pleasant that are by nature pleasant, and such are the actions of virtue" (1099a7, 1099a11–14). No one is truly virtuous who does not love doing virtuous acts, and life for one who does love them is intrinsically so pleasant that it has no need of "extraneous pleasures" (1099a15–16). Finally, the activity that composes such a life is good as well as noble and pleasant. "Therefore happiness is the best, noblest, and most pleasant thing, and these are not separated, as the inscription at Delos has it: 'Noblest is what is most just, but best is to be healthy, / And most pleasant by nature is to attain what one passionately desires'" (1099a25–28). Nothing could be more appealing than a life that promises such wholeness, freeing us from inner discord and bringing our pleasures into perfect alignment with all that we find best and noblest. If Aristotle can deliver on his promise to show us a happiness that does this, his account will be compelling indeed. The test must of course await his full elaboration of the virtuous life. For now we observe only that in promising such wholeness, Aristotle is in fact breaking with one of the oldest and most authoritative of human opinions: the pious view, inscribed on nothing less than the temple at one of the classical world's holiest sites, that virtue needs divine support precisely because it is so hard. For virtue seems to demand that we give up much of what is best and most pleasant by nature, including a long life when courage or justice requires it, and often the satisfactions of erotic yearnings, which are so powerful that they can defy all legal constraints. Can Aristotle's gentlemanly ethos answer the challenge of piety? Or, considering from a different direction the eros Aristotle here alludes to, can his gentlemanly ethos answer the challenge of Socratic thought, according to which the power of eros broadly understood, the power of the yearning "to have the good always," is so great that it will in fact assert itself afresh even through the very actions of heroic self-overcoming that seem most to oppose it?[29]

The perspective of piety is closely linked to the perceived importance of fortune and to the general belief that virtue and even virtuous activity is not enough to assure the happiness that we associate with "blessedness," mentioned at 1099b2, or "having a good guardian spirit," as *eudaimonia* literally means. Aristotle makes an important concession to common opinion and common sense at the end of 1.8 by allowing that it is impossible or at least not easy to do what is noble if one lacks the external equipment that consists in wealth, political power, and even friends, if one's life is marred by ugliness or low birth or childlessness, and still more if one's children or friends turn out badly or die. But he gently insists that virtue is the core if not quite the whole of happiness. Aristotle is encouraging here a high-minded sobriety, which makes room for our strong natural attachments to goods we cannot control, while calling on us as much as possible to place our happiness in what we do control and to regard other good things as mere supports or supplements to our own virtuous activity.

In 1.9 Aristotle continues wrestling with the twin problems of fortune and piety. Raising the question of whether happiness is acquired "through learning, habituation, or some other practice, by some divine allotment, or even through chance" (1099b9–11), he first says that if anything is a gift of the gods to humans, it seems fitting that happiness, as the best of all things, would be.[30] But then he moves gently to the also inspiring thought that even if happiness is not god-given but instead comes through "virtue and a certain learning or practice," this "prize and end of virtue" is still somehow "among the most divine things" (1099b14–18). From there he proceeds to consider whether our situation might in fact be best if happiness should turn out not to be god-given, for then it would be more broadly accessible "through a certain learning and care to all who are not impaired with respect to virtue" (1099b18–20). Regarded as the prize of virtue in need of a prize-giver, happiness is out of our hands and dependent on beings that, if not automatically just, seem capricious. Would it not be better, Aristotle asks, for happiness to be available through learning and care "than through chance" (1099b20), suggesting now that these are the two fundamental alternatives—and that happiness is rather an end secured through virtue than a prize required by it? Learning, habituation, and practice have reduced to the learning and care that are up to us, while the gift of the gods has been assimilated to chance: so quietly does Aristotle register how problematic it is either for virtue to depend on being well habituated by another or for happiness to be in the hands of providential gods. "And if it is better to be happy this way than through chance, it is reasonable that it is so, if in fact the things that are in accord with nature naturally are in the noblest possible state, and similarly too what accords with art and every cause, and most of all what accords with the best" (1099b20–23). Aristotle encourages his readers to place their trust not in providential gods but in a benevolent nature that puts happiness within reach of virtually everyone. Or does it? He offers no demonstration that nature is so benevolent; the mention of art reminds us of all the needs that nature does not directly meet and that human ingenuity must address; and observations he will make later suggest that nature may not in fact equip us all well for virtue.[31] So another, soberer way of reading this statement is that "what accords with nature" is not what we can naturally expect but what we ought to do to make use of the resources nature gives us (in uneven measure) in order to best satisfy the needs and desires that nature also gives us, without teaching us how to do so.

How much, then, can we hope from the happiness that may be available in this way? This question brings us back to the concern for completeness: not only do we want completely satisfying activity but we want to enjoy it for a complete lifetime. Thus equipment is needed; thus we do not call animals happy; thus we cannot yet call children happy, both because they have not attained their full potential and because at best they have thrived for only a small part of a full lifespan, for "both complete virtue and a complete life are required" (1100a4–5). Even a man like Priam who has prospered for most of his life can meet with terrible reversals in old age, and no one would call such a man happy. If we are not willing with Homer to attribute Priam's sufferings to the gods' inexplicable hostility to a city that has steadfastly honored them,[32] nevertheless fortune seems to make most vulnerable the happiness that we wish might depend on us alone. With this sober thought Aristotle ends the chapter.

HAPPINESS AND MORTALITY (1.10–11)

Nor is this all. For the case of Priam draws Aristotle into the question of whether even at the end of a rich and successful life we can definitively call a person happy. Aristotle explores this question with a complicated series of questions, objections, and counterobjections in 1.10 and 1.11 as he provides a subtle dialectical response to a most serious objection to the thesis he is developing. Raising the question of whether we should follow Solon's dictum and "look to the end" before judging a man happy (1100a11),[33] he first rebuts a naïve interpretation of Solon on Aristotelian premises—arguing that it would be strange to call a dead man happy if happiness consists in activity—before challenging a more sophisticated interpretation of Solon on Solon's own premises. "Yet if we do not say that the dead person is happy—and this is not what Solon meant either—but that a man might then safely be called blessed once he is beyond the reach of evils and misfortunes, this admits of dispute as well" (1100a14–18). If Solon is right in accepting the popular supposition that happiness consists in good fortune and good success, Aristotle asks, is there not also force in the popular supposition that these do not altogether end even with a person's own death? This is believed to happen in three different ways. First, the dead are sometimes thought to be capable of perceiving or learning of what happens among the living, as Homer shows the shade of Achilles doing when Odysseus visits the underworld in the *Odyssey*.[34] Second, even if we never impute to the dead any further awareness, the honors and dishonors given to them or to their families, friends, or countries are thought to reach them somehow. Third, the happiness or misery of those they cared for and the posthumous success or failure of their own efforts can all affect our assessment of their lives and our inclination to call them happy. Now Aristotle never concedes that the dead do have any further awareness, and his statements elsewhere gently deny it.[35] Nor is he willing to concede that honor is ever decisive for happiness, let alone posthumous honor. But the third consideration is stronger. If a man endeavored throughout his lifetime to benefit friends and family and country and seemed to leave them secure and thriving, but immediately after his death everything he worked for is destroyed, must we not conclude that he ended his days in something of a fool's paradise? And do such considerations not show that even or especially for the most serious among us, happiness extends beyond our own activity in ways that leave us inescapably vulnerable to fortune?

This is an important challenge, which provokes one of the most stirring passages in the *Ethics*. Again weaving together his sublime sobriety with his inspiring high-mindedness, Aristotle defends the activity of virtue as the core of a happiness that is durable and resilient. If we must wait until we are beyond the reach of fortune to call ourselves happy, we can never do so, and it is not clear when anyone else can either, but that is good reason to suspect Solon's criterion for happiness. True happiness, Aristotle argues, is something lasting and not easily subject to reversals. It is possible to have it and lose it, but this does not happen easily, since a noble character is of all things one of the most stable. To become happy requires time, then, but not a whole lifetime.[36] Yes, fortune matters, "but it is the activities in accord with virtue that have sovereign control over happiness" (1100b9–10), inasmuch as without virtue there can be no true happiness, and with it there can be no true wretchedness. Good fortune can complete the happiness whose core lies in virtuous activity; ill fortune can curtail happiness by impeding action or by inflicting overwhelming pain, but "even in the midst of these, nobility shines through," when one endures misfortune calmly and shows one's greatness of soul (1100b30–31). What fortune cannot do is make a happy person wretched, "for he will never do things that are hateful and base" (1100b34–35). If Priam came to a wretched end, then, he never was truly happy: he possessed good fortune for a time but not greatness of soul.

Most important, so long as fortune leaves us any scope for action, we can take satisfaction in making the most of such opportunities as we have. "For we suppose that one who is truly good and sensible bears all fortunes in a becoming way and from what is available does what is noblest, just as a good general uses the army he has with the greatest military skill and a shoemaker makes the most beautiful shoe out of the leather given him" (1100b35–1101a5). The examples of a great general and a humble shoemaker are both important. Aristotle strengthens his case for virtue precisely with his realistic refusal to claim, as the Cynics were already doing and the Stoics would later do, that happiness is equally available to the oppressed and the privileged, to the ignorant and the well educated. To be sure, it is more impressive to fill a life with virtuous activity and to accomplish great things with poor opportunities than with good ones, but it is harder. Aristotle does nevertheless insist that the indispensable core and some substantial degree of happiness are available to all those who act well, so long as fortune is not altogether malignant. Thus he offers no guarantees, but he does provide a powerful portrait of the spirit in which we all might give ourselves the best chance for happiness and secure ourselves against wretchedness. No small part of what is impressive in that portrait is the brave, wise, robust realism with which Aristotle calmly accepts and depicts the noble person as accepting the limits of what life offers. "We will say that those among the living who have and will have available to them the things stated are blessed—but blessed human beings" (1101a19–21). For of course as humans we are still mortal.

Is this enough? Can a life of virtuous action add up to what Aristotle led us to expect happiness would provide as he defined it in 1.7? Saint Thomas says it cannot, since we yearn for immortality.[37] Aristotle himself has repeatedly acknowledged and even evoked this yearning with his discussion of "completeness" as a key feature of the happiness we are seeking, although without explicitly conceding that such completeness as we yearn for is unavailable. Yet as he returns to the issue of completeness at the end of the chapter, he introduces a note of doubt. The statement that we will call the man who lives well without serious reversals of fortune a blessed human being is in fact part of a conditional sentence, and in that sentence Aristotle takes a step back from his earlier insistence that we need not wait until the end to evaluate the happiness of a life. It is as if Aristotle himself is still intent on calling a full human life happy, in the spirit of the general who fights well with the army he has and accepts the results with equanimity rather than cursing fortune for what it does not give him—and yet somehow he is starting to run into a strong headwind.

At the beginning of 1.11 that headwind increases, and Aristotle cedes further ground in the face of it. "But that the fortunes of a person's descendants and all his friends contribute nothing whatever appears to be excessively unkind [or unfriendly—*aphilon*] and contrary to opinion" (1101a22–24). We see now that an important part of the objection represented by Solon has yet to be met. Aristotle's arguments in 1.10 were all about bearing up well under our own misfortunes and making the best of our opportunities, keeping our attention focused squarely on our own actions and not on what happens to us. Fair enough: that looks both sensible and impressive. But what about the fortunes of those we love? Aristotle here calls attention again to the inescapable human vulnerability to fortune that virtue in many ways counteracts but in some ways actually heightens, inasmuch as serious people naturally care especially about the results of their efforts and the happiness of their loved ones. This vulnerability they can feel even more keenly on behalf of others than themselves, because pride can make them resolute in the face of their own suffering and death, while giving less protection against that of others. In a certain way, the human vulnerability to fortune is more clear in the dead than in the living, even if they perceive nothing at all: they are helpless to do anything for those they cared about; there is no question now of their resolutely focusing on acting well and making the best of what fortune brings. Human love and the human concern with what one leaves behind after death—two expressions of eros, as Plato depicts it[38]—thus converge in a serious challenge to Aristotle's claim about the happiness available to human beings through virtuous action.

Aristotle's response to this challenge is to grant that these things matter, but to return to his gentle insistence that they matter much less than a person's own actions. If anything at all does "get through" to the dead, he says, it is something slight or at any rate not so weighty as to make happy those who are unhappy or to deprive those who are happy of their blessedness (1101b1–5). Do the dead have some awareness after all? Can they still enjoy happiness? Commentators generally agree that Aristotle is not expressing genuine uncertainty as to whether the individual soul survives the death of the body, that his serious thought is merely that subsequent events make at most a small addition to the sum total of phenomena that should be considered in assessing a life, and that we should not reevaluate a life as *having been* unhappy if it was happy when the person was living.[39] But his language opens the door to a more hopeful reading, at the cost of opening himself to a charge of inconsistency. Is this studied ambiguity just an endeavor to avoid wounding readers' feelings? I believe Burnet is right to point to the dialectical character of the argument here, and Pritzl is right to insist that it is also doing serious work.[40]

This passage is in fact a fine example of how Aristotelian dialectics can accomplish different things with several different kinds of readers at once. Aristotle has argued so explicitly and emphatically that happiness consists in activity that only a careless reader could think he means seriously to hold out hope of eternal happiness in any but the most attenuated sense. But he is making his teaching about the substance of happiness more palatable to the pious reader who cannot give up hope of some kind of afterlife, however shadowy, while gently shifting that reader's attention toward what is under his own control in this life. Significantly, however, Aristotle refuses any encouragement at all to the thought that the virtuous need or should expect rewards in the afterlife or that vengeful gods will punish the wicked. Recalling with the mention of Priam in 1.9 the tragic spirit of Homer's poems, in which heroic virtue cries out for reward and providential gods are all-important, Aristotle turns his more pious readers' attention instead to the intrinsic rewards of the life of virtuous activity and to the benevolent nature that makes this life possible. To a tougher and more skeptical kind of reader he is encouraging a more sober spirit of self-sufficiency, and the more sober reading that what happens after death "gets through" only in the sense of being relevant to an assessment of a life after the fact. And yet for this reader too he evidently thinks that it may be helpful—that it may paradoxically contribute precisely to his spirit of self-sufficiency—to leave a faint glimmer of doubt about the finality of death and the possible support of providential gods. "I can face my mortality and the limits of the happiness life makes available," such a reader will be inclined to think, "and my virtue is in need of no divine reward. But who knows? Perhaps after all there are gods who care about human beings, even after we die, and if there are, surely they will care especially for those who live nobly and intelligently as I do" (cf. 1179a24–29). Would not just this glimmer of doubt make it easier for many people to accept adversity, injustice, and ingratitude without bitterness, and in that way really to be as self-reliant as possible? But for the most philosophic reader who is most averse to self-deception Aristotle offers something different: a lesson on the power of the yearning for completeness, which though it does not make happiness impossible, certainly casts a long shadow over such happiness as is possible, and likewise renders perfect clear-sightedness most difficult.[41]

Thus, on the question of happiness after death as on many important questions throughout the *Ethics*, Aristotle is not presenting a tidy doctrine but is exploring, raising questions, suggesting considerations, and engaging in multiple conversations at once as he prods different kinds of readers to take what steps they are ready to take toward clarity, while also offering them different possible stopping points along the way. In the same way, he presents his account of happiness not as settled doctrine but as a hypothesis to be tested through the elaboration of the rest of the *Ethics* and in the lives of those who are inspired by it. His project of teaching that the activity of virtue has authoritative control over happiness makes no sense unless he truly thinks that a life lived on this premise is possible and is the best available for most of us, yet its exact strengths and limitations remain to be fully explored. As he proceeds, he will challenge us to reflect deeply on what nature gives us, what it makes us yearn for, why we all find great acts of virtue so inspiring, and how far the life of moral virtue can in the end answer our deepest yearnings. He will suggest in book 10 that it is the activity of philosophy and not of moral virtue that can provide the most complete happiness, and he will spell out some but not all of his reasons for that conclusion. But he devotes the bulk of the *Ethics* to a defense of an active moral life that only at the end comes to light as second best, because for the majority of people it will be the best possible, and because even for potential philosophers, a deep, sympathetic exploration of its meaning is precisely the best path forward. Aristotle's account of happiness is broadly inclusive, in order to capture and prod us to reflect on what we all yearn for; it is narrowly inclusive, in order to encourage us all to place our happiness as much as possible in excellent activity and to minimize the importance of other goods; and it is exclusive, in order to encourage those with a theoretical bent to concentrate every effort on what is highest. There is not one teaching in the *Ethics* because there is not one kind of reader, and because in fact both kinds of readers are better served by a complex, layered unfolding of Aristotle's thought.

HAPPINESS AND VIRTUE, HONOR AND PRAISE (1.12)

In 1.12 Aristotle closes his discussion of happiness with a final question that at first seems merely semantic and rather more germane to rhetoric than to ethics: whether happiness is among the things that we praise or those that we honor.[42] But the question turns out to open a significant difference between happiness and virtue. "Now everything praised appears to be praised for being of a certain sort and for its condition relative to something: for we praise the just person and the courageous person and altogether the good person and also virtue on account of their deeds and works" (1101b12–16). But we do not or at least should not praise the gods, Aristotle says, and we do not praise happiness either, for what is appropriate for the best and highest things is simply to honor them as blessed or divine. As Saint Thomas puts it, "There are two kinds of excellence. One is absolute and in this sense honor is due to it. But the other is an excellence in relation to some end, and in this sense praise is due. . . . The best things are not ordered to anything else but rather other things are ordered to them."[43] If we sometimes praise divine beings, it would seem to be in the way that we praise human leaders, for their perceived contribution to our good or for the way they meet a standard by which we measure ourselves, but Aristotle indicates that this is not really appropriate. Happiness, on the other hand, we are not even tempted to praise: it is final and complete, the end for the sake of which we do everything that we do.

The praise we give to virtue, then, implies that there is something incomplete or only conditionally good about it, even in comparison with pleasure, which, as Aristotle notes, we also do not praise. Is virtue's limitation, then, just that its possession does not guarantee the ability to exercise it without impediment? Aristotle does say that we praise virtue because "it inclines people to do noble things" (1101b32), but then why do we also praise noble actions? Perhaps this is an error, inasmuch as noble activity is precisely the substance of happiness, but this Aristotle does not say. Perhaps such praise is appropriate only in the limited sense that beginners in virtue need encouragement to persist in cultivating the habits that will ultimately bring them the best chance of complete happiness, but this he does not say either. Rather than pursue the question further, he stops short: "perhaps to be precise about these things belongs to people who have worked on encomiums" (1101b34–35). Would a precise account of the praise we give to virtue and virtuous actions call too much attention to the common perception that both are in need of praise, having their chief value in their results and often benefiting others more than the virtuous person himself? Aristotle has of course steadfastly refused to treat virtue as a means, but by pointing out the different spirits in which we praise virtue and cherish happiness, he sharpens the critical question of precisely what virtue's standard is and how reason grasps it.

THE PARTS OF THE SOUL (1.13)

Something holds Aristotle back from giving the simple if still formal answer that virtue's standard is nothing more or less than happiness, in the direct sense that virtues are nothing other than those abilities and inclinations of the soul that lead it to engage in the activities that are most deeply and naturally satisfying. Perhaps, then, this is the core of the matter, but the needs of the political community give important secondary standards for virtue. This seems to be the direction Aristotle is moving at the beginning of 1.13. Recalling his definition of happiness as "a certain activity of the soul in accord with complete virtue," and referring back to "the choice made at the beginning" (1102a13)—evidently the choice to treat the study and promotion of human virtue as part of the political art—he proposes that we examine what "the practitioner of the political art in the true sense" is properly aiming at as he seeks "to make the citizens good and obedient to the laws" (1102a5–10; cf. *Politics* 1276b16–18). To the extent that virtue's standard still needs clarification, we would expect our task to be a deeper investigation of the human soul and its well-being with special attention to its political context, the qualities that individuals need in order to thrive within that context, and the ways that the political community can best be deployed to foster these traits in its members. Moreover, to the extent that there is something higher and more divine in the common good than in the individual good, as Aristotle suggested in 1.2, or simply prior and more urgent, we would also expect the task to include giving a fuller account of what that common good is, what it demands of the individual, and in what way and how completely the requirements of individual happiness and the common good can be harmonized.

But this is in fact not the task Aristotle is calling for. Rather than investigate happiness further with a view to clarifying the standard for virtue, his proposal now is to study virtue "that we may better theorize about happiness" (1102a5–7). As Zeller observes, when Aristotle takes up his detailed study of the moral virtues, he will not derive them from any comprehensive account of happiness or measure them by their contribution to happiness.[44] Indeed, he will fall silent on the subject of happiness. For as he zeroes in on the virtues he will give unprecedented attention to the serious person's opinions about them, and central to those opinions is the view that virtue is good precisely in the unconditional way that Aristotle in 1.10 attributes only to happiness.[45]

Accompanying this turn away from the subject of happiness is a certain reticence on investigating the soul, whose thriving constitutes happiness. "If these things are so, it is clear that it is necessary for the statesman to know in *some* way about the soul, just as the one who is going to treat the eye to know about the whole body. . . . The statesman too ought to contemplate the soul, but he must do so for the sake of these things, and as far as is sufficient for the things sought" (1102a18–25, emphasis added). And for such practical purposes, Aristotle continues, some of the teachings even in his popular writings are sufficient. Now if it were Aristotle's core project in the *Ethics* to elucidate and teach the statesman how to promote the happiness of individuals according to nature, he could no more dispense with a precise account of the soul than the art of medicine can dispense with precise knowledge of physiology. The statesman could not even afford to be ignorant of any part of the individual soul's material and political context without first ascertaining that this context is not important for happiness. Thus it seems that his need for knowledge is even more comprehensive than that of the eye doctor, whose concern with other parts of the body extends only to their potential effects upon the eyes. Strangely, however, Aristotle compares knowledge of the only sometimes relevant context of the eye doctor's art, general physiology, to knowledge of the soul itself. Thus he limns the strange approach that will characterize the *Ethics*, an approach to the soul that steadfastly insists on investigating it not as an independent natural being through a fresh, radical investigation of human nature, or as a political being beginning from the needs and demands of the political community, or even as both as once, but instead in a way that eschews precision, that studies the "how" and the "well" without first specifying the "what," and that dismisses as only loosely relevant context the very thing whose excellent activity it seemed to be setting out to clarify.[46]

Aristotle now focuses his inquiry on the good functioning of just one part of the soul, the part involved in moral virtue, even though in doing so he relies on claims that he acknowledges belong to "popular" teachings that may be misleading. "But some points about the soul are stated sufficiently even in the exoteric arguments, and one ought to make use of them—for example, that one part of it is non-rational and another possesses reason. Whether these things are divided like the parts of the body and of every divisible thing, or are two in speech but by nature inseparable, like the convex and concave in the circumference of a circle, makes no difference for the present task" (1102a26–32). Aristotle thus encourages us to think of the soul as comprising separate rational and nonrational parts that can act independently so as to rule, obey, rebel against, tyrannize over, and persuade one another. He assures us that this model will work well enough for his student legislators, even as he suggests that thinking and feeling may truly be just two different aspects of, expressions of, or ways of considering the same movements of the soul.[47] Precisely our central question, then, the place of reason in the human soul and in its excellent activity, will be treated in a way that Aristotle assures us is good enough for practical purposes but perhaps in fact misleading. Does this distinction really make no difference?[48]

As Aristotle proceeds to elaborate his account of the parts of the soul, further doubts arise as to the proper way to classify them. After dividing the soul into a nonrational and a rational part, he provisionally divides the former again into one that governs nutrition and growth and is common to all living beings and another that possesses reason only in a limited sense. He infers the existence of the latter as a distinct part from the fact that *something* in uncontrolled people seems to resist reason in the way that a paralyzed part of the body fails to carry out the choices of the mind. But after offering this evidence for a threefold division of the soul only with a hesitant "perhaps," he goes on to affirm that the way the intermediate part differs from the rational one "does not matter" (1102b25). In the self-controlled person this part, whatever it is, obeys reason, he says, adding that "perhaps it is even more obedient to reason in the moderate or courageous one, for everything harmonizes with reason" (1102b27–28). Thus the intermediate part is the seat of the appetites and desires, fundamentally nonrational but able to be persuaded by reason. Or, "if we must affirm that this part too possesses reason, then what possesses reason will also be twofold, one possessing it in the authoritative sense and in itself, the other in the sense of listening to it as to a father" (1103a1–3).[49] Either way, the highest of three parts is the seat of the intellectual virtues, Aristotle concludes, while the intermediate one is the seat of the moral virtues.

Aristotle has in fact just offered three quite different ways of thinking about the parts of the soul, leading to quite different ways of thinking about moral virtue. If we view the soul as having a twofold nonrational part and a single rational one, virtuous action would seem to consist in passion's obedience to the autonomous commands of reason, a reason that is able to see what is noble and choose it for its own sake without any reference to desire, commanding well-habituated passions as a master commands a well-trained dog. Virtue on this account would mainly entail the proper habituation and subordination of passion to reason, while vice would represent reason's capitulation to passion. According to this picture, however, the seat of the moral virtues, like the obedient dog, has only enough "reason" to be able to grasp commands and not enough to assess arguments or to understand what makes a right thing right. This part's only real virtue will be obedience, and in following the strictures of one's elders and of tradition, moral virtue would seem to be dependent on the wisdom of an authority extrinsic to it.

Perhaps it is significant, then, that Aristotle takes as his analogue for the well-habituated seat of the passions and of moral virtue not a dog but an obedient son, not yet wise but possessing the capacity for reason and hence able to be persuaded by admonitions and exhortations, and not yet able to love virtue for its intrinsic goodness but still able to love it provisionally as a result of loving those who embody and honor it. This image suggests that reason in the best case does not just overrule the passions but educates them to respond to experiences in a different and better way.[50] This image also fits with Aristotle's last schema that classifies the intermediate part of the soul not as the higher of two irrational parts but as the lower of two rational ones. But now we have a most complicated account of the intermediate part, as the seat of both passions and imperfectly developed reason. In what sense does the incomplete reason present in this part differ from the more complete reason present in the higher one? And how are the passions and the reason that both reside in the intermediate part related?

Such puzzles bring us back to the first of Aristotle's three ways of describing the soul as perhaps best after all. According to this schema, which he briefly alluded to as possibly truer but not relevant for the practical purposes of the *Ethics*, the soul is not composed of separate ruling and ruled parts but rather is a single whole in which passions and judgments are two aspects of the same inclinations toward the good and away from the bad, no more independent of one another than are the convex and concave sides of a single arc. Then good character would consist in a single quality of seeing well, understanding well, taking pleasure in, and embracing what is good, and likewise seeing, understanding, disliking, and rejecting what is bad. The moral and intellectual virtues would be closely related and interdependent, as Socrates suggests. The tangles that seem to involve the mind's approving one thing while the passions desire something else would still need explaining, but on this account they would have to be understood in terms of contradictory desires and confused judgments rather than the opposition of separate parts. Aristotle will proceed through books 2–6 on the premise that the parts of the soul and the virtues governing each part are separate and distinct, but here at the outset he alerts us to consider whether this premise may not ultimately be misleading, and likewise whether, in treating as mere "context" what is in fact the very subject we most need to understand—the nature of the human soul—we will not be at least ostensibly bypassing questions of the greatest moment.

CORRECT REASON AND THE MEAN (BOOK 2)

Taking up at the beginning of book 2 the distinction between the moral and the intellectual virtues as perfections of two different parts of the soul, and now explicitly answering the question of 1.9, Aristotle says that intellectual virtue arises mainly through teaching and moral virtue results from habituation. Perhaps the clarity and simplicity of this distinction rests on the choice made in 1.13 to treat the soul as more cleanly separated into parts than it is, but surely there is much truth to it. Then, without comment and even with a shift in language that soon begins to imply that the moral virtues are the virtues simply (1103a24), Aristotle postpones discussing the intellectual virtues and devotes the rest of book 2 to outlining the various moral virtues and their common and distinctive features. He will not return to the intellectual virtues, whose task is to grasp well the end of action, until book 6, when his treatment of the moral virtues has been completed. Likewise, as we have seen, he will set aside any further discussion of happiness as the end. But he will listen most carefully to what people say about the virtues and watch most observantly what they do, as the student that he is of both human behavior and human nature. In quiet ways, nature will remain a theme of the discussion, and so will reason.

Instead of drawing a sharp contrast between nature and convention as the pre-Socratics did, our philosopher, in keeping with his thesis that man is by nature political (1097b11), depicts a subtle relationship between nature and convention in 2.1. What arises by habit, Aristotle says, is neither given by nature, as sense perception is, nor contrary to nature, for nothing can be habituated to do what is truly against its nature. "Thus neither by nature nor against nature do the virtues arise, but they do so in us who are of such a nature as to receive them and are completed through habit" (1103a23–26). It is part of our nature that we can be habituated at all, that we can be habituated in various ways but not in just any way, and that proper habituation is needed to perfect us.[51] What is natural for human beings in the highest sense according to Aristotle is not automatic or even common, then; it is an unfolding that takes direction from nature just as the arts do, in deploying innate abilities to meet needs that nature gives us but leaves unaddressed. Indeed, in a passage whose strangeness the translators invariably obscure, Aristotle even compares the virtues to "the *other* arts" (1103a32).[52] As with the ordinary arts, we acquire the virtues not chiefly by study but by practice, yet this does not mean that we can acquire them without knowledge, as Aristotle acknowledges in speaking of the need for a teacher in cithara playing. Moral virtue is in every way something that takes root and flowers somewhere in between our animal natures and our purely intellectual capacities. Yet Aristotle ends 2.1 by stressing the importance of practice over teaching: "It makes no small difference, then, whether one is habituated in this or that way straight from childhood but a very great difference—or rather the whole difference" (1103b23–25). This chapter gives a subtle teaching on nature but perhaps also downplays the importance of nature, for Aristotle claims that even courage arises wholly through habituation and is silent on natural virtue (cf. 6.13). The chapter is likewise silent on the importance of insight into what is good.

In the next chapter, 2.2, Aristotle underscores the importance of actions that form good habits, reiterating that "we are conducting an examination not so that we may know what virtue is but so that we may become good" (1103b27–28). But if habituation makes all the difference, knowledge should be unnecessary for right action; if we have been well raised, we should not need Aristotle's study to be virtuous. Yet Aristotle insists that somehow the knowledge that the *Ethics* teaches is essential not just for the statesman but for anyone who wishes to be virtuous. And indeed, as soon as he takes up the question of what correct action looks like, the first answer he gives is "acting in accord with correct reason [*orthos logos*]" (1103b31–32). "Correct reason" is an important but, as Bartlett and Collins observe, an ambiguous formulation, which can mean either true reason or a morally correct reason that may or may not be true.[53] To our dismay but by now no longer our surprise, however, Aristotle no sooner raises the standard of correct reason than he says he will postpone discussing it and its relation to the "other virtues"; instead he gives another statement on the necessary imprecision of moral and political matters. More than ever, we suspect that Aristotle's reticence in stating the standard true reason looks to in guiding human life and the imprecision of the subject matter are one and the same. In our quest for an accurate picture of the strange animal that is moral virtue, one of the first features to come clearly into view, then, is moral virtue's resistance to a precise statement of its own standard.

If we were taking happiness as virtue's standard, correct reason would be the insight into what is most beneficial for promoting happiness in us and those we care about. Aristotle alludes to the beneficial as a relevant aim even as he is insisting on the impossibility of precision:

> Matters of action and those pertaining to what is beneficial have nothing stationary about them, just as matters of health do not. And since such is the character of the general argument, still less precise is the argument concerned with particulars, for it does not fall under any art or any set of rules. Instead, those who act ought themselves always to examine what pertains to the opportune moment, as is the case with both medicine and piloting. (1104a3–10)

Aristotle now claims that his subject, involving as it does particular, changing conditions, is not only impossible to reduce to universal rules but impossible to reduce to an art—and this despite the fact that he has just spoken of virtue *as* an art (1103a32) and despite the explicit reminder he is giving of the arts of piloting and medicine, which are not only precise in their aims but capable of taking ever-changing particulars into account in pursuing them with intelligence. But perhaps the good that virtue pursues is even more deeply changeable than the ends of these arts are.

This fifth and final statement in books 1–2 on the imprecision of the subject matter of ethics marks another important transition, coming just after Aristotle has raised "correct reason" as a potential key to clarity on the moral virtues but has postponed discussing it, and just before he introduces the new doctrine of the mean. The doctrine of the mean now replaces correct reason. The mean is clearly something rational, consisting in a correct balance between extremes that builds and sustains each good quality, just as the right amounts of food and exercise sustain good health. There is, however, this difference: in the case of food and exercise, the goal of health stands outside the activity as a standard, whereas in the case of the virtues, virtuous activity itself is the standard, and Aristotle will seek specificity not in anything virtue produces but in the particular kinds and qualities of action that we praise and blame.

Reason recedes further from view in 2.3 as Aristotle argues for the importance of pleasure and pain in the moral virtues and vices. "Moral virtue is concerned with pleasures and pains: it is on account of the pleasure that we do base things, and it is on account of the pain that we abstain from noble ones. Thus one must be brought up a certain way straight from childhood, as Plato says, so as both to enjoy and to be pained by what one ought, for this is correct education" (1104b10–13; cf. Plato *Laws* 653a ff.). Each characteristic shows itself in its relations with the things by which it becomes better or worse, and "it is through pleasures and pains that people become base, by pursuing or avoiding the ones that one ought not, or when one ought not, or as one ought not, or in as many other such conditions as are defined by reason" (1104b21–24). This is reason's only appearance in this chapter: it somehow fixes the mean, even while character formation seems to be entirely a matter of habituation.

Aristotle presses more deeply into the relative weight carried by reason, habituation, and pleasure and pain in constituting moral virtue in 2.4. He begins with the question of how it is that acting justly is the cause of becoming just, rather than confirmation that one is already just. To address this he returns to his comparison between virtues and arts: in both one learns by doing, and in both action and production it is possible to perform well only by chance or under the direction of another without possessing the relevant skill or characteristic. But there is also a difference. The arts require a know-how that comes partly by instruction and largely by practice, whereas virtuous action requires three elements, only one of which is shared with the arts: one must act "knowingly"; one must act "by choice and while choosing the acts in question for their own sakes"; and one must act "while being in a steady and unwavering state" (1105a26–33).[54] This is an important statement on the criteria of virtuous action. Yet no sooner has Aristotle made it than he qualifies the first part of it. "These factors do not count when it comes to possessing the other arts, except knowledge itself. But in the case of the virtues, knowledge has little or no force, but the others have no small power, but rather the whole power" (1105a33–b4). Aristotle ends the chapter with a stern rebuke of "the many" who imagine that they can become good by taking refuge in argument, "supposing that they are philosophizing," and acting no more sensibly than the sick who seek medical advice but fail to follow it (1105b12–16). Knowledge—or at least "philosophizing in this way" (1105b18), which may or may not be true philosophizing—is neither sufficient nor even essential for virtue.

This denigration of knowledge prepares us for Aristotle's specification of the genus of moral virtue in 2.5. Referring now to moral virtue simply as virtue and to the part of the soul that contains it simply as the soul, he specifies the three things that the soul contains as passions, capacities, and characteristics, leaving understanding silently aside. The moral virtues are neither passions nor capacities, he says, taking his evidence especially from the fact that we do not praise and blame people for these. What remains, then, is that they are characteristics, "those things by which we are in a good or bad condition in relation to the passions" (1105b25–26)—for example, the tendency to become angry at the right things and to the right degree. "Moreover," he adds, in explaining why the virtues are not passions, "we become angry and afraid without choice, but the virtues are certain choices or not without choice" (1106a2–4). Thus he puts quietly on the table the puzzling question of just where choice and responsibility lie in moral virtue. For if the virtues are habitual ways of feeling, they would seem to be even less susceptible to the direct influence of choice than the individual passions themselves are.

In 2.6 Aristotle takes up the challenge of defining more specifically what kind of characteristic moral virtue is. Although he remains silent on happiness, he does return to the idea of a natural work or function: "Every virtue both renders that of which it is the virtue in a good condition and causes the work belonging to that thing to be done well," he says (1106a15–17). As examples, he says that the characteristic virtue and work of an eye is to see and that of a horse is to run, to carry its rider, and to stand its ground in battle. More generally, we might say, the work of an eye is to serve the organism it belongs to and of a horse to serve its master; more metaphorically, the work of the eye is directed to contemplation and that of the horse to the political community's security. But what is the chief work of a human being? To whose good is that work directed, and is it fundamentally contemplative or active? Aristotle merely says that "how this will be, we have already said," and that we will gain further clarity if we "contemplate what sort of thing the nature of virtue is" (1106a24–26). Yet the nature of virtue, he has been arguing, is to be a mean between extremes, and in defining the mean in each case, clarity of purpose seems indispensable. For as Aristotle now explains, the mean to be sought in moral virtue is not the mean in relation to "the thing itself"—that which is equidistant from both extremes—but the mean "in relation to us" (1106a28, 1106a31, 1106b7). He gives the example here of a trainer determining the right amount of food for each athlete, again pointing implicitly to natural need or health as the standard for moral virtue, and now making explicit the need for knowledge. "Thus every knower [*epistēmōn*] flees the excess and the deficiency but seeks the mean and chooses this, the mean not with respect to the thing but with respect to us" (1106b5–7). If *every* knower does this, is knowledge after all not sterile but by itself sufficient to ensure correct choice? Virtue seems now to be a kind of science or art, or even "more precise and better than every art, just as nature is" (1106b14–15).[55] Is it, then, through perfect knowledge of the mean to be found in each case that moral virtue attains its great precision and excellence? But no sooner has Aristotle suggested this than he reminds us that moral virtue is chiefly a matter not of knowledge or even skill but rather of passions and habits, a matter of feeling pleasure and pain and every other passion "when one ought and at the things one ought and towards whom one ought and for the sake of what one ought and in the way one ought" (1106b21–22). Without explaining how the passions may become so precisely shaped and directed, or specifying the relation between passion, knowledge, and choice, he adds that in actions, too, virtue involves hitting on the one right way among many ways of going wrong. He concludes, "Virtue, then, is a characteristic involving choice, consisting in a mean with respect to us, a mean defined by reason and in the way that a man of active wisdom [*phronimos*] would define it" (1106b36–1107a2). Active wisdom is clearly relevant, then, but this is the last we will hear of it until book 6. Indeed, a few lines later Aristotle will identify not reason but virtue itself as that which "discovers and chooses the mean" (1107a5–6). In listening carefully to the self-understanding of the serious man of virtue, Aristotle seems to have found a respect for reason alongside a deep resistance to specifying any external end or measure or standard of virtuous action. Deferring for now to that self-understanding, he turns to examining the particular virtues one by one, looking to see how each of them comes to sight in the serious person's life and what achieving the mean looks like in each case. But as he does so, the primary meaning of the "mean" itself begins to shift. The spotlight moves away from identifying the perfectly appropriate emotional response and the perfectly best action to take in each circumstance—a task for sophisticated reason if ever there was one, given the ever-changing character of human things (cf. 1104a4)—and onto the best disposition as a single, stable point on a line between two extremes. It is now at the end of 2.6 that Aristotle goes furthest in affirming the existence of moral absolutes, against the passage just cited and the claim in 5.7 that among human beings natural right "is all changeable" (1134b29–30).[56]

In 2.7, however, Aristotle provides a sketch of the moral virtues that shows how much more complex his project is than one of either deriving virtues from nature or merely listening to and codifying what respectable opinion honors and considers each virtue to be. As he now populates his catalogue of virtues and vices by combining widely praised and blamed qualities with others of his own introduction for which he must coin new names, as he points to ambivalences in the way "we" regard certain qualities such as ambition, as he rejects at least one widely praised quality, shame or reverent awe (*aidōs*), as not truly a virtue at all, and as he identifies one virtue, righteous indignation (*nemesis*), only to drop it from his subsequent catalogue of virtues, he makes it clearer that his project will be a complicated amalgam of deferential listening and critical reflection, meant mainly to support but sometimes to improve traditional moral judgments, and likewise meant partly to conceal but occasionally to reveal his own critical perspective. And somehow key to understanding that perspective will be grasping the reasons for Aristotle's unconventional view of both *aidōs* and righteous indignation, which we will try to do in chapter 3.

The promise Aristotle has held out so far is that it will be possible to identify a perfect balance in each virtue and to find a happy harmony of inclinations, pleasures, and moral judgments in the well-cultivated life. In the last two chapters of book 2, however, a certain shadow begins to fall over that picture. Beginning gently in 3.8 from the observation that to the coward the brave man may look rash and to the rash he may look cowardly, Aristotle addresses the fact that people often identify certain virtues not as means between extremes but as one of a pair of opposites, such as courage and cowardice. The problem is not confined to skewed judgment caused by the observer's defective character. Some means such as courage really are closer to one extreme than another, he says, and in some things human beings naturally incline more to one extreme than to the other. Thus, for example, immoderation is far more common than the other rare and hence nameless extreme Aristotle calls "insensibility." Nature is neither a perfection that unfolds of its own accord nor even one that is easily attained with a little cultivation: it is in some ways positively recalcitrant to the virtues that nonetheless somehow compose our natural perfection.

But perhaps the problem is even more complex than this. In 2.9 Aristotle speaks of the difficulty of hitting the right mean, illustrating it with a cascade of evocative images that point in different directions. First he alludes to the problem of finding the middle of a circle, which "belongs not to everyone but to a knower" (1109a25–26). In almost but not quite the same way, he says that striking the right mean when it comes to anger and money "does not belong to everyone" but rather is "rare, praiseworthy, and noble" (1109a28–30; cf. 1099b18–20). Then he calls on us to steer clear of whatever is most contrary to the mean, quoting Odysseus's advice to his men on approaching Charybdis to "keep away from this smoke and swell" (1109a32 and Homer *Odyssey* 12.219). He then acknowledges that our challenge is after all not to identify the precise mean, but rather to devise a second-best expedient that will at least avoid the worst extreme, or indeed to make a "second sailing" (1109a34–35), a proverbial expression for resorting to rowing when the winds fail. The need for knowledge returns as Aristotle enjoins us to examine ourselves well—but this with a view to "dragging" ourselves away from the extremes to which we ourselves are most inclined, or forcibly opposing what is recalcitrant in us "as people do who straighten warped timber" (1109b4–7). Finally, urging us "above all" to guard against pleasure, which does not leave our judgment "unbribed," he offers another image from Homer, approving the judgment of the Trojan elders that as beautiful as Helen is, Troy would be better off sending her back (1109b7–12 and Homer *Iliad* 3.154–60).

Our task, in short, turns out to be one not of fine-tuning a delicate instrument but of forcibly straightening warped timber. Has nature after all made us vicious? Does virtue require even less thought than the doctrine of the mean has suggested, and instead just brute habituation? And is the moral life even at its best one not of happy harmony but of hard self-restraint? These are serious questions that Aristotle prompts at the outset of his detailed account of the moral virtues, which we must bear in mind even as he allows them to drop from view in the coming books. But we also should note that he here gives hints of something more complex and perhaps more positive in these images. First, we see with his two references to knowledge that while the kind of knowledge a geometer has is not sufficient and perhaps not even altogether helpful for moral virtue, self-knowledge may still be very important. Second, the reference to Odysseus's encounter with Scylla and Charybdis points to an alternative reason for virtue's difficulty besides a natural recalcitrance to doing what is good for us individually. Aristotle claims that the advice to steer clear of Charybdis is Calypso's, but Homer gives these words to Odysseus, who is silently reflecting to himself as he speaks that it is pointless to tell his men that in order to avoid the risk of losing the whole ship and crew to Charybdis they must hew close to Scylla, who will devour six of them (*Odyssey* 12.222–25). Odysseus is wrestling with the terrible political fact that often the good of some must be sacrificed for the security of the community, and Aristotle, in speaking as Odysseus, is perhaps signaling the way in which moral virtue is necessarily shaped by this imperative. Finally, with the second reference to Homer, Aristotle alludes to the intoxicating power of eros, which the Trojan elders connect to the divine: while they say that the city could scarcely be blamed for keeping Helen, so terribly does she resemble a goddess, still they judge it best to give her up, lest she be a grief to them and their children (*Iliad* 3.154–60). If it is best for the city to put a firm lid on eros, is it best for every individual? If it is best for the political community that individuals' encounters with what is divine be mediated by the laws, is that, too, best for every individual? We recall that the story of Scylla and Charybdis follows immediately upon the story of the Sirens, in which Odysseus judges it best for his men to have their ears stopped against the Sirens' song but for himself to hear it. We recall as well that the metaphor of a "second sailing," which Aristotle uses for turning away from seeking mathematical precision to forcibly countering our worst tendencies, is used by Socrates to describe his turn from natural philosophy to dialectics, a study in which he questions law-bred opinion, tests the claims of the Delphic Oracle, and plumbs the meaning of his own extraordinary insight into eros. The obstacles to complete self-knowledge and complete inner wholeness are formidable, but perhaps not insuperable.

Chapter 2

KNOWLEDGE, CHOICE, AND RESPONSIBILITY FOR CHARACTER

VOLUNTARY AND INVOLUNTARY (3.1)

Aristotle begins his discussion of choice and character in book 3 with the observation that "Since virtue concerns passions and actions, and since praise and blame are given for what is voluntary, and sympathy and sometimes pity for what is involuntary, it is perhaps necessary for those who are investigating virtue to distinguish the voluntary and the involuntary, and it will also be useful for lawgivers with a view to both rewards and punishments" (1109b30–35).[1] This formulation immediately raises a puzzle: when we hold people responsible for their virtues and vices, we regard those virtues and vices as voluntary; yet as we have seen, virtue and vice seem to involve unchosen passions as well as deliberate actions (cf. 1106b16–23). As Aristotle has stressed from the outset, it is essential to virtue that one not only do the right thing but do it for the right reason, and among the reasons for acting that we do in fact blame and praise are such passions as greed and the love of justice. If virtues and vices concern both choices and the unchosen dispositions that precede and inspire them, how can we draw a line between the voluntary and the involuntary in such a way as to do justice to our intuitive sense that virtue and vice fully deserve praise and blame and also rewards and punishments?[2] Or will that intuitive sense have to undergo serious revision to become theoretically sound? For example, might praise and blame for virtue and vice turn out to be rational only in the limited sense in which praising beauty and blaming ugliness are, and might rewards and punishments be rational only as forward-looking instruments of policy? But if healthy communities require a robust belief in moral responsibility to ground civic virtue and the rule of law, the investigation into the voluntary and the involuntary will be politically delicate. By saying that such an inquiry is *perhaps* necessary for those who are investigating virtue and also useful for lawgivers, Aristotle signals that his account may be tempered so as to be morally and politically salutary, even if this renders its value to students of philosophy less certain. And indeed, the complex analysis of 3.1–5 cannot be reduced to coherence without bearing this dual purpose in mind.[3]

Aristotle devotes the first chapter of book 3 to distinguishing the voluntary from the involuntary. He begins with the latter: it is easier to say with certainty what is not voluntary than what is. The voluntary is of course easily grasped on an intuitive level. It is what is done spontaneously, of one's own accord; it is what is "up to us," in the sense that we could do it or not do it as we choose; it is that of which the individual is the true source and cause. But all of these ideas, when analyzed, involve us immediately in a host of difficulties. What do we mean when we say that something could be or could have been otherwise? What do we mean by a true source and cause? Something that is itself caused by further things, or something uncaused? Perhaps all that we clearly mean by the word voluntary is that the individual who acts is *not* forced into the act by compulsion from outside and is not acting under a delusion. It is here, on this solid ground, that Aristotle begins.[4]

Compulsion

"Those things seem to be involuntary that occur by compulsion or through ignorance," Aristotle says (1109b35–10a1). His only examples of pure or unequivocal compulsion are cases in which a man is carried somewhere by a wind or by others who have him in their power. But at such times a person cannot truly be said to "act" at all, which Aristotle all but concedes when he says that in a case of compulsion, "the one doing [*prattōn*] or suffering [*paschōn*] something contributes nothing" to the result (1110a2–3).[5] The use of the word *paschōn*, which is related to the word for passion, *pathē*, points to the similarity between passions and the other unchosen forces that can carry us away without our consent and prevent us from acting voluntarily. Every human occurrence, if it is to be an action at all, would seem to need to be in least *some* sense voluntary.

Those actions that are actions in the full sense but are done under constraint Aristotle terms "mixed," but closer to the voluntary than the involuntary. To illustrate the mixed class, he cites what one does "through fear of greater evils or for something noble, for example, if a tyrant commands one to do something shameful, holding one's parents and children in his power, so that if one does it they will be saved, and if one does not do it they will die" (1110a4–7). This example may be taken either as a case of doing something through fear of greater evils or as a case of acting for the sake of the noble. Another example of the "mixed" class is jettisoning cargo in a storm. "Considered simply, no one jettisons things voluntarily, but every intelligent person would do it to save himself and his fellows" (1110a9–11). Taken "simply" or "in themselves" all such actions are involuntary (1110a18, 1110a19, 1110b3), but considered, as they should be, in the light of circumstances, they are mixed, and indeed more voluntary than involuntary. Actions are not rendered involuntary because they are done under the pressure of circumstances, for all acts are chosen from alternatives limited by circumstances and hence are properly assessed in light of those circumstances (1110a12–15, 1110b3–7). In arguing that even such desperate acts as jettisoning property are in an important way still voluntary, Aristotle appeals to the common sense of the matter: "the source of the movement of the instrumental parts of the body in such actions is in oneself, and when the source of something is in oneself, it is up to one to do it or not" (1110a15–18).[6]

Aristotle uses examples of dire situations to illustrate the mixed class, but we may well wonder how many ordinary acts, how many even of the noblest acts, would fall under the rubric of acts choiceworthy not in themselves but only because of the pressure of need or the threat of greater evils.[7] Would this class not include virtually all acts of courage, most acts of justice, and perhaps much of moderation and generosity as well? Aristotle's hints here about noble acts that are not simply choiceworthy anticipate what he will say more frankly in book 10: that there is something constrained or less than perfectly choiceworthy in most of moral and political life. Perhaps only such an activity as philosophizing would meet the test of voluntariness to the highest degree.

Aristotle offers further support for his claim that things done under pressure are still largely voluntary by adducing the praise and blame that they evoke. While acknowledging the difficulty of making the right judgment in such cases, he suggests that one can always find a course of action that is right, however unattractive it may be. The right course may be hard because one must endure painful and even shameful things in pursuing a noble object, things that would bring reproach if undertaken for no good reason.[8] Aristotle offers no rules for determining "what should be chosen for the sake of what" (1110a30, 1110b7), acknowledging the difficulty not only in making correct decisions but in "abiding by one's judgment" in hard cases (1110a29–31). What he is clear on is that acts must be judged in light of their particular circumstances and particular consequences, leaving it up to us to decide when the stakes are sufficiently high to merit making exceptions to normal rules of moral conduct.

Even when a base act is not justified by circumstances, Aristotle says, it may still elicit sympathy or understanding if it was done "under a strain greater than human nature can bear and that no one could endure" (1110a23–26).[9] By speaking of sympathy rather than justification, Aristotle upholds the decent view that in every case there is a right course of action and that terrible pressure does not turn wrong into right. But he does suggest that such pressure may turn voluntary into involuntary, since, as he said at the beginning of the chapter, praise and blame are given for what is voluntary while sympathy is accorded to what is involuntary. Without defining the magnitude of pressure that strains human nature to the breaking point, Aristotle reminds us that *some* degree of overwhelming evil to be avoided makes nearly everyone excuse an act and hence implicitly treat it as involuntary. Is there a clear and rational line to be drawn between such evils and the lesser ones that we think leave our voluntariness intact? Or could our moments of sympathy in the extreme cases be moments of unusual insight?[10]

Immediately afterward, however, Aristotle says that "some things it is perhaps not possible to be forced to do, but instead one should die suffering the most terrible things" (1110a26–27).[11] His example is Euripides' Alcmaeon, who was induced by his father's threats to murder his mother, Eriphyle. Euripides' play is now lost, but the story goes that Eriphyle had been bribed with a necklace to persuade her husband, King Amphiaraus of Argos (whose name means "double cursed"), to join in the doomed expedition of the Seven against Thebes. Learning of her treachery before his death, Amphiaraus ordered his sons to avenge him, cursing them with barren lands and childlessness if they did not kill their mother. Aristotle calls the things that forced Alcmaeon to do this ridiculous, but he also implies that nothing could justify such a murder, and that while considerations of good and bad outcomes may justify many acts, they do not justify the worst acts. Saving a ship by throwing away cargo is reasonable, but preventing starvation in the land by killing a woman is necessarily wrong . . . at least if that woman is one's mother. Whether it is ever permissible to sacrifice one life for the sake of many others, Aristotle does not say.

At the core, then, of the Aristotelian gentleman's decency is something sacred that underlies both what he will not do and what he cannot bear. It expresses itself not in rules or in categorical imperatives, but in a seriousness about human ties and especially the closest of human ties. In his sympathetic account, Aristotle supports the sensible gentleman who stands at the opposite pole from the Platonic character Euthyphro, who prosecuted his own father for impiety.[12] Aristotle stands with those who divine that without a sense of humanity that extends widely but that begins at home, without reverence for parents and all that they represent, moral virtue is in danger of becoming a cold fanaticism. Aristotle does not expose the limitations of this core of gentlemanliness. In particular, he does not mention that in at least one version of Alcmaeon's story, Alcmaeon was commanded to kill Eriphyle not only by his father but by the Delphic Oracle.[13] He does not, in other words, explicitly draw our attention to the evils and contradictions that men's deepest loyalties may involve them in. He implies that one can always do what is noble by, in the worst case, accepting a painful death for oneself. But what if the cost is higher and involves the destruction of parents, children, and city? And under pressures that strain human nature to the breaking point, is it possible to choose not to break? In the two sentences about things that human beings cannot bear and things that they cannot be forced to do at 1110a23–27, Aristotle captures a contradiction that inheres in morality precisely to the extent that it is decent and humane. On one hand, such morality sees the circumstantial nature of all human actions, the need to weigh actions by their intended results, and hence the need to allow or excuse evils done under great pressure to attain a great good: it recognizes in some way the power of the good to compel us. On the other hand, it denies precisely this power, for we also sense that if our determination to do what is right is strong enough, we can always resist temptation.

These two different perspectives accord with two different ways of understanding the structure of the soul that Aristotle sketches in 1.13. Looking at it from the perspective that treats the seats of reason and the passions as separate, we can say that the passionate part sometimes obeys reason as it should and sometimes refuses or is overcome by such pain that it is unable to. But if the division into parts is an inaccurate way of thinking about the soul, if passions and judgments about good and bad are inseparable aspects of our responses in the same way that the concave and the convex sides of an arc are, then perhaps we have in the heroic resistance to temptation and the capitulation to it not two fundamentally different phenomena but one and the same thing: the human being's natural and invariable pursuit of whatever at each moment seems best to him.

First Objection

Aristotle now presents a version of this thought as the objection of a nameless interlocutor, whom he will allow to interrupt the first five chapters of book 3 repeatedly, turning it into a kind of Socratic dialogue with some unusually deep implications.[14] In response to his suggestion that acts done strictly under compulsion are only those in which "the cause is external and the one acting contributes nothing" (1110b2–3), Aristotle acknowledges now the possible objection that "pleasant and noble things are done under compulsion, since these exercise compulsion from without" (1110b9–10). His answer has three parts. First, he says that if this were so, then "everything would be a matter of compulsion, since everyone does everything for the sake of these things" (1110b10–11).[15] Like both the interlocutor and Socrates, Aristotle rejects the most extreme notion of human freedom according to which human beings freely choose between good and evil. But if we concede that every choice is made for the sake of the pleasant or the noble, how is that different from saying that the pleasant and the noble compel us?[16]

Aristotle addresses this difference with his second response. "Things done under compulsion and involuntarily are painful, but things done on account of the pleasant and the noble are done with pleasure" (1110b11–13). Or so, at any rate, we tend to assume. The interlocutor is raising the possibility that we are in the habit of thinking of acts done under compulsion as painful only because we do not recognize that the good is compelling us all the time. Still, Aristotle's point is sensible: whatever freedom one may or may not ultimately have to choose one's ends, there is a clear difference between what one does because one wants to, such as killing an enemy, and what one does without ever having wished it, such as running aground in a storm or leaving a sinking ship. This distinction is important both for thinking clearly about human action and for assessing character. Only what is done voluntarily reveals the kind of person one is. If we are "compelled" by the good, it seems to be in such a different way from the way that we can be compelled to act against our wish that it is misleading to use the same word at all. When we act voluntarily we are precisely not puppets on strings but autonomous agents pursuing our own ends. If there is a kind of necessity at work here, it is very different from the blind necessity we call "compulsion."

Third and finally, Aristotle says, "It would be ridiculous to assign responsibility to externals, and not to oneself for being easy prey to such things, and to oneself for noble actions, and to pleasures for shameful ones" (1110b13–15). There is to this reply the same sensible core: things that we desire do not compel us in the same way as winds that blow us off course, for when we act on our desires, the efficient cause of the action is within us. If we are an easy prey to temptations, we may ourselves be responsible for our inflamed desires or weak characters. Accordingly, the interlocutor will return in his next two objections to the question whether people should be held accountable either for their desires or for their characters. But if this response has a sensible kernel, it is also unfair to the interlocutor, who never claimed that noble acts are more voluntary than ignoble ones. Aristotle is casting aspersions on his questioner's motives, suggesting that his objection was prompted by a dishonest effort to escape censure for his faults. This rhetorical assault assures every reader who prides himself on his virtue that Aristotle will not countenance such evasions of responsibility.[17] In concluding his discussion of compulsion, Aristotle leaves maximum scope for moral responsibility by calling compulsory only "that of which the cause is external, and to which the one being compelled contributes nothing" (1110b15–17).

Ignorance

Aristotle turns next to ignorance, the second factor after compulsion that can render an act involuntary. He divides acts due to ignorance into those that are subsequently regretted, which he classes as truly involuntary, and those that are not, to which he gives the name nonvoluntary. In his discussion of sailors jettisoning cargo, Aristotle has insisted that we must look to the moment of action and the end one had in view at the time in order to determine if one acted voluntarily or not. Hence some commentators have asked how subsequent regret can render an act involuntary.[18] Aristotle's point, however, is not that regret changes the act but that it reveals the key fact that it was not at all what one meant to do. For a human act is properly understood not just as the moving of one's limbs but as the bringing about of some result, and it is truly voluntary only if both the movements and at least their chief immediate effects are intended or accepted. This is why ignorance of what one is doing can render an act wholly involuntary in a way that compulsion cannot. But regret is a crucial confirmation that this is the case. To sicken one's guests by serving fish one did not know was contaminated is involuntary; to sell sometimes contaminated fish because one cannot be bothered to handle it properly is nonvoluntary. As Burnet puts it, even if the result was not intended, the agent "makes it his own by his acquiescence in it."[19] The distinction between the involuntary and the nonvoluntary is not only sensible but necessary if we are to give due weight to the importance of the agent's intentions in evaluating actions.

At the same time, however, Aristotle's distinction opens the door to the troubling line of questioning pressed by Socrates. If acting voluntarily means doing what one intended to do, is not every crime, inasmuch as it harms the soul of the perpetrator, involuntary to the extent that the perpetrator is ignorant of its true consequences? Socrates takes this thought and presses directly to the radical conclusion that all vice is involuntary. Aristotle, by contrast, maintains a sensible middle ground: the ignorance that renders an act involuntary is ignorance of one's present action and of its immediate, easily foreseeable consequences, to others as well as to oneself. When a tyrant orders a subject murdered in hopes of benefiting himself, that act is voluntary and blameworthy even if its ultimate results are not what he hoped, for it springs from and reflects his own wicked priorities.

This commonsensical line of analysis is open to an objection, however, which Aristotle recognizes: often people really are ignorant of the immediate and easily foreseeable consequences of their actions, and we still blame them. To accommodate the intuition at work in this blame, he draws a distinction between acts "due to ignorance" and acts done "in ignorance" but due to something else, such as intoxication or anger (1110b24–27).[20] While he has called the former involuntary, he implies that the latter are not. What is the difference, however, if neither act was chosen or anticipated and if both are regretted? Why do we blame the drunk driver who strikes a pedestrian in a crosswalk, even though he was unaware that he was going too fast to stop, and even if he regrets it bitterly? Behind this judgment is the thought that his ignorance is culpable, that he should have known better than to take the risk of causing an accident. Or rather, he did know better and chose to disregard what he knew.

Now our Socratic interlocutor might well ask whether there was not, behind that choice, a deeper ignorance of how bad it was. Aristotle in fact makes a dramatic concession to this position.

> Every wicked man is ignorant of what he should do and of what he should abstain from doing, and it is through this sort of error that men become unjust and generally evil. But the term "involuntary" is not meant to be used when someone is ignorant of what is advantageous. For ignorance in choice is the cause not of the involuntary but of depravity, nor is ignorance of the universal (for men are blamed for this) but rather ignorance of the particulars. (1110b28–33)[21]

When we blame people for wrongdoing, we tend to think that they know what is right but fail to act upon this knowledge. Aristotle will recognize the failure to act on what one somehow knows is good under the rubric of lack of self-control, but true wickedness, he insists now, runs deeper: it consists in having the wrong ends altogether. Not the man who kills accidentally and regrets it but the one who is unrepentantly negligent, and even more the one who kills in cold blood, thinking it is perfectly all right to destroy anyone who gets in his way, is the wicked man. Therefore, Aristotle concludes, only ignorance of particular facts and circumstances renders actions involuntary. In drawing this distinction he again follows common sense: we excuse those acts done in ignorance that we think could happen to anyone and blame those that seem clearly due to bad principles.

But if we may, for a moment, ask an unsavory question, why do we blame the wicked man who is ignorant of universals, any more than we blame a two-year-old who takes what is not his because he does not yet know that stealing is wrong?[22] In the case of adults, we think that any such ignorance is no excuse. Saint Thomas voices this idea when he distinguishes the culpable ignorance of the wicked man from the innocent ignorance of one who is mistaken about particulars. For, he says, "everyone is bound to be solicitous about knowing what he is obliged to do and to avoid."[23] But what can this mean except that the wicked man *knows* he ought to think carefully about right and wrong and fails to follow this knowledge? And why would someone who knows that something is important be so negligent about it? In the passage quoted above, Aristotle characterizes the deepest ignorance underlying wrongdoing in three ways, as ignorance of what is advantageous, ignorance in choice (perhaps ignorance of the particular act that is most choiceworthy in a given situation), and ignorance of the universal, the fundamental principle to be applied or end that should govern choice. Might not ignorance of virtue's importance as the core of happiness be the cause of negligence in pursuing knowledge of the right ends and principles?

Now one might still argue that ignorance of virtue's value to oneself is no excuse for vice: whether one knows that virtue is good for oneself or not—whether indeed it is good for oneself or not—one is obliged to follow its dictates simply because it is noble. Behind this thought is, of course, the widely shared conviction that the wicked man, unlike the toddler, does in the crucial sense know better. But this Aristotle never concedes. Nor does he ever say that one would be obliged to do what is right even if it were fatal for one's own happiness; the quiet suggestion of the whole of book 1 is that there is no standard of morality higher than human happiness. Nor, finally, does he argue that one who (erroneously) imagines that virtue is essentially a sacrifice of one's own good is obliged to persist in and follow this erroneous view. It may seem that nearly everyone is clear about virtue's specific demands even when ignorant of its essential character as the core of happiness, and that the only belief anyone is obliged to follow is this knowledge of particulars. Aristotle casts doubt on this assumption by characterizing the wicked man's ignorance both as ignorance in choice and as ignorance of the universal. Whatever knowledge one has of what one is "supposed to do," in fact this "knowledge" has a terrible tendency to turn to confusion when one faces a choice between what looks like happiness and what looks like a nobility that is fatal to happiness, as Aristotle himself acknowledged in his discussion of hard cases at the beginning of 3.1. He has not yet conceded to Socrates that ignorance is *the* cause of vice, but he has taken a large step in Socrates' direction in conceding its presence at the deepest levels of the thinking of those who do wrong. This step is surprising, yet it is only an unfolding of the full implications of the thought with which Aristotle opens the *Ethics*, that every choice aims at the good.

Pulling back for the time being from these deepest and most troubling implications of his premise, Aristotle now pauses to spell out all the kinds of particulars ignorance can pertain to—the particulars that define an action. He lists these as "who" it is that acts, "what" one does, "with respect to what or in what circumstances; sometimes also by what means, such as an instrument, to what end, such as safety, and how, such as gently or violently" (1111a3–6). Ignorance is possible about any of the particulars that characterize one's own action except the first (the agent), and each can render an act involuntary, Aristotle says, especially ignorance about the "most authoritative" things, which he identifies as "that in which an act consists and that for the sake of which it is done" (1111a15–19). Aristotle's thought would seem to be that what most defines an act is the immediate thing one does and the purpose or end for which one does it, and these are indeed the things we chiefly consider in assigning praise and blame. But what exactly does it mean to be ignorant regarding one's own purpose? Socrates would define this as ignorance as to whether the purpose one pursues is good or bad, calling this the greatest ignorance and one that makes an act most involuntary of all. Aristotle's example suggests that he has in mind something more limited, the act's immediate result: one might give someone a drink in order to save him, he says, and in fact kill him. Still, the fact that Aristotle speaks here of ignorance about the purpose rather than ignorance about the result is curious, reminding us that the greatest ignorance in action is ignorance of what is and is not good to do, and leaving us to wonder just what it is that could ever make *this* ignorance voluntary.

Second Objection

Aristotle, in sum, has defined the involuntary narrowly. An act is involuntary only if the immediate cause was not in oneself (compulsion) or if the immediate result was not at all what one intended to do, through no fault of one's own (ignorance).[24] But the interrupting interlocutor seems not at all satisfied to draw the lines in this way, and as if he has just objected again, Aristotle says, "It is perhaps not noble to say that things done through anger or desire are involuntary" (1111a24–25). If ignorance can make an act involuntary, are people not often blinded by passions? If Aristotle were to assent to this much, the interlocutor might go on to question whether all human action is not ultimately the result of passions. But Aristotle rejects the premise, arguing that on this view all the acts of animals and children would have to be counted as involuntary, since all are due to passions. He asks moreover whether everything we do through desire and spirited passion is involuntary, or whether the ignoble acts are involuntary while the noble ones are voluntary, again calling it ridiculous to make such a distinction when "the cause is the same" (1111a29). Since the passions are just as much a part of us as reason is, it is irrational to call involuntary or to disown the acts that arise from them. Certain passions it is praiseworthy to feel; errors based on passion are just as much to be avoided as those made through calculation; the passions are an integral part of our characters and should not be treated as alien forces that overcome us. In all of this Aristotle makes a strong case for defining the voluntary broadly in a way that supports holding adults responsible for all their voluntary acts, but he also calls attention to the considerable common ground in the motivational structure of the acts of noble and base adults, children, and animals. Indeed, while he implies for now that passion-driven acts are one class of acts and reason-directed acts are another, later he will say that "thought alone moves nothing" (1139a35–36).

What is clear, however, is that Aristotle is defending a distinction of great practical importance. When he says that it is not noble to call involuntary what is done through spiritedness or desire, he means much more than that it is not good form: it is truly a bad thing. It is good to excuse mistakes due to ignorance because such mistakes tell us little about one's character and what we may expect from that person in the future. Passionate acts that involve no ignorance of particulars, even when regretted, are more revealing: they truly belong to the one who does them. When we blame them we hold them up as things that can and should be avoided. The belief that we are the passive playthings of passion is dangerously misleading; the belief that "it is up to us whether to be ruled by our passions" is true in the important sense that those who determine to govern themselves by reason can make progress in doing so and thereby become better people. Whatever the ultimate truth about the necessities that do or do not govern our souls, Aristotle's treatment of voluntary and involuntary action does justice to the effectual truth that the language we use has power to shape our souls for better or for worse.

CHOICE (3.2)

If animals and children, like adults, have enough awareness of what they are doing for their acts to be termed voluntary, and especially if adults, like animals and children, are motivated even at their noblest moments by passions (though the objects of these passions may be quite different), we are left to wonder what the critical difference is that makes us hold only adults morally responsible. This distinction would seem to be justified by adults' capacity for deliberate choice, the topic to which Aristotle turns in 3.2. "Choice," he begins, "seems to be most closely related to virtue, and to provide a better basis for judging character than actions do" (1111b5–6). Aristotle has already indicated the central role of choice in moral acts in book 2: to be virtuous, an act must be done knowingly; it must be done by choice and "chosen for itself"; and it must be done on the basis of a stable character (1105a26–33). Actions that outwardly conform to the requirements of virtue do not reveal a virtuous character if they are not chosen in the right way and for the right reason. At the same time, even acts that are unjust or otherwise base may not reveal a corrupt character if they result from a sudden, thoughtless impulse (cf. 1111b9–10). We may well ask, however, whether choices reveal the true character of a soul because there is a distinct, autonomous part of the soul that comes into play in making choices, or simply because choices are a distinct kind of act, one that draws more than impulsive acts do upon the deep and settled passions and judgments that make up who we are. Translators and commentators routinely assume that Aristotle is offering a theory of the "will" or of "free will" in his account of choice, but Aristotle in fact has no term for either of these. Choice is for him an activity, not a separate part or even faculty of the soul.[25]

Instead of probing into the part of us that makes choices and arguing for the radical freedom or autonomy of that part, Aristotle devotes 3.2 to distinguishing choice (*proairesis*) from four things with which he says it is incorrectly confused: desire or appetite (*epithumia*), spirited passion or anger (*thumos*), wish (*boulēsis*), and opinion (*doxa*). He never tells us who makes these mistakes, and at first sight it seems strange that anyone would, especially since he has just reminded us that choice is voluntary and the other elements he discusses are not normally considered voluntary. However, as Aristotle argues against the identification of choice with each of these four things, it becomes increasingly clear that what they share is their importance as causes or sources of choice. By framing his discussion of choice in terms of its root causes, Aristotle leads the reader to consider the possibility that all choices are nothing but the consequences of passions, wishes, and opinions. But to consider this possibility is to become even more puzzled as to just what it is that turns nonvoluntary passions and thoughts into responsible choices.

Aristotle begins with *epithumia*, a word for desire that refers especially to appetites for the pleasures associated with the body. Such desires are shared with animals, as Aristotle points out, whereas choice is not. What is more, it is possible to act from desire but without choice, as people do who lack self-control, or against desire and by choice, as self-controlled people do. Self-control comes into play precisely when one opposes and resists what is, at that moment, one's most intensely felt desire. But is it something altogether different from desire that gives one the strength to resist temptation, or is it another desire for a more distant good that ultimately inspires such a choice? Aristotle implies here, at least, that self-control involves resisting desire and pursuing something different in kind for which no desire is felt. He continues, "Desire opposes choice, but desire does not oppose desire. And desire is concerned with the pleasant and painful, but choice with neither the painful nor the pleasant" (1111b15–18). To be sure, while desires can be incompatible, they cannot be precisely opposed; one can desire both to keep enjoying a meal and to feel less full, for example, but one cannot both desire and feel aversion to the same thing in the same respect at the same time.[26] And what motivates choice often feels very different from the immediate pull of pleasure. It is not clear, however, that some form of desire is not ultimately the cause of all human choice. In *On the Soul* (433b5–10), Aristotle gives just this role to *orexis*, desire or wanting broadly conceived, which he there defines as the sum of *epithumia*, spirited passion, and wish. And indeed, at the end of *NE* 3.3, he will define choice as deliberate desire (*bouleutikē orexis*).

Aristotle quickly dismisses the second element that he says is incorrectly identified with choice, spirited passion or anger (*thumos*). *Thumos*, even more than desire, can drive people to act impulsively, and acts of sudden rage seem to be among those that are done most blindly and least by deliberate choice. Yet surely a spirited concern for such things as honor, dignity, fairness, and the well-being of oneself and one's own does lie at the root of many actions that are quite deliberately chosen, and in particular many or all acts of justice.

Third, Aristotle distinguishes choice from wish. He observes that wish can be for the impossible and for that which depends upon fortune or the actions of others, whereas choice is only for that which depends on oneself to perform.[27] But he concedes that choice is especially closely related to wish. Unlike desire and spirited passion, but like choice, wish is uniquely human, for only human beings can hold opinions about what would be good to do or to have. Aristotle points to an even closer connection between wish and choice as he continues to distinguish them. In an important statement at 1111b26–29, he says, "And further, wish is more for the end, and choice is for what contributes to the end [*tōn pros to telos*]; for example, we wish to be healthy and choose that through which we will be healthy, and we wish and say we wish to be happy, but it would not be fitting to say that we choose to be happy." What "contributes to the end" need not be only the means to the end; it can include the constituent parts of the end.[28] Nevertheless, if wish is the essential basis of all acts that are deliberately or rationally chosen, then every choice would seem to be governed by something else that is not chosen: one may make many choices in pursuit of one's wishes, but one cannot choose what to wish for.

Finally, Aristotle distinguishes choice from opinion. Opinion, he points out, can take for its object not only what is unattainable by us or altogether impossible, as wish can, but even what is eternal and unchanging. Yet might choice not be identical to a certain class of opinion, opinion about what it is best for us to do at the present moment? Aristotle still insists on a distinction: "It is by choosing good and evil and not by opinions that we are the sort of people that we are" (1112a1–3). If this statement suggests that opinions about good and bad can be quite sterile and choices quite disconnected from opinions, Aristotle suggests a closer connection between choice and knowledge of the good in the next statement: "We choose what we most of all know to be good, but we opine about what we do not know well at all" (1112a7–8). But then he states even more strongly the divergence between opinion and choice in the next lines: "the same people do not seem to make the best choices and hold the best opinions, but some hold rather good opinions and yet through wickedness fail to choose what they should" (1112a8–11). When good opinions are ineffective, are they simply overpowered by something else in the soul that is the real cause of choice? Or might the uncertainty of opinion that Aristotle has just alluded to not be at the bottom of these failings? For the present he leaves such divergences unexplained, observing in conclusion only that it is immaterial whether opinion precedes or follows choice, since the two are different. But of course this question is not at all immaterial to the deeper question of what it is that causes choice. While emphasizing the distinctiveness of choice as a unique and uniquely human act, he thus quietly puts on the table the question of whether the essential cause of choice may not always be the opinion about what is best to do that is most persuasive in the moment of acting. And this suggestion is at least consistent with his conclusion. Choice, he says, is "a matter of prior deliberation" (1112a15), and the result of deliberation would seem to be an opinion about what is good to do.

DELIBERATION (3.3)

Since deliberation is the activity that distinguishes acts of choice from other voluntary acts, Aristotle next takes up deliberation. Deliberation is an inquiry of a particular kind, distinguished by its specific range of objects. People do not deliberate, Aristotle says, about what is eternal, such as the cosmos and the facts of mathematics. Nor do they deliberate about things that come to be through necessity, such as solstices or sunrises, or through nature (this would include all the living things), or in variable ways as the weather does, or through chance, or even by the agency of other people. The objects of deliberation are rather things that "are up to us and practicable, and these are in fact what remain. For nature, necessity, and chance seem to be causes, but so too are intellect and all that comes about through a human being" (1112a31–33). By suddenly bringing into view every kind of investigation into every kind of object of knowledge and every kind of cause, Aristotle stresses the limited scope of deliberation, while also inviting reflection on the relation between deliberation and other kinds of investigation, and likewise between the kind of cause at work in human choice and other causes. How independent is intelligent deliberation in fact from other investigations into things, including the whole cosmos, over which we have no control but which we must perhaps understand in order to live well?[29] And how are the different kinds of causes related? Aristotle does not address these questions here, although he does affirm that choice is a unique kind of cause distinct from the necessities that govern the nonhuman world.[30] Depending on deliberation, it is essentially bound up with the intellect; yet as Aristotle proceeds, he makes clear that deliberation is also essentially bound up with uncertainty. For in any art or science that is exact and self-contained, he says, there is no room for deliberation: a literate person does not deliberate about how to spell each word. Deliberation occurs when one is at least momentarily perplexed and forced to reflect. One unstated consequence of this thought is that a being with perfect knowledge, whether human or divine, would never deliberate and hence never make choices.

Even among fallible humans, Aristotle stresses, the uncertainty that deliberation resolves is uncertainty not about the ends to be pursued, but only about how they may be attained. "We deliberate not about ends but about what contributes to the ends [*tōn pros ta telē*]," he reiterates. "For the doctor does not deliberate about whether to heal, nor the orator about whether to persuade, nor the statesman about whether to establish good government, nor any of the others about the end; but establishing the end, they investigate in what way and through what it may be attained" (1112b11–16). Nor, although deliberation begins in uncertainty, is there necessarily any uncertainty remaining at the point of choosing. Aristotle's paradigm for rational deliberation is the analysis of a geometric figure, which ends in certain knowledge of how to proceed, or knowledge of the "first cause" (*prōton aition*) that is required to set in motion the sequence of events that will bring the desired result (1112b19). Although fields of knowledge such as politics can never be reduced to such certainty, Aristotle suggests that all those who deliberate are ultimately engaged in the same sort of investigation as the geometer, seeking the surest, simplest path to their predetermined ends.

In the conclusion to this chapter Aristotle returns to the thought that "a human being is the source of his actions" (1112b31–32). This, like his identification just before of the initiation of action as a "first cause," might sound like an endorsement of the strongest view of human autonomy. Does the mind's investigation, then, bring one to a point of decision at which one freely chooses to act or not to act, and in choosing does one intervene in the flow of natural necessities and bring about what was by no means necessary? This Aristotle does not say. Instead, he says that if what we seek turns out to be attainable, "we begin to act" (1112b26–27), as if nothing at all intervenes between the conclusion of deliberation and the initiation of action, or as if the conclusion of deliberation is itself the initiation of action. Moreover, he spells out a corollary of the thought that deliberation is not for the end but only for "that which contributes to the end": the acts about which we deliberate are done "for the sake of things other than themselves" (1112b33–34). Evidently to explain why we do not deliberate about ends, he adds, "if one always deliberates, one will go on to infinity" (1113a2). The ultimate causes or principles of action, then, must somehow be simply given. He concludes this thought with the observation that "the object of deliberation and of choice is the same, except that the object of choice has already been determined, for it is what has been decided by deliberation" (1113a2–5). But this means that the object of choice is never simply an end. How are we to square this analysis, then, with the statement in book 2 that the virtuous person chooses the right action "for itself" (1105a32)? In fact Aristotle seems now to be silently correcting that assertion. Moral choice first comes to sight as something that is neither instrumental nor conditional in any way but simply the kind of thing a decent man does. But under philosophic interrogation, we see that since choice requires deliberation, it always implies a standard. Evidently for this reason, after 3.5 Aristotle will begin to replace the statement that the virtuous man does the right thing "for itself" with a series of other formulations that reflect his deepening analysis, beginning with the statement that the moral person acts "for the sake of the noble."[31]

So far it seems as if the only difference between an individual at the point of deliberating and at the point of choosing is that in the latter the uncertainty that called for deliberation has been resolved. And yet, as if to underscore that the moment of choice is not a point like any other in an endless and uniform web of causation but is uniquely determinative, Aristotle adds, "Each person stops investigating when he traces the source of action to himself and to what is sovereign in him, for this is that which chooses. This is clear from the ancient regimes, which Homer recalls: the kings would proclaim to the people what they had chosen" (1113a5–9). However mechanical deliberation and choice seem to be in Aristotle's account, there is something at work in us when we choose that is, if not an uncaused cause, still in a significant way a source or starting point, something sovereign that is most truly ourselves. Its importance is attested by the way we tend to regard our own choices, in comparison with both passions and thoughts. Passions seem at times to take "us" over; thoughts seem at times to pop into "our" minds and even to plague "us," but it is always "I" that chooses, and in momentous choices, we have the sense that what is most important in ourselves is fully engaged, an intuition Aristotle supports with this observation that it is what is "sovereign" in us that makes choices. When we act on aberrant passions or uncharacteristic thoughts, we often say that we have not really chosen to do so but that something else was driving us.

But is it a separate part that exercises this sovereign capacity for choice? Aristotle seems rather to consider choice a distinct and distinctly important activity that in fact unites the affective and rational aspects of our natures. "Since what is chosen is what is desired through deliberation among those things that are up to us, choice would be deliberate desire for what is up to us. Judging on the basis of deliberation, we desire according to the deliberation" (1113a9–12).[32] Thus desire, which generates deliberation, is in turn guided and shaped by deliberation. Deliberation sometimes makes clear which of our felt desires is most worth pursuing now in light of our ultimate concerns and sometimes generates new desires for activities that we have not previously considered. In the acts of choice in which we are most of all ourselves, desire and thought are both deeply engaged and converge on the same point.

It is this unity of desire and thought that explains the moral significance of choices and Aristotle's statement that choice is especially closely related to virtue and a better indicator of character than are actions (1111b5–6). When we act with full awareness of what we are seeking and of the alternatives before us, and especially when important alternatives are in play, we show especially clearly what our true ends are. As G. E. M. Anscombe has argued, what Aristotle means by choice is not just any decision to do one thing with a view to another but rather an exercise of reason that expresses a settled understanding of what it means to live well.[33] And this helps us to see why Aristotle says that children as well as animals are incapable of choice. When a child selects a flavor of ice cream or a story for bedtime, he chooses in a sense, but he does not do so with a view to anything further than immediate pleasure. When he tells a lie to avoid punishment, he is indeed calculating, but still not acting in a morally responsible way. Aristotle has observed that children and youths are guided overwhelmingly by pleasure and pain (1095a2–6; cf. 1156a31–33). Their actions are similar to those of uncontrolled people who may calculate in their pursuit of pleasure, but do not act by choice (1142b18–20, 1179b13–14). The pleasures and pains felt by children may of course include the pleasures of generous and kindly deeds and the pain of shame: there would be no point to habituation unless it had the effect of giving opportunities for and strengthening such pleasures and pains.[34] Yet even when they act for such higher pleasures, the immature are not yet making moral choices.

What changes, then, when an immature child becomes a rational, responsible adult? His experience of the pleasures and pains by which he has hitherto lived comes to inform and be informed by thought, so that instead of merely following the impulse of the moment, he acts in ways that begin to articulate a settled character, at the core of which is a vision of the appropriate way to conduct one's life. Only when one approaches the end of childhood is one able to think comprehensively about different ways of life and different principles of action and adopt overarching goals. Only then can others begin to speak with confidence about one's character as something more permanent than passing phases and shifting proclivities. This is why we say to a child, "You were a good girl today," knowing that it is not certain whether she will be as good tomorrow. Only gradually, in a process that is completed with the onset of adulthood, do choices come to have full moral significance as the reflection of principles of action that one has implicitly or explicitly made one's own. Not the capacity to calculate but the capacity to hold and follow such ends is what makes deliberate choices morally significant. Particularly important in both defining and revealing character are those acts that are chosen not merely as means to some further end, but as direct fulfillments of a central end one holds, a possibility Aristotle allows for with his careful formulation that choice and deliberation pertain to that which "conduces to the end," a formula that can cover both means and constituents of the end. Thus, for example, a choice to stand one's ground in battle might be made not as a means to a separate end but as a direct fulfillment and an integral part of the agent's purpose of living nobly.[35]

CHOICE, DELIBERATION, AND ENDS

Still, we might ask, do we really not choose ends? While Aristotle is surely right that the realm in which the most significant choices take place, the realm of moral and political action, is especially fraught with uncertainties, the uncertainties are arguably about more than the best way to realize predetermined ends. In the most difficult choices, the doubts people face often seem to be doubts about the proper weight to give different ends. Is it not precisely the freedom to choose and rank different ends that makes us morally responsible agents? Aristotle's highly technical account of deliberation is, however, strangely silent on the complexity and the moral seriousness of important choices, beginning with the fact that this chapter says nothing about choices between right and wrong. A number of modern commentators have thus argued that it provides an inadequate account of the phenomenon of human decision-making. Unlike the process of selecting the best way to attain a well-defined end, they argue, real-life deliberation tends to involve uncertainty about the right end to be followed, frequent efforts to get clear what one really wants, and investigations into whether the means required to secure the end one has immediately in view entail acceptable or unacceptable costs to other ends one has. And, it seems to many of these commentators, unless deliberation does include the weighing of ends as well as technical reasoning about how to attain ends, it cannot serve as the defining feature of responsible human choice that sets it apart from the nonresponsible acts of animals.[36]

The deeper inquiries into the proper ranking and balancing of ends, which seem to be a frequent part of or at least adjunct to all serious deliberation, are perhaps clearest in public debates. Especially when great statesmen are confronting great issues, but even when petty politicians are pursuing selfish or partisan goals that have little to do with the true ends for which the community was formed, political discourse often seems to include attempts to strengthen the listeners' commitment to certain ends over others—by arguing, for example, that national security should be the paramount consideration in foreign policy, or alternatively that a country should run risks for the noble goal of freedom. Indeed, Aristotle speaks at length about how to make just these sorts of appeals in his *Rhetoric*. In a similar way, personal deliberation often seems to involve inquiries into the proper weight that should be given to such ends as honor, invigorating challenges, knowledge, friendship, and simple pleasures. Such reflections frequently carry us into the investigation of what each end really is, whether it truly is an end in itself or is ultimately resolvable into some other end, whether it is coherent or confused, and, once seen for what it is, how compelling it remains. Two examples of this last type of analysis from the *Ethics* itself are the discussions of pleasure, honor, virtue, money, and knowledge as potential ends in 1.5, and of honor and affection in 8.8. But this process of clarifying, weighing, and reevaluating life's ends is strangely absent from Aristotle's model of deliberation in 3.3.

In part, Aristotle's reason for this silence may be a technical one. If he does not emphasize, he also does not deny that deliberation can lead us into the kind of inquiry that seeks a better articulation of our ends. Certainly deliberations about what to do often lead us to question aims we took before as given. A doctor may at one time deliberate about the best means to bring down a fever, at another about whether reducing a fever is the best way to cure a disorder, and at another about whether a patient should continue to be treated at all. Ends that are assumed in one context may indeed be subject to scrutiny and rejected in others. Still, there can be no deliberation unless *some* end is accepted as a standard by which to evaluate possible courses of action.[37] Deliberations about what to do can also lead us into the kind of investigation about who we are and what we want that the whole of the *Ethics* seeks to foster. But this investigation, as Aristotle might point out, is not itself an act of deliberation but a philosophical inquiry.[38]

Still, it is significant that in this part of the *Ethics* such an inquiry is not being explicitly pursued. The discussion of the voluntary, choice, deliberation, wish, and responsibility for character falls within the section of the *Ethics*—books 2 through 5—that gives a rich depiction of the moral life and especially, with some modifications, of the ethos of the classical gentleman. Our contemporary uneasiness with Aristotle's account of deliberation helps make clear an important difference between the classical way of thinking about morality that Aristotle supported and refined and the way that has become second nature in a world deeply shaped by Christian thought. For the Christian, morality is all about making free choices between the good we should desire and the evil that poses an ever-present temptation. For the Aristotelian gentleman, by contrast, being moral means acting as a matter of course according to a habituated, deeply ingrained love of the noble. Such a man does not deliberate about his ends because his ends are firm and unshakeable: he always chooses what is noble above all else.

But even if Aristotle's gentleman never chooses between what is noble and anything else, how does he understand and, more important, how does Aristotle intend for us to understand, the times when other people seem to choose between separate and incommensurable ends, neither of which is simply a means to or even a part of the other—as, for example, the young Hercules evidently does in Prodicus's story, adapted by Socrates in Xenophon's *Memorabilia* (2.1.21–34), when Hercules ponders which course to take in life, and virtue and vice appear before him in the guise of two beautiful women who vie in speeches to win his loyalty? Aristotle avoids discussing such choices by separating his discussion of choice and deliberation from his more theoretical reflections on happiness in books 1 and 10. If we pressed Aristotle to bring them together, he would doubtless insist that the inquiry into happiness is also determined by a standard that we do not choose. But in this case, it is a standard given by nature that we must simply discover, as the substance of the happiness that we most deeply want and that stands as the comprehensive end of all human activity.

Aristotle does not directly explain how deliberation works when it is the choice of a whole way of life that is at stake, or how he understands choice and deliberation to work when what is noble seems to oppose happiness, but he does give a few clues. These clues, if we follow them carefully, lead to the surprising conclusion that in Aristotle's judgment no one ever does choose what he considers right at the cost of what one understands as one's own greatest good, or choose what one considers best for oneself at the cost of what one understands to be the demands of virtue. If happiness is the comprehensive end of all that we do, it makes sense that the desire for it would have sovereign power over our action, and if virtue is the core of happiness, it makes sense that the wicked who follow bad ends would do so only in a deep ignorance of what is good, as Aristotle has said in 3.1. But Aristotle indicates that even for those who do not see the unity of virtue and happiness, there is something so compellingly good about both of them that they cannot bear consciously to choose one and leave the other behind. Of course we all want happiness, but Aristotle will also say in book 5 that "no one wishes what he does not suppose to be morally good [*spoudaios*], but the uncontrolled does what he thinks he should not do" (1136b7–9), suggesting that violations of what we suppose is the decent course of action take place not by choice but only through lapses of self-control. Conversely, Aristotle will say in book 6 that moderation is needed to "preserve active wisdom" (1140b11–12) or correct conviction. As Cooper puts it in an interesting gloss on this passage, if the desires do not learn to follow reason, then reason tends to become corrupted and begins trying to justify the desires, for "we cannot very readily or contentedly let the contradiction stand."[39]

Thucydides, in his masterful reconstructions of political deliberations, confirms this thought on the way what we desire or perceive as good and what we think right tend to sway one another. In the debates and resolutions that he records, he shows that even when people seem most clearly to face a choice between virtue and self-interest, they never deliberately choose to pursue either one over the other. Leaders never advocate acts of justice while conceding that they are disadvantageous or advocate advantageous acts while conceding them to be unjust. It seems that political men are in fact always trying—in endlessly complicated and frequently disingenuous ways—to reconcile these two ends that are both unquestioned. For even when doing the most terrible things, they often appeal to necessity, not as a reason for disregarding justice but precisely as a justification. And perhaps in personal deliberations, too, both goodness and happiness are somehow always accepted as unquestioned ends. No one ever asks whether one should be an admirable person or a scoundrel, any more than anyone considers whether to pursue happiness or misery. Even when Prodicus's Hercules ponders which course to take in life, he does not recognize vice for who she is but has to ask her name: the question of whether to be good or bad was not quite what he was pondering (*Memorabilia* 2.1.26). Even when one wrestles with the question of how much weight to give to one's own welfare and how much to the needs of another, one seeks a path that is both good for oneself and morally justified, and a path that satisfies as well as possible all the concerns that one finds oneself to have. Likewise, when one chooses to make sacrifices for others or for what is noble, such choices are perhaps invariably accompanied by the thought that any happiness worthy of the name requires that one be the sort of person who chooses that way—that one would not be able to live with oneself if one did otherwise.

If, as Aristotle has argued throughout book 1 of the *Ethics* and especially in his challenge to the inscription in the temple of Delos, there is a single comprehensive end for human beings, a flourishing life that is noble inasmuch as it is good in itself and pleasant inasmuch as what is noblest is most pleasant for the healthiest human being, then all deliberate choice in some way aims at this one end. Aristotle of course acknowledges that the pleasant, the beneficial, and the noble as they appear to most people are frequently misaligned. But his claims about the ultimate unity of the good supports our analysis of ordinary choice as involving a groping toward a good that we intuit must somehow be able to combine what is noble or at least justified with what is in the long run and the final analysis best for ourselves.

WISH (3.4)

If choice is not of the end but only of that which contributes to the end, then the most morally significant differences by which we judge human beings will be found not in how well they deliberate and choose, but in the ends they hold. A complete theory of virtue requires that we be able to evaluate ends themselves. But if ends are not chosen but only wished for, is there still a compelling sense in which we can say that one *ought* to wish for and choose in accordance with one end and not another? If so, what exactly is the character of that "ought"? The challenge that Aristotle faces in 3.4 is to give an account of wish, or human directedness to the various good and bad ends that determine choice, and to do so in such a way as to support moral responsibility.[40]

Modern commentators, in thinking about the nature of wish, have focused on the question of how the ends that we have are grasped—whether it is through the habituation of the passions that one desires what one does, so that active wisdom follows well-habituated passions, or whether the correct ends are seen by an act of mental insight and desired as a result of being seen as good. This question is intriguing and difficult to answer, and Aristotle never draws the clear distinctions here that many would like to see.[41] Quite possibly, however, his silence on it is both intentional and significant. It is a basic feature of Aristotle's moral philosophy that he never grants the existence of human desire unaccompanied by at least an implicit judgment that the thing desired is, taken in itself, good, or the possibility of judging something good for oneself or for others that one cares about without to that extent desiring it. Of course we often desire conflicting things; this is the same as to say that we are of two minds about what is best. The knowledge that something pleasant would be harmful does not necessarily make the desire evaporate, for to the extent that it announces itself as pleasant it still appears good.

Aristotle's question rather is what the true object of wish (*boulēton*) is.

> Wish . . . seems to some to be for the good, and to others to be for the apparent good. And so for those who say that the object of wish is the good, it turns out that one who chooses incorrectly wishes for something that is not an object of wish (for if it were an object of wish it would be good, but in this case it is bad). For those, however, who say that the apparent good is the object of wish, there is no object of wish by nature, but only what appears so to each person. (1113a15–21)

Do all human beings wish for what is good, however dimly they perceive it and however badly they miss the mark, or do they wish only for the specific goals they in fact pursue? What would it mean to say that something ought to be wished for when it is not? This is a problem for Aristotle because he refuses to grant the existence of the "good in itself" as an absolute standard that stands above nature and our natural needs and inclinations. Nature itself is the standard. Hence he does not even explore a third possible claim, that the true object of wish is that which is simply intrinsically good, whether anyone in fact wishes it at all. But if we refuse to grant a perspective from which to say that lions ought not to desire to eat lambs, how can we say that predatory human beings ought not to wish to gain power by destroying their fellows? And if we do not say that, how can we avoid relativism?

The first group of people Aristotle identifies here, those who think of the object of wish as the good, are Socrates and his followers. Socrates can affirm the existence of an objective standard of wish because he holds that all people do in fact have the same ends, so that the right ends are what everyone truly wants and cares about, even if not everyone knows it. In his exchange with Polus in Plato's *Gorgias*, for example, Socrates says, "tyrants have the least power in their cities . . . for they do nothing, so to speak, of what they wish to do, even though they do whatever seems best to them" (466d7–e2). What they really wish, according to Socrates, is not to make the particular movements and utterances that they make but to benefit themselves, whereas in ruling others unjustly they in fact harm their own souls. Socrates thus calls their evil-doing involuntary. This argument of course flies in the face of both the common understanding of wish and the assumptions of decent people and laws everywhere about moral responsibility. Without addressing the morally pernicious tendency of the argument, Aristotle refuses to bend the commonsense meaning of "wish" so far out of its natural course. Where Socrates insists that the object of everyone's wish is genuine happiness, Aristotle hews closer to common sense in including as objects of wish the particular content or subordinate ends that people conceive as making up happiness.

However, to accept this second alternative without qualification is morally even less attractive. If the object of wish were only whatever seems good to each person at each moment and if nothing were naturally and inherently choiceworthy, then there could be no basis for distinguishing the apparent good from the true good. We would then be left in the position of saying with Protagoras that "man is the measure of all things"[42]—at any rate of the good and the bad—and meaning by this that each and every man is equally the measure of the good and the bad. Such relativism is fatal to morality, and Aristotle avoids it also.

Instead, Aristotle stakes out a third possibility, more in accord with moral common sense. He says that "simply and according to truth the object of wish is the good, but for each person it is the apparent good" (1113a23–24). He is able to speak of the true object of wish or the true end for man, in spite of endless differences among people's actual wishes, because he at least implicitly takes the healthy soul as a standard. What seems good to the morally serious person truly is good, he says, in just the way that what seems wholesome to the healthy person truly is so.

> The morally serious person judges each thing correctly, and in each case what is true appears as such to him. For what is beautiful and pleasant differ with different characters, and the morally serious man differs perhaps most in this, that he sees the truth in each of them, being as it were the standard and measure of them. But in the majority the deception comes through pleasure. (1113a29–34)[43]

In this way, Aristotle partially agrees with Protagoras: man is himself the measure of things and not the other way around, but only man at his best.

The healthy soul thus emerges as a standard of ends in two distinct but interrelated ways. First, the ends that are naturally or "simply" good are such because they are the satisfying ends for human beings in a flourishing state, human beings as nature meant them to be. Good ends are good for a healthy soul to achieve in just the way that vigorous exercise is good for a healthy body: it is satisfying to engage in and beneficial afterward, contributing to a lasting good condition and sense of well-being in a way that unhealthy indulgences do not, and contributing to a whole life that is harmonious and free of inner divisions and regrets. The standard of goodness is thus provided by the needs and inclinations of human nature. Second, man in his healthy state seems to be a correct judge of things, even of such things as the heavy and the light, which are not as such good or bad for him, because he has a clarity of judgment not distorted by sickly imbalances and disorderly passions. Once again, good vision turns out to be essential for virtue.

What does all of this imply about the ends of the unhealthy? Some of their wishes, such as the wish to sleep long hours, are good for the unhealthy but not good simply, but in other respects unhealthiness obscures the judgment, so that what people wish is not good even for them. In comparing the person with bad ends to the physically unhealthy, Aristotle indicates that on his own terms and in his own experience his condition betrays its defectiveness. A predatory human being is not like a thriving lion but like a rabid cat, whose disordered condition is clear in itself even without reference to its bad effect on others. Perhaps a human being who feels no wish for friendship cannot truly be said to wish for what he does not want, but he does wish for a happiness that is unattainable on such a narrow plane as he imagines it; it is for this reason that friendship is properly an object of wish for him even if he does not feel it to be so. But Aristotle will go further: even when the vision of what is good and noble is most obscured, it is not absent entirely. Glimmerings of what is best are present even in the most depraved, making their souls incapable of wholeness or harmony (see 1136b5–9, 1162b34–36).

Aristotle thus agrees with Socrates that the true object of wish is what accords with the natural health of the soul. He disagrees in insisting, sensibly, that some people wish for what is bad. But his agreement is deeper. If, as he indicates now, the clear vision of the virtuous is what sets them apart, then knowledge and ignorance are at least as important as desire in determining character. Just as faulty deliberation is due to errors that no one would ever voluntarily make, so aiming at an illusory good suggests an ignorance that no one would ever choose to have. But if no one would choose such ignorance, can one be responsible for it? This is the challenge that Aristotle must still confront as he begins the fifth and final chapter in his discussion of moral responsibility.

RESPONSIBILITY FOR CHARACTER (3.5)

In 3.5 Aristotle makes his most emphatic defense of moral responsibility and comes as close as he ever does to asserting the existence of free will, yet he also makes his most dramatic concessions to the Socratic interlocutor. He begins with the thought that the activities of virtue precisely fit the description of acts that are both "according to choice" and voluntary, and from this he concludes: "Virtue is up to us, then, and likewise vice. For in things in which it is up to us to act, it is also up to us not to act, and to that to which we can say no, we can also say yes. So that if acting is up to us when acting is noble, likewise not acting is up to us when acting is base, and if not acting is up to us when acting is noble, acting is also up to us when acting is base" (1113b6–11). Throughout this chapter Aristotle will insist not only on our responsibility for virtue but on the symmetry between virtue and vice and hence on our equal degree of responsibility for both. But what does he mean when he says our choices are "up to us"? To say that we act by choice is to say that we are free to do otherwise, if we so choose. But are we free to choose otherwise, circumstances and our character and understanding of the good and the bad being what they are? Aristotle never says that we are. What he asserts and defends in 3.5 is not the radical freedom of the will, but individuals' responsibility for shaping their own characters.[44] What exactly is the nature of this responsibility for character, then? If responsible acts are those that are not just voluntary but chosen with full knowledge of what one is doing, do people choose their characters in such a way as to meet this standard? Let us trace Aristotle's development of this important argument step by step.

Aristotle begins his elaboration by taking issue with the saying that "no one is voluntarily wicked [*ponēros*] or involuntarily blessed [*makarios*]." While agreeing that no one is involuntarily blessed, he insists nonetheless that "depravity [*mochthēria*] is voluntary" (1113b14–17).[45] The saying, attributed by the Aldine Scholiast to the poet Epicharmus,[46] is of uncertain origin. It does seem, however, that Aristotle has interpreted it contrary to its original meaning, for the word *ponēros* means primarily "wretched" and only secondarily "wicked"; especially when opposed to "blessed" it would normally be taken in the first sense. Thus the proverb would be making only the uncontroversial claim that no one is voluntarily wretched. Aristotle, however, interprets and takes issue with it as an assertion of the Socratic thesis that vice is involuntary. Yet by calling attention to the connection between virtue and happiness on one hand and vice and wretchedness on the other—on which he fully agrees with Socrates—Aristotle reminds us of this agreement and so only sharpens the question: why would anyone voluntarily choose what makes one unhappy?

Leaving this question unaddressed, Aristotle insists that we must accept that wickedness is voluntary, or else "contradict what we have just said, and deny that man is the cause [*archē*] and begetter of his actions as he is of his children. But if these things seems right, and we are not able to trace actions back to causes other than those within us, then those things of which the causes are within us are up to us and are voluntary" (1113b17–21).[47] This is the closest Aristotle comes to affirming a free will. While he never goes that far, still he reflects his awareness of the powerful attraction of the thought that we are somehow first or uncaused causes. Yet in fact it would be difficult to find a more richly ambiguous analogy for the autonomy of the moral agent. Parents are the cause of their children's natural endowments without choosing them, and even when parents provide good guidance, children often go on to do many things against their wishes. On the other hand, to the extent that a parent does have the power to shape a child's character, that child, when grown, is not the cause of it. And as Aristotle said in 2.1 of this parental influence: "It makes no little difference whether one is habituated from early childhood in this way or that, but a great difference—or rather, all the difference" (1103b23–25). We are all enmeshed in a web of causes and effects, stretching indefinitely into the past and future, and Aristotle's reminder of parents' responsibility for their children, in both a natural and a moral sense, reminds us of how far we must abstract from fact to regard the individual as an uncaused cause of his own character. These lines, then, while purportedly proving that virtue and vice are radically up to us, actually point at least equally in the opposite direction.

And somehow, in holding ourselves and others responsible, we want to move in both directions. The acts we praise and blame cannot be just a necessary result of prior causes, we think, for then the one who does them could not have done otherwise. But Aristotle's argument forces us to see that we want equally to affirm the opposite. These acts also cannot be just random, meaningless events like muscle spasms, or indeterminate ones like the movements of subatomic particles, for it would make even less sense to hold people responsible for those. Hence in the same breath that we affirm that a morally responsible agent was free to do otherwise, we affirm that the acts we hold him responsible for are not random but are meaningful acts, caused by and hence indicative of his character. But again, can we hold a person responsible for the character that determines his actions if that character is ultimately caused by natural endowments and parental upbringing? Could we hold him responsible if it were caused by nothing?

Aristotle quietly alludes to the political importance of such tangled attributions of responsibility in his next argument, in which he offers support for his claim that we are responsible for both virtue and vice by citing the practice of private men and of lawgivers. Both of them, he says, use punishments and honors to discourage wicked acts and to encourage noble ones, but no one tries to persuade another to do "what is not in his power and not voluntary," for example to stop feeling heat or pain or hunger (1113b26–29).[48] By calling attention to the power of incentives and disincentives in controlling behavior, Aristotle in fact underscores again the extent to which individuals are not the makers of their own actions or characters. This argument supports not the existence of radical freedom, then—the freedom, at the moment of acting, to do otherwise, one's options and one's judgments of them being exactly as they are—but only the freedom to do otherwise when one's options or one's assessment of them have altered. A sensible lawgiver who is sure of only this much will use rewards and punishments as incentives and disincentives for future behavior, which is just what Aristotle attributes to lawgivers, but will not punish in a retributive spirit. Indeed, the process of shaping character as described here does not necessarily even entail choice on the part of the subject. Whereas Aristotle's standard of responsibility at the beginning of the chapter was what is based on choice, voluntary, and hence "up to us," he now describes the actions that we reward and punish and that shape character only as up to the individual and voluntary. He has thus silently broadened the range of morally responsible action to include all actions that are subject to the incentives and disincentives that are used alike to rule adults, to educate children, and to train animals.[49]

Still, is it not significant to show that acts of vice are voluntary, and is this not what Socrates denies? Sometimes he certainly seems to, as in the passage from the *Gorgias* cited above (466d7–e2), but perhaps this is misleading. At his trial Socrates denies not voluntarily conversing with the youth, but voluntarily corrupting them. Evil is what is involuntary, according to Socrates, and it is involuntary because of ignorance. As if in reply to this argument, Aristotle reiterates that a crime committed in ignorance and even ignorance itself may be punished, "if the person is thought to be responsible for his ignorance" (1113b30–31), and if the ignorance seems due to negligence. Those who penalize such acts assume that beneath a person's particular ignorance of the law or of the effects of his action is a deeper knowledge that such ignorance is bad and needs correcting. They hold him responsible for having disregarded this knowledge, believing that he was free to do otherwise.

Third Objection

But already at 1110b28–1111a1 Aristotle has cast doubt on the assumption that wicked people know what is best. The assumption that they know the importance of informing themselves and are free to regard or disregard that knowledge is now called into question by the nameless interlocutor, who in effect interrupts Aristotle's argument for the third time on behalf of the determinative power of nature. "Perhaps," Aristotle allows him to say, the man who carelessly fails to inform himself about the law is simply "of such a sort as to be careless" (1114a3–4). But Aristotle replies that "by living carelessly, these people are themselves responsible [*aitios*] for becoming so" (1114a3–5).[50] Individuals make themselves unjust or self-indulgent by behaving unjustly and passing their time in dissipation, just as people training for a contest become good runners by running, so that one would have to be "altogether insensitive" not to see that individuals shape their characters by their own actions (1114a10). We may wonder, however, whether the man who becomes an alcoholic by drinking and the one who becomes a champion runner by running are quite parallel cases. It is all very well to say that one who has habitually drunk too much ought to have known what he was doing to himself. This is still not to say that he did know, or that he knew in more than isolated flashes of insight, quickly repressed, or least of all that he chose to become an alcoholic. The runner is intently focused on his goal and chooses each practice session as a means to reach it, but the drunkard chooses only this drink, as good or pleasant in itself. Aristotle emphasizes how unreasonable it is for the one behaving unjustly or self-indulgently not to wish to become unjust or self-indulgent or to allege as an excuse that he never wished this, since the outcome was entirely foreseeable.[51] Yet a development that is foreseeable is not always foreseen, as Aristotle himself will concede at 1114b31–15a1, and those who know a principle and can apply it to other cases often fail to apply it to their own, as he will observe in his rich discussion of self-control and lack of self-control in book 7.

Aristotle insists, however, that vice is still voluntary.

> If someone who is not ignorant does those things from which he will become unjust, he would be unjust voluntarily, although he cannot stop being unjust and become just by wanting to, any more than an ill person can become healthy. And it may happen that he is ill voluntarily, living without self-restraint and failing to listen to the doctor. Before it was possible for him not to be sick, but in time it no longer is, just as it is no longer possible for one who has thrown a stone to recall it. But nonetheless the throwing was up to him. For the cause was in him. (1114a12–19)[52]

But why would one ever want to recall a stone, unless one did not realize what harm it would do? This example recalls the earlier example of the person who accidentally sets off a catapult and regrets the result, which Aristotle gave as a case of action that is involuntary through ignorance (1111a10–11). The involuntary firing of the catapult is in fact an even closer analogy to the process of contracting disease or bad character than is the voluntary but subsequently regretted throwing of a stone. One cannot throw a stone without meaning to, even if one does not intend to break a window with it, but one can set off a catapult, contract heart disease, or become a dissolute person without meaning to at all. Aristotle has to lower his own standard for what constitutes voluntariness, then, in order to call such a process voluntary.

Fourth Objection: Natural Vision

In the destruction of health or character the disjunction between wish and effect is possible because the moments of decisive action and the moments of clarity do not coincide, so that the irremediable consequences of what was done in a haze are seen only later in the clear light of day. Aristotle has stressed how easy it should be to see what one is doing to oneself as one develops a bad character, but the Socratic interlocutor insists that an unchosen lack of clarity is nevertheless the root cause of every bad action. This is the thrust of his last and most powerful objection, which shows that even if he attributes full causality to the actions of the human soul, he by no means attributes to them a blind or mechanistic causality.

> Suppose someone should say that everyone aims at what appears good, and that people do not control the way things appear to them, but that of whatever sort each is, thus the end appears to him. If each is somehow responsible for his own character, he will somehow be responsible for the way things appear to him. But if not, no one is responsible for his own bad actions, but through ignorance of the end he does these things, supposing that they will bring him the greatest good. And his aiming at the end is not of his own choosing, but one must, so to speak, have a natural vision, by which to judge nobly and choose what is truly good, and he to whom this is nobly given by nature is naturally well endowed. For this is the greatest and most noble thing, which it is not possible to acquire or learn from another, but one will have it just as it is given by nature, and to be well and nobly provided by nature with this is to be perfectly and truly well endowed by nature. (1114a31–b12)

Aristotle does not immediately rebut his interlocutor as he did in the case of the earlier interventions but instead gives or allows the interlocutor to give an elaboration of his objection and its implication. It is in fact hard to tell precisely which lines should be given to the interlocutor and which to Aristotle himself.[53] At any rate, both within and immediately after the passage quoted Aristotle presents two alternatives, both now representing a departure from the strong claim he made for responsibility for character earlier in the chapter, which was at odds with his own standard of the voluntary. Each individual now is "somehow responsible" for his own character and for what appears good to him, or else virtue and vice are wholly determined by a kind of natural vision, a new possibility that is described in beautiful and compelling terms. Let us consider both alternatives.

The statement that each individual is "somehow responsible" for his own character seems to lend support to those who believe that we are uncaused causes of our own virtues and vices. But it need not mean more than that our acts are responsible for our characters in the way that heavy rains are responsible for a flood, as the natural cause of a necessary result. And in fact Aristotle has given the careful reader no grounds for interpreting this expression in the strong sense of an uncaused cause.[54] He has shown that actions shape character, which in turn shapes one's sense of good and bad and hence one's subsequent actions. But the chain of causation, which he never calls into doubt, is not an absurd circle only because somewhere, at some beginning point or points, one was moved by desires or wishes or opinions of the good that one did not create but simply adopted from others or discovered within.[55]

The second possibility presented here, which is in fact not incompatible with the first but rather one possible specification of it, is that in human action we find neither uncaused causes nor circular causes nor endless chains of mechanical causes as we find in weather systems, but rather a sequence containing one overwhelmingly decisive cause, the individual's good or bad natural ability to see clearly the ends that are truly good. On this account, it is insight or vision that gives the distinctive character and dignity to human choice. The most important division between different kinds of actions is not that between those that are undetermined and those that are necessitated, but rather that between those that follow from insight into the good that one truly wants, and all the more or less compelled or confused or blind acts that do not rise to the level of intelligent choices. The dignity of human beings, in contrast to the lower animals, would then lie not in human free will—which this interlocutor might say could only mean blind willfulness or a disconnect between insight and action—but to the contrary, in the capacity for intelligent action that springs naturally and even necessarily from true insight. This insight is powerful not just as an explanation of what is but as a source of what can be, for to see what is good and to see that it can come about through one's own actions is to begin to be able to achieve it.

Aristotle gives here such a compelling account of the centrality of natural vision in shaping character that we may ask what relation it has to the other factor he earlier called decisive for character. Here, where Aristotle comes closest to endorsing a Socratic account of virtue, he identifies vision or understanding as key; in book 2, where he expresses a more gentlemanly and civic view of virtue, he identifies habituation as key (1103b23–25). This puzzle will reappear in book 6 as the puzzle as to whether it is the passions, correctly formed, that constitute the virtues to which active wisdom looks in guiding choice, or whether it is active wisdom's independent insight into the good that defines the end that the virtuous man looks to in choosing correctly.

For now, however, what is striking is the extreme mildness of Aristotle's reply to the Socratic interlocutor's last intervention, which consists chiefly in a rhetorical question: whether the individual contributes "somehow" to his character or whether character is wholly the result of natural vision, how will vice be any less voluntary than virtue? Thus Aristotle concentrates all his fire on the Socratic-sounding saying that virtue is voluntary but vice is not. He ends the chapter with a firm insistence that everyone must accept equal responsibility for one's own virtues and vices and with a not very subtle suggestion that his interlocutor is guilty either of claiming credit that he does not deserve or of evading blame that he does. But this insinuation is unfair.[56] The interlocutor has not been claiming any credit. And while his thesis explains good and bad actions as largely parallel pursuits of the apparent good, it also provides grounds for answering Aristotle's question. For if to act voluntarily is to do what one intends with knowledge of what one is doing, the deliberately chosen actions and the consequent positive character formation of a virtuous person will meet a higher standard of voluntariness than the thoughtless, often regretted actions and especially the consequent moral decay of one with murky vision. And Aristotle shows that in fact he agrees with the crux of this analysis, for he concedes that vice involves not only ignorance of the right ends but regrets, once the truth about what one has done to oneself becomes clear. The account Aristotle sometimes gives of vice as wholehearted and unwavering thus seems even by his own account in book 3 to be suspect, as he himself finally concedes in 9.4.

It therefore turns out that in the end Aristotle's position is in fact very close to that of Socrates. Both present virtue as the only basis for true health and harmony in the soul, and both recognize the decisive importance of knowledge for virtue. If so, then both must agree that virtue is in fact more voluntary than vice, inasmuch as the acts and possession of virtue can reflect the true wishes and fully informed choices of the whole man in a way that those of vice do not.[57] By ending the chapter with the insistence that virtue and vice are equally voluntary, Aristotle diverts attention from the extent of his own retreat. He diverts attention from his crucial concession to Socrates that at the root of every vice and every act of vice is a mistake about what is good and what will make one happy. He diverts attention, above all, from the problem of circularity in his account of moral responsibility, as he explains action as the result of character and character as the result of action without showing how anything other than unchosen passions, habits, and insights can be the cause of either of these. Thus while Aristotle comes close to conceding at the beginning of 3.5 that to be fully responsible we would have to be the uncaused causes of our own characters, he manifestly fails to show that we are.[58]

Aristotle's Political Purpose

Because this evident attempt to defend human freedom and responsibility is so problematic, some scholars have denied that Aristotle is making any such argument and have suggested that he instead subscribes to a thoroughly Socratic or deterministic view.[59] Others have argued that Aristotle is not even engaging the question of the ultimate causes of human action in 3.1–5 but is merely addressing legal and political problems and offering improvements to the legal concepts in use in contemporary Athenian society. Thus, it has been suggested, Aristotle is improving upon the Athenian dichotomy between involuntary killings and premeditated killings by offering such new categories as intentional acts committed without premeditation and acts of culpable negligence.[60] I believe Aristotle does intend to make such improvements and that these scholars are on the right track in seeing the present chapters as somehow political; indeed it is his political purpose, I would submit, that makes sense of the tensions and obscurities we have observed. But the deeper political purpose of these chapters has not yet been discerned.

Healthy political life, as Aristotle indicates in many places, requires a legal system that does more than discourage the forms of behavior that are socially destructive. Healthy political life requires support also for precisely the common moral opinions regarding obligation and culpability that Socratic psychology calls into question. It requires support for the view that individuals are obligated—and hence free—to rise above their concern for their own good and to give precedence to duty, and that punishment for those who fail to do their duty is not just socially advantageous but deserved. It requires that society, in its most solemn acts and pronouncements, give satisfaction to the righteous indignation of the dutiful citizen against the criminal. Aristotle agrees with Socrates that that righteous indignation has at its root a false opinion, the opinion that doing what is right is good for others but bad for oneself, and doing what is wrong is bad for others but good for oneself, and that hence those who attempt to get away with crime should be made to pay as a way of evening the scales and avenging the wrong. Aristotle contests the presuppositions underlying this common view of right and wrong, most strikingly in the opening lines of the *Eudemian Ethics*, and he tries throughout his ethical works to move the reader toward a different, more Socratic understanding of virtue and vice, an understanding that is *also* universally if dimly grasped, and that renders incoherent the unreflective moral opinions from which we all begin. This alternative is the view that virtue is the perfection of the soul and activity according to virtue the substance of happiness, so that vice calls not for indignation and revenge but for pity and correction.

Yet while trying to move his readers away from the outlook that focuses on the agent's freedom and duty to do right and on retribution as the proper response to wrongdoing, Aristotle nevertheless recognizes the powerful grip this view will always have on virtually everyone, and the consequent necessity for political and legal life to respect it by giving some satisfaction to the thirst for vengeance it entails. Thus he speaks with apparent approval in the present chapter of lawgivers' use of retributive punishment (1113b23–24), and he observes in book 5 on justice that retributive as well as corrective punishment is a necessary part of a well-ordered state, even as he acknowledges the defective rationality of those demands (see also *Rhetoric* 1378a30–33, *Politics* 1332a12–16).

Thus I believe it is incorrect to say that Aristotle lacked a theory of the freedom of the will or failed to take an interest in the question. To the contrary, he gives every evidence of having thought hard about this idea as it presented itself in ordinary unreflective opinion and having recognized its practical importance; he never attempted to develop it into a rigorous philosophic theory because he considered it fundamentally mistaken. It seems then that Aristotle has, at the least but probably also at the most, a rhetorical quarrel with Socrates. From Aristotle's perspective, Socrates (as opposed to the Athenian Stranger) had an insufficient concern for his effect on those who would never become philosophers. Aristotle's more careful education of moral citizens not only contributes something new to political life but helps us see better the truth of political and moral things, the effectual truth, in the realm of action. It makes theoretical sense to show the grounding of every act in unchosen opinion, but it makes practical sense to stress more the dynamic and cumulative process of character formation and the power we do have to shape our destinies. This power is too easily obscured by the Socratic claims that everyone does the best he can and that vice is merely ignorance, and an irrational carelessness or fatalism can too easily be the result.[61]

And thus we may say that Aristotle's insistence on holding everyone equally responsible for his actions is not merely rhetorical; it also reflects an important truth. For even if Aristotle has found no rational basis for the kind of praise and blame that assume the agent's freedom to choose between good and evil and that assume that the one calls for rewards and the other for retribution, still there is good reason for praise and blame in a more moderate spirit, the celebration of good and the censure of what is bad that are given in order to inspire and deter and keep us all on a better course. The act of praising and blaming is rational because it reminds us of something all-important: that our acts of virtue and vice are voluntary, and that every one of them is etching beautiful or ugly forms into the bedrock of our souls.

These chapters of the *Ethics*, when read casually, support moral seriousness of a fairly conventional kind, but when read carefully they support something better, a seriousness about virtue that is uncompromisingly clear about the difference between good and evil and truly gentle and humane at the same time. It is a seriousness that has no illusions about the difficulty of acquiring virtue and wisdom, and that is thus free of harsh moralism, and a seriousness that sees the worth of virtue above all for the happiness of one's own soul, and that hence is free of harsh vindictiveness. It is, finally, a seriousness that is sober about the importance of natural endowments and yet that takes comfort in this thought: that if we grasp Aristotle's teaching about virtue and pursue it with wholehearted determination, we can become good and wise. And that proves we are as free as anyone could rationally wish to be.

Chapter 3

REASON AND PURPOSE IN THE MORAL VIRTUES

THE ENDS OF MORAL VIRTUE

So how, precisely, does reason function in moral virtue? To what extent is virtue dependent on good vision—and vision of precisely what? As we have seen, moral virtue is resistant to interrogation on the question of the end that reason looks to in guiding it. Aristotle, in his most dogged but respectful investigation of virtue, begins with the moral man's own starting point: you know virtue when you see it if you have been well brought up. As every good parent will say, there are certain things that you just do because they are noble and right, and certain things that you just never do because they are base and wrong. This would seem to mean that the acts are chosen just for themselves, and so they first come to sight in *NE* 2.4.1105a33. We have seen that in book 3 Aristotle begins to offer a correction to this first account. If choice and deliberation are not of ends but of what conduces to the end, and if moral acts are of necessity deliberately chosen, then they must at least be chosen with a view to some goal or standard. Beginning in 3.6, Aristotle will characterize this standard as the noble.

What, then, is this nobility? Is it an irreducible quality that is not explicable by or commensurable with anything else? Always taking his bearing especially by the gentleman's own self-understanding, Aristotle listens carefully to the way such a man describes what is noble. Virtue always involves doing the right thing, at the right time, in the right way, and for the right reason. It means finding the correct mean between two incorrect extremes, a mean that is not equidistant from both but closer to one or the other depending on the case. These ideas all imply an important role for reason in discerning what is noble, but again, we ask, how exactly does reason locate and give precision to what the noble demands? To the extent that moral virtue looks to the needs of the body or of the political community or even of philosophy in identifying the noble, it threatens to collapse into a cleverness in achieving nonmoral ends. But if the philosopher can look closely enough at the kinds of actions and qualities that morally serious individuals agree in admiring and listen closely enough to the things that they themselves admire about them, perhaps he can flesh out a portrait of the noble that stands as virtue's own internal standard, as something autonomous and high, irreducible to and incommensurate with other ends, grasped by its own intellectual virtue, *phronēsis*, loved by a well-cultivated heart, and attainable through long habituation. If so, moral virtue would seem to be especially immune to the troubling Socratic reduction of virtue to mere knowledge. In this way moral virtue might be confirmed to be "for its own sake" but still rational, and the moral person might be said to choose well not merely because he reasons better than others about ends that everyone shares, as Socrates suggests, but even more because of the excellence of his character.

THE STUFF OF COURAGE (3.6)

In the remainder of book 3 and books 4 and 5, Aristotle turns to painting a series of portraits of the virtuous life as he fills out an account of each of his eleven moral virtues. His discussion of the first virtue, courage, is especially revealing about the meaning of nobility, and hence especially worthy of close scrutiny. "And first," he begins, calling attention to his ordering of the virtues without explaining it, "let us speak about courage" (1115a6). Does he begin with courage because it is traditionally the core meaning of virtue or *aretē*? Because it is the most necessary of virtues, inasmuch as the community's survival depends upon it? Because it, with moderation, is most rudimentary, inasmuch as these two "seem to be the virtues of the irrational parts" of the soul, as Aristotle says not here but in introducing the less splendid virtue of moderation at 1117b23–24? Or is it, to the contrary, because courage is the noblest and most splendid of all, as he does not say but certainly implies with his unusually dense references to the noble in 3.6–9? Closely related to the puzzle of the order of

Aristotle's virtues is that of their ranking, for he arranges them in a progression, with two distinct peaks or comprehensive virtues among the moral virtues—and active wisdom in book 6 appearing as a comprehensive virtue also in a different way. In beginning with courage, Aristotle begins where the traditional gentleman does without imposing more clarity on his priorities than he finds there, but with a gentle persistence in querying those priorities (cf. *Laws* 630a ff.).[1]

While courage is the most immediately impressive and traditionally the most deeply admired of virtues, it poses a special challenge to Aristotle's claims about the goodness of virtue and the happiness of the virtuous life. For as he says at the outset in 3.6, courage is concerned with fear, fear is the expectation of evils, the most frightening of all things is death, and yet the courageous man is "someone who is fearless" and in particular "fearless when it comes to a noble death" (1115a16, 1115a33). How is such fearlessness possible?

Whatever the explanation may be, Aristotle insists that noble fearlessness is not blindness. The courageous man who dies on the battlefield "is deprived of the greatest goods knowingly" (1117b12–13), and in doing so he follows or at least acts in conformity to the dictates of reason: "The courageous man suffers and acts in accord with what is worthy and as reason would command" (1115b19–20). Yet Aristotle equally rejects the Socratic view that courage is knowledge. In saying the courageous man acts as reason would command, he leaves open the possibility that one could be completely courageous without oneself possessing knowledge of what is best and why, so long as he imitates the one who has knowledge and exercises it. In delineating a number of qualities that resemble courage but fall short of it in 3.8, Aristotle says, moreover, "And experience regarding particular things seems to be courage; hence even Socrates supposed courage to be knowledge" (1116b3–5). But, Aristotle continues, the coolness in battle that comes from experience and is seen especially in mercenaries is far from true courage. Aristotle's insinuation that the Socratic doctrine arose out of a false inference from observing mercenaries is unfair, but perhaps not quite so unfair as might first appear.[2] For Socrates does argue that courage is nothing other than knowledge about what is terrible and what is not, and it is indeed this knowledge that allows seasoned mercenaries to remain calm when raw citizen recruits are prone to take fright. As Socrates presents his reasoning to an assembled gathering of distinguished Athenians and sophists in Plato's *Protagoras*,

> "Isn't it the case," I said, "that no one voluntarily approaches the bad or what he supposes to be bad, nor, it seems, does this belong to human nature, to go voluntarily towards what one supposes to be bad instead of the good things; but when one is compelled to choose one of two bad things, no one chooses the greater one if it is possible to choose the lesser?" All of us agreed to all of these things. (*Protagoras* 358c6–d4)

Then, defining fear as the expectation of something bad, Socrates concludes that no one voluntarily advances toward what he fears most, but that in every courageous deed one is in fact pursuing the lesser of two evils or risking harm for the sake of a greater good one hopes to achieve. The difference between the cowardly and the courageous, then, comes down to the fact that cowards are ignorant of what is truly terrible, foolishly judging death to be the worst of all evils, whereas the courageous possess "wisdom about what is terrible and what is not terrible" (*Protagoras* 360d4–5; cf. *Laches* 194d7–95a1). To be complete, such wisdom would require an accurate assessment not only of one's immediate situation and its dangers and opportunities, but also of what risks are worth running for what gains, grounded in a knowledge of one's own nature, one's capacities and limits and needs, and how all one's important concerns rank and fit together. Such wisdom, if available, would allow one to judge each thing at its true worth with a clarity undistorted by irrational hopes and fears and to keep these judgments steadily in view. If the wise determine that it is worth waging war against an enemy to preserve freedom for themselves and their loved ones, they will fight hard and intelligently, taking sensible risks; if suddenly ambushed they will not lose their heads; if overwhelmed by the enemy they will withdraw in good order in hopes of living to fight another day. Such a soldier perhaps was Socrates himself, who was famous not for fiery exploits but for a calm, slow, deliberate retreat that saved his life and that of Laches at the battle of Delium.[3] To act as he did he doubtless needed not only theoretical knowledge but also a strong constitution and a level head; yet in calling courage wisdom he suggests that courage may be nothing other than the ability to keep one's wits about one and conduct oneself intelligently in the face of the most frightening dangers.

Now Aristotle's entire treatment of courage in *NE* 3.6–9 may be said to be an experiment in resolutely resisting just this Socratic reduction of courage to knowledge or wisdom. To be sure, the ordinary, decent man in the street, to whose opinions Aristotle listens with exquisitely close attention, is of two minds on Socrates' claims about courage, as about all the virtues. Such a person can be brought to agree that if courage is good, it must be good for something, such as safety, freedom, or glory; that courage is not recklessness and that life should not be risked to no purpose; that courage may indeed be an ability to keep one's head. But something else in him—in us—is not satisfied by this line of analysis, sensing that it risks turning into an instrument of lesser goods what is in fact supremely good and supremely noble in itself. Lincoln beautifully encapsulates both of these intuitions in his Gettysburg address, which in a few words gives moving expression to the high end for which the fallen soldiers fought and in a few more suggests that nothing can ever match the intrinsic value of the brave deeds they performed in pursuit of that end. Churchill does the same in rallying the British people to fight for freedom as a prize worth the ultimate price in blood, toil, tears, and sweat, even while calling their most anguished moment of struggle their finest hour.[4] Civic oratory and national patriotism have seldom burned brighter than in the spirit these two statesmen kindled and kept alight. Yet if it ultimately does not make sense to say that what is most excellent, most intrinsically worthy of all is properly in the service of something else, how should we untangle this knot? Might Socrates in attempting to untangle it have cut the nerve and destroyed the noble essence of courage? That is the challenge Aristotle takes up as he gently draws out and isolates for us the other strand of the citizen's intuition about courage, the strand that denies that any virtue is reducible to knowledge of what is good, and that uncompromisingly reveres courage in particular as a free, uncalculating choice of what is supremely noble for its own sake.

While Aristotle begins his treatment of courage with a direct challenge to the Socratic position—recalling Socrates' definition of fear as the "anticipation of something bad," conceding that "we fear all the bad things" (1115a9–10), and yet still insisting on behalf of common opinion and common sense that the courageous man is "fearless" (1115a16, 1115a33)—he devotes this first chapter on courage not to addressing the question of how such fearlessness is humanly possible, but to the seemingly unrelated question of courage's domain. Yet in delimiting true courage narrowly as fearlessness on the battlefield, Aristotle isolates the nerve of what makes courage, in the eyes of hero and common citizen and Protagoras alike, so resistant to being reduced, as Socrates would reduce it, to another form of wisdom. Aristotle thereby begins to limn the unique concern—the love of the noble—that may somehow make it possible to be unafraid precisely of what is most frightening. Now if the essence of courage were simply bearing up calmly under necessary evils and keeping one's head in difficult straits, courage would be a kind of reasonableness or wisdom that might indeed be exercised in meeting evils of every kind.[5] But if we are to do justice to the decent citizen's intuition that courage is a virtue worthy of the very highest honors, we must consider what is so impressive and so moving about the fallen hero. Aristotle indicates the answer: he faces not only the greatest but the "noblest dangers"; he faces them willingly; he is "fearless when it comes to a noble death"; he shows what he is above all "in circumstances where prowess is possible or dying is noble" (1115a30–31, 1115a33, 1115b4–5). Steadfastness in the face of such unavoidable evils as illness and shipwreck, by contrast, is perhaps too much like the suffering of a mute mule to be a true virtue and even the peak of virtue: Aristotle calls it courage only in a partial and analogous sense.[6]

If the hero's death is noble in large part because it is willingly chosen, it is also chosen because it is noble, simply in itself. And, this chapter clearly brings out, that nobility has everything to do with the grave risk or sacrifice the hero willingly accepts. Aristotle does not attribute to the man of courage the calm calculation of Socrates in Plato's *Apology*, who purports to be unafraid of death because it is, after all, nothing bad. Nor does he here depict him as one who scorns death and cares only for the virtue that is his and cannot be taken from him, just as a good Stoic refuses to trouble himself over rude men's insults (but cf. 1104b1–2). If death were something beneath his concern, then facing it staunchly in battle would hardly be anything remarkable (cf. *EE* 1228b9–11), whereas in fact the brave man cherishes his bravery as something supremely difficult and noble. Somehow the brave man is fearless in battle not despite but precisely because of the very great and hence very noble sacrifice he is prepared to make. But if this is courage, is it rational?

COURAGE, COWARDICE, RASHNESS (3.7)

In the next chapter Aristotle sheds more light on the judgment that informs true courage by distinguishing it from its corresponding excess and deficiency. In doing so he brings reason and judgment to the fore and at the same time offers a correction. The courageous man is not after all completely fearless, but "intrepid as a human being" (1115b10–11). For some things everyone who "has sense" will fear, and "a person would be mad or insensitive to pain if he should fear nothing" (1115b8–9, 1115b26–

27). Rather, in fearing things that are terrible, the man of courage will "endure them as he should and as reason commands, for the sake of the noble" (1115b11–13). Does he differ from the ordinary man not in his emotions but in his actions, then? No, his virtue shapes both: "He, then, who endures and fears what he ought and for the sake of what he ought, and as he ought and when, and who is similarly confident as well, is courageous" (1115b17–19). Finding the right mean in courage thus involves a complex problem of getting the object, end, manner, and time right, regarding both acts and emotions. Moreover, while Aristotle defines courage as "a mean with respect to fear and confidence" (1115a6–7, 1116a10–11), this is not quite the same as saying that it is a simple mean *between* fear and confidence. In both the *Rhetoric* and the *Eudemian Ethics* he treats fear and confidence as simple opposites (*Rhetoric* 1383a15 ff.; *EE* 1228a27–b3), but in his subtler discussion in the *Nicomachean Ethics* he suggests that fear and confidence stand in a more complex relationship, both being subject to excess and deficiency and potentially moving independently. For neither of them is the right mean simply an intermediate amount: in some circumstances it seems that both fear and confidence should be high. Aristotle says that "the courageous man suffers and acts in accord with what is worthy and as reason would command" (1115b19–20), but how exactly does reason determine the right mean in each circumstance in respect to object, end, manner, and time? Aristotle gives few details, and in some cases more than one standard seems to apply. Are the objects one should not fear the ones that are not even bad, such as thunder and black cats, or are they the things it is not noble to fear, such as the enemy charging at a run upon one's phalanx? Will the brave man after all fear the enemy to just the extent that the enemy is dangerous, as Aristotle does not quite say in the *Nicomachean* but does say in *Eudemian Ethics* (1229b26), but endure that fear anyway? But then, if he is not after all fearless but must endure painful fear, is his courage a true virtue, exercised with pleasure or at least without pain as Aristotle has claimed virtue always is (1104b3–9), rather than a painful case of self-control (*enkrateia*)?[7] Or will he somehow, without becoming reckless, fear a noble danger less that the threat alone would seem to dictate? It is tempting to identify the rational purpose or end of courageous endurance as a well-chosen military objective, but Aristotle insists that the end for the sake of which the courageous man acts is nothing but the noble itself (1115b12–13, 1115b21–22, 1115b23, 1116a11–12, 1116b3, 1116b31, 1117a17, 1117b9, 1117b14–15), without further specifying its contents.[8] What Aristotle most strikingly does not say is what every eulogist over fallen soldiers invariably does say, that the noble death is one in which one dies for one's fatherland. Precisely this we must not say if we are most resolutely to resist allowing virtue to become a means to other goods.[9] Neither wealth nor empire nor freedom nor safety can be the most important end of war, but instead war must be the stage on which virtue is tested and honed and given scope for action. The proper manner would seem to be "as reason commands" (1115b12, 1115b19), but this criterion remains formulaic since Aristotle does not specify what kind of fear, endurance, and confidence reason dictates. Finally, is the wrong time to fear the enemy the time when it no longer poses a danger, or precisely when it is most dangerous but it is also most noble not to be afraid?

Rather than explain how the courageous man determines what, why, how, and when he should endure, Aristotle goes on to contrast courage as a proper mean with its improper extremes. In keeping with his complex analysis of courage in the *Nicomachean Ethics* as a mean with respect to both fear and confidence, he identifies a nameless and, among sane people, evidently nonexistent excess of utter fearlessness and a separate excess of confidence that he calls recklessness. Opposite both of these is the single vice of cowardice, entailing both too much fear and too little confidence. Now if every sane person has a realistic fear of what is dangerous, it would seem that the courageous are distinguished after all not by fearlessness but by their high levels of confidence. But how does courage differ in this from recklessness? Is recklessness taking risks that are too great in relation to what one stands to gain from them? This Aristotle does not say, presumably because to do so would again be to define courageous acts as instruments of lesser goods. Instead, he gives a definition of recklessness that is incomplete. The majority of reckless men, he explains, are reckless cowards who make a show of fearlessness but flee in the face of real danger. What, then, of those who remain steadfast? How does recklessness that never quavers differ from true courage? Or is this distinction impossible to draw, and is the correct reason that governs courage impossible to specify, without resorting to prudential considerations that are alien to the noble core of courage Aristotle is trying to isolate?[10] Aristotle's definition of cowardice is incomplete as well: the coward has too little confidence, he tells us, in contrast to the courageous man who is "of good hope" (1116a3–4), but exactly what the courageous man's hope rests on he does not say.[11] By insisting that courage is a mean on two different scales, respecting both fear and confidence, by contradicting himself on the courageous man's fearlessness, and by leaving the source of the courageous man's confidence unstated, chapters 3.6 and 3.7 have the effect of highlighting the puzzle of how courage can combine a rational assessment of real danger with fearlessness or at least great confidence.

DEFECTIVE FORMS OF COURAGE (3.8)

In 3.8 Aristotle sheds additional light on courage by contrasting true or complete courage with five defective forms of it.[12] This is a procedure he follows with none of the other virtues: somehow it is especially hard to get courage right, and the defective forms all involve acting correctly (at least initially) but for incorrect reasons.[13]

Political Courage

First and least defective is political courage, which is virtuous insofar as it takes its sights by what is noble and shameful but defective in doing so in the partial and somewhat misguided form of loving honor and fearing dishonor (cf. 1116a10–12 with 1116a27–29). True virtue according to Aristotle is rooted in a love of what is noble for its own sake and a disgust at what is shameful quite apart from any consequences (cf. 1117a17, 1117b9), and it recognizes virtue and vice as themselves the most important parts of the noble and shameful, but it is characteristic of the citizen soldier that he is moved especially by honor and dishonor. Moreover, it belongs to the citizen's perspective that he thinks nobility needs such a reward and baseness such a penalty. Aristotle's examples are startling, however. He says that those peoples who especially dishonor cowards and honor the courageous—a category that would surely include the Spartans—appear to exceed in true courage but actually have only a defective form of political courage; then he quotes speeches of the great Homeric heroes Hector and Diomedes expressing their fear of reproach (*Iliad* 22.100, 8.148) to illustrate the concern with honor and shame that rules men of such defective courage. If the Spartans and Homeric heroes fall short of true courage, who possesses it? Does Achilles, or is Achilles not an even clearer example of one for whom honor and disgrace are all-important? Aristotle gives no examples of men who embody his "true" form of courage, leaving us to wonder whether it actually exists.

The picture Aristotle paints with his quotations from Homer is complicated, however. Hector is indeed afraid of reproach from his friend Polydamas, but what Hector anticipates Polydamas will reproach him for—what he is now so ashamed of that he would rather face death at Achilles' hands than return to the city—is the fact that he has been imprudently risking Troy's safety by fighting far out beyond the city walls in search of personal glory (*Iliad* 22.99–107). In other words, Hector is *ashamed* of himself for acting almost as if noble fighting were an end in itself and for forgetting that his first duty is to protect his city. Thus while he agrees with Aristotle that there is something defective about his own courage, he and Aristotle understand that failure differently. In a similar way, the preeminent warrior Achilles fights and acts in single-minded pursuit of his own glory until that pursuit results in the death of his friend Patroclus, at which point he, too, regrets what he has done (*Iliad* 18.22–126). Might it be that flesh-and-blood human heroes in fact always feel a duty to put the good of friends and fatherland above their pursuit of their own honor and even above their own honorable deeds, in a way that presents a problem for Aristotle's effort to make the noble an end in itself?

As a member of the attacking Greek army, Diomedes is not fighting for his fatherland as Hector is, but neither is he moved chiefly by shame as the words Aristotle quotes might suggest: piety works more powerfully than honor and shame both to inspire and to limit his daring. Diomedes performs his greatest exploits under the conviction that Athena herself has breathed "strength untremulous" into his limbs, and on that basis he scorns to seek safety at Sthenelos's urging, calling it "not noble" (*Iliad* 5.125–26, 5.252–56). Later, when Nestor echoes Sthenelos's call to retreat and points out that Zeus has now turned against him, Diomedes does briefly resist with the thought of Hector's imagined reproaches, but his fear of shame is soon overcome by his greater fear of Zeus's thunderbolts (*Iliad* 8.138–44, 8.161–71).[14]

Curiously, it is precisely fear of a greater power or a greater evil that constitutes the other and lower side of political courage as Aristotle presents it. In his third quote from Homer he cites Agamemnon's threatening words to the cowards among the Achaians as an example of what is needed to move such men, but he also cites the use of rear guards to punish deserters, which every army needs to maintain order. Is it only a few bad apples who fight out of fear of something worse, and without whose infectious example no one would flee? And what about those who fight well in hopes of booty or new lands? Political courage seems in fact to draw upon all these fears and hopes.

Experience

Second after political courage Aristotle treats the defective form of courage that arises from experience in battle. He cites especially the example of professional soldiers, but of course experience was also a crucial reason for the outstanding courage of the highly trained citizen soldiers of Sparta. Aristotle brings out professional soldiers' immunity to the panics that plague amateurs but also the limits of their courage when the odds are against them, for their courage rests on calculation about their chances of facing either death or gain. But then Aristotle draws a contrast with the citizen soldier that subtly revises what he said before about its basis. For to citizen soldiers "it is shameful to flee and death is more choiceworthy than such preservation, while those who from the beginning were taking risks on the assumption that they were stronger flee when they recognize how things are, fearing death more than what is shameful. But the courageous man is not of this sort" (1116b19–23). Is the citizen soldier guided after all not by honor and reproach but by love of the noble itself or at least fear of the shameful, which perhaps amounts to the same thing (cf. 1117a17 with 1117b9)?[15] And in shifting his point of contrast from political courage at the beginning of this comparison to courage simply at the end of it, is Aristotle now suggesting that political and true courage are after all the same? But perhaps, putting this passage together with Aristotle's earlier characterization of political courage and his quotations from Homer, we should say rather that Aristotle is giving a subtle and accurate account of political courage as being *essentially* complex and shifting in its foundation. The citizen's cluster of reasons for fighting well center especially on honor and disgrace but include also devotion to the fatherland, hopes of gains and fears of losses of a mundane sort, piety (which is suggested again with the mention of citizen soldiers fighting steadfastly before a temple of Hermes at 1116b18–19), and not least but never exclusively, an intrinsic love of what is noble and scorn for what is shameful.[16]

Spiritedness

After this discussion of calculation as a defective form of courage, Aristotle turns third to an opposite quality that seems even more crucial to the phenomenon: spiritedness or anger (*thumos*). Clearly spiritedness alone does not constitute the virtue of courage: it is shared by animals; it is an elemental passion that may support what is noble or base; it can be wholly without reason.[17] Animals are spirited out of fear or frustrated desire and often rush impulsively and blindly into danger; human adulterers, Aristotle observes, are often daring out of desire, and people driven by the pain of anger or the pleasure of anticipated revenge often fight fiercely, but none of this is courage. With these examples Aristotle sketches the outlines of spiritedness as a fundamental psychological force. It is the passion that flares up in defense of our own or in pursuit of what we need or want when our desires encounter obstacles. It is a love of victory so intense that it easily becomes heedless of death. It is the anger that in humans always involves judgments, however hasty or prejudiced, about wrongs for which it seeks revenge (cf. 7.6). And, as the allusions to the Homeric heroes remind us, it is felt in human beings as an intense concern for dignity. How, then, is the passion of *thumos* related to true courage?

At 1116b31 Aristotle calls spiritedness a "fellow worker" with or within the courageous; then in a complex passage we have already alluded to he adds,

> That which arises through spiritedness seems to be most natural, and with the addition of choice and the end ["that for the sake of which"], to be courage. And when human beings are angry they are pained, but when they get revenge they feel pleasure; and those who make war on account of these things are warlike but not courageous, for they do not do so on account of the noble or according to reason but through passion; yet they have something closely resembling courage. (1117a4–9)[18]

Spiritedness seems by turns to be an ally to courage, the natural foundation of courage to which reason and choice must be added to give it proper direction, and a mere simulacrum of true courage. The thought that spiritedness is the natural *foundation* of courage is of a piece with the thought that courage is the perfection of the spirited part of the soul and with the civic perspective according to which courage is the disciplined expression of the natural inclination to fight in defense of one's own. Reason then would function as a supplement, allowing human beings to be fully aware of the danger they face and so to act fully by choice, and putting limits on anger to prevent indiscriminate slaughter.[19] But while repeatedly reminding us of this essentially civic perspective on courage, Aristotle never endorses it. Is spiritedness, then, just reason's *ally*, as Socrates claims in the *Republic*? But if it is, what motivates reason, and how are these two disparate motivations related?[20] Does reason make an independent assessment of what is noble and enlist the energy of spiritedness whenever it aligns with reason's judgment? Or is even that picture granting too much to spiritedness, since Aristotle says those who fight on account of anger are *not* courageous, evidently because they seek not the noble but revenge? But since "thought alone moves nothing" (1139a35–36; cf. *On the Soul* 433a15–24), what is the desire within the choice or deliberate desire that fuels true courage, and what ensures that it will outweigh the blind love of one's own or desire for vengeance?

Pondering the relation between spiritedness and the core motivation of genuine courage, we are forced to wonder whether reason does introduce a separate motive that gives to the animal energy of spiritedness a new, noble purpose, like a rider directing the strength of a great horse—or whether reason just gives voice to the passionate love of one's own or yearning for freedom or honor or revenge, affirming that it is noble to defend these things at all costs and that one's own dignity should never have to bow to any considerations of mere advantage but is the highest thing in the world. There is, at any rate, a curious resemblance between spiritedness's tendency to leave behind all prudent calculations in pursuit of dignity and the spirit of high courage as Aristotle captures it, with its insistence on doing what is noble for its own sake. Might it be precisely spiritedness that resists the Socratic reduction of virtue to knowledge and of courage to an unshakeable knowledge of what truly is and is not terrible and what is worth risking for the sake of what? In our belief that in virtue we have found a higher purpose than all of the mundane goods that we and our communities need to be happy, perhaps we are still being carried away by spiritedness.[21]

That spiritedness has an uncanny power to inspire us is undeniable. Aristotle's quotes from Homer all point to the way people fired with spiritedness can feel themselves infused with divine wrath or with superhuman strength. The heroes in the scenes from which Aristotle quotes here believe the gods are breathing might into them or fighting alongside them. Some, like Diomedes and Achilles, become so spirited that they even challenge the gods, while others, like Hector, come to seem to their fellows if not to themselves to be in fact divine.[22] In their moments of greatest fear, human beings most long for and pray for divine protection, although to need it is no reason to believe we deserve such help. But when anger convinces us that we are in the right, it calls more confidently for divine aid; when it fires us to be very brave without flinching, it fuels the hope that we do deserve it. Indeed, if we are brave enough, perhaps we can even somehow rise above needing that help and become invulnerable to death itself. Such, at least, seem to be the hopes of the figures who admired and cultivated courage most single-mindedly and brought it to its highest glory, the Homeric heroes.[23] Aristotle opposes their angry demands for glory; he refuses to endorse their hopes for divine favor for those who are brave; he works throughout his account to build a calmer, more autonomous spirit in the warrior; but he cannot dispense with their nonetheless inspiring examples.

Hope

So deeply is spiritedness entwined with hope that hope is the next topic Aristotle turns to. Those who are of good hope because they have often been victorious before—again we are reminded of the Spartans—resemble the courageous, Aristotle says, but the truly courageous are confident not for this reason but "for the reasons already mentioned" (1117a12–13). Aristotle has indeed said that the courageous are confident, but what they place their confidence in beyond knowledge and experience is never entirely clear. Can it be that the courageous not only endure but are positively confident or hopeful simply because it is noble to feel this way (cf. 1117a16–17)? The confidence that is noblest seems at any rate to rest on something other than calculation. For it is most evident, Aristotle says, in sudden dangers where one cannot have recourse to "calculation and reason" and must rely instead on character (1117a17–22). Despite the importance Aristotle places on choice in virtue, we see that in the splendid, paradigmatic virtue of courage, reasoned choice is much less important than is deeply ingrained habit or character. Such character is perhaps also more evident in the soldier who simply obeys hard orders than in the commander who must calculate with a view to the practical task of winning while suffering the fewest casualties.

Ignorance

Reflecting on these questions, we are not wholly unprepared when Aristotle turns fifth and last to the ignorant as a group who bear a misleading resemblance to the truly courageous. He attributes to those who are fearless only because they do not know what they are up against the same failing he has attributed to recklessness and even to the defective form of courage that is based on knowledge or experience: insufficient staying power in the face of great danger once that danger becomes manifest. But is a determination to be confident merely because confidence is noble itself altogether immune to collapse when it becomes clear that one's side cannot after all overcome the enemy?

Perhaps, however, we have not yet identified correctly the object of courageous soldiers' confidence. Perhaps what they count upon is not safety but ultimate victory for their side, or the rightness of their cause. Surely they often do, but this does not yet explain how confidence works to counteract fear. Or perhaps the object of the confidence that matters most is simply their own courage that they value more than either life or victory and that they know will prevent them from panicking in extreme danger or behaving shamefully to save their lives.[24] In courage we seem to have a purpose that is its own purpose and a confidence that is its own ground. But perhaps in many such heroic souls there is something else at work that Aristotle is alluding to in his reference to the heroes' sense of divine inspiration. Aristotle by no means presents courage as dependent on piety, but he quietly indicates why piety may be such a helpful support to it. Mustering a confident frame of mind in the conviction that it is noble to do so, courageous soldiers are likely to see themselves as deserving protection or victory on account of their nobility, and to be confident that one deserves divine favor is perhaps reason enough to hope for it. Of course to be certain of divine aid would again mean fighting well only out of knowledge that one has the advantage on one's side, and this again seems less than sublimely noble. Courage cannot be folly, but if its promise of great nobility is to be sustained, it may have to be grounded in something other than solid knowledge.

COURAGE AND HAPPINESS (3.9)

This thought would seem to be behind Aristotle's opening sentence in his fourth and final chapter on courage, 3.9. Although courage is indeed concerned with confidence as well as fear, he reminds us, it is especially concerned with fear: courage is by no means a sensible assurance that all will be well. But Aristotle pushes so hard to uphold courage's nobility that he risks toppling the claim he has also been building in the *Nicomachean Ethics* about the happiness of the virtuous life. If happiness is the final end of life and of all action, if happiness requires a "complete life" (1098a18), if the courageous man is not running a calculated risk to win some great gain for himself or his loved ones but instead is fighting and facing death bravely just for its own sake, how is that not folly? This is a serious challenge, but Aristotle faces it squarely. Yes, the courageous man suffers fear and pain and often death, and no, the exercise of courage in itself is not pleasant, and yes, in possessing a noble soul he even gives up a happier life than does the worthless man when he dies.[25] But no, he is not enduring all this and gaining nothing in return.

Aristotle compares the courageous man to the boxer, who also voluntarily endures terrible things, but for the sake of a goal that is sweet, though easily obscured by pain and suffering: the crown and the honors that accompany victory. Like the boxer, the courageous man endures great evils for the sake of a goal that is in fact pleasant. But what is the goal in his case? The brave man, Aristotle says,

> to the extent that he has all virtues and is more happy, will be more pained by death. For such a man life is most worth living, and he will be deprived of the greatest goods knowingly, and that is painful. But he is no less courageous, and perhaps even more so, because in war he chooses what is noble in exchange for these. For pleasant activity is not available in all the virtues, except insofar as they attain their end [*telos*]. (1117b9–16)

Aristotle attributes to the completely brave man, then, full knowledge of what he is doing and what he is giving up. But precisely what, we ask again, is this end for which the courageous man fights and sacrifices? Is it the same as the boxer's, the crown and the honors that the champion wins? Especially in the last line above Aristotle invites us to wonder whether a courageous life can be happy if it is not pleasant, or pleasant if no such rewards are forthcoming, but he does not identify the courageous man's end as being honor as the boxer's is, and he has given good reasons not to do so. Not only is honor not available for those who die, since death is "a limit or end [*telos*], and there seems to be nothing else for the dead, either good or bad" (1115a26–27; cf. 1111b23), but more important, honor is the end only for a defective form of courage Aristotle took up in 3.8, political courage. Even if we interpret 3.8 to mean that true courage in its pure form is vanishingly rare and that political courage with its mixed motives is the best of the existing forms of courage, still the love of honor is not the highest strand within that courage.

It seems that we must say that what courage at its purest and highest moments attains is rather just the great, completed act of heroism itself, or the nobility of this act and nothing subsequent or extrinsic to it.[26] Not every courageous warrior who enters the fray is able to do anything splendid; one may be wounded by grapeshot in the first moments of the battle and never manage to engage the enemy. But to fight well, steadfastly standing one's ground in the face of a terrible onslaught, overcoming fear to use strength and skill and wits to fight superbly, or dying without flinching as Leonidas and his men did—perhaps this is an end so noble and splendid that it is itself worth everything one might lose.[27] Aristotle suggests as much in a passage in 9.8 that echoes this one, and that introduces a motive he has scrupulously avoided attributing to courage in book 3.

> It is true of the morally serious man that he will do many things for the sake of his friends and his fatherland, and if necessary he will give up his life for them. He will give money and honors and all the contested goods, seeking above all the noble for himself. He would choose to feel pleasure intensely for a short time rather than mildly for a long time, and to live nobly for one year rather than indifferently for many, and to perform one great noble act rather than many small ones. Those who give up their lives perhaps achieve this, and they choose great nobility for themselves. He will give away money so that his friends may have more, for they thus get money, but he gets the noble: he assigns the greater good to himself. (1169a18–29)

In book 3, where the stress is on the idea that true virtue must be embraced for itself, Aristotle is silent on the idea of dying for friends or country. In book 9, where the theme is love and friendship, he does introduce this idea, but still in the context of insisting that the morally serious man loves and seeks the noble for himself most of all.

So once again and for the last time, what exactly is this thing, the noble, which inheres in courage and is so fine and splendid that it is worth even the "greatest goods" that the courageous man sacrifices to attain it? Here is where everything becomes very strange. For it is of the essence of nobility, Aristotle shows, that one understands oneself to choose the noble act just for its own sake. What is most noble in courage seems to be just this hard act of overcoming fear, risking death, and above all actually sacrificing life in battle, especially when a life is rich and satisfying and full of good things. We have then something deeply paradoxical at the heart of the courageous man's self-understanding. He sees his activity as hard and bad for himself and thinks it is above all this that makes it noble; but he sees this very same activity in its nobility as something good for him, best for him, indeed the greatest prize of all, and it is this that makes it choiceworthy. He is somehow hopeful, despite or even precisely because of his sacrifice, but what he puts his hope in refuses to come clearly into focus. It is perhaps simply that he will fight well, but this Aristotle does not say. It is perhaps also, then, that he will win divine aid, as do the Homeric heroes Aristotle alluded to in the previous chapter, for surely he must deserve it if he is very brave. The aid he hopes for, in turn, is perhaps simply help in being supremely brave, but perhaps also help in winning and enjoying the fruits of victory, for surely one who sets his sights only on being brave deserves victory if anyone does. Or perhaps it is a hope that in dying he will enjoy a reward for his courage, a reward that seems less conceivable if death is the end or if gloomy Hades is all that awaits the dead, but a reward that seems nonetheless all the better deserved by one who faces this grim prospect squarely, and in being better deserved it is more inspiring of hope, if only the dimmest of hopes against hope.

The deepest problem in all this is not that the courageous man is secretly mercenary; rewards may be far indeed from his thoughts. The deepest problem, rather, is the self-contradictory understanding of what the nobility in virtue consists in. Glaucon in Plato's *Republic* insists on a simple question that the noble man cannot satisfactorily answer: is the noble on balance and in the final analysis good for the noble person or bad for him, and why? Aristotle asks it less obtrusively but lays out for anyone who looks closely the ambivalence in the noble soul that makes him so resistant to giving a clear answer. This ambivalence is present to some degree in all of moral virtue but is especially visible in courage, inasmuch as courage seems especially to embody the nobility of self-sacrifice, with its extraordinary power to stir us to admiration and to tears.[28]

For a different but related reason, courage understood as an end in itself is open to a further difficulty: the hero not only suffers but inflicts terrible things. Aristotle is silent on this fact here, where he makes the best case for the courageous man's own self-understanding, but he does bring it up in book 10 when he turns to a defense of the philosophic life as a life more intrinsically choiceworthy than the life of practical activity. While we engage in work in order to live and recreation in order to rest from our labors, Aristotle says, we choose the activities of leisure for their own sakes, and preeminent among these is philosophy. "The activities of the practical virtues in political life and war and the actions concerned with these seem to be unleisured, and the warlike ones wholly so. For no one would choose to make war for its own sake, nor to foment war. For one would seem to be totally bloodthirsty if one should make war on one's friends so that there could be battle and killing" (1177b6–12).

If, then, our original, untutored admiration for courage is incoherent, regarding acts of courage as noble precisely because they are so bad or unchoiceworthy and as good and choiceworthy because they are so noble, if in our admiration for virtue we intuit that the highest things in life must be ends in themselves and yet we see that choosing courageous acts just for their own sake would be bloodthirsty, how should we understand what is best in courage? Aristotle's experiment in resisting the thrust of the Socratic analysis of courage as wisdom and good sense shows us the necessity of restoring to our account what he refused to grant to that analysis for the purposes of this experiment. An act of courage must involve accepting the risk of pain and death for the sake of something else, some benefit to the fatherland or some service to a further virtue that makes the risks worth taking. But if courage is to be regarded as itself a noble virtue—and every nation and good citizen soldier must regard it as such—it necessarily must combine the belief that it is a means to a further end with the thought that it is in itself admirable and perhaps supremely admirable. Political courage is in fact better than the pure courage that would entail a choice of courageous acts solely for themselves, if such purity were possible, but it is also even more intractably tangled.

In the discussion of courage we have a striking example of Aristotle's method. He gives the strongest, most sympathetic case he can for each virtue as an end in itself. He draws on the most distinguished, most serious segment of commonsense opinion to make his case. He imposes nothing on that opinion from outside, but neither does he sweep away tensions that actually exist within it, especially when both sides of a tension turn out to be essential to the outlook he is exploring. Rather, he reproduces the tensions so that they show up more clearly than they usually do in the heat and dust of active life, pointing only obliquely to the different plane on which they might be capable of a wholly satisfactory resolution.

What might that resolution look like? It would have to keep clear the fact that risk and sacrifice and killing are as such nothing good, while recognizing that the unwavering strength and steadfastness that battlefield courage requires may be good as a means to other goods of different kinds. On the highest plane, it might be in service to the philosophic life, which requires the courage of facing difficult truths, holding firmly to what one knows in the face of temptations to despondency or unreasonable hopes, and persevering in running risks that one has correctly calculated are worth running. This ability is not merely a means; it is good also as a quality desirable in itself in the way that health is. It is even noble inasmuch as it combines what is rare, difficult, and beneficial in a noncontradictory way—even if it is also very close to the wisdom that Socrates identifies with true virtue, or at least to the ability to hold onto and follow such wisdom. It is, however, only a foundation for the best life and by no means its chief substance; it is not heroic; it belongs to a life so austere as to include little of what makes ordinary lives rich and serious.

Yet the active life too requires the strength at times to take risks without losing one's head, to endure suffering without collapsing, and to confront hard truths without flinching. Even if the active exercise of such endurance is neither an end in itself nor the substance of happiness, might it not be nobly enlisted in the service of something else, such as justice, whose activity could be shown to constitute a satisfactory end in itself and the focus for a satisfying life? At least in the case of very strong and sober citizens or leaders, a certain form of political courage might then be coherent, not as the peak of virtue but as an important subordinate virtue. We must see whether the discussion of the other virtues gives a basis for understanding the moral life fully in this way.

MODERATION (3.10–12)

Turning from courage to his second virtue, moderation, Aristotle begins, "After this let us speak about moderation [*sōphrosunē*]. For these seem to be the virtues of the irrational parts" (1117b23–24). In 1.13 he suggested that all the moral virtues are perfections of a single part of the irrational part of the soul, the one that includes the passions and is capable of listening to reason. But now it appears that the cardinal virtues of courage and moderation are especially closely involved with our subrational natures. Perhaps we could say that courage is the perfection of the spirited passions and moderation that of the desires, or more precisely, since Aristotle defines both narrowly, that courage governs the most basic fear and moderation the most basic desires.[29] For moderation according to Aristotle concerns only the desires for bodily pleasures, and indeed only the lowest of these, involving food and sex. This restriction of scope is especially striking given that the Greek word *sōphrosunē* can mean not only moderation but sanity or sobriety or good sense altogether. In Plato's *Republic* Socrates defines it as the harmony of all the desires of the soul under the guidance of reason, a harmony that "stretches literally throughout the whole" of the healthy soul, making all its elements "sing the same chant in unison" (430c, 432a). In Plato's *Charmides* Socrates and Critias explore the possibility that moderation really comes down to wisdom and especially to a comprehensive self-knowledge—a view that Socrates interrogates critically, to be sure, but in such a way as to suggest that Critias's understanding needs to be refined rather than abandoned. Aristotle once again offers for a cardinal virtue a treatment that seems designed especially to resist the thrust of the Socratic thought by which all the virtues become only different expressions of the single virtue of wisdom. But in returning in the opening sentence of 3.10 to his division of the soul into parts in 1.13, a division he made a point of saying might well be misleading, Aristotle reminds us of the road not followed in his analysis of *sōphrosunē*. That road, which would begin from the close interdependence of judgment and passion, might well make better sense of the full range of meanings of the virtue and show better how they are related.

Aristotle begins by addressing just this question of scope. Setting aside all the higher, more complicated, and uniquely human pleasures that sometimes carry people away but that also characterize precisely the lives of cultivated gentlemen in a free republic, Aristotle exempts from the purview of moderation and immoderation not only the nonbodily pleasures of honor, learning, and storytelling, but also the more refined pleasures of the senses, including those of seeing beautiful sights, listening to music and drama, and even enjoying hot baths and discriminating refined flavors. Moderation seems not to involve directing and limiting any of the pleasures that the mind itself partakes of, then, but to be a simple mastery of the lowest animal passions, the raw desires to eat and to copulate. "So licentiousness pertains to the most common of the senses, and it might be held to be justly subject to the greatest reproach, because it belongs to us not inasmuch as we are human but inasmuch as we are animals" (1118b1–4). To enjoy these sorts of things and to be fond of them most of all Aristotle calls both slavish and brutish. Curbing these inclinations would seem to be not a complex work of finding the perfect mean but a simple task of restraint, which might be accomplished by good habituation with little need for thought. Accordingly, apart from a single mention of correct reason at 1119a20, Aristotle is silent on the role of reason until the end of the three chapters on moderation.

As with courage, then, Aristotle defines the virtue of moderation especially by what it is not: the courageous man is unafraid, the moderate man is not slavish or piggish in his pleasures. This gives some guidance; does it give enough? If Aristotle had defined moderation as a harmony of all the desires under the guidance of reason, he would have to explain with more precision what the correct ranking is of the desires, what the correct limits are of each one, and what the standard is that yields this ordering. But by defining it narrowly, does he avoid the need to make a precise demarcation of the proper ranking and limits of the higher desires, or even of the lower ones? And does he really show what is bestial about licentiousness or in general how this vice arises? For in fact, the paradox of 3.10 is that we never see animals in the wild overeating and growing obese or falling prey to an obsession with sex or anything else. Licentiousness is a uniquely human failing, and indeed part of human nature, as Aristotle brings out at the end of his discussion of moderation: "Whatever desires shameful things and can undergo much growth ought to be chastised, and appetite and a child are especially of this description: children too live according to appetite, and the desire for pleasure is present in them especially" (1119b3–7). But if we so easily go wrong right from the start, why is this? How is nature still a standard for us? And in what way is the virtue of moderation a mean between extremes at all rather than a case of forcible self-control to avoid the single vice of licentiousness?

Aristotle points to the answer to the first of these questions already in 3.10 as he distinguishes human pleasures from animal ones. Animals' pleasures are strictly tied to their needs: if a lion enjoys the sound of a cow lowing, it is only as a direct signpost to the meat it wants to eat. But human pleasures are open-ended and easily take on a life of their own. What carries us wrong is the restless, fluid character of human thought and imagination as they invent new forms and sources of pleasure, making possible all the higher pleasures unknown to animals, but also making us prone to unchecked licentiousness right from childhood.

Aristotle indicates the sense in which nature is a standard in the next chapter but also introduces a subtle shift in the argument. Nature is the standard regarding the appetites nature herself gives us: "The natural desire is for the satisfaction of need" (1118b17–18). What instinct does for the animals in keeping desires within the bounds of true need, habituation can do for humans. The gentleman takes pride in his freedom from being the slave to his stomach and his lust, and such mastery is essential to his life as a free, cultured person, even if in itself it is nothing exalted. But in fact, as Aristotle concedes now, this is not the front on which the greatest challenges lie. Perhaps there have been human beings who have grown obese on barley cakes, but the real problem is the invention of rich sauces. Not the animal inclinations but the flexible and unbounded character of human pleasures causes almost all the problem with immoderation. The problem is especially bad when the higher human faculties are enlisted to sharpen and indulge the lowest desires for food and sex, but cocaine and gambling present similar problems, which Aristotle implicitly takes under consideration as he expands the discussion in 3.11 to every kind of pleasure, conceding that it is after all the "idiosyncratic" ones that cause the most trouble (cf. 1118b8–9, 1118b15–16, and 1118b21–22). Thus the chapter in fact addresses a higher meaning of moderation as a virtue that governs the manifold, endlessly varying, and characteristically human pleasures, a virtue that, however, will require us to draw subtler and more difficult distinctions. The person of true moderation will take the right attitude toward all human pleasures, desiring those that are conducive to health and fitness in a measured way and enjoying others only insofar as they neither impede the healthy ones, oppose what is noble, nor outstrip one's resources. Such a person will rate each of them at its true worth, as correct reason commands (1119a20), and will be passionately attached to none of them.

This is all most sensible in outline, but has Aristotle really given us a reasoned basis for judging what different pleasures are worth? The noble gentleman's moderation seems characterized more by a general sense of balance and freedom from any intense yearnings than by precision about what things matter and why. His is not the single-minded spirit of Menelaus and Achilles, whose thirst for vengeance makes the one unmindful of safety and the other indifferent to sex in the two passages Aristotle quotes from Homer in 3.10 and 3.11 (*Iliad* 3.24, 24.129). Still less is it that of the needy, resourceful Socrates, who attributes his own freedom from enslavement to his stomach and sleep and lust to the fact that he has other pursuits that absorb his whole attention, and who tells his friends it is better to decline an inheritance than risk becoming possessed by one's own possessions (Xenophon *Memorabilia* 1.6.8 and 1.5.6). Aristotle, by contrast, reproduces the gentleman's imprecision in not quite letting himself be pinned down on the question of whether it is permissible for the moderate person to be so devoted to any particular pleasure that he can be called a lover of this or that thing (a common expression in Greek, as in the term *philosophia*), for Aristotle seems both to distinguish such lovers from the truly immoderate and to count loving something to an unusual degree among the three ways an immoderate person does in fact go wrong (1118b22–27). Is it not part of gentlemanliness to give great attention to cultivated pleasures and at the same time to take them all lightly, to wish to be dependent on no one and nothing, and to consider a single-minded pursuit of anything beneath his dignity? And might not a certain imprecision about how much each source of pleasure or happiness is worth in fact be necessary to him? For neither a life ordered by urgent necessities—even the necessity of learning what one needs to know and does not know—nor a life conducted according to careful calculation displays the sublime freedom that seems especially noble to such a person. Thus, although Aristotle will end the discussion of moderation with an affirmation that "the desiring part of the moderate person ought to be in harmony with reason, for the target of both is the noble" (1119b15–16), the precise character of the noble that is the goal seems again to take its meaning from what one opposes or rises above; its positive content remains elusive.

In the final chapter on moderation, 3.12, Aristotle takes up the connection between moderation and licentiousness and the voluntary and involuntary. If we are responsible for our vices, then they or at least the actions that form them must be voluntary. In discussing courage and cowardice Aristotle did not raise the question of whether acts of cowardice are truly voluntary, but now he concedes that their voluntariness is at least significantly curtailed by the fact that they are driven by pain, for "pain unhinges a person and destroys the nature of him who undergoes it, whereas pleasure does no such thing." Thus acts of cowardice "seem to be compelled [*biaia*]" (1119a23–24, 1119a30–31). But, he adds, "it might seem that cowardice is not voluntary in the same way the particular instances of it are. For it itself is without pain" (1119a27–29). Thus Aristotle saves the appearances regarding moral responsibility in cowardice by suggesting that the quality is voluntary, even if particular expressions of it are not. But he does not quite say that cowardice is voluntary, and he hedges what he does say here with an "it seems." The reason for this hedging soon appears when he questions the voluntariness of licentiousness: "for no one desires to be licentious" (1119a33). Surely no more does anyone desire to be cowardly. Is each individual act of licentiousness, at least, then fully voluntary? To the extent that such an act is driven by pleasure, Aristotle says "it is more voluntary and hence more subject to reproach" (1119a24–25). Yet a moment before he pointed out that the licentious are pained by being deprived of what they want (1118b27–19a5), and soon he will acknowledge that the longing for pleasure, too, is "insatiable" and when strong can overcome reason (1119b8–10). As Aristotle turns his spotlight on each vice, he gives the impression that either it or the acts that engender it are fully voluntary, but in every case we find statements elsewhere that call this suggestion into question. Might every vice in fact develop and operate in a way that is at the deepest level involuntary?

Aristotle closes his discussion of moderation with the comparison we have noted between the naturally licentious tendencies of desires and of a child, with the conclusion that both need to be chastised and subjected to the rule of reason, exercised by the higher part of the soul or by a child's tutor, and taking the noble as its target. Affirming the character of virtue as a subjection of what is low to what is high, this image raises the question of whether the parts and concerns of the soul can ever be a single harmonious whole. So long as it is reason's task to master passion with a view to this elusive thing, the noble, such a division seems inevitable. If, on the other hand, reason's true task is to come to understand all one's own concerns and their power to create happiness and to order one's life accordingly, harmony would seem more possible, but then the virtue of moderation would again come close to its Socratic meaning as a form of wisdom.

LIBERALITY (4.1)

In Aristotle's treatment of the other moral virtues, we see similar problems, but we also begin to get a fuller picture of what the noble means in the moral life and what the tangled elements of it are that so much resist reduction to any simple formula. Third, and "next in order" (1119b22), Aristotle takes up liberality (*eleutheria*), another virtue that governs our disposition respecting the most basic human passions and needs, here the concern for money and all that money can buy. Liberality is the virtue of a free human being, one who gives freely and is free of excessive concern for material things. So far is liberality from the spirit of petty calculation that the words for calculation and reason are almost entirely absent from the chapter.[30] Because generous giving is more noble, more rare, more praised, and more loved than the correct acquisition of wealth and the abstention from theft, Aristotle identifies not prudent household management or justice but liberality as the true excellence in the handling of material goods. Like courage, liberality is very much concerned with the noble, and just as in the case of courage, we see a cluster of different meanings that attach to the nobility of liberality, pulling it, as it were, in different directions.

Liberality, like courage, seems impressive inasmuch as its possessor willingly gives up the things that others are most attached to—life itself in the latter; money, the means to life (1120a2–3), in the former. In contrast to his depiction of the courageous, Aristotle speaks directly of the benefits that the liberal confer on others: "Of all those who act on the basis of virtue, liberal human beings are perhaps loved most, for they are advantageous to others, and this consists in giving" (1120a21–23). But Aristotle also insists that liberality does *not* mean making painful sacrifices, for the liberal person gives freely and with pleasure. What comes to sight as especially noble about liberality is the liberal person's sublime indifference to the so-called goods of fortune that hold others in their thrall: the liberal person "does not honor money" (1120a32). Perhaps, however, this indifference is not perfect indifference, for then the readiness with which the liberal person gives would not seem impressive. Nor would such indifference be sensible, for money is good for many things and foolish to throw away. Liberality cannot be mere prodigality any more than courage can be mere recklessness. Thus the nobility of liberality must also involve meeting real needs thoughtfully, effectively, and gracefully.

Liberality is an attractive virtue, then, in the way it brings together a sense of perspective, a sublime sense of freedom, a kindly and lovable benevolence, and an intelligent exercise of judgment to deploy one's resources wisely and upon appropriate objects. But something in this cluster of meanings of the noble, as Aristotle depicts it, makes it hard to be consistently and rationally liberal. To take liberality seriously as a virtue would seem to mean taking seriously the correct and thoughtful use of something that one scorns to take seriously at all. Perfect liberality would have to combine a certain carelessness and a certain carefulness in a way that is not easy. To insist that every dollar be well spent and accounted for is the mark of a businessman or a bourgeois, and liberality is a quintessentially aristocratic virtue. Only by spending freely does one show that one is above pettiness, above greed, above seriousness about mere material things. Here we see the aspect of nobility that is most immediately impressive, even if negative in orientation: it is beneath the noble person's dignity to cling to mere life at all costs, to be the slave to his stomach, or to be attached to possessions. To be noble is to be free of all such reins and spurs as can control lesser human beings. Is such freedom really possible, or are those who profess it in some degree always self-deceiving? And to the extent that it is possible, how is it?

Aristotle never raised either question in his discussion of courage, but he does give the beginnings of an answer to them here. In fact, liberal people tend strongly toward prodigality: "Excess in giving very much belongs to the liberal person, so that there is little left for himself, for it is typical of a liberal person not to look out for himself," and "he is inclined neither to take nor to safeguard money; rather; he is inclined even to throw it away" (1120b4–6, 1120b15–16).[31] Prodigality deviates from liberality in a way never quite precisely specified. The prodigal person "has the traits of the liberal person: he both gives and does not take, but in neither case as he should, or well" (1121a22–23). He is curable, and "his character does not seem to be base, since to exceed in giving and in not taking is the mark of neither a wicked nor a lowborn person, but of a foolish one" (1121a25–28). For as Aristotle said at the outset, to be prodigal is to destroy one's own resources or substance (*ousia*, 20a1). Is Aristotle gently suggesting that the liberal person is one who does not know the value of a dollar? The chapter at any rate contains no clear statement on what money is really for, in the liberal person's view, except to give away. And perhaps Aristotle is suggesting something more—that the liberal person knows in a way that money is important to his life, but believes that it will always be there for him. If so, he fails to know himself and his own vulnerability to fortune. This problem comes out in Aristotle's observation that those who inherit money are more liberal than those who earn it, not only because the moneymaker loves his earnings as his own but because those who have inherited money "are without experience of need" (1120b12–13). Time often corrects (or overcorrects) this error, for "age and every infirmity seem to make people stingy" (1121b13–14). While life is in full flood, these people's good fortune allows them to believe that it is beneath their dignity to concern themselves with what they in fact count on never being without. Unlike the soldier on the battlefield, then, the liberal person rarely confronts squarely the full dimensions of the risks he is running, and to this extent he may be even less clear-sighted.

But second, insofar as noble-minded people really can rise above the universal human concern with the goods of fortune—and to some considerable extent they clearly do—how do they do so? Is it through having some higher activities, loves, or pleasures so splendid as to be able to cast these basic natural concerns into the shade? To this question the spirit of nobility resists giving an answer. Nobility is not a carefully considered "this for the sake of that" or "not too much of this so as to leave room for more of that." Nobility wants to be freer than such calculations imply; noble action wants to be an end and indeed the highest end in itself.

Hence, as Aristotle insists repeatedly in this chapter, liberality means being generous simply for the sake of the noble. It is this focus on his own virtuous activity that gives the liberal person such a spirit of proud independence, just as it seems to be the brave man's own courage that is the grounds of his confidence. Neither another activity for which he wants to free his energies nor his usefulness to beneficiaries can be his highest purpose, if virtue is to be an end in itself. This seems to be the reason why, as often as Aristotle insists that the liberal person must give "for the sake of the noble and correctly," that is, "to whom he ought and as much as and when he ought, and anything else that accompanies correct giving" (1120a24–26), he offers no specific guidelines for doing so beyond a suggestion at 1121b5–7 that the recipient must be decent and deserving. But can liberality be an end in itself? Can giving well and properly even make sense without careful thought about the effect one wishes to achieve, whether it is worth the time and expense, and how it is to be done most effectively? Do we have here again a case of human spiritedness trying to make its own act of self-assertion an end in itself in a way that ultimately is not altogether rational?

What can be perfectly rational and admirable, albeit on a lower plane than the sublime contempt for money that the born aristocrat shows, is the excellence of spending useful resources wisely and effectively, with full attention to the result one seeks to bring about. It is always a fine thing to do one's job well, even if one's job is growing turnips, and it is certainly a fine thing to run a hospital or a charitable foundation well, especially if one needs a job. More impressive still is the wise assessment of what needs are most worth meeting and the use of one's intellect to solve important and thorny problems. Here the virtue of liberality arguably comes closest to being just the virtue of wisdom. For wisdom would include the wisest possible use of all the resources at one's disposal, rating each of them at its true worth, and doing intelligently what reason judges to be most worth doing.

Nonetheless—and here the aristocratic spirit boldly presses an important question that our democratic sensibilities shrink from—why should philanthropic activity be the chief focus of the very best life, the life most to be wished for, the life least constrained by unfortunate necessities and most devoted to activities good in themselves? How does the life of the serious, careful benefactor avoid putting what is high, virtue and intelligence, in the service of what is lower, the needs of the body, or at best putting the capacities of a great intellect in the service of educating ordinary intellects? Again, there is something both satisfying and admirable about using intelligence well for any honest purpose. But perhaps to find a generous activity that is noble in the fullest sense of the word, we must turn to the activities of the higher virtues that Aristotle takes up next and, as it were, in response to the limitations of liberality that he has allowed us to glimpse.

MAGNIFICENCE (4.2)

In the following chapter, on the virtue of magnificence, Aristotle's references to the noble reach their crescendo. Magnificence, or liberality on a grand scale, is a quintessentially aristocratic, proud, republican virtue, equally far from the spirit of the Bible and the spirit of modern liberal democracy. While liberality is possible for a person of moderate means under any regime, magnificence is not, for it involves large and tasteful expenditures on such projects as building and adorning temples, equipping warships, and outfitting and sponsoring tragic choruses. It is thus a virtue that flowers fully only in communities that are small and self-governing as well as aristocratic and highly cultivated—perhaps, then, only in a few times and places.[32] This virtue surpasses liberality in quality as well as quantity, for it flowers not in meeting basic needs or conferring mere pleasures but in promoting and giving grace to the highest of human activities, the political and religious life of the community and the arts. Moreover, while it is possible to be generous without good taste, magnificence requires knowledge of what is graceful, harmonious, and a suitable adornment for one's intended object. "The magnificent person resembles a knower, since he is able to contemplate what is fitting and to spend great amounts in a harmonious way" (1122a34–35). Knowledge now reenters the discussion with a suggestion that the activity of magnificence has a share in or at least a similarity to the contemplative life. In the exercise of good judgment and taste to bring dignity and grace to the public life of one's community, do we not finally have a suitable sphere in which moral virtue may be deployed for the sake of what is noble and beautiful, through serious activity that is choiceworthy for its own sake and worthy of the best kind of leisure? Indeed, the importance of magnificence in Aristotle's catalogue of virtues is underscored by the fact that this virtue, involving as it does the honoring of the gods with festivals and temples, comes the closest of Aristotle's virtues to replacing piety, which he has omitted from the ranks of the moral virtues (cf. Plato *Protagoras*

329c ff.).[33] But unlike piety, the very Greek virtue of magnificence is in its essence not fearful obedience or even reverent devotion but contemplation and celebration of all that is best in the cosmos and in humanity itself. For, beginning with Homer, even as the Greeks honored their gods they honored themselves, in the perfected humanity that they attributed to the gods and in the noble austerity and quiet grace that they gave to their temples, statues, and dramatic festivals. Might we even say that the construction of such beautiful things is from the highest perspective just the occasion for the exercise of this graceful virtue of magnificence, which engages both mind and heart in activities that are truly choiceworthy for their own sakes?

Aristotle's account of magnificence invites all these reflections, but it also contains important countercurrents of thought. Most fundamentally, making the activities of magnificence ends in themselves threatens to untether them from the high purposes that make them serious. For throughout this chapter on the virtue most concerned with the beautiful, Aristotle speaks again and again about what is appropriate or fitting (*prepon*) to its object: the word we translate as magnificence, *megaloprepeia*, means literally "that which is fitting to greatness." To be sure, the expression "fitting to greatness" is ambiguous, as it can mean fitting to the greatness of the recipient or of the giver. Thus the magnificent person will display his magnificence even in the choice of beautiful gifts for a child and in adorning his own house in a suitably impressive way. But Aristotle makes it clear that what is most splendidly beautiful is what properly honors the highest things, the fatherland and the gods, and that here and only here does magnificence come fully into its own. This is to say, however, that the activity of this especially high virtue, which is constrained by none of the urgent necessities or mundane practicalities that largely define courage, moderation, and liberality, is still not quite its own end but is aimed at finding a fitting adornment for something beyond itself and especially above itself. As soon as the activity of spending great quantities becomes one of producing a splendid spectacle for its own sake, it degenerates into ostentation and self-display, the vice of vulgarity. For tastelessness is partly just a lack of discernment about what is beautiful, but even more an excessive regard for displaying one's own possessions or resources or even one's own abilities. The opposite vice of niggardliness is in a curious way similar, an excessive concern for money instead of what is suitable for the object one is spending it on, for in the midst of spending a great deal it prompts small attempts to economize that mar a fine effect. Once again, although in a different way from its first appearance in the virtue of courage, the noble, when construed as simply for itself, fails to be either as sensible or as serious as we sense it ought to be. This may explain why, in his treatment of all the virtues subsequent to magnificence, Aristotle no longer says that the one who possesses the virtue acts "for the sake of the noble," for the noble or beautiful, when serious, turns out to be a fitting adornment or tribute to something still higher.[34]

Might the problem of empty display not be overcome, however, if the magnificent man puts his focus not on displaying his own wealth but on exercising his own intelligence—and on giving others suitable objects of reflection, both high and low? But here we are sobered by Aristotle's qualified formulation: he says not that the magnificent man is a knower but only that he "resembles a knower" (1122a34). After all, such a gentleman is neither artist nor architect nor poet but only one who knows how to use the works of others appropriately. Such a supervisory position is especially congenial to the gentleman, to whom "precise calculation is petty" (1122b8) and precise technical knowledge seems slavish. One might object that the magnificent person exercises the most important knowledge in knowing what is fitting to each object and how to achieve it, as Aristotle says. Surely there is something to this, but how well can one understand what is fitting for the city or the gods if one does not have precise knowledge of politics or the divine, or even of the human passions one evokes in orchestrating a sublime spectacle?

If Aristotle's gentlemanly description of each of the virtues points through its limitations to a more satisfactory version of the virtue that would rest on thorough knowledge such as a philosopher would have, this virtue points upward to the activity of the wise poet who pays fitting tribute to gods, heroes, and statesmen, and who understands well the different meanings of "the fitting" and how they must be balanced against one another—if indeed there have been among the poets such paragons of wisdom.

GREATNESS OF SOUL (4.3)

If the gentleman in cultivating the virtue of magnificence feels and perhaps must feel a certain ambivalence as to whether his activity is an end in itself or ministerial to something higher, the next virtue, greatness of soul, carries to its ultimate conclusion the thought that the activity of the highest virtue must be simply an end. If this is so, the peak of virtuous activity cannot consist in sacrifices one makes for the sake of something else, as the brave citizen soldier does for his fatherland, or in deeds done to honor something higher than oneself, such as the gods. And indeed, if the city is not more but rather less capable of partaking in happiness and thought than an excellent individual, if the gods that the great Greek architects and artists and their patrons celebrated were even perhaps the creation of other artists, the poets, might not the virtuous individual in fact be the very highest thing? Or if those creations provide popular images of divine beings that are in fact more distant and sublimely self-sufficient, might not the best human lives still imitate and approach theirs? This is the hope Aristotle takes up in his depiction of the man of greatness of soul, who considers himself worthy of "that which we assign to the gods," namely, honor (1123b18–20; cf. 1.12), and whom Aristotle compares to Zeus in his wish to be splendidly self-sufficient. In greatness of soul, the claim that virtue is the very highest thing and an end in itself makes a last and most interesting stand.

Even more than magnificence, greatness of soul is an aristocratic and even quasi-divine virtue.[35] It is the pride of a man so excellent and so self-assured that "nothing is great to him" (1125a3; cf. 1123b32, 1125a15). He acts rarely, disdaining petty challenges and small efforts. His is never the error of viewing what is high as a means to what is low. Politics, war, and philanthropy are alike canvases on which to deploy and display his virtues, and he accepts only the best of canvases. Greatness of soul is the "crown" of the virtues, requiring all the others as its preconditions; it is likewise the keystone of the arch of virtue, supporting and strengthening the others by instilling high expectations of oneself and a disdain for acting in a manner unworthy of one's dignity. Because of the way such pride protects virtue, Aristotle judges it better to have an excess than a deficiency of it: in a striking disagreement with both biblical and democratic morality, he calls humility or smallness of soul a worse vice than vanity. But the great-souled man is only "thought to be haughty" (1124a20; cf. 1124a29–31). His pride is in fact justified by his virtue, and his virtue is complete.

Yet this virtue of greatness of soul is in fact only one of three complete virtues, as Ronna Burger has pointed out, for Aristotle will also say that justice is complete virtue exercised toward others and that active wisdom guarantees the existence of all the other virtues.[36] If the political virtue of justice is above all the virtue of a citizen or ruler, and the intellectual virtue of active wisdom is aimed primarily at the individual's own good and especially at the acquisition of theoretical wisdom (1141b29–30, 1142a1–2, 1143b33–35, 1145a6–9), the crowning moral virtue of greatness of soul stands in a puzzling relation to both justice and active wisdom. Indeed, there has been much controversy about the meaning of greatness of soul, about the focus of the great-souled man's life and attention, and even about whether Aristotle's account of him is simply laudatory or is in fact gently ironic or quietly but deeply critical. Some commentators have portrayed the life of the great-souled man as thoroughly political, some as philosophic, and others as essentially ambiguous.[37]

To add to our puzzles, Aristotle gives an account of greatness of soul in the *Posterior Analytics* (97b14–17) that raises the question of whether it is a single phenomenon at all. Introducing greatness of soul to illustrate the inquiry needed to determine whether two groups of objects or individuals belong in a single class or merely share a name, he cites on one hand men like Alcibiades, Achilles, and Ajax, who he says are all intolerant of *hubris* or of dishonor, and on the other hand Socrates and Lysander, who he says are alike in being unaffected by good and bad fortune. If indifference to fortune and intolerance of dishonor are expressions of one common element, Aristotle continues, this common element would give us the single definition of greatness of soul; if not, there are two forms of it. But he does not identify a common element, and we may well question whether there is one, especially since receiving or failing to receive the honor one deserves would itself seem to be a matter of fortune. In *Nicomachean Ethics* 4.3 Aristotle describes the great-souled man in a way that resembles both of these descriptions but is not simply either. Here the great-souled man comes to sight as one who claims to deserve great honors and does deserve them but is not fiercely intolerant of dishonor, and likewise one who is moderate with respect to fortune but not simply indifferent to it. What seems to connect his attitude toward honor and toward fortune is a sublime sense of self-respect and self-command. The great-souled man deserves honor but would evidently consider it beneath his dignity to fly into a towering rage as do Achilles, Ajax, and Alcibiades when dishonored; he knows he deserves good fortune and with Aristotelian realism knows that virtuous activity at its peak requires equipment, but he also knows he can make the best of whatever fortune brings. In this portrayal we see Aristotle bringing to a culmination his subsumption of civic and philosophic virtue into a new synthesis, a moral virtue that involves a most impressive independence and strength. Yet the source of the great-souled man's independence is still not perfectly clear, and several striking features of the discussion suggest possibly important limitations even to this peak of moral virtue.

First, Aristotle is almost silent on knowledge and reason in describing greatness of soul. The great-souled man is not—for virtue is not—foolish or mindless (1123b2–4), but is he wise? He is inclined to be truthful, for he despises deviousness, but he is not quite a lover of wisdom; indeed, he shows no wonder, the starting point for philosophy, for his mind is not inclined to focus on what he does not understand (1124b26–25a2; cf. *Metaphysics* 982b12–13). Ashamed to receive benefits from others, he remembers only the benefits he bestows, not those he has received.[38] Nor, in competing for the coveted position of benefactor, does he think through the problem that he is relegating even his friends to a less desirable status. Perhaps for these reasons, while Aristotle attributes lack of self-knowledge to the two vices that correspond to greatness of soul, smallness of soul and vanity, he never actually says that the great-souled man possesses self-knowledge or active or theoretical wisdom.

Second, the great-souled man turns out to have a curiously tangled view of honor. Aristotle begins to reveal this with his innocuous-sounding statement that "it makes no difference whether we consider the disposition or the person who has it" (1123a35–b1). Whenever Aristotle says that something makes no difference, he seems in fact to mean that it makes almost no difference—unless we want to understand the matter at hand in the most precise and deepest way. Since greatness of soul entails judging oneself worthy of the greatest things and truly being worthy of them, and the greatest of external goods is arguably honor (1123b20–21; but cf. 1169b8–10), it makes sense that the virtue is particularly concerned with honor and indeed consists in a correct attitude toward it. But is the great-souled man himself particularly concerned with honor? It seems that he is and he is not. He regards honor as his rightful desert; he chooses his actions with a view to what is most honorable; he considers honor as the rightful prize of virtue (1123b18–20, 1123b35; but cf. 1095b22–30, 1099b11–18, 1101b10–1102a4, 1159a14–27). In all these ways he seems to take honor seriously. Yet Aristotle also says that "toward honor he is not disposed as if it is anything great" (1124a16–17). The great-souled man actually despises small honors and the honors of the many and is only moderately pleased by those of worthy judges. But is this because he is so self-sufficient that small honors are for him truly insignificant and the favor of the people worth nothing? We learn in the next chapter that it is a virtue to rate all honors neither more nor less than they are worth; the man of greatness of soul is perhaps not quite rational in his scorn for some of them. Might this scorn betray a sense that honors from inferiors inevitably fall short of what he deserves and even needs? To be sure, Aristotle agrees with him that "there could be no honor worthy of complete virtue" (1124a7–8). Now this statement could be taken, and it seems would most properly be taken, to mean simply that fitting honor, as a full recognition and acknowledgment of merit, is possible only from an equal or superior. Thus a mathematical genius who far outstripped all other humans could never be properly appreciated by them, and neither could a divine being, yet both might be entirely happy in their own activity and untroubled by that gulf. But it could also be taken to mean that perfect virtue requires honor as its just reward and yet that, tragically, no honor can ever pay the debt that the most virtuous are owed. Considering these two possibilities, we sense that the great-souled man as Aristotle portrays him is fundamentally ambivalent on just this point: he thinks honor is nothing great at all, merely a confirmation of a worth he already is fully confident of; yet he is also inclined to view his claim to honor as a serious claim of justice and even to view honor as the prize of virtue (1123b19–20, 1123b35), a prize that ought perfectly to crown his happiness and yet that somehow never can. And considering this, we are sobered by the fact that Aristotle never actually calls the great-souled man happy.

Third, the great-souled man "does not pursue things that are generally honored, or in which others hold first place"; he tends to be "idle and a procrastinator" (1124b23–24), since sufficiently grand and honorable opportunities for action do not often come along. But this idleness must put a serious limitation to his happiness, if as Aristotle has said happiness consists in activity. If the best activities are ends in themselves, why would the best man not find them easily and embrace them simply for their capacity to engross and satisfy him, without needing them to bring him distinction? What he gives his time to is not clear; indeed he seems altogether to be defined more by what he is not and does not do than by what he is and does. Observing the great-souled man's idleness, his detachment, his sense that "nothing is great," and his scorn for gossip, for ordinary activities, and for ordinary praise, and observing that Aristotle attributes to him complete virtue, which would seem to include theoretical virtue, Gauthier and Jolif connect these features with Plato's account of the philosopher in the *Republic* and *Theaetetus* as one who eschews petty speech, contemplates all time and all being, and considers human life nothing great. They argue that the great-souled man is not indeed philosophic (for he wonders at and hunts after nothing) but wise, and happy in his absorbing activity of contemplating what he knows.[39] Other commentators have rightly objected that if this is what Aristotle meant he ought to have said it, that all the actual actions Aristotle describes the great-souled man as undertaking belong to the active life, and that what he seems to aspire to most of all is to be a great benefactor.[40] I would add that we are seeing positive limitations to the great-souled man's understanding. Yet the resemblance between the depiction of the great-souled man of the *Ethics* and Plato's loftiest depictions of the philosophic soul is, I think, more important than most commentators have yet acknowledged.

Cleaving closer to the text, other commentators have argued that since the great-souled man wishes to do great deeds and especially to be a benefactor, his real sphere is political. They connect this discussion to Aristotle's statement at *Politics* 1325a34–37 that the most complete virtue is developed and exercised in political rule. This would imply that the great-souled man needs supreme power in order to attain supreme fulfillment—a logic that by itself, Collins suggests, implies that he should seek tyranny, although justice will prevent him from doing so.[41] But oddly, Aristotle portrays the great-souled man not as tempted to seize high office but as scorning to pursue it even lawfully, evidently because while "political power and wealth are choiceworthy on account of the honor they bring" (1124a17–18), honor is nothing great to him.

The problem of identifying a positive, absorbing focus of activity in the great-souled man's life is closely connected to a fourth and final problem in Aristotle's portrait of him in *Ethics* 4.3: the difficulty of ascertaining what the principle of action in his life is. Just as he does not order his life with a view to amassing honor, neither does he order his life with a view to justice. Of course the great-souled man scorns to do injustice, but Aristotle again expresses his reasoning negatively: "For the sake of what would he do shameful things, he to whom nothing is great?" (1123b22). What Aristotle does not say is that the great-souled man dedicates his life to making the world just, likely because dedicating his life to any cause would imply looking up to that cause as something higher than himself. Does he act, then, for the sake of the noble? In fact Aristotle scarcely mentions the *kalon* in the chapter on greatness of soul and, unlike in previous chapters, never as the virtuous person's end. His only reference to the *kalon* as an object of love or desire or choice is in the statement that the great-souled man "is such as to possess beautiful and unproductive things more than useful and productive ones, since this is more the mark of a self-sufficient person" (1125a11–12).[42] Why does Aristotle not say the great-souled man is guided by his love of the noble in everything that he does?

The progression of Aristotle's unfolding thought about the noble or beautiful in the discussion of choice and deliberation and then in the virtues running through courage, moderation, liberality, and magnificence to greatness of soul would seem to be this. To say that virtuous activities are chosen simply for their own sakes turns out to be misleading, as every choice is made with a view to some end that serves as its standard. Thus it is better to say that all activities are chosen either for their intended results or for some quality of the activity that makes its performance intrinsically satisfying. The nobility of an activity at first seemed to be such a quality, but this intuition has not withstood scrutiny. For the nobility of actions has resolved into two things: either a labor, risk, or sacrifice undertaken for some worthy end; or the grace, effectiveness, and suitableness of the action to its aim. In the discussion of courage we saw that nobility in the first sense does not ultimately make sense as an end in itself; in the chapter on magnificence we saw that in the second sense it does not either, since to be the source of seriously and movingly beautiful things is precisely to bring fitting adornment or honor to something higher than oneself. Only when grace and harmony function on a lower plane, as ornaments for ordinary life, can they be beautiful just for themselves, as harmonious lines and pure colors can be in the visual arts or in domestic architecture. It would seem to be for these qualities that the great-souled man values the beautiful and useless objects he possesses. In such beauty but evidently only here he finds a nobility that is simply an end.

Or might it be the case that even here, beauty of form points to a more serious kind of beauty that might have been, perhaps ought to be, of central concern to the great-souled man? What are especially beautiful to us are living beings, and beautiful creatures are invariably strong, healthy, thriving ones; in them beautiful form and line and movement suggest an abundance of vitality and a capacity to meet one's own needs effectively and even effortlessly. Why does the great-souled man not strive to live beautifully or nobly in this sense, enjoying and displaying his self-sufficient capacity to meet his own needs harmoniously and with intelligence? In a sense he does. But perhaps he is, paradoxically, too noble-minded to think of himself chiefly in this spirit. His focus is on moral virtue and on what it makes him worthy of. Although he yearns to be self-sufficient, he yearns also to do great deeds, such as saving his city. To be sure, he cannot do so in the spirit of a public servant, who makes it the focus of his life to serve his city as well as possible at all times: the great-souled man "is incapable of living with a view to another, except a friend, since doing so is slavish" (1124b31–25a1). He wants to be able to say, "The city needs me; I don't need it. My life is rich and full and complete already, but if the city is in serious need and only I can save it, I will interrupt my happy self-sufficient life to do so." We may ask whether it is not already a deficiency of self-sufficiency that allows his happy self-sufficiency to be intruded upon by others' problems, but in fact his life as Aristotle portrays it is less a rich succession of rewarding activities than a long wait for an occasion suitably magnificent to stir him out of his magnificent idleness. The great-souled man needs objects worthy of his dedicated efforts and sacrifices, yet if moral virtue is the highest end and the virtuous man is the highest thing in the world, a being for whom nothing is great, there can be in the realm of practical activity no such objects. This is the reason for his static, almost paralyzed, and even faintly comic appearance, evident in Aristotle's depiction of his deep voice, slow gait, and small self-deceptions. The great-souled man is ambivalent not only toward honor but toward action itself. He is all dressed up with nowhere to go.

In his leisured, independent, and contemplative spirit the great-souled man points beyond himself toward the philosophic life that he does not in fact share in, and even more toward the divine life as Aristotle depicts it, a life not of wondering and seeking but of perfect wisdom contemplating itself.[43] This highest life needs nothing beyond itself and desires nothing that it is not or has not yet been able to do, for all such desires imply a condition of something less than perfection.[44] All of these considerations help us understand Aristotle's claim in book 1 that we honor but do not praise the gods, since praise implies measuring up to a standard or serving a purpose beyond oneself, and likewise his statement in book 10 that it would be ridiculous to think of the gods as performing acts of moral virtue. The moral virtues are all grounded in our natures as vulnerable, social beings; they involve meeting well, individually and collectively, needs that perfect beings would not have. Now of course human beings do praise gods for their virtues; they pray to them and consider them their benefactors. It is this popular model of the divine and not Aristotle's that in fact captivates the great-souled man and inspires his desire to be a benefactor, even while he is sublimely self-sufficient. But the great-souled man finds himself impaled on the inner contradiction of this vision, a contradiction that the church has always acknowledged in speaking of the impenetrable mystery of divine charity. Aristotle might well ask, however, whether this is not to impute to the divine being a contradiction that resides only in ourselves. In the quiet realism of the philosopher who is as self-sufficient as is humanly possible yet realistic about his own limitations, by contrast, we find the form of greatness of soul that is, humanly speaking, most rationally consistent.

THE SOCIAL VIRTUES (4.4–9)

Aristotle's catalogue of virtues began with the cardinal virtues of courage and moderation and ends with those of justice and wisdom; in between he has ascended to the less celebrated but in fact preeminent virtue greatness of soul, in which the logic of choosing what is noble for its own sake is carried to its ultimate if problematic conclusion. After greatness of soul comes what appears to be a descent to five virtues that govern the everyday social intercourse of human beings, and indeed only of more ordinary human beings, including as they do the correct ambition according to which "we" neither overvalue small and moderate honors nor despise them as the great-souled man does, and the friendliness or affability such a man can scarcely be imagined to show. But what is a descent from the perspective of nobility may be a certain further ascent in sobriety if not in rationality altogether, for if the wisest souls are unlikely to devote themselves to battlefield heroism or to getting or spending money, they may certainly show such virtues as gentleness and wit. Yet Aristotle still says little explicitly about reason in his treatment of the social virtues. As we try to ferret out the standard to which reason must look in governing these virtues, the cause of this reticence becomes clear: the goal of virtue is again becoming more complex. Leaving behind his formulas that the virtuous person does what he does for itself or for the sake of the noble, Aristotle now appeals to multiple standards. He brings in the good and the pleasant, and likewise what is good for oneself, one's family and friends, and the political community. He complicates matters also by citing Socrates explicitly and Aristophanes implicitly as examples of deviations from the mean—or perhaps better, as alternative claimants to the true mean—leaving it to us to ponder how all these different standards should be balanced or ranked.

In his treatment of correct ambition or the love of honor (*philotimia*) in 4.4, Aristotle says one should seek honor to the right degree and from the right sources and in the right way, but he says nothing now about either the right end or the standard by which to find the mean. Indeed, he is silent on reason altogether and seems to confine himself to the plane of opinion, focusing on a curious ambivalence that "we" feel toward ambition. For, he says, we alternate between blaming ambition as something almost sordid—an excessive, ungentlemanly thirst for praise or for power—and praising it as a sign of spirit and of love of the noble. Ambition seems good especially in the young, as a spur to attempt great and difficult things. Is there, then, a right degree of ambition that values honors precisely at their true worth and pursues them just so far as is reasonable? Or in order to act well, especially but not only in youth, do individuals need and do their communities need them to need an unreasonable infatuation with little gold stars? If so, people's unstable opinions about ambition and Aristotle's unwillingness to jettison either side of these opinions reveal that we have here a virtue with two ultimately conflicting but indispensable standards: what is good for a wise person who sees correctly the truth of things, and what is needed by the political community.

The next virtue, gentleness, involves the right disposition toward anger (4.5). Since anger arises especially from slights to oneself or one's own, this is in a sense the last and perhaps most rational of a series of three virtues that govern the concern for honor that Aristotle has taken up in 4.3, 4.4, and 4.5. At the same time, inasmuch as the social virtues of ambition and gentleness both concern *thumos* and manliness or the lack of it (1125b11–12, 1126a19–21, 1126b1–2), they are perhaps also supplementary or even higher alternatives to the first virtue that governed *thumos*, courage. Might gentleness in fact be the highest and most truly rational virtue governing *thumos*?

Be this as it may, Aristotle brings out the way gentleness, like ambition, is a subject of ambivalent and shifting judgments about where the virtue lies and where its excess and deficiency. Here, however, he more openly expresses his own judgment that the true virtue lies far on the side of what is normally considered an unmanly deficiency. As with ambition he speaks of the right amount, objects, and manner of anger, adding the right time and maintaining his silence on the right end, but unlike with ambition, he speaks directly here of correct reason: "The gentle person wants to be undisturbed and not led by passions but as reason may command, and so to be harsh at such things and for as long as it does. But he seems more to err in the direction of the deficiency. For gentleness is not vengeful but rather sympathetic or forgiving [*suggnōmonikos*]" (1125b33–26a3). Does the gentle person then actually err or only seem to? How much harshness or vengeance does reason call for, if any, given that Aristotle has said that ignorance of what is best is a cause or the cause of the wickedness that provokes anger (1110b28–32)? This Aristotle does not spell out. Instead he shows why people tend to admire those near the other end of the spectrum: the gentle seem too neglectful of their own dignity, and a fighting spirit seems indispensable for ruling. Again we are prompted to wonder whether, in the dictates of strict reason on one hand and in the requisites of common life on the other, we do not have a dual standard for gentleness that underlies our ambivalence, and whether successful leadership might require an eagerness to punish unhealthy malefactors that is less than rational, or at the least a readiness to indulge such a spirit in others.

The next virtue, amicability or *philia* (4.6), likewise looks to more than one standard—this time the noble, the advantageous, and the pleasant. But amicability is especially concerned with pleasure, a fact that links it to moderation, although in this case the focus is not on bodily pleasures but on the high pleasures of conversation (*logos*) and of social intercourse in general. As with moderation, so in the case of amicability, the proper giving and taking of pleasure is limited by what is noble and what is beneficial. But now, unlike in his discussion of moderation or of any other virtue, Aristotle says that the exercise of this virtue involves pursuing not the noble but pleasure "for its own sake" (1127a2–3), so long as the pleasure is not outweighed by something ignoble or harmful. Thus the noble and the advantageous do not completely trump pleasure but are only considerations to be weighed against it: the amicable person will be gracious in letting his guests smoke and will overlook small acts of pettiness rather than giving offense by censuring them. To be sure, the virtue of *philia* is a minor social grace, not as important for happiness as the true friendship Aristotle discusses in books 8–9. The great-souled man would in fact seem to lack it, since Aristotle says he does not accommodate himself to another except to a true friend (1124b31–25a1). But is this altogether a point in the great-souled man's favor, or does he take himself a little too seriously? By elevating pleasure after ceasing to identify virtue with choosing the noble for its own sake, Aristotle does not clarify the standard reason looks to in governing moral virtue, but he leaves us with much food for thought.

The next virtue, truthfulness (4.7), likewise seems to be the perfection of a higher aspect of the soul than any that came into play in the first series of virtues that pertained especially to bodily and external goods. But with truthfulness it becomes especially clear that Aristotle is presenting the social virtues primarily as they appear in and to the gentleman, whose chief concern in matters of truth is honesty and not the search for wisdom. To that extent truthfulness and the following virtue of wit are both extensions of the virtue of social grace or *philia*, governing the ways people represent themselves to one another in the ordinary give-and-take of "speeches [*logois*] and actions" (1127a20). And in each case we find quietly implied a dual standard, this time expressed not in terms of different principles of action but in terms of different individuals who embody rival models of excellence. Our example of truthfulness is the unnamed perfect gentleman, whose habit it is to speak the truth even or especially when no gain or loss is at stake, simply because this is the sort of person he is (1127a33–b3). He is in a sense a lover of truth, at least of the truth he already knows, and he is certainly a hater of deceit, judging it shameful (1127b5–6). This is as far as Aristotle goes now in specifying the truthful person's motives, but we are reminded of his earlier remark that the great-souled man "is open in both hate and love, since concealment is the mark of a fearful person, as is caring less for the truth than for people's opinion" (1124b26–27). Perhaps, then, it is the noble air of fearlessness and independence that draws the gentleman to love truthfulness. But, as if to remind us that something more is at stake in this virtue, Aristotle mentions among his examples of the corresponding vice of boastfulness those who make false claims to prophecy and wisdom (which false claims he curiously says most people make), and as an example of the opposite vice of irony, Socrates. From the perspective of the ordinary gentleman, Socrates lacks manly frankness, but from the perspective of Socrates the unphilosophic gentleman is a boaster who imagines himself both wiser and more invulnerable than he is and who fails to grasp how explosive the truth can be. The gentleman's graceful frankness resembles something in the soul of the true lover of reason without altogether sharing in it.

Fifth and last of the social virtues (4.8) is wit (*eutrapelia*), a proper mean between buffoonery and dourness. It is closely related to amicability in its focus on pleasure and to truthfulness in governing the proper conduct of conversation, and it shares with all the virtues a spirit of "rising above" or of holding lightly what others are too attached to, but now turned in new directions. At first sight it would seem to be the least serious of all, belonging as Aristotle says to moments of relaxation. Again we observe the curious hybrid character of the social virtues as Aristotle presents them: they extend beyond the plane of strict morality to touch what are potentially very high matters, yet they seem to come within the sphere of moral virtue only by being viewed through the eyes of the gentleman as minor social graces, and this is most obviously true in the case of wit. No morally serious person could regard his capacity to contrive good jokes as an important quality, but the capacity for cultivated playfulness at appropriate moments is a grace that seems to put the finishing touch upon the perfect gentleman, rendering him more charming while no less impressive. Somehow this seems exactly right, and we are grateful to Aristotle for refusing to let his gentleman be a ponderous bore. The playfulness Aristotle praises here involves quick wit, tact, and a sense of propriety that Aristotle says makes the refined and liberal person "like a law unto himself" (1128a32).

If all of this is impressive, we must still wonder what the real meaning is of this quality that, as Aristotle brings out, has at its core a flexibility, a tendency toward insolence or slander, and a refusal to be quite serious about serious things. Does it really make sense that an intermediate if still small amount of insolence and ridicule is better than much or none at all—even if it is hidden in innuendo? If so, what deeper insight does this intuition point toward? In this perplexity we are at first only more puzzled by Aristotle's examples, for he suggests that the new comedy of such poets as Menander better illustrates the proper mean than the more scurrilous and obscene old comedy, whose greatest exponent was of course Aristophanes. Menander may have been less shocking, but he was also less funny and less thoughtful, whereas in Aristophanes we have a poet of the first rank who launched a radical challenge to many aspects of conventional morality and piety. It is characteristic of the *kalos kagathos* in his sublime spirit of balance to want to cultivate an appreciation for everything good, including comedy, while pursuing nothing with abandon. But will he laugh only at the foibles and pretenses of boasters, or will he go further and share just a bit in Aristophanes' recognition that there is something absurd about gentlemanliness itself? And how far will this recognition carry him if he takes it seriously? Does it make sense to stop short of plumbing the question to its very depths?[45]

Aristotle ends book 4 with a disposition that is sometimes regarded as a virtue but that he denies properly is: *aidōs*. This word can be translated as shame, and Aristotle here treats it chiefly as such, but it can also mean reverence or awe, especially toward the divine. Again we are reminded of

Aristotle's silent demotion of piety from the ranks of the virtues, and all the more so when we recall that in book 2 Aristotle followed his overview of shame with one of *nemesis* or righteous indignation. There he suggested that even if neither *aidōs* nor *nemesis* was quite a virtue because both are passions and do not sufficiently involve choice, still there is a proper mean to be attained respecting each one. Here in book 4, however, he insists that there is no proper degree to which a decent, mature person should feel shame, since he should have no defects to feel ashamed about.[46] The denial that shame need play any part in the life of complete virtue is important for our question on the place of reason in the moral virtues, for shame is required as a motive only to the extent that one's own autonomous understanding of and love of what is good is defective or still incomplete. Thus shame befits the young but not the mature, and shame and honor are the twin motives to political courage but allegedly not to true courage. Even while Aristotle concedes that shamelessness (or being unafraid to say or do what truly is shameful) is bad, then, he holds up a certain sublime freedom from shame as best. But who exemplifies this perfection? Even the man of greatness of soul does not quite attain it: he is ashamed to receive a benefaction (1124b9–10). His shame is occasioned not by vice but only by his human limitations. But it is still a defect, inasmuch as his displeasure at being reminded of favors others have done him makes it hard for him to show gratitude and implies an inability to face the full truth about what he needs and where he stands. Might we get more guidance, then, from the alternative models Aristotle has introduced into the discussion of the social virtues? Aristophanes was more frankly accepting of human limitations in himself and others—and also a prime example of shamelessness, at least in speech. But does Socrates, in the gentleman's eyes, fare much better? Considering especially the portrait Socrates paints of eros in Plato's *Symposium* (203b ff.), as the child of resource and poverty, barefoot and threadbare, dogged and shameless, and altogether reminiscent of Socrates himself, we must wonder whether a certain shamelessness, conventionally understood, might not be a necessary accompaniment to the most clear-eyed rationality of the wisest human beings. Especially with Aristotle's help, this model is somehow glimpsed and admired by the *kalos kagathos*, but only dimly through a distorting haze.

In contrast to shame, to which Aristotle concedes a limited place in the moral life, he now entirely drops righteous indignation or *nemesis* from his discussion of the virtues. In 2.7 he called righteous indignation a mean between envy and spite. The righteously indignant man is appropriately pained, it seems, by undeserved success; the envious man is pained too much, being vexed at everyone's success; and the spiteful one feels too much pleasure when he should not, enjoying the suffering even of those who do not deserve it. The person whose indignation is righteous will show only a moderate amount of envy and a moderate amount of spite, but is any amount of either in fact good or rational? The righteously indignant person is angry that anyone should do well or succeed who is not virtuous, but Aristotle began the *Ethics* by denying that in the most important respect anyone ever does, and in his important discussion of choice in book 3 he has shown the unenviable ignorance or confusion that always accompanies wickedness. His very qualified praise of *aidōs* and his omission of both righteous indignation and piety from his full discussion of the virtues continue to signal his departure from ordinary moral opinion.

Chapter 4

JUSTICE AND THE RULE OF REASON

THE MEANING OF JUSTICE (5.1)

In book 5 of the *Ethics* Aristotle continues his treatment of the virtues governing our relations with others, now ascending again to the very high and comprehensive virtue of justice. If noble activity does not in the end quite make sense as being altogether for its own sake, and if the life characterized by greatness of soul seems impaired by a lack of worthy objects for the best man's energies, might justice not provide an adequate focus for a whole lifetime of serious activity and perhaps a better organizing principle for virtue altogether? Book 5 on justice is an especially rich one; we can here examine it only selectively, focusing on our questions of how reason works to guide this virtue and what end or standard it looks to in finding the right mean. Bringing these questions to the forefront, we observe that Aristotle is surprisingly silent on correct reason as a guiding principle in justice, and likewise on the aims of the just person. He does say at the outset of 5.1 that justice is a quality "from which people act justly and want just things" (1129a8–9; cf. 1134a1–2), but he does not explain the grounds for this wish. In particular, he never says that the just person does just things either for their own sakes or for the sake of the noble. Indeed, the noble is another concept that is almost entirely missing from book 5, although its two appearances are both suggestive. The first is in 5.8, where Aristotle says it is "noble" not to count acts done from anger (*thumos*) as premeditated (1135b25–26): here the noble refers not to sublime self-denial or to anything sought as an end in itself but merely to an object or thought that is admirably fitting. The second use of the term comes in 5.9, where Aristotle, discussing the problem of an individual assigning to himself too much of what is good, gives as his examples "reputation or what is simply noble" (1136b22). Here we do have an echo of Aristotle's earlier suggestion that the noble is properly loved just for itself—but now with the troubling additional thought that for those who love it, the noble itself can become an object of competition and conflict.

Not only is book 5 relatively silent on both reason and the moral purpose that serves as its standard, but it is not even clear on the passions that shape and are perfected by the virtue of justice.[1] Each of the other virtues, we have seen, is a *hexis* or characteristic disposition governing the way the individual experiences and responds to a particular passion—fear in the case of courage, desire for bodily pleasure in the case of moderation, and so on. Does the desire for justice govern and modify a new passion, or one that Aristotle has already discussed? In part it seems to be a limitation on the love of money, but Aristotle treated that passion under liberality, extending the virtue to cover not only the correct use but the correct acquisition of money. In part the desire for justice seems to be an expression of *thumos*, especially insofar as it involves a thirst for retribution. But instead of identifying righteous indignation as a foundation for justice, Aristotle in his overview of the virtues in book 2 gave that passion a separate treatment just before taking up justice, denied there that it was a virtue, and declined even to mention it when he reached the corresponding place in his full explication of the virtues in book 4. Aristotle's entire discussion of justice in book 5 in fact tends almost comically to abstract from the passions that drive claims of justice and the conflicts that they ignite.

Aristotle does indirectly shed light on the question of the passions related to justice and injustice, however, as he proceeds in 5.1 to take up a problem of ambiguity. *Dikaiosunē* and *adikia*, he explains, each have two closely related but distinct meanings, the former encompassing both the lawful and the fair, the latter the unlawful and the unfair. Modern English does not have quite the same ambiguity, although the older term "righteousness" captures the fuller sense of justice that Aristotle is concerned with here. Now of course law, through its necessary generality, can never be uniformly fair, a problem to which Aristotle will return in his treatment of equity in 5.10. But with his exploration of the two meanings of justice in 5.1 he is pursuing a deeper problem.

Focusing first on injustice, which is somehow more salient and unmistakable than justice, and on its second meaning as unfairness or grasping for more than one's share, he elaborates:

> Since the unjust person is a grasper, he will be concerned with good things, not all of them, but as many as are matters of good and bad fortune, which are always simply good, but not always for a particular person. Human beings pray for and pursue these things, but they ought not to; rather, they should pray that the simply good things might be good also for them, and should choose the ones that are good for them. (1129b1–6)

The proper passion pertaining to justice as fairness, then, is nothing less than our concern with all the good things that depend on fortune or on others, including money, possessions, freedom, security, offices, opportunities such as access to education, honor, gratitude, and many sources of pleasure. Justice as fairness governs all of the external preconditions and supports for happiness; it would seem to govern not a particular passion but the desire for happiness itself.

Justice as lawfulness turns out to be even more comprehensive.

> Since the criminal was said to be unjust and the lawful man just, it is clear that everything lawful is in a way just. The things stipulated by the art of legislation are lawful, and each of these we say is just. The laws make pronouncements about everything, aiming at the common advantage either of all or of the best or those who are sovereign on the basis of virtue or in some other such way. Thus in one way we call just the things that produce or preserve happiness and its parts for the political community. (1129b11–19)

Here mentioning happiness for the only time in book 5, Aristotle goes on to outline the ways in which law codes order each citizen to act in accordance with the dictates of each of the virtues, "the one laid down correctly doing so correctly, and the one laid down at random less well" (1129b24–25). Thus justice as lawfulness, as practiced unevenly by every actual political regime but as articulated clearly by the philosopher, aims not only at the external goods but at the complete well-being of each citizen: again, but now in a different way, the desire for happiness is the passion that it governs. This is a meaning of law that was, to be sure, more prominent in ancient than in most modern regimes, but it is common to all regimes and is visible, for example, in our own provisions for public education.

In beginning his treatment of justice by identifying this ambiguity in the meaning of justice, Aristotle brings out that justice takes two strangely different stances with respect to the desire for happiness. As fairness, justice calls on each person to refrain from taking too much of what conduces to happiness; but as law, or as the highest aim of law properly understood, justice looks to promote as much as possible the common good and thus the complete happiness of each citizen (cf. *Politics* 1282b14–18). True, in the second passage quoted above Aristotle alludes briefly and gracefully to the massive problem of the partisan character of every actual regime, the subject of so much of the *Politics*; this is a major reason for the law's invariably limited success in attaining a true common good. But here in the *Nicomachean Ethics* he is pursuing a more fundamental problem at the heart of justice itself. If it is a matter of prayer that the simply good things should be good for us, how much more is it a matter of prayer that our fair share of all the limited goods should be the amount that is best for us? Is that ever simply the case?

Yet in hoping to close the gap here—in hoping that each person's fair share might be brought into alignment, at least in most cases, with the requisites for at least minimal well-being—we still have not yet gotten to the deepest layer of the problem Aristotle is raising. This becomes clear in the last section of 5.1 in his beautiful account of why justice among the virtues is so impressive and so moving. This turns out to be for two reasons, corresponding to the two meanings of justice he has been elucidating, between which we find now not just a gap but a collision. For if justice in the most comprehensive sense is the completest fulfillment that each citizen is capable of, a key demand of justice will be that the great-souled man be allowed to exercise and hone his virtue in meeting great challenges and accomplishing great things for his fellows. Hence "in justice all virtue is united together," and "office will show the man" (1129b29–30, 1130a1–2; cf. 1094b7–10). High political office, like the Olympic Games, is the arena in which the best can exercise and display their excellence and receive fitting honor from everyone. And yet, looking at the same thought with attention to the other side of justice that Aristotle has been highlighting, office shows the man because exercising virtue toward others is so difficult and acting unjustly is so tempting. For justice considered as fairness inevitably calls upon those who could seize the greatest share of everything good to refrain, as the just man "does what is advantageous to another" (1130a4–5). Justice is so impressive because it looks like the complete excellence that is most choiceworthy of all things to have for oneself, but justice is *also* so impressive because it looks like the most difficult self-denial. Thus with rare clarity Aristotle limns the fundamental problem of justice that will render it so recalcitrant to rational analysis and to a consistent exposition as the work of correct reason.

Aristotle further underscores the tension between justice as self-fulfillment and justice as self-denial in the conclusion to the chapter. While he identifies the worst person as one who treats both others and himself badly, he says the best is one "who makes use of virtue *not* in relation to himself but in relation to another" (1130a5–8, emphasis added). The asymmetry here—silently corrected by several commentators[2]—suggests that the perfect exercise of virtue toward oneself and toward others may not be compatible. This thought, however, is again submerged in Aristotle's conclusion: justice and complete virtue are the same, although their "being," or way of being in the world, is different, justice being simply the exercise of complete virtue toward others.

COMPLETE AND PARTIAL JUSTICE (5.2)

Already at the start of the second chapter, however, Aristotle begins smoothing over the troubling rupture in our understanding of justice that he has just brought to light. He devotes this chapter to attempting to show that justice as fairness is indeed distinct from justice as lawfulness, but only as one part of a greater whole. Now it is certainly true that some laws aim narrowly at fairness while others aim at the well-being of citizens more broadly: details of the tax code and provisions for public health would be examples of each. But law as Aristotle presents it now is ordered to cultivating *every* aspect of virtue and completely subsumes partial justice as fairness: "everything unfair is unlawful" (1130b12). This is an account of law not as it actually is but as it aspires to be at its highest and most comprehensive. Yet we soon learn that Aristotle is outlining this understanding of law as complete justice and justice as complete virtue only to set it aside (1130b18–20), so as to isolate justice as fairness and to explain what fairness adds to the dispositions and habits already provided by the other virtues. This means that book 5 will in fact be not about justice as a comprehensive virtue and a rival to greatness of soul, but only about that part of it that is now coming to sight as just one more particular virtue.[3]

In fact, however, Aristotle has a strangely difficult time setting justice as complete virtue aside, and likewise distinguishing the complete and partial forms of justice and injustice he has just identified. At the beginning of 5.2, as evidence that there are kinds of injustice that are *not* a matter of grasping for more than one's share of the good or less than one's share of the bad, he gives as examples "someone who throws down his shield out of cowardice, who speaks viciously on account of his harshness, or who does not help another with money on account of his stinginess" (1130a18–19). Then he contrasts two cases of adultery, one done for money and the other done out of desire and involving some financial cost, calling the second a case of immoderation and the first a case of injustice without immoderation. This is not unreasonable, although we recall that in 4.1 Aristotle also described the acquisition of money from shameful sources as an aspect of illiberality. Next Aristotle cites adultery, desertion in battle, and assault as acts of comprehensive injustice that are due to the vices of licentiousness, cowardice, and anger, contrasting them with the acts of partial injustice that are due to the desire for gain—although again declining to mention the illiberality to which he earlier assigned improper gain (1130a28–32). Then he dramatically broadens partial injustice by pointing out that "gain" need not be monetary but can be anything the grasper takes too much of, so that the partial form of injustice "pertains to honor, money, or preservation—or to some one thing if we were able to encompass all these by a single name" (1130b1–4; cf. 1129b2–5). Finally, after distinguishing fairness in public distributions from fairness in private transactions, he includes among examples of unfair private transactions adultery, assault, slander, and outrage (1131a5–9)—just such things as he before counted *not* as examples of partial injustice as unfairness but as examples of other vices, falling under complete injustice as lawlessness. All the examples of other particular virtues allegedly not attributable to unfairness reappear as examples of unfairness; unfairness itself expands from an improper stance regarding material goods to an improper stance regarding everything good. What is going on?

Aristotle is in fact giving us not two forms of justice related as part to whole, but two ways of looking at justice and at moral virtue altogether. According to the first perspective, justice is the individual's highest good, the perfection of one's soul, the full development of those qualities whose active exercise constitutes the substance of a happy life, including the courage that makes one take noble risks, the moderation that prevents overindulgence in low pleasures, the liberality that prevents greed, and the proper degree of ambition that causes one to claim only those honors one deserves. According to the second perspective, justice is a curtailment of the individual's good, a willingness to take no more than one's own fair share of safety, pleasure, wealth, honor, privilege, and opportunity, so that others might get their fair share as well. Aristotle flatters the laws of every existing community but also exhorts future lawgivers to set their sights high by identifying virtue understood in the first way with justice as lawfulness. The vast majority of individuals and every law code in fact waver between these two perspectives, but it is the latter perspective that always predominates, as Glaucon and Adeimantus so eloquently complain in the *Republic*. Laws, especially in the ancient world, do seek to promote citizens' welfare in many ways, but they give their most concerted attention, Aristotle acknowledges even as he sets justice as lawfulness aside, to ensuring basic fairness of some kind and to preventing the vices that harm others. It is not the higher aspect of justice but the higher perspective on all of justice that Aristotle will at least ostensibly set aside through most of book 5.[4]

And in restricting our attention to justice as fairness, Aristotle notes, we must also postpone the grave question of whether a good human being and a good citizen are the same, and whether the art that educates individuals to be good human beings is after all the political art or some other (1130b26–29). In the *Politics* Aristotle will argue that the good man and good citizen are the same only in the best regime, and indeed that even then, complete individual excellence is possible only for the ruler (1276b16–77b33, 1293b5 ff.). Here in the *Ethics*, however, the incompletely described comprehensive individual virtue of justice will be followed by the perhaps higher comprehensive individual virtue of active wisdom in book 6 and the clearly higher individual virtue of wisdom in book 10, casting even stronger doubt on the claim that the simply best individual and the good citizen are ever the same or are educated by the same art.

To return to justice as fairness, the morally decent gentleman as Aristotle has already depicted him will be free of the vices that spark much of the conflict between individuals. But how will he experience the additional claims that fairness seems to make upon him, especially since, as Aristotle finally observes in 5.5, justice as fairness is a mean "not in the way the other virtues are"—not, that is, as a point of perfection between two defective states of the soul—but rather as "a mean between doing injustice and being done injustice, the one entailing getting too much and the other too little" (1134b30–33)? This suggests that there are indeed demands of justice not covered by the other virtues, then, but their character will involve denying oneself what would be best for oneself. How will reason guide the just man's assessment of the proper mean in this respect, and what natural passions will support him in desiring it?[5]

PROPORTIONAL, CORRECTIVE, AND RECIPROCAL JUSTICE (5.3–5)

While book 5 is on the whole silent on correct reason as a guiding principle, as Aristotle begins his explication of justice as fairness in 5.3, the discussion takes on a curiously mathematical and hence ostensibly very precise character, turning on the idea of proportion or ratio, for which he uses the word *logos*. Indeed, chapter 5.3, on the just distribution of common funds and especially of honors and offices, seems a model of that mathematical precision that Aristotle protested in book 1 should not be expected in moral and political matters. Aristotle captures a universal moral intuition when he says that those who are more deserving should have more of what the community has to distribute in proportion to their merit—which he says is apparent to all "without argument" (1131a13–14): our sense of basic justice is in our very bones. Yet the chapter achieves its appearance of precision only at the cost of abstracting from often violent human passions, from conflicting claims about what constitutes merit, and even from the difference between living human beings and inanimate shares, as Aristotle slips into a digression on continuous proportions. He alludes only briefly to the partisan disputes that erupt over the relevant standard of merit, and thus over whether the community should distribute honors and offices on the basis of freedom, wealth, birth, or virtue—contests that will always prevent reason's dictates from being perfectly implemented. More gravely, 5.3 leaves unaddressed the question of precisely how and why just distributions ought to reward merit at all. Perhaps the worst tangle Aristotle shows on this question comes *within* most of those who recognize virtue as the true claim to honors and offices. For to agree to this is not yet to determine whether the best individuals deserve the greatest honors and other rewards as a recompense for services rendered in the past or simply as recognition for their intrinsic excellence. The great-souled man will lean to the latter view, but the city perhaps necessarily toward the former, as Aristotle suggests in the next chapter when he says that distributions should be in proportion to "contributions" (1131b29–31).[6] Indeed, political communities and statesmen are invariably of two minds even as to whether offices should be given to the best as rewards—whether for virtue or for past services—or as a service that the community requires from those most able to promote the common good, even at cost to themselves. In accord with the diverse meaning of justice as both the common good and as an individual virtue and of individual justice as both self-perfection and self-denial that Aristotle has brought to the fore in 5.1, we are forced to allow that the morally serious person invariably thinks all of the above. Reason wants to be the guide to distributive justice in applying correctly the principle of proportionality that it easily grasps in the abstract, but it cannot do so as long as these tangles lie unresolved and even unrecognized.

Chapter 5.4 on corrective justice in exchanges contains the same veneer of mathematical precision, beneath which we find a similar problem of unresolved ambivalences as to the principles to be applied, ambivalences so serious now that Aristotle must concede that what people's sense of fairness demands is really an improper application of the concepts of gain and loss.

> If one person is struck and the other strikes, or if one kills and the other dies, the suffering and the doing involved are divided into unequal segments. But the judge tries to restore equality by inflicting a loss, thereby taking away the gain. For the term *gain* is used as a way of speaking simply in such circumstances, even if in certain cases it would not be the proper name—for example, for the person who struck another—and the term *loss* is used for him who suffered. (1132a7–14)

Aristotle's mathematical language again holds out hope that the administration of justice can be made perfectly rational, even as his language of gain and loss directs attention to the crucial, seldom clearly answered question of whether the criminal really is better or worse off after a crime. From the truest and highest perspective the answer is clear: it can be no gain to maim or kill a fellow citizen in a brawl; the indulgence of base passions only makes one's soul more unhealthy; the assailant does not even come away with a material good the way a thief does; and even the common thief is not on balance better off.[7] But law, regarding citizens' relations not mainly from this perspective but from the perspective of fairness with respect to bodily and external goods, must respond as if the assailant did come out ahead. The law must satisfy the desire of victims, their families, and even law-abiding citizens at large to "get even" with the assailant, the demand that the criminal not be allowed to "get away with his crime" but suffer a punishment or loss that "fits the crime," as we say, thus "restoring equality" (1132a10, 1132a25).[8] These demands are so passionate that law and order can never be established without satisfying them, but Aristotle quietly insists that the premises about gain and loss that they rest on are not rational. "A judge wishes to be, as it were, the just ensouled," he says (1132a21–22), but every real judge finds himself forced to mediate between unhealthy offenders and angry victims and to content himself with finding a middle way between reason and unreason that will restore the peace. Aristotle does retreat into another geometrical analysis of lines that gives the impression of perfect rationality and even of precision of a kind that in book 1 he repeatedly warned us was inapplicable to ethics, but as he does so he also retreats into language about what people say and assume and assert justice to be (1132a27 ff.).

In the next chapter, 5.5, Aristotle probes more deeply into the irrational claims that the concern for justice as fairness leads people into, even or especially as they demand mathematical precision in the calibration of punishments. In 5.4 Aristotle ostensibly endorsed a purely restorative form of corrective justice, while in fact ceding considerable ground to the irrational demand that justice harm the perpetrator even when he has gained nothing tangible. Now Aristotle goes further in questioning the rationality of retribution. Simple reciprocity, he says now, in fact "fits neither with the just in the distributive sense nor with the just in the corrective sense" (1132b23–25). The claim that people should suffer what they inflicted is part of traditional piety, as Aristotle reminds us by associating this view with the Pythagoreans, who taught the immortality of the soul, and with the mythical son of Zeus and judge of the dead, Rhadamanthus, but Aristotle raises three weighty objections to it. First, it is not simply true that in corrective as opposed to distributive justice the parties should be treated as equals and consideration be given only to the harm done, as Aristotle said in 5.4—or perhaps rather, the harm that must be taken into account includes the greater harm done when the person assaulted is an officer, especially an officer of the law. Crimes against those in authority make especially clear something that is true of all crime, that it is an attack not only on its immediate victim but against the whole fabric of society.[9]

Second, Aristotle says, simple reciprocity does not properly take into account the difference between the voluntary and the involuntary. Thus he again alludes briefly to the whole thorny question of whether acts that truly harm oneself are truly to be considered voluntary, and, less radically, to the way in which crimes committed knowingly show vice in the perpetrator in a way that inadvertent acts do not, and hence ought not to receive the same punishment.

Third, Aristotle shows that to focus on simple retaliation as if it were an end in itself is to miss the deeper meaning and purpose of reciprocity, the purpose that makes not simple tit for tat but some kind of proportionality the essential thing. "By proportional reciprocity the city holds together. For people seek to return either evil—if they do not, that seems to be slavish—or good" (1132b33–33a1). Bowing to irrational demands for vengeance is not just an unfortunate necessity but in a certain way positively just—but because and only because it is essential for holding the community together. To suffer assault and to be unable to hit back, even against one whose soul is overrun with such disorderly passions as to render one incapable of real happiness, is enough to leave people feeling like slaves.[10] People's anger betrays their ambivalence about the goodness of justice. They want to look down on the lawbreaker—in the best case they want to believe as Aristotle teaches that injustice is bad for the victim but worst of all for the unjust person himself (1138a28–b5)—but they are unsure of this. In seeking punishment for the offender they are attempting to make absolutely certain that crime does not pay, and thus to shore up their own belief in justice.

By endorsing a modified version of reciprocity, then, Aristotle leaves standing something close to the ordinary view of corrective justice that he has both associated with traditional piety and shown to be irrational. But he is pointing lawgivers to the strongest reason for accepting it—the common good, beginning with the most basic requirement for peace and social cohesion—and thus providing a basis for moderating the fierceness of angry *thumos* when possible. More explicitly and more positively, Aristotle is working to encourage another aspect of reciprocity, *thumos*'s more pleasing and graceful counterpart, gratitude. In this chapter that is unusually full of references to the gods and to piety, Aristotle connects this aspect of reciprocity also to the divine, the Graces whose statues he says people have erected by the roadside to encourage gratitude and reciprocal giving. "For this belongs to gratitude: one ought to serve in return someone who has been gracious, and ought oneself in turn to take the lead in being gracious" (1133a4–5). Thus distancing himself from the viewpoint associated with Rhadamanthus while praising the Graces, Aristotle nudges traditional piety in a direction both gentler and more rational.

The remainder of 5.5, on reciprocity in economic exchanges, speaks again to the universal wish for a perfectly defined, perfectly rational standard of justice that might regulate all human transactions. Yet Aristotle's elaborate equations about fair prices and wages leave much unexplained. If workmen should each be compensated in proportion to their worth, is that worth to be measured by the time expended, the effort expended, some inherent value that may be assigned to their skill, their ability to meet a real need, or their ability to meet any market demand at all?[11] Aristotle encourages the thought that all goods have an intrinsically fair price and laborers an intrinsically fair wage that may be identified with mathematical precision, but his analysis in fact points to need or even popular demand as the standard that justice in economic matters must bow to. For again, what is just in the primary sense is the common good, the common good requires first and foremost that the community hold together, and this it will do only if people can get what they want from their voluntary exchanges and find satisfaction for their indignation when they suffer in involuntary ones.

At the end of 5.5 Aristotle sums up: it is now clear what justice and injustice are and in what sense justice is a mean—not as a point of optimal perfection between an excess and a deficiency as in the case of the other virtues, but as the midpoint between having more and having less than one's share of what is good. But in getting clarity on the troublingly different way in which this virtue is a mean, we are forced to confront again the question of why anyone would love it. We have seen why people seek vengeance when things go wrong, but what is it that disposes one to take for oneself precisely one's fair share and no more? In pointing us again to this question, Aristotle indicates that his account of justice is not complete after all. So far he has not provided the motive for wishing to conform to the demands of justice, and to do this he must consider more deeply how justice belongs to our nature as political beings.

POLITICAL JUSTICE (5.6)

Before Aristotle takes up political justice in 5.6, however, he deepens the puzzle of what it means to have a just disposition. Doing an act of injustice does not by itself reveal that one is an unjust person, he says, if one acts from passion and not by choice. Yet as important as what he says here is what he does not: he does not say that a just person chooses what is just for its own sake or for the sake of the noble. We have seen how both formulations have proven problematic and have been dropped in the discussions of earlier virtues. It is here that Aristotle points out that it is especially political justice that we are seeking. Justice may not be lovable just for itself, but perhaps it can be loved as a feature of the political community that we are naturally inclined to belong to and to care about, and in an analogous but less complete way, as a feature of smaller and closer communities such as the family.

Aristotle's precise way of framing the introduction of political justice is most ambiguous, however. What he says is—depending on how we render the repeated word *kai*—either "It must not escape our notice that what is being sought is both [*kai*] the just simply and [*kai*] the politically just" *or* "It must not escape our notice that what is being sought is also [*kai*] the just simply, namely [*kai*] the politically just" (1134a24–26).[12] Is Aristotle distinguishing justice simply from political justice or identifying them? Perhaps he is deliberately inviting the pleasing thought that there is something truly and perfectly just that transcends the political realm, even as he prepares to show why justice in the true sense is political and requires law. His statement at the beginning of the next chapter that natural justice is part of political justice will lend further support to our suspicion that Aristotle recognizes no justice higher than political justice. "But," he continues here, in a way that for now maintains the ambiguity while according better with the identification of political justice with justice simply, "this exists among those who share a life in common with a view to self-sufficiency, who are free and equal either proportionally or arithmetically. Thus for those for whom this does not exist, there is nothing politically just in relation to one another, but only something just in a certain sense and by way of a similarity. For the just exists for those for whom there is law in relation to one another" (1134a26–30). Where there is law and justice there is also injustice, which consists in giving oneself more of what is unqualifiedly good and less of what is unqualifiedly bad. "Therefore we do not allow a human being to rule, but reason, because a human being does this for himself and becomes a tyrant" (1134a35–36). In the context, the rule of reason can only mean the rule of law.[13] As he puts the same thought in a fuller formulation at the end of the chapter, political justice and injustice "accord with law and exist among those for whom law is natural, namely, those for whom there is equality in ruling and being ruled" (1134b13–15). Law is essential for justice in two ways. Most obviously, law is essential if citizens and their property are to be protected from one another and those charged with protecting them are to be kept from becoming predators. But more fundamentally, if justice in the full sense is not merely insecure but nonexistent except where citizens stand in a relation of equality to one another, that can only be because the equality fixed by law is essential to make acting fairly a common good, and hence just. For all individuals between whom there is no reliable common good to be found in restricting themselves to what is fair according to the mathematical principles Aristotle has elaborated in 5.3–5, there is no justice or injustice in the strict sense.

But are fixed laws really essential to create a common good for citizens in treating one another fairly?[14] Can a wise and virtuous ruler not accomplish the same thing as well or even better? Aristotle does go on to say that a ruler (evidently a proper ruler, as opposed to a tyrant) is guardian of the just. But no sooner does the idea of a just ruler arise than it brings with it a new tangle.

Aristotle says that if he is just, he will not assign more of what is simply good to himself, unless it is proportional to his merit. But if it is proportional to his merit, should he give himself most of all? To take the best for oneself seems to be the mark of a tyrant and proof that one is not deserving, but to labor for everyone else and to give oneself no reward for one's pains is to confirm the troubling claim that justice is the good of another: paradoxically, being just seems to require being unjust to oneself. Again we see the collision between two views of justice and good statesmanship, the view that justice means fairness and so a fair return for all individuals on their contributions and investments, and the view that just rule means service and sacrifice for others, which is what makes it noble. Aristotle's purported solution is that "Some wage must be given" to the good ruler, evidently by others, "and this is honor and privilege" (1134b6–8). But is this really a solution? The great-souled man's sense that he deserves the highest honors and yet that no honor can ever do justice to his desert betrays his sense that his great deeds are not simply fulfilling for himself but are a loss to him and a gain to others that should be but cannot be repaid; in this way his belief in his unselfishness and his claim to get his fair share are inextricably entangled in the noble soul. As Aristotle says a few lines later in a different but related statement on justice in the household, "no one in fact chooses to harm oneself" (1134b11–12). To try to devote oneself to a life of service is invariably to rack up debts in the back of one's mind, and to do this is to store up trouble for oneself and others.[15]

By contrast to the political sphere, Aristotle says that in relations within the household, justice in the unqualified sense does not exist, for one's possessions and dependent children are one's own and no one chooses to harm oneself. But if family members are the people who are most of all one's own, fellow citizens with whom one shares in living together under law and in ruling and being ruled in turn are also, if less intimately, one's own. And if in the family the love of one's own provides such a strong motive to share what one has that justice seems scarcely to apply, does love of one's own fellow citizens not also provide some motive to want to treat them fairly? Law may indeed be essential to make fair dealings a common good and hence to bring justice in the full sense into being, but affection for those who thus become one's fellow citizens, and the satisfaction of being part of a community that treats all of its members fairly, would seem to provide an important emotional foundation for the virtue of justice as fairness. Yet curiously, Aristotle does not explicitly ground this virtue in the natural passions that make us political beings. Possibly his reason is that the blind love of one's own, even when extended to a whole city or nation, can as readily encourage savagery as decency. The citizen, in his fairness as in his courage, must draw upon disparate motives to do his part, but Aristotle finds in respect for and fear of the law the most important and reliable of these motives.

NATURAL JUSTICE (5.7)

Aristotle's famous but cryptic statement on natural justice or natural right in 5.7 holds out hope that nature can always and everywhere provide clear standards for reason to look to in directing a community or a life justly. Yet to our disappointment, we find that this chapter, like most of book 5, is in fact silent on reason. Less surprising is that Aristotle never says, as his commentator Saint Thomas will, that natural justice is based on divine justice. To the contrary, Aristotle suggests that whatever it is that naturally pertains to the gods—leaving open for now whether that includes justice, which he will ultimately rule out (1178b8–12)—it bears little resemblance to the natural justice that pertains to us. Indeed, Aristotle cites provisions regarding sacrifices, in one case to a human being, among his chief examples of what is just by convention. He gives no examples of natural justice, however, from which a rational standard might be deduced. Nor, finally, does he present nature here as a universal, uniform standard that transcends the invariably narrow and partisan judgments of the political sphere: natural justice, he says explicitly at the outset, is part of political justice (1134b18–19).[16] For our highest standard of justice we can look neither to the divine nor to pure reason nor to the simply uniform laws of nature, but only to our own experience as beings for whom it is natural, as Aristotle paradoxically but helpfully put it at the end of the previous chapter, to create and live by legal conventions (1134b13–15), arbitrary and changeable as those conventions may be.

Indeed, so much of what goes by the name of justice is so clearly arbitrary, Aristotle says, that

> it seems to some people that all [just things] are this way, since what is by nature is unchanging and has the same power everywhere, just as fire burns both here and in Persia, but they see the just things changing. But this is not so, although it is in a way. Among the gods, at any rate, it is perhaps not so at all, but among us there is something that is so by nature, though it is all changeable. Nevertheless, some of it is by nature and some not by nature. (1134b24–30)

Challenging early Greek philosophy's sharp bifurcation between nature (*physis*) and convention (*nomos*), Aristotle contends that between the natural beings that are governed by uniform necessities and the human constructions that are wholly conventional is an intermediate category of natural justice that is *all* changeable. In what way is natural justice related to conventional justice? In what way is it changeable, and how does it still retain the same power everywhere?

A clue may be found if we consider Aristotle's examples of things just by convention: the amount of a ransom, the particular animals offered as sacrifices, and the sacrifices offered by the people of Amphipolis in honor of Brasidas. Each of these is arbitrary, and at least the last rests on a falsehood, but none is simply arbitrary. Together they point to the importance of such things as ransoming prisoners, supporting divine worship, and honoring benefactors, so as to promote the humanity in warfare, the civic unity, the reverence for the laws, and the desire of good men to be benefactors that a healthy polity requires. Each, we may say, rests on a universal natural need or rule of prudence that, because it is natural, is naturally costly to disregard.

While Aristotle gives no examples of natural justice, he does offer a pregnant analogy for it. Just as, among the things in the political realm that admit of being otherwise, there are some things that are by nature, "the same distinction will apply in other cases. By nature the right hand is stronger, although it is possible for all to become ambidextrous" (1134b33–35). Is natural justice a natural tendency that habit may suppress, a natural order that habit may corrupt, or instead a natural limitation that habit may overcome? Could it be in different ways all of these?

Saint Thomas in his commentary answers, in effect, that natural justice is a natural order that habit may overturn, but never completely. For he insists that there are practical principles that are naturally known and hence known everywhere, which bear witness to what is right even in a corrupt soul or city. This, however, Aristotle himself never says. According to Saint Thomas, this natural conscience gives access to universal rules of justice that underlie and provide a standard for the particular enactments of particular law codes. Thus, for example, the fact that all law codes forbid stealing reflects their common basis in natural justice, even if they enforce this prohibition with different penalties.[17] The basis for the traditional law of nations or *jus gentium* is this general recognition that there are certain principles that should always be upheld and certain lines that should never be crossed, such as targeting civilians in warfare, using torture to extract intelligence, and executing people without trial. But on this reading natural justice itself would be a fixed standard for the shifting conventions that attempt unevenly to put it into practice—and Aristotle says explicitly that what is just by nature all changes.

The Latin Averroist Marsilius of Padua gives a different account of natural justice that better fits Aristotle's description of natural justice as all changeable. Marsilius agrees with Saint Thomas that what is called natural justice consists in the principles of conduct upon which all or "almost all agree," including such things as the worship of the gods and the honoring of parents. Marsilius goes on to say that these generally recognized rules are thought to be natural by a kind of "transposition" or reasoning from the effects: because they are recognized in all lands with a uniformity that resembles the uniform way fire burns in Greece and in Persia, they are considered natural. But in fact they depend on "human enactment." Thus, as Leo Strauss puts it, Marsilius in fact judges them only "quasi-natural."[18] This account and critique of natural justice is consistent with one statement in the corresponding chapter of the *Magna Moralia*—that what is naturally just is what "prevails for the most part" (1195a3).[19] But it is not consistent with the account of natural justice in the *Nicomachean Ethics*, where Aristotle explicitly acknowledges that justice exists only where there is law (5.6), explicitly denies that justice manifests itself the same way everywhere as fire does, and nonetheless insists that natural justice exists and has the same power everywhere. Clearly Aristotle means by this power something less obvious than that all peoples recognize it equally.

However, Marsilius goes on to suggest a second and deeper objection to the idea of natural justice as a consistent and always at least dimly recognized rule of true reason underlying positive or legal right. Natural justice, he says, is according to "some" (clearly including Saint Thomas) an expression of divine justice and always follows "the counsel of correct reason." Yet to make this identification, he continues, is to confuse the quasi-naturalness of generally recognized principles with the true naturalness of correct reason. "For there are many things which accord with the dictate of correct reason but which are not granted to be honest in all nations, viz. those which are not self-evident to all and in consequence not admitted by all either."[20] Common opinion does converge more or less on certain alleged principles of justice, but these principles are deficient in the light of the correct reason that is evident only to the wise. As Strauss puts this thought: "Civil society is incompatible with any immutable rules, however basic; for in certain conditions the disregard of these rules may be needed for the preservation of society; but, for pedagogical reasons, society must present as universally valid certain rules which are generally valid. . . . The unqualified rules are not natural justice but conventional right."[21]

Could the true principles of natural justice, then, be principles of correct reason that are generally *not* recognized but nonetheless valid? Could natural justice be like a right-handedness that is in fact everywhere irrationally suppressed? This thought too is suggested by a statement in the *Magna Moralia*, although one that is in tension with the statement that what is naturally just is what "prevails for the most part" (1195a3). Immediately before taking up natural justice, in a passage parallel to *NE* 5.6, the author of the *Magna Moralia* says that political justice "consists chiefly in equality, for fellow citizens are partners in common, and want to be equals by nature, though different in character" (1194b8–11). Although the force of this last phrase is not quite clear, the thought seems to be that political communities impose a false equality on individuals who are equal neither by nature nor by character. And surely they do: democracies treat all voters as if they were equally good judges of policy and of candidates for office; oligarchies and aristocracies treat as equals or "peers" all those with wealth or superior education, although as individuals they differ greatly from one another and most are no better by nature than the general run of the excluded poor. Is true natural justice, represented by right-handedness, the rule of those who are truly best, even if it is generally opposed by law and convention? Perhaps, or perhaps in part, although Marsilius does not take this step: he evidently sees the rule of reason as leading away from politics altogether. But perhaps to call the rule of the best natural justice still does not do justice to the complexity of the way in which natural justice is changeable.

Strauss suggests that the key meaning of justice that Marsilius does not consider in his implicit denial that there are any principles of justice that are universally valid is the common good. The common good, we have seen, is the most solid standard of justice for Aristotle, but its demands are especially complex and unstable. Pursuing the common good intelligently requires that a leader take into account the low but often pressing needs of survival as well as the true happiness of each citizen; the demands for fairness, including reward for service, honor for excellence, and punishment for wrongdoing; and the need for reciprocity, gratitude, and fellow-feeling. Pursuing the common good intelligently means recognizing that these aspects of the common good are not simply aligned and cannot even be consistently ranked in importance. To say that natural justice exists though it is "all changeable" (1134b29–30) is to suggest that there is always a right thing to do, even if there is no rule that it is always right to follow. Breaking the rules is itself at times a demand of justice and even of natural justice. Aristotle's analogy of ambidexterity is well chosen to capture this thought. Most people do not cultivate ambidexterity, but some deliberately do and find it advantageous, especially in times and situations of pressing necessity such as war. They find it good to sacrifice some dexterity and precision to gain the flexibility that, for example, allows them to shoot around corners in both directions. In this way not just right-handedness but ambidexterity is natural, as an adaptability that nature itself makes possible: nature itself is changeable. Nonmetaphorically, ambidexterity then would represent the necessary and appropriate flexibility of a wise leader who willingly makes exceptions to generally sound rules and practices, as, for example, suspending civil liberties in national emergencies. Justice has the same power everywhere because both violating its normal dictates when not forced by extreme circumstances and failing to make exceptions when necessary is likely to exact a serious price.

Just as there are no absolutely valid specific rules of conduct and no always-binding principles such as those of commutative or distributive justice, so there are no rules of decision-making that a leader can use to determine when exceptions are justly made or which aspect of the common good is most important to attend to at any given point. Nonetheless, as Strauss suggests, it is possible to discern, within the different aspects of the common good that a wise leader must weigh, elements that are higher and lower: nature gives no guidance in the form of "universally valid rules of action," but it does in the form of a "hierarchy of ends" that puts the goods of the soul higher than those of the body.[22] The great honor due to wise statesmanship follows from the fact that it takes rare character and judgment to discern how best to balance the various ends that the community must attend to and how to allow the more urgent to take precedence over the more noble when necessary, without allowing the citizens to fall deaf to their higher aspirations or, as one such statesman put it, to the better angels of their natures.[23] Part of what is so impressive about this way of regarding natural justice is its eminent, quiet sobriety: Aristotle refuses to allow us to take our sights by utopian possibilities or to despise the messy necessities of real political life in light of the imagined purity of some other unattainable possibility. Natural justice is part of political justice.

However, to leave it at this would be to neglect another and even deeper layer of Aristotle's cryptic chapter on natural justice. Justice is especially changeable, he indicates, according to the regime. Thus after mentioning ambidexterity he goes on to explain that conventional justice changes as measures for grain and wine do, depending on whether those who fix them are buyers or sellers. The serious meaning here seems not to be the innocuous fact that in retail markets commodities are sold in smaller quantities than in wholesale ones,[24] but that, for example, a grain-exporting country calls a "bushel" a smaller quantity than a grain-importing one does, and in the same way different regimes tailor the laws to the interests of those in power. To say that justice is the common good is not yet to address the question of whose good it is, since every regime attends most to the common good of those who hold power, and no regime ever empowers everyone equally. To be sure, Aristotle insists that this regime-dependence is characteristic only of conventional justice: "The just things that are not natural but human are not everywhere the same, since the regimes are not either; but everywhere there is only one regime that is in accord with nature, the best regime" (1135a3–5). This statement invites the reassuring thought that in this respect nature does give a single, unchanging, perfect standard, which all actual regimes may always fall short of but which we may at least clearly fix our sights on as on a polestar and steer by. The best regime is the one that would distribute power according to true merit, and above all according to wisdom. Where a single outstandingly wise person is available, the best regime would be the rule of that person, using intelligence flexibly to meet the complex, shifting needs of the whole community and not any one part of it.[25]

If the rule of the wise is true natural justice, this itself would seem to be an unchanging standard of justice. But while Aristotle says there is only one best regime, he does not say there is only one just regime. If what is right by nature is all changeable, then what is right is not normally the best simply. In each time and place there is one regime that is the best attainable under the circumstances, the one that best fits the unique temper and habits of its people while striving as much as possible to put the "natural *aristoi*" into authority,[26] and this regime Aristotle declares to be just. It is no more just to try to impose a regime that cannot succeed than it is to enforce a law when doing so will do more harm than good. Thus if a city has a large mass of ill-educated urban poor, or a dangerous enemy that requires enlisting everyone energetically in the city's defense, it may be best and therefore most just to expand the franchise for the sake of strength, even if that means diluting the city's seriousness about virtue (*Politics* 3.11; cf. Xenophon *Education of Cyrus* books 1–2). The metaphor of ambidexterity captures nicely the trade-off involved in such a choice, the most important dilution being the dilution of the claims of wisdom by the concession to popular consent. When, as is usually the case, a regime that involves such compromises is the best available, it is just to give it our full support. Natural justice belongs to real political life with its shifting, urgent demands and its terribly imperfect participants, not to some unattainable realm of perfection above politics.

If we look more closely at Aristotle's discussion of the best regime, however, we see further and deeper reasons for his statement that natural justice is all changeable: there is something unstable or profoundly elusive about the standard of the best regime itself. We have seen that the common good turns out to be not one thing capable of precise specification even in principle, but rather a collection of things good in different ways that always involve tensions and trade-offs. In the same way and for much the same reason, the best regime turns out not to be a single, perfectly coherent, and unproblematic thing. We may set aside the complication that in the *Politics* Aristotle at different times and in different ways calls more than one regime best; aristocracy, polity, the mixed regime, and the rule of the single wisest person without law are all by turns declared to be best. For it is the last of these to which Aristotle gives a clear statement that it should trump the others when it is possible (*Politics* 1284b25–34, 1288a29). We must leave aside the objection to all actual human rulers that their wisdom is invariably limited and their characters are rarely if ever incorruptible; the premise of Aristotle's claim is that *if* there should arise a single outstandingly wise and virtuous man in a community, it is best that unfettered rule be given to him. We may even leave aside such grave practical issues as the problem of succession and of the danger of granting extensive prerogative to a wise ruler when the same prerogative may then more easily be claimed by an unworthy one. All of these considerations are only grounds for accepting a constitutional order that is arguably second best in order to prevent grave problems later; they do not refute the claim that best of all would be the direct, unfettered rule of true wisdom if it were always available.

But there are still two deeper reasons for at least doubting this. The first has to do with what the rule of a supremely wise ruler would do to his subjects—or put differently, what the rule of perfect reason that is not in our own possession would do to each of us. How could we escape becoming perpetual children in our dependency—or in our foolish rebellion? It might be objected that the best education consists in helping students think for themselves, and surely the wisest ruler would give the highest priority to educating others to serve as trustworthy subordinates and as capable replacements when he is gone. This process, however, would require that those being trained should be given a free hand to make many mistakes and to learn from their mistakes. But mistakes can be catastrophic for those who are the objects of them; would it not be better if mistakes were never made? Besides, to depict the best ruler as one who needs lieutenants and successors is to make the goodness of wisdom's rule dependent on the limitation of that wisdom, either in reach or in duration. We are now considering, however, whether precisely the unfettered rule of reason would be best of all, and at the end of that road would be the direct, all-seeing, minute-by-minute supervision of each of us by a perfect intelligence. This is at least a hard question. Certainly there are grave authorities that assure us it is only foolish pride that inclines us to doubt it. But we may at least wonder whether what is best in humanity might not depend on our having to stand on our own feet and think for ourselves. Not only modern republicanism but the ancient republicanism that Aristotle supports would seem to have as a premise the goodness of some such collective self-reliance that sharpens the virtues and the judgment through ruling and being ruled in turn. Surely it is best if we can do this with considerable help from the wisest who have come before through their books or in their laws, and likewise from those contemporaries who are further along the same path as ourselves and can offer instruction, but who, perhaps unfortunately but perhaps fortunately, have neither the time nor the inclination simply to take charge of our lives.[27] Yet it is not altogether clear from all that Aristotle says whether he thinks the collective autonomy of decent men of ordinary ability is better for them than rule by one who is truly wise.

These last thoughts bring us to the second—and admittedly more explicitly Aristotelian—reason for doubting whether the unfettered rule of a single supremely wise human being would be the unproblematically best of all possible regimes. And this is Aristotle's judgment, shared by all of the classical philosophers, that not the life of rule but the life of contemplation is the best and happiest life. If direct rule by the wisest were most beneficial for the less wise and most fulfilling for the wise, it would achieve a true common good. But if, as Aristotle has said in his discussion of distributive justice, those who are inherently best and who contribute the most should get the greatest rewards, and if the life of ruling is less good and less happy than the life of contemplation, then Aristotle's best regime seems to be precisely *unjust* to the one who is most deserving of all. Of course in times of crisis it might well be best for all including the wisest that they take personal charge, but this is a desperate expedient for a dangerous emergency and no longer a lasting arrangement to be wished for.

All of these thoughts return us again to consider the merits of the rule of reason understood very differently, as the rule of law. Arguably best for everyone including the philosophic is that citizens should live together under wisely framed laws that give dignity and a share in governing to all who are capable of it and who wish it, while giving a protected, if shadowy place on the margins of society to the philosophers, just as the nocturnal council does in the regime of Plato's *Laws*.[28] This thought accords with Aristotle's statement in *Ethics* 5.6 that justice exists where there is law and an equality of citizens in ruling and being ruled. But in the chapters that immediately follow the discussion of natural justice in 5.7 Aristotle will offer many reflections on the very grave limitations of even the best laws.

Thus our thoughts on natural justice point us upward to the rule of reason, yet the rule of reason as we try to bring it sharply into focus turns out to take two very different forms: on one hand the rule of law, which is stable, uniform, and impartial, yet blunt and blind; and on the other, the rule of a living intelligence, which is perceptive, responsive, and adaptable, but also embodied, limited, mortal, guided by its own desires and concerns, and in itself better suited to educating by ones and twos than to governing by brute force. The step of positing an intelligence wholly other, wholly unlimited, unneedy, free of partiality, yet engaged and benevolently concerned with humanity is one that Aristotle refuses to take. Natural justice, Aristotle insists, is part of political justice.

VOLUNTARY AND INVOLUNTARY REVISITED (5.8)

In the last part of book 5 reason and knowledge come into the discussion of justice more frequently, as Aristotle gently offers reforms for legal standards, discusses the limitations of law, and points to a perspective beyond that of legal justice. Chapter 8 takes up again the distinction between voluntary and involuntary acts and the problem of responsibility that were the subject of 3.1–5, now from the perspective of legal justice. Aristotle draws a sensible and useful distinction between involuntary mishaps that occur contrary to reasonable expectation, involuntary acts resulting from errors of judgment, unjust acts that are voluntary but impulsive, and unjust acts that are premeditated and hence show a vicious character. In this way he improves on traditional Greek law's simple distinction between involuntary crimes and crimes of malice aforethought. Knowledge is relevant to these distinctions but in a limited way: the pertinent knowledge is chiefly or perhaps exclusively the simple knowledge of what one is doing. While Aristotle repeats his earlier observation that one can be ignorant of or knowledgeable about the person acted upon, the act, the means, and that for the sake of which (*hou heneka*) one acts, his only example of the last is the immediate result, in the case of one who strikes another in order to wound him (1135b14–15). Aristotle does not say that a virtuous act must be done for its own sake or for the sake of the noble. He does concede that an act such as returning a deposit, if done out of fear, is just only incidentally, and that acts of justice and injustice that show just and unjust characters must be done by choice, but the precise character of the motivational state of one who acts justly still refuses to come into clear focus. As Burger points out, this problem is related to the fact that justice, unlike the other virtues, is not a mean state of character or characteristic passions between two extremes, but a mean between doing injustice and suffering it (1133b30–32), a standard that defines relations between individuals and not a perfection of some aspect of the soul.[29]

What Aristotle does not say that would give us a mean on the model of the other virtues is that a just disposition is a correct understanding of the comprehensive good that is of concern to an individual, an understanding that neither underrates nor overrates the value of each element of it, including the external goods that are objects of competition and the good relations with one's fellows that a thriving life requires. Aristotle neither reduces a just disposition to knowledge nor explicitly grounds it in a deep knowledge of this kind; to do so would perhaps too seriously challenge the wisdom of punitive laws. Yet he allows questions about the motivations behind just and unjust acts and their relation to knowledge to emerge quietly but repeatedly throughout this series of chapters. One way he does so is to reproduce and so put on the table for reflection certain common ambivalences, for example, our conflicting opinions as to whether, in order to act unjustly, one must know that one is doing wrong. Evidently the plotter knows, but a person who acts in anger, Aristotle points out, supposes that the other party is wrong and that his retaliation is justified, for anger is always at "apparent injustice" (35b28–29). Somehow we assume nonetheless that angry people know that they are wrong to lash out at the objects of their wrath. But do they? And is the appearance of injustice not as present in the case of slow-burning as of red-hot anger? Aristotle speaks likewise of the sympathy or forgiveness we are inclined to feel when the whole cause of a harm was ignorance, and the lack of sympathy we feel when the cause was "a passion that is neither natural nor human" (1136a6–9), but what about the cases in between, acts done in knowledge of the facts and out of an anger that is both natural and human? We both blame and want at least partially to excuse them, especially when the provocation was very great, an ambivalence that Aristotle reproduces by calling harms inflicted in anger both unjust acts *and* errors (1135b22–23). And if we sometimes sympathize with people overcome by "natural" anger, why should we not sympathize even more with those whose souls are so unhealthy that they are driven by unnatural passions? Of course no law code can dispense with punishments for most harms inflicted in anger, but is that because the legislators are bowing reluctantly to the citizens' irrational anger as the Athenian Stranger does in Plato's *Laws*, or because they share their conflicted thinking?

INJUSTICE TO ONESELF (5.9)

Aristotle finds it difficult to extricate himself from the Socratic paradoxes that he has allowed to intrude into his discussion of justice. Can people do injustice with full knowledge, if or to the extent that this harms them?

Can they either suffer injustice voluntarily or do injustice to themselves? In attempting to dispose of these questions in 5.9, he probes more deeply the relation of knowledge to virtue. At the bottom of each question is whether anyone ever voluntarily accepts what is bad for oneself, either when one seems generously to put others first or when one harms one's soul through one's own vice or lack of self-control. If to do injustice is simply to harm someone with knowledge of what one is doing, Aristotle says, then one can voluntarily do injustice to oneself and can voluntarily suffer injustice. But he suggests that the definition cannot be right. One obvious problem here is that injustice is something that we feel the law ought to correct, but the law cannot step in every time a transaction or an action turns out to be bad for someone. If a legal system were to work from the premise that acts in order to be just must be good for all parties concerned, no contract would be secure and no election beyond challenge. Perhaps for this reason, Aristotle proposes a further test: an injustice is a harm done not only knowingly but "against the other's wish" (1136b4–5).

This stipulation does let the political community off the hook for having to inquire into the justice of any transaction that was voluntary on both sides. But in fact "wish" introduces a higher standard than the voluntary, since many impulsive acts and all lapses of self-control are voluntary but not wished for. Aristotle's new standard will at least briefly open up a radical chasm in our way of thinking about justice. Does anyone truly *wish* to be harmed, or to harm one's own soul? If not, how many judgments would we have to change to be true to this insight? Aristotle continues to insist that one can voluntarily suffer harm and that the person lacking self-control does: this seems to accord with ordinary opinion. But does anyone voluntarily suffer what one knows to be bad at the moment of acting or acquiescing, as opposed to voluntarily suffering what is in fact bad? Ordinary opinion is not clear on this. But such opinion is at least clear in holding that no one wishes to suffer injustice. Aristotle then generalizes *this* thought in an important statement. "No one voluntarily suffers injustice, for no one wishes for this, not even the person lacking self-restraint, but instead he acts against his own wish. For neither does anyone wish for what he does not think is of serious worth [*spoudaios*], and the person lacking self-restraint does not do what he thinks he should do" (1136b6–9). Wish is in accord with what we believe to be decent or of serious worth. No one, then, wishes to be done injustice—but neither, Aristotle suggests now, does anyone wish to do injustice, as much as people voluntarily do things that in fact are unjust. What we all truly wish, Aristotle suggests, is to be happy in a way that is also admirable. This is an insight that the law cannot follow. It must allow citizens to do harmful, essentially unjust things all the time, as long as they are somehow consented to, just as it must punish as wholly voluntary acts that harm the doer as well as the victim. Political communities have no real alternative, but this necessity casts a dark shadow over the rule of law.

Covering over again the chasm he has just opened, however, Aristotle quickly retreats to a less stringent test of the voluntary than true wish. One who gives away his own things in an unequal exchange, as Glaucus does in exchanging his gold armor for Diomedes's bronze in book 6 of the *Iliad*, does not suffer injustice, he says, since "the giving is up to him" (1136b11–12). This example carries us from Aristotle's deliberately pedestrian treatment of unfair exchanges to Homer's richly suggestive portrayal of what may drive human beings both to heroic acts of self-sacrifice and to many of their less costly acts of imprudence, in one of the most famous scenes in the *Iliad*. Stepping forward to challenge the Greek hero Diomedes, and asked his name and lineage, Homer's Glaucus answers with a frank and moving statement of the transience and ultimate insignificance of all things mortal:

> "Great-hearted son of Tydeus, why ask of my generation?
> As is the generation of leaves, so is that of men.
> The wind scatters leaves on the ground, but the burgeoning wood
> puts forth others when the season of spring returns.
> So one generation of men grows and another perishes.
> Yet if you wish to learn all this, so that you may know well
> our genealogy, there are plenty of men who know it.
> There is a city, Ephyre, in a corner of horse-pasturing
> Argos; there lived Sisyphus, who was the most cunning of men,
> Sisyphus son of Aeolus, and he sired a son, Glaucus,
> but Glaucus sired incomparable Bellerophon . . ."
>
> (*Iliad* 6.144–55)

Yes, we are all as ephemeral as leaves, but the soul that grasps this truth loses it again in the next breath, and the conscious leaf that has just accepted its fate of joining its predecessors in oblivion again throws out tendrils of hope and faith that, after all, it may not quite be so. Glaucus's family story is full of hardship and betrayal but also of bravery and honor; with Glaucus's help and especially with Homer's, the memory of the good Bellerophon who killed the Chimaera will never be wholly forgotten as long as human civilization endures. For Glaucus himself that memory is more than "not forgotten": it confers at once the burden of obligation to prove a worthy heir, so as "not to shame the stock of my fathers" (6.209), a sacred trust to preserve Bellerophon's memory, and a source of bright if hazy inspiration.

When he hears Glaucus's story, Diomedes proclaims that through their fathers he and Glaucus are guest-friends and must not fight; he proposes instead the exchange of armor to seal their friendship. Yet, Homer says,

> Then Zeus the Son of Cronos stole the wits of Glaucus
> who with Diomedes the son of Tydeus exchanged armor
> of gold for bronze, the worth of nine oxen for that of a hundred.
> (*Iliad* 6.234–36)

Is it really Zeus, whom Homer treats with subtly playful skepticism throughout the poem, that steals away Glaucus's wits? Or is it the faith Glaucus places in Zeus, a faith rooted in his belief in his own nobility, his belief that he can in a moment of courage transcend his fear of death and in a moment of friendship transcend self-interest, and all will be well with him? Neither Homer nor Aristotle tells us. But Glaucus's failed attempt to accept the necessity of his own oblivion does offer one important answer to Aristotle's question of how it is that a human being, never wishing "for what he does not think is of serious worth" (1136b7–8), may nonetheless voluntarily do what causes him harm.

This example leads into the argument of the second half of 5.9. Here Aristotle makes clear that he has by no means disposed of the question of whether it is possible to do injustice to oneself. For if anyone who gives another more than is merited does injustice, this should be possible. And indeed, giving oneself less than one deserves is just what a decent person is thought to do. But perhaps it is not so simple, Aristotle says, for one who makes such a distribution may be "grasping for more than his share of another good—for example, of reputation or what is unqualifiedly noble" (36b21–22). As we have seen, we cannot really do an act for its own sake, and even the noble seems to point beyond itself to something else that is being done well or honored well. But to the extent that we do view the noble as an end, we tend to think of it as a prize we want for ourselves. The noble is in fact another contested good, and the contests over it are not unselfish, even if their true motives are deeply buried.[30]

But if someone who gives away more than his share of what is good *may* be grasping for more of his share of another good, what of the cases where he is not? Is he necessarily doing himself an injustice then? Aristotle implies not, for in any case, he continues—whether one is grasping for more of something else or not—such a person "is suffering nothing against his wish" (1136b23–24). To give up one good and not to grasp for more of something else is possible only if one gives without surreptitious motives and without moral confusion, clear-sightedly seeing that it accords with one's true wish to benefit another.[31] And to act in accord with one's true wish is not to suffer injustice.

Aristotle turns then to the person who receives or, as he keeps putting it, who "has" more than his share of something good (1136b16, 1136b18, 1136b26): is he guilty of injustice? The clearest case of this would be many members of Aristotle's primary audience, the gentlemen who sit in comfortable possession of property that was acquired through an impeccably respectable process of inheritance, but often originally seized violently from others. Aristotle places at least the chief blame on those who act and not on their passive recipients, but he has allowed a question about the foundations of all lawful possession to creep into a discussion that is coming to reflect more and more on the problems with law and the assumptions that underlie it.

Turning back to the distributor, and evidently thinking now of one who originally allocated goods from a common fund or of a judge who has redistributed that which belongs to others, contrary to merit, Aristotle says that if this person acted in ignorance, his act is not legally unjust but it is "in a sense," for "the legally just and the just in the primary sense are different" (1136b33–34). After beginning book 5 by identifying complete justice with justice as lawfulness, Aristotle now explicitly allows daylight to appear between legal justice and "justice in the primary sense." The verdicts of juries and judges that are trying their best to dispense justice, even if ignorant of relevant facts, are one thing: the law must generally recognize their verdicts as just even if they are not simply so. The judgments of crooked judges are another matter, and Aristotle again attributes to such people (in this case without a "perhaps") a kind of *pleonexia* and to their actions real injustice: if the distributor "knowingly judged unjustly, then he himself too is grasping for more, either of gratitude or of vengeance" (1136b34–37a1).

What, then, is justice in the primary sense? It would seem to be what the law at its best aspires to achieve but does not: the unerring judgment of unbiased wisdom. This would be judgment based on full knowledge of each case, a judgment that would see the part ignorance and self-destructive confusion play in crime and so that would not seek retribution, a judgment that would seek out the true good of each person involved and the common good of all of them to the extent possible. And precisely this meaning of true justice seems to be implied in what Aristotle goes on to say. For now he criticizes those who suppose that "what is just is easy" (1137a5–6) and imagine that "to know the just and unjust things is in no way to be wise, because it is not difficult to comprehend what the laws say (but these are not the just things, except incidentally)." The gulf between true justice and law widens again. "But how the just things are done and how they are distributed—this is indeed a greater task than to know what is healthy." Being familiar with drugs and medical procedures is perhaps not hard, "but how one should apply them with a view to health, and to whom and when, is as great a task as to be a physician" (37a9–17). True justice now turns out to require wisdom; it is comparable to but higher than the art of medicine; it is nothing less than the art of tending to souls. It is at the same time itself a good condition of soul, from which one never would do injustice, for it is another and kindred error to suppose that "doing injustice belongs no less to the just person" than to the unjust (37a17–18). Complete justice, in sum, is the active expression of a wise and healthy soul in one's conduct toward others.

Already at the end of 5.9, however, Aristotle begins to descend from this very high perspective on justice. In the last few sentences he returns to identifying justice not with the art of caring for souls but with fairness in the distribution of things of which it is possible to have an excess or a deficiency. And this descent forms the horizon within which he will consider the relation of justice to equity in 5.10.

JUSTICE AND EQUITY (5.10)

In light of Aristotle's comparison of justice to the art of medicine in 5.9, we might have expected him now to revisit the question of whether it is best for human beings to be ruled by law or directly by the reason of the wisest human being without law. He does indeed say at the beginning of chapter 10 that it "follows next in order" to discuss the place of a certain kind of flexible intellect in administering justice—the virtue of equity (*epieikeia*)—and the equitable man (1137a31–33). But the spirit of equity as he describes it here and the perspective on justice he sketched in the previous chapter are not the same.

The Greek *epieikeia* is broader than the English "equity." It refers both to the virtue by which a good judge corrects legal justice and to the spirit of a generally decent or good person, especially one who is not a stickler for strict justice in his own affairs. Thus equity comes to sight as diverging in two ways from strict justice, and in both ways potentially casting a shadow over justice. Is strict justice not sometimes a bad thing, when mercy is needed, as Shakespeare's Portia says, or at least equity, to avoid a cruel result? And is an equitable man not one who takes less than his due and is noble in doing so? Aristotle's explicit answer is hardly coherent: there is no divergence between the equitable and the truly just, but only between what is equitable and "a certain justice," for "the equitable and the just are the same, and while both are serious, equity is superior" (1137b8–11). He goes on to make the cogent statement—perhaps a simple correction—that what equity is superior to and a correction of is legal justice, which requires occasional correction because of law's necessary generality. But perhaps the problem that caused Aristotle's uncharacteristic lapse into incoherence is something more complex. Might it be that legal justice aspires to a standard that it cannot consistently achieve, and yet that this standard itself—fairness as the law understands it—falls short of the highest standard?

For the most part, the equity that improves on legal justice reaches only so high as to correct for the occasional inadvertent unfairness of general law. Thus the sentence of death normally prescribed for sentries who fall asleep on the watch is suspended in the case of a soldier who volunteered for a double watch after an extraordinary march to help a sick comrade; unpaid taxes are forgiven for one whose house was washed away in a storm. That this is still not the spirit of the soul doctor is clear from Aristotle's way of framing the problem that equity is needed to solve: it is needed to correct the "error" that the lawgiver made in laying down laws that are invariably too general and that are no less correct for all that.

> The error resides not in the law or the lawgiver but in the nature of the matter. . . . Whenever the law speaks generally, then, but what happens in a given case constitutes an exception to the general rule, then it is correct, where the lawgiver omits something and erred by speaking unqualifiedly, to rectify that omission with what the lawgiver himself would have said if he had been present and would have legislated if he had known of this case. (1137b17–24)

What we have now is not the doctor of souls who treats every case individually, with deep insight into human nature and careful attention to the different needs of every patient, but an administrator of fairness who knows that in exceptional cases rules should be bent. The only limitation of law addressed now is its generality. Aristotle is silent in 5.10 on the deepest problems we have seen with law: its tendency to focus on fairness more than on the health of citizens' souls and to assume that criminals are benefiting themselves unfairly through their crimes. Thus the equitable man as Aristotle describes him shares not the purpose and outlook of one who grasps and embodies "justice in the primary sense," but only those of ordinary lawgivers. To be sure, some of the exceptions such a man will make come from his readiness to forgive when he sees someone breaking under "pressures that perhaps no one could bear," but it belongs to his spirit also to believe there are some things so terrible that no one can be forced to do them (1110a23–27). It is not part of his spirit to be exacting in his thought and to pursue to the bottom the tension between these two opinions. The spirit of equity and the spirit of gentlemanliness are of a piece.

Aristotle underscores the massive concern with fairness that lies at the heart of what we think of as equity, as well as the confusion as to whether in being just one secures one's own highest good or denies oneself even one's fair share, when he closes the chapter with a statement that the equitable man "is not exacting to a fault about justice, but instead is disposed to take less for himself" (1138a1). Whether in claiming less for himself he is "taking more than his share of another good, such as reputation or of what is unqualifiedly noble" (1136b21–22), Aristotle does not now say. We must, however, suspect that he often is, and that he only partially and intermittently shares the perspective of the wise, who see that most of the time other things matter more than getting their fair share of contested goods and who willingly forgo pressing their fair claims in order to gain goodwill, to advance a common interest, to help a friend, or merely to win themselves freedom from troubles. The different elements of the equitable man's outlook are in tension, yet together they produce an impressive soul that is calm, dignified, gentle, generous, and self-reliant. In these ways the equitable man resembles the philosophic soul on a lower plane.

JUSTICE AND COMPLETE VIRTUE (5.11)

In the final chapter of book 5 Aristotle returns yet again to the question of whether one can do injustice to oneself, showing that there is a problem here he still has not disposed of. And indeed, the spirit of lawful justice and even the spirit of equity remain unresolved on this point. Both at times treat deliberate self-harm as possible and wrong, yet both also assume that no one wishes to be harmed. Aristotle himself agrees with the latter judgment, and on this basis will again deny that injustice to oneself is possible. In the process, however, he shows more about the problematic relationship between the spirit of lawful justice and reason.

Aristotle considers now the ultimate case of self-harm, suicide. Communities treat suicide as wrong as part of their concern with justice in the extended sense of complete virtue: does this not imply that they view it as injustice to oneself? He says that suicide is "against correct reason" (1138a10), a striking formulation inasmuch as this is his only mention of correct reason in book 5. Since suicide is the most fatal blow one can strike against one's own happiness, this suggests an especially close connection between correct reason and the wise pursuit of happiness. But maintaining his outward deference to the perspective of law, Aristotle embeds the statement that self-harm violates correct reason in a discussion of law that goes in a very different direction. Suicide is an injustice, he says, since communities punish it with dishonor, but an injustice against the community, not oneself. In support of this thought he even cites approvingly the view of law that grants the community maximal claims on the individual: "What the law does not command it forbids" (1138a7).[32] This is an extreme formulation of the perspective according to which the purpose of virtue is to fulfill one's obligations as a citizen. It is a perspective largely at odds with the *Ethics*' stress on the good order and thriving of the individual human soul, but it is one Aristotle finds himself forced to appeal to now in order to resist the whirlpool of Socratic dialectics that he has conjured up and that threatens to pull him all the way to acknowledging that injustice, marring the happiness we all want, is at the deepest level involuntary.

Turning to the other meaning of justice he has pursued through most of book 5, justice as fairness, Aristotle adds that in this respect too it is not possible to do injustice to oneself, either in the full sense of a deliberate injustice or even in the lesser sense of an action that is unfair although not the result of vice—and this for the simple reason that it is not logically possible for the same person at the same time and in the same respect to gain unfairly and to lose unfairly. Fairness makes sense only as a quality of transactions between people; every act of unfairness is in pursuit of some good that the doer desires or wishes for; unfairness against oneself makes no sense. This is technically true but it again evades the problem of whether law does not necessarily treat as voluntary acts whose chief victims are the perpetrators themselves. And this question Aristotle implicitly answers in the affirmative as he reiterates that justice is a mean between doing and suffering injustice, adding that doing injustice is intrinsically the worse of the two. And as he concedes his agreement with this Socratic claim, he returns to his medical analogies for virtue as the health of the soul.

What Aristotle will not do is agree with Socrates in the *Republic* that justice means simply the right ordering of the elements of the soul. Aristotle, the teacher of lawgivers, insists that justice is still primarily a virtue governing one's external relations with others, and that it is in at most a metaphorical sense the proper relation of internal parts. In his account of this metaphorical inner justice, moreover, Aristotle departs from Socrates in the way he describes the relevant parts. In line with his account in *Ethics* 1.13, the good order Aristotle describes now is not that of *thumos*, parallel to the trusty auxiliary class of Socrates' little republic, assisting reason in ruling desire, but rather the direct rule of reason over a single irrational part as a master or household manager over his subordinates. In the rule of a master or household manager, Aristotle said in 5.6, there can be no justice or injustice in an unqualified sense, for no one wishes to harm what is "like a part of oneself" (1134b11–12); still less does anyone wish to harm his own soul. Thus reason's rule over the passions, when effective, seems to be a benevolent despotism. Here and here alone reason is assured of having sufficient motive to exercise rule. But whether it does so with a view to the fulfillment of every part or merely uses and otherwise curbs the lower desires in a more genuinely despotic spirit, Aristotle does not say. He does, however, explain the possibility of this metaphorical injustice as following from the fact that it is possible for these "parts" to "suffer something contrary to their respective desires" (1138b10–11): reason too has its desires.

And with this thought, perhaps significantly, Aristotle closes his book on justice, having shown us a rich and even bewildering range of meanings, each valid in its own way and each implying a different standard or set of standards, not framed in terms of action for the noble or action for its own sake, but all in terms of different aspects of the human good that is of concern to us.

Chapter 5

WISDOM AND ACTIVE WISDOM

The Intellectual Virtues

THE PROBLEM OF INTELLECTUAL VIRTUE (6.1)

We take up Aristotle's discussion of the intellectual virtues in book 6 with questions that Aristotle himself acknowledges have grown only more puzzling and more pressing. In 1.7 he defined the human good as an activity of the soul in accordance with reason, or with virtue; in 1.13 he turned to the investigation of virtue, dividing it first into intellectual and moral; in 2.2, while granting that all virtue must be in accord with correct reason, he postponed the question of just what correct reason is and how the intellectual virtue that assures it relates to the other virtues, in order to investigate the moral virtues; in 2.6 he defined virtue as "a characteristic involving choice, consisting in a mean with respect to us that is defined by reason and in the way that a man of active wisdom would define it" (1106b36–1107a2); and in the following three books he gave a rich description of each of the virtues as it comes to sight in ordinary moral life, showing how it functions as a mean between improper extremes. Yet in all of this he has not fully specified what the standard is that correct reason looks to in determining the mean. In a curious way, even as he sharpens the question of virtue's standard, he will continue this oblique approach in book 6 as well. In each of the moral virtues, he explains,

> there is a certain target [*skopos*] that the one who possesses reason looks to in tightening and loosening, and there is a certain measure [*horos*] of the mean, which we say is between the excess and the deficiency, being in ac-

> cord with correct reason. But while speaking this way is truthful, it is not at all clear. For in all the other concerns also about which there is a science, it is true to say that one ought not to strain or slacken either too much or too little, but according to the mean and with correct reason. Yet having this alone, one would know nothing more—for example, what sorts of things should be applied to the body, if somebody should say, "as many things as the medical art commands and in the way that the one who has it says." Therefore it is necessary also, concerning the characteristics of the soul, not only to state this truly but to define what correct reason is and what its measure [*horos*] is. (1138b22–34)

In this strikingly clear statement of what has not yet been accomplished, Aristotle once again points to the art or science of medicine as a possible model for his own investigation. Just as the medical art looks to the health of the body as the target in accordance with which it seeks to bring each bodily function within the correct parameters, so the art of virtue must look to the health of the soul as the target in accordance with which it seeks to bring all the passions and habits of character into the right condition. Then the question would be, what is the health of the soul? But while Aristotle points to this line of inquiry, once again he does not follow it. Instead, having raised the question of both the target of virtue and the measure of the mean, he silently drops the question of virtue's target to focus on the question of the measure—and that no longer of the mean that accords with reason, but rather of reason itself. Thus the investigation of intellectual virtue, as of moral virtue, quickly becomes one of describing the work and defining the proper boundaries of each part of it, so that the question of its goal will again disappear into the interstices of the discussion.[1] But it will be there; we simply have to ferret it out.

Because Aristotle takes up the intellectual virtues in book 6 with the moral purpose of clarifying their role in the rest of virtue, he will give pride of place to *phronēsis* or active wisdom, that intellectual virtue that is more than merely intellectual, that is intimately bound up with the correct shaping of all the passions that constitutes the moral virtues, that is always found together with those virtues, and that guarantees the presence and continuation of each of them while itself being preserved by moderation.[2] This intimate connection between active wisdom and moral virtue is of course the fascinating feature of active wisdom that allowed Socrates to claim that virtue is knowledge. The connection might be understood in several ways. Active wisdom might be considered wholly dependent on character, a virtue that belongs to the intellect inasmuch as it involves calculation, but that draws both its guidance and its energy from the well-formed tastes and passions and habits that make up moral virtue. Or, reflecting its apparent in-between character, active wisdom might be regarded as the perfection of a distinct part of the soul that somehow includes both practical understanding and the passions that obey that understanding. Or active wisdom might, as Socrates suggests, be simply an understanding of human nature, the human good, and one's own soul so clear and comprehensive as to be always compelling and efficacious in guiding its possessor to what is best.

In fact, however, Aristotle makes a new beginning in the middle of 6.1 at 1138b35, stating that the discussion of the moral virtues is complete and proposing now to turn to the intellectual ones, as if the purpose of book 6 were after all not to address a key unanswered question about moral virtue but to treat intellectual virtue as a new topic in its own right. This second beginning prepares us for the complex character of this book, which will survey all aspects of human reason, but chiefly from the perspective of the moral life.[3]

Launching this new investigation, Aristotle begins with the soul. He reminds us of his prior division of the soul into a rational and an irrational part in 1.13, which he said was adequate for practical purposes but not perhaps wholly correct. There he further divided the irrational part into two, one governing nutrition and growth and the other comprising the passions but capable of heeding and obeying reason. Then at the end of that chapter he said of the latter, "if we must affirm that this part too possesses reason, then what possesses reason will also be twofold, one possessing it in the authoritative sense and in itself, the other in the sense of listening to it as to a father" (1103a1–3). Thus we seemed to have three elements in the soul, the middle one not definitively assigned to either the rational or the irrational part. Now, however, as if he had earlier made only a single division of the soul into rational and irrational parts, he says,

> Now we must divide the one that possesses reason in the same manner. Let it be assumed that there are two that have reason: one by which we theorize about those beings whose principles do not admit of being otherwise, and the other by which we theorize about those that do admit of being otherwise. (1139a5–8)

There are several curious things about this formulation. First, this division is set forth as an assumption. Is it in the final analysis any more adequate than Aristotle's original division of the soul into rational and irrational parts? Or might this division be adequate and even excellent for most practical or educational purposes although ultimately inaccurate? Second, while the first part sounds like the seat of wisdom and the second that of active wisdom, Aristotle says that both "theorize." Third, we have a different cut, as it were, from the one in 1.13. Is Aristotle further elevating the intermediate part, the seat of the passions and of moral virtue, and now attributing to it greater rationality than he did before—and perhaps more rational autonomy than it really has? Counting against this reading is the fact that in 6.12 Aristotle will finally speak of four parts of the soul, two rational and two irrational. But if there are two rational parts, what is their relation? For, fourth and most important, the division Aristotle is articulating now looks much cleaner than it is. He seems at first to be distinguishing as two spheres of knowledge the changing and the unchanging—the heavens and the mundane world of living things, perhaps. The precise cut he makes, however, is rather between the things whose *principles* do not admit of change and the *things* that change.[4] Might the things whose principles are unchanging not include many or possibly all of the things that themselves admit of change—stars, rocks, fishes, triangles, and even human beings? For are not all knowable things knowable by means of principles that do not change, including the fundamental principles of human nature? Are even conventions such as current English usage really knowable unless one knows what language is and what it is for and how its universal functions differ from the varying conventions by which meaning is expressed? But perhaps this is to use the concept of knowing too restrictively: in some sense toddlers and even dogs can know that they are not supposed to jump on the couch. Does the second part of the rational part of the soul—that which governs moral action—grasp only the changing aspects of what exists by opinion or fiat, then? Surely not: surely there can be no moral virtue without a grasp of principles. Yet we recall that Aristotle said in 5.7 that what is just by nature is all changeable—the "all" evidently encompassing the principles as well as the applications. Practical reason would seem to belong to this strange realm of things that exist somehow by nature even as they are profoundly mutable. But can it possibly "theorize" correctly about these things if it lacks what our guide Aristotle certainly has and uses throughout this treatise, a knowledge of human nature? And yet if such knowledge is essential, we must wonder whether it really makes sense to assign reasoning about justice to a part of the soul distinct from that which theorizes about nature, and whether it would not be better to say that there is just one part of us that theorizes about all things knowable, including all of nature both nonhuman and human, the justice that is natural and yet changing, and the many human languages and opinions and customs and laws that are expressions of human nature.

Aristotle defends his division of the rational part of the soul into distinct parts on the grounds that objects different in kind must be grasped by parts of the soul that differ in kind, "if indeed it is by a certain similarity and kinship that knowledge comes to be for them" (1139a10–11). He here leaves this difficult premise as an undemonstrated hypothesis.[5] Something in it certainly seems right, if puzzling: somehow the mind must have the capacity to reconstruct within it the forms and the relations between them that it finds in the world, although just how it does this is a mystery. Given that the chief division Aristotle is drawing here between objects of thought is between changing and unchanging ones, perhaps it is well that he does not delve into this mystery here: would what grasps unchanging truths have to be itself unchanging? Or, if this is impossible for any living being, would the part of the mind that grasps unchanging truths both hold within itself their fixed principles and also change as it learns and grapples with new manifestations and implications of those principles? But is that not what the mind in fact does in thinking about objects of every kind?

More light is shed on the character of this purported second part of the soul by Aristotle's next step, which is to identify the divisions of the rational part by their activities. Yet the way he defines these is also curious: he calls the two parts the "scientific" (*epistēmonikon*) and the "calculative" (*logistikon*), adding that calculating and deliberating are the same thing (1139a12–13). Naming the second "deliberative" would anchor it firmly in the realm of human action, but naming it "calculative" calls to mind especially the activity of mathematics.[6] Aristotle has already compared deliberation to geometrical analysis in 3.3, but now he is assigning both deliberation and calculation to a single part of the soul, separate from that which grasps unchanging principles. Again, does a mathematician grasp the principles of mathematics with one part of his soul and work out how to construct a figure or solve a mathematical problem with another, which also is the seat of moral reasoning? Would it not be better to say that we have a single faculty of reason that engages in different activities, sometimes studying what is and how and why it is, sometimes grasping how it changes, and sometimes applying this knowledge to reasoning about what else might come to be? Is it not by a single faculty of reason that Aristotle is engaging in political philosophy as he writes this book, studying what is true of human nature and political life and how to promote the good condition of souls and healthy political regimes, in the same way that it is through a single intelligence and a single medical art that the doctor both studies and heals human bodies?[7]

PERCEPTION, INTELLECT, DESIRE (6.2)

In order better to identify the intellectual virtues and especially the one that provides guidance for moral action, Aristotle opens the next chapter with a new division. "There are three things in the soul that are sovereign over action [*praxis*] and truth: sense perception [*aisthēsis*], intellect [*nous*], and desire [*orexis*]" (1139a17–18). Unlike the division in the soul drawn in 6.1, this one seems very clear. Sense perception might seem to be especially important as a foundation for at least some of the activity of the "scientific" part of the soul, but Aristotle immediately sets it aside on the grounds that it is "not the origin of any action" (1139a19), thus underscoring that in this book he is examining the intellectual virtues chiefly with a view to illuminating the form of reason that guides correct action. Thought is concerned simply with what is true and false, but desire in a certain way is also, and its conformity to correct reason is essential in moral virtue.

> What affirmation and denial are in thinking, pursuit and avoidance are in desire. Thus, since moral virtue is a characteristic involving choice, and choice is deliberate desire, it is necessary on account of these things for the reasoning to be true and the desire correct, if the choice is to be morally serious [*spoudaios*], and for the former to affirm and the latter to pursue the same things. (1139a21–26)

The big questions, of course, are what sets the standard for the correctness of reasoning and desire, and what ensures their alignment. By reminding us of his analysis of deliberation in 3.3, Aristotle points to one way of understanding the harmony of desire and reason, as outlined there: thought alone moves nothing; choice is deliberate desire; the reasoning that constitutes deliberation is instrumental reasoning that finds the best means to attain the end that desire seeks; thus reason if carried out correctly will accord with desire because it follows it; and both will be correct when desire is for what is truly good.[8] The problem, as Saint Thomas brings out, is that "if the truth of the practical intellect is determined by a right appetitive faculty and the rectitude of the appetitive faculty is determined by the fact that it agrees with correct reason, as was previously shown, an apparent vicious circle results." Saint Thomas offers an appealing solution, more clear and simple than anything Aristotle provides: "the end is determined for man by nature," an understanding of which is the starting point for both the practical and the theoretical intellect.[9] A full understanding of our natural needs and of the happiness we naturally desire would on this account give us the ends that correct choice pursues, so that naturally healthy and well-understood desire, properly directed by reason to the happiness according to nature that is desired most of all, would be the unified starting point for action. Yet in this important passage on intellect and its contribution to moral life, Aristotle himself is silent about both nature and happiness.

Instead, he stresses again the peculiar structure of moral choice:

> Of action, then, the source is choice, from which comes the motion but not the purpose [*hou heneka*], but the source of choice is desire and reasoning for the sake of something. (1139a31–33)

While it is choice that sets us in motion, we choose not for the sake of choosing but rather for the sake of an end given by desire. Thus we have a chain of causes, beginning with desire for some object, desire initiating deliberation or instrumental reasoning, desire and reason together determining choice, and choice initiating an action, which is for the ultimate sake of the good that is desired. But in the case of moral action, the first cause and the resulting action turn out to be one and the same.

> Thought itself moves nothing, but thought for the sake of something and concerned with action. And this is also the source of making. Everyone who makes makes for the sake of something, and the thing made is not the end simply, but with a view to something and for the sake of something—but an act is. For acting well [*eupraxia*] is the end, and desire is for this. (1139a35–b4)[10]

Making and its product are both instrumental, but, returning to the formulation from book 2, Aristotle suggests again now that good action is "for itself." Thus even if desire for some particular object is what sets us in motion when we do move (e.g., a desire for a new fence), and deliberative reasoning seeks the appropriate steps to secure that object (e.g., negotiating with the neighbor to share the cost), in virtuous action this process is in fact only the occasion for the acting well (e.g., justly) that is its own end, the truest end of desire, when action is morally good.

This is a subtle formulation. Is it cogent? As we have been seeing, there are two major and related clusters of problems with it, one having to do with the motivation for virtuous action and the other with its standard. The first is the question of precisely how the desire that has acting well as its object is related to the initial desires that set us in motion. Are these initial desires embraced merely as the occasion to exercise virtue, so that the desire to act well in this sense now becomes *the* desire motivating choice? The picture here is complicated by the dual meaning of *eupraxia* in Greek, which includes both acting well and faring well or being happy. Even granting that, as Aristotle has insisted, virtuous action is the core of happiness, and granting that, as he has also insisted, we would choose virtue for itself even if nothing further resulted from it (1097b1–5), acting well and being happy are not simply identical, and a great deal depends on the extent to which acting morally is experienced as intrinsically satisfying. The more important honor and other rewards are to the virtuous person, the more this becomes doubtful. The second set of problems concern the great difficulty of defining "well" or "nobly" at all except as measured by some specific goal or goals, such as getting the fence rebuilt, getting help with the cost, and maintaining good neighborly relations, but these are all extrinsic to the act itself.[11]

A further set of questions is provoked by Aristotle's contrast here between action and production, which he will use as the basis for his treatment of art in 6.4. As an example of the contrast we may consider a soldier firing at the enemy on one hand and a factory worker producing ammunition on the other. The basic thrust of Aristotle's teaching is clear: the factory worker's labor is for the sake of his product, which is itself for the sake of something further; his activity is thus neither an end in itself nor particularly dignified; whereas the soldier's activity is an exercise of courage that has great dignity and as such is inherently choiceworthy. But this is perhaps not quite how it all appears to the commander in chief, who deploys both to defeat the enemy and would be loath to waste the efforts of either, but perhaps especially those of the soldier, to no purpose. Does the commander not define the excellence of his own activity and that of everyone he oversees primarily in terms of the victory he seeks?[12] As Aristotle says in book 10, we would have to be bloodthirsty to want to fight battles for the sake of fighting battles (1177b6–12). And conversely, may the patriotic factory worker who puts in long hours to do his part for the war effort not see his own activity as satisfying and meaningful in a way that goes beyond the value of the bullets produced? In general, is the line between making and action really so clear?[13] This is a problem that will recur in the discussion of art in 6.4.

If ordinary moral activity seems more directed to ends beyond the activity than Aristotle's formulation here suggests, Aristotle's next sentence hints at a different realm of activity that is possibly more self-contained and noninstrumental. "Therefore choice is either desiring intelligence [*orektikos nous*] or thoughtful desire [*orexis dianotike*], and such a source is a human being" (1139b4–5). Choice as thoughtful desire would seem to characterize the practical choice in which thought helps to clarify the object of desire and to guide the pursuit of it; choice as desiring intelligence by contrast would seem to be thought with its own curiosity to know, as an end in itself. Yet by calling "such a source" a human being, Aristotle invites the question of the relation between these two partnerships of thought and desire. Is the desire to know wholly autonomous, or is it given its most serious direction by other needs of the human being that manifest themselves as nonintellectual desires? The language here suggests, at least, a close relation between our desire to know and our need to know in order to choose and to live well: it presents us as single wholes whose desires infuse our thought and whose thought infuses our desires. If so, our recognition of the good that we need and do not yet have would be what lights up the scene for us, making us attend closely to what is before us rather than surveying it idly. Likely this is what Plato means when he says that the idea of the good is the source of all knowledge in book 6 of the *Republic*. But this would suggest that wisdom and active wisdom are intimately related perfections of a single soul, impelled by both need and curiosity to seek above all to know its own nature and its place in the cosmos. And central to that concern would be the desire to know what necessities govern the universe and our human life and how those necessities are related to the accounts we hear about the divine. Does knowable necessity govern all beings, or are there one or more divine beings with mysterious powers to overturn every apparent necessity? Possibly this is the reason Aristotle ends the chapter with a curious line of poetry about the divine from a lost work of Agathon's: "For of this alone even a god is deprived: To make undone whatever things have been done" (1139b10–11). If the past is irrevocable, is it really plausible that that is the only necessity? If aspects of the present and the future also follow necessities, which necessities are these, and how do they affect our own choices?

But all of these sources of wonder about the essence of human nature, necessity, and the divine Aristotle barely hints at here. Instead, concluding that that it is the work of both intellectual parts of the soul to attain the truth, he prepares for yet another new beginning in the next chapter.

MODES OF KNOWLEDGE (6.3)

"Let those things by which the soul tells the truth by affirming or denying be five in number," Aristotle begins 6.3. "These are art [*technē*], science [*epistēmē*], active wisdom [*phronēsis*], wisdom [*sophia*], and intellect [*nous*]" (1139b15–17). How does this enumeration relate to the statement at the start of chapter 2 that the three things sovereign over action and truth are perception, intellect, and desire? It would seem that Aristotle has now set aside both perception and desire to articulate the five subdivisions or modes of activity of the intellect—except that intellect is itself one of the five. But this still seems right, for intellect has a comprehensive meaning for Aristotle in addition to the narrow and indeed quite mysterious meaning he will give it in 6.6.[14] This dual meaning of *nous* is only the first of many ways in which the divisions Aristotle makes so briskly at the beginning of book 6 will prove far less clean and more complicated than they at first seem. And do these five things characterize separate parts of one being or just different activities of it? Although translators and commentators often treat the five as distinct faculties or even parts of the soul, Aristotle calls them *hexeis*, characteristics or dispositions (e.g., 1139b31), the same word he uses for the characteristic ways of feeling and acting that constitute the individual virtues, so that it may indeed be most accurate to view these five as characteristic activities or perfections of a single intellect. Supposition (*hupolepsis*) and opinion (*doxa*), he adds, are not modes of knowing, for they can be mistaken. Still less does he suggest here that they constitute or govern separate parts of the soul.

What might be the principle of order in this list of art, science, active wisdom, wisdom, and intellect? There seems to be an ascent in rank as we move from the most mundane applications of knowledge, art; to a contemplative activity that depends on experience and induction, science; to the highest form of understanding in matters of choice and action, active wisdom; to the most complete form of theoretical understanding, wisdom; and finally to the purest form of knowing that directly grasps first principles, intellect. But when Aristotle sets out to discuss these five in detail, he changes the order, reversing art and science and likewise wisdom and intellect. Active wisdom alone retains its place in the center—a fitting position given that book 6 is especially concerned with distinguishing the activity and features of this characteristic. The new order suggests a particularly close relation between art and science on one hand and wisdom and intellect on the other. If the list is an ascent, it also entails an elevation of both art and wisdom. Might these two both be higher than they seem at first sight, perhaps in a similar way?

Science

Epistēmē is a fitting starting point since in its most nontechnical sense it means "knowledge" simply, of both theoretical and practical kinds (cf., e.g., 1146b31–35). In book 6, however, Aristotle confines himself to the technical meaning, best translated by the English word "science," but this too has both a narrower and a broader sense, as Aristotle's treatment of it in the remainder of 6.3 brings out. First, he says—or rather says that we suppose, using a cognate of the word translated above as "supposition," which is subject to error—that what is known scientifically does not admit of being otherwise but exists of necessity. Therefore, he adds, it is eternal—or at least what exists of necessity in the "unqualified sense" is eternal—and is not subject to generation and decay (1139b23–24). The objects of scientific knowledge would seem to be not the living and dying plants and animals and eroding rocks and such around us, then, but only the divine beings and the parts of the universe that are presumed eternal, such as the stars. But do we know that anything exists eternally, or do we merely suppose it? Might there be another kind of knowable necessity in a "qualified sense" that pertains to things like mathematical truths that are perhaps in a sense eternal but not beings that have existence, or to the natural being that do come into being and change, although their principles are unchanging and hence knowable?[15] Aristotle elsewhere treats such fields of science at length, but here he does not mention them.[16] He is indeed astonishingly silent in this discussion of science about nature altogether, perhaps necessarily so since in the *Physics* and elsewhere he identifies the beings that in the fullest sense exist according to nature with the living beings that are all subject to decay and death.

Second, Aristotle gives a rather different account of scientific knowledge as teachable and therefore grounded in either induction or syllogism or both: "Induction is in fact the starting point of the universal, whereas syllogism proceeds from the universals" (1139b28–29). It is induction based on observation that gives us knowledge of the world around us and its division into distinct kinds of beings with distinct natures. According to this account, science should comprehend not only astronomy but meteorology, geology, metallurgy, and biology in all its branches, including anatomy, medicine, and agriculture. And each science should contain its own first principles or *archai* in the particular observations it rests on, subsumed into universals through induction, which serve in turn as the first principles for deduction. But perhaps there is always in such studies something less than knowledge of ironclad necessities. For Aristotle concludes his account of science with the statement, "When one somehow trusts and the starting points are recognized by him, he knows. But unless he knows these more than the conclusions, he will have knowledge only incidentally" (1139b33–35). Only with extensive experience of observable particulars can one have a solid grasp of the universals formulated through induction, and only with a solid grasp of these principles and their manifold applications can one be confident of conclusions deduced from them. But at a deeper level, does all of science not involve trust in the general reliability of perception, the real existence of the things we perceive, and the assumption that the patterns and regularities we perceive in things rest on underlying necessities? Without such necessities we could scarcely speak about the nature of anything, but it is not clear that science itself is ever able to prove that these necessities exist. In sum, Aristotle's account of science in 6.3 gives the impression that its scope is more restricted to ironclad necessities and its certainty is more perfect than seems warranted by what he says elsewhere, or even by a careful reading of what he says here.

ART (6.4)

Aristotle turns explicitly in the next chapter to the realm of changing and contingent things: "But of what admits of being otherwise is a thing made and an action, but making and action are different" (1140a1–2). By almost giving the impression that the realm of what admits of being otherwise and the realm of human activity are the same, Aristotle continues to sharpen the suggestion of a clean dichotomy between the sublime, eternal necessities contemplated by science and the mundane, practical world of human affairs, as if there were no intermediate science of natural and living beings, including a science of human nature, which might inform and give guidance to life.[17] It is characteristic of the whole of book 6 to leave this crucial intermediate realm of knowledge and thought in the shadows.

As he begins to define art (*technē*), Aristotle builds on his distinction between making or production (*poiēseis*), often relegated to slaves in aristocratic societies, and action (*praxis*), which constitutes the core of a morally serious citizen's activity, claiming now that for this distinction we can "trust" in his exoteric or popular writings (1140a2–3). In the process of defending the distinction between production and action, however, he in fact calls attention to their similarities. Both belong to the realm of contingencies, both involve human activity, and both are characteristics (*hexeis*) accompanied by reason. Then he identifies art with making and on that basis distinguishes it from action. But if the line between making and action is not perfectly clear, that between art and action is even less so. Certainly many arts are forms of making, including the very high art of poetry that takes its name from the general term for making. Yet such arts as medicine, navigation, and war produce no products. And what about the architectonic art of politics, which aims at the common good of a whole community and seems virtually the same as the activity of statesmanship?

Aristotle draws a further connection between art and all of the higher activities of soul by describing art as a process of "artfully contriving and contemplating [*theorein*] how something that admits of either being or not being may come to be, of which the principle or source [*archē*] is in the maker and not the thing made" (1140a11–14). This latter formulation raises the question of whether at least some of the arts do not involve a considerable degree of thought, of a kind at least sometimes not altogether different from the thought that goes into science and philosophy. Indeed, as he proceeds Aristotle briefly alludes to the study of how other beings that admit of change come into being, either by "necessity" (1140a14) or by nature: is not knowledge of these processes essential to many of the arts? Immediately afterward he alludes to a necessity of a different kind, now in the realm of human activity and the logic that governs it: since making and action are different, art is "necessarily" concerned with making but not with action (1140a16–17). If science is the understanding of necessities of all kinds, it would seem to have an important role in informing action and all of the arts.

In particular, Aristotle has indirectly brought art and science into close association by treating them together and reversing the order between them in his list in 6.3 and his subsequent discussion in 6.3 and 6.4. Clearly the sciences that rest on induction provide the foundation for many of the arts. Might the arts also provide starting points for the sciences by provoking much or most of the thought that leads to discovery? Aristotle even calls the entire distinction between art and science into question elsewhere in the *Nicomachean Ethics* by using the terms interchangeably (e.g., 1094a6–18, 1094a24–b7), as if they are in fact two facets of a single activity of contemplating and contriving.[18] True, he leads in a somewhat different direction at the end of 6.4 by asserting a kinship between art and chance, citing the poet Agathon's cryptic saying that "art loves chance and chance art" (1140a19–20). Perhaps there is an affinity here inasmuch as many artful practices rest on chance discoveries—but these would be chance discoveries about nature, even natural necessities. There is also a less positive connection between art and chance inasmuch as the arts are often contrivances for diminishing the destructive power of chance—again by allowing us to understand necessities that make it possible to counteract or anticipate and so be forearmed against it. Does art in this way not hate chance as much as it loves it? Or should we say that every artist and all of us are indebted to the spurs of shifting fortune to rouse us to making and to acting and to thinking of every kind, including the actions of moral virtue, the writing of poetry, and philosophizing? We may at least wonder.

ACTIVE WISDOM (6.5)

Aristotle begins the crucial fifth chapter on active wisdom in an unusual manner: "As for active wisdom, we may get hold of it in this way, by theorizing about who we say possess active wisdom" (1140a24–25). Somehow active wisdom is especially bound up both with character and with opinion. In framing this question Aristotle also calls attention to his own theoretical activity. Does he theorize about active wisdom with a different part of his soul than the part that possesses it? But that would mean that active wisdom is itself bereft of the knowledge about virtue and the human soul that it would most seem to need.

He continues,

> It seems to belong to the person of active wisdom to be able to deliberate nobly about his own good and advantage, not in a partial way, regarding what sort of things are conducive to health or strength, but regarding what sort of things are conducive to living well as a whole. A sign of this is

> that we also say that people have active wisdom regarding something when they calculate well with respect to some serious end, about which there is no art. (1140a25–30)

With a certain tentativeness, Aristotle now identifies the end that the person of active wisdom has in view as his own good. He connects this person's nobility with his excellence in thought, a meaning of nobility that we have encountered before and that seems especially serious and solid. And he says that active wisdom comes into play where there is no art to prescribe the right course: as art seeks to address the defects of fortune, active wisdom would address the defects of art. What kinds of challenges are the arts unable to meet that put us in need of active wisdom? Is it the challenge posed by changing circumstances and needs, unlike the controlled conditions of a workshop? But in fact every art requires some adaptation to new demands, and judgment and innovation that could never be reduced to simple rules are essential especially to the more architectonic arts such as war. Does active wisdom, then, take the activity of the arts to the next level, grasping the proper end, value, and limits of each, and combining and deploying them well for the final goal of happiness, which it comprehends as the particular arts do not? Does active wisdom, in other words, govern a single all-encompassing art of living?[19]

Aristotle at least encourages this hope. As he does, he points to a better way of ranking activities, not according to whether they result in a product but according to the comprehensiveness of the understanding that they require and of the choice that they involve. On this basis we could distinguish all of the arts, productive and otherwise, humble and dignified, each of which pursues a limited end merely postulated as good, from the complete grasp of the human good which is active wisdom. Aristotle does not make much of this alternate criterion, however. His reason is perhaps in part that to do so would be to emphasize the high rank of some of the arts and thereby undermine the claim that *praxis* is entirely different in kind from the lowly, instrumental arts. He could say, however, that *praxis* properly speaking is distinguished from every partial art by the fact that it takes its guidance from a complete understanding of the human good, whereas they need not and rarely do. Yet for a reason that is not yet clear, he is reluctant to insist that noble action is possible only for one who has complete active wisdom or that active wisdom entails a complete understanding of the human good.

Indeed, while active wisdom would seem to require deeper thought than any of the arts, it also seems harder to give a clear rational account of its doings than it is for the arts, since, as Aristotle does not quite say but strongly implies, active wisdom governs things whose "principles admit of being otherwise" (1140a33–b2). What he does precisely say is that active wisdom can be neither a science nor an art, yet for both he gives problematic reasons. He says it cannot be a science because matters of action are matters that admit of being otherwise—yet this alone would not exclude active wisdom from being a science in the extended sense, if it grasped and applied the unchanging principles governing changing things, just as biology does. Nor can it be an art, he says, because *praxis* differs from making—but as we have seen, not every art is a form of making. Something prevents active wisdom from being both a certain kind of science and a certain kind of art, but Aristotle has not persuasively shown that this impediment is either its domain in the realm of changing things or its lack of concrete products.

We return, then, to the glancing suggestion at 1140a33–b2 that the problem is that active wisdom's principles admit of being otherwise. This suggestion recalls again the fluidity of natural right, the highest principle governing the realm in which active wisdom operates. And now Aristotle makes clearer than he did in chapter 5.7 on natural right what the deepest element is that changes: "The principles of action are that for the sake of which the actions are undertaken" (1140b16–17). Where active wisdom is especially needed is in a realm in which the ends themselves are mutable. Aristotle points out that pleasure and pain can *seem* to make the ends change—they can indeed make the proper end wholly fail to appear, a problem for those who claim that people who err truly know what is best—and he says that moderation (*sōphrosunē*) is needed to preserve steady judgment in the face of temptations. But why might the ends of action actually change?

Several possible answers are provided by the context. First, Aristotle opened 6.5 by asserting that active wisdom is about seeking one's own complete good, or living well in general: its goal is happiness, but the exact parameters and contents of happiness are elusive and perhaps not simply fixed. Second, unlike the arts, which do have purposes if not products beyond themselves that remain clear, active wisdom governs the *praxis* that is supposed to be itself an end. It is somehow about good and bad but not about any further good and bad beyond itself, and this makes it exceedingly hard to pin down what its principle is. As Aristotle gives his definition of active wisdom in the center of the chapter, he continues to raise doubts about how far it makes sense to consider *praxis* to be truly just for itself, while introducing a third potential reason for the mutability of the principles of active wisdom:

> It remains, therefore, that it is a true characteristic accompanied by reason, pertaining to action and concerned with things good and bad for a human being. For the end of making is separate, but that of *praxis* would not be: for good action is itself the end. For this reason we suppose Pericles and those of that sort have active wisdom, because they are able to contemplate what is good for themselves and for human beings. And we consider that household managers and political men are of this sort too. (1140b4–11)

After calling art "a certain characteristic pertaining to making that is accompanied by true reason" at the end of the previous chapter (1140a20–21), Aristotle now echoes but subtly changes this formulation in calling active wisdom "a true characteristic accompanied by reason, pertaining to action" (1140b5), allowing the word *true* to migrate from reason to characteristic or character.[20] Could it more properly be said of the man of active wisdom that he has a heart that is true than that his mind grasps the truth in the way that a philosopher or even an artisan does? Then, immediately after reiterating his action-production contrast and his claim that action is its own end, Aristotle indicates that a great statesman like Pericles, who seems a model of active wisdom, acted not for the sake of his own action but to secure the good of the city. Or was the existential threat Sparta posed to Athens merely the occasion for Pericles to engage in activity that was really for his own fulfillment? This is not what Aristotle says now, however, nor what Pericles or his admirers would be likely to say either. Was Pericles quite clear on what his highest principle was, or on whose good he most sought to secure? Might it be that active wisdom, governing as it does the highest arts of household management and politics, is inveterately unclear on whether it seeks chiefly the good of oneself, one's loved ones, one's friends broadly speaking, one's whole community, those who are best within one's community, or as much as possible everyone who comes within one's sphere of action? Is it enough to say that active wisdom is concerned with all of these and that one "simply knows" which should take precedence in each new circumstance one faces? Something in that seems right, but the elusiveness of the ultimate ordering principles of the active citizen's self-understanding as Aristotle has been portraying it suggests a deeper imprecision here that is fundamentally resistant to clarification. Yet if active wisdom proceeds without a precise account of happiness, without clarity on whether the practical activity of household management and politics is a final end or is for the sake of some further good, and without clarity on whose good it most seeks, active wisdom is less than fully wise.

This conclusion, troubling as it is, is just the one Aristotle will quietly draw at the end of this chapter. He prepares us for it when he connects active wisdom (*phronēsis*) to moderation (*sōphrosunē*), saying that what moderation preserves (*sōdzō*) is not knowledge but a "supposition" (1140b13) regarding the principles or starting points of action. It is this supposition that we have seen refuses to stay put. Building on this thought, Aristotle then identifies active wisdom as the virtue of one of the two parts of the soul that possess virtue, the "opining" part (1140b26).[21] At 6.1 he divided the soul into scientific and calculative parts; at 6.3 he seemed to improve on this by identifying art, science, active wisdom, wisdom, and intellect not as the soul's parts but as its five modes of attaining the truth, leaving aside supposition and opinion as defective modes of thought that can err (1139a12, 1139b14–18). But now he returns to the idea that the rational part of the soul is divided into separate parts, now not the scientific and the calculative but one that attains knowledge and one that forms opinions. Is it really plausible that we attain knowledge and form opinions with different parts of the soul? Or could active wisdom as now described be the "perfection" not of a rational part of the soul or even of one of the soul's chief rational activities but merely of one of its defective activities or conditions?[22]

Yet despite its connection to mere opinion and to changing things, despite even its susceptibility to corruption by pleasure and pain, Aristotle insists that active wisdom is especially durable: one can forget the chemistry one learned in college, but not active wisdom. This thought is connected to his observation just before, at 1140b21–24, that while there is excellence or virtue (*aretē*) in art, there is not in active wisdom, and while voluntary errors are better to make than involuntary ones in the arts, this is not so of active wisdom: active wisdom is a deep aspect of character, not a tool one can pick up and set down. But how can it be so durable if it is so changeable, and how can something so important depend on mere opinion? Indeed, it is not even completely clear that it fully qualifies as a virtue: in the same section Aristotle compares it to "the virtues" and then calls it "a certain virtue" (1140b24–25): is it after all a virtue in only a qualified sense?

If active wisdom is merely a perfection of ungrounded opinion, yet the opinions in question are deeply ingrained, revered by the authoritative figures in one's community, and hedged round with powerful threats and powerful hopes, it makes sense that it would be both shifting and all but ineradicable. And so what often passes for active wisdom is. But if real knowledge of the human good should be in fact attainable, this might form the basis for a different form of active wisdom, the perfection not of a distinct part of the rational part, still less of a defective condition, but rather of all modes of knowing that bear on action and choice, grounded in a science of human nature and extending to comprise a complete art of living, the work of a single rational capacity of the soul, stable not because it is instilled in us by powerful authorities but because it concerns the good that is of central importance to us at every moment of our lives, which for that reason we cannot truly grasp and still forget. If active wisdom in fact appears in two such different forms, one a shadow of the other, it would make sense that it would appear especially changeable, even if the higher form is in fact virtually incorruptible.

INTELLECT (6.6)

The next chapter gives a remarkably cryptic account of intellect or *nous*. On the surface this chapter confidently assures us that intellect gives unerring access to first principles, but Aristotle's mode of proceeding gives ample reasons for doubt. Returning to his first, more rarified account of science as that which proceeds not from observation and induction but from direct insight into what cannot be otherwise, Aristotle begins, "Since science is a supposition [*hupolēpsis*] concerning universals and of the things existing by necessity, and since there are principles [*archai*] of demonstrable things and of every science . . ." (1140b31–33). Now we have learned to be uneasy at the word "supposition." At 1139b17 Aristotle excluded supposition as a means by which we attain truth since it can be mistaken; three lines later he introduced science with an observation that we all suppose that what we know scientifically does not admit of being otherwise; now he casts an even darker shadow over science by characterizing it as itself a supposition. Science, understood as a process of attaining truth about what exists of necessity, must assume the validity of two kinds of *archai*—the assumptions from which it begins and the principles of reasoning that it applies in deriving conclusions from them. But, Aristotle proceeds to ask, what is it that grasps with certainty these *archai*? Might it be ultimately impossible to attain certainty about the necessities that we intuit but cannot prove, even if thinking cannot proceed except on the assumption that these intuitions are correct? Without either demonstrating that we have access to such knowledge of principles or explaining how we have it, Aristotle simply argues by a process of elimination that "*if* the ways by which we attain the truth and are never mistaken about the things that do not (or even do) admit of being otherwise are science, prudence, wisdom, and intellect, and it cannot be any one of these three—by three I mean active wisdom, science, and wisdom—what remains is that it is intellect that pertains to the principles" (1141a3–8, emphasis added). Does it indeed?[23]

Much is strange here. First, Aristotle simply assumes that we have access to certainty about the starting points of science—even while he calls science a supposition. Second, he merely affirms that wisdom does not include its own starting points—even though he will call this assumption into question in the next chapter. And third, he assumes that the modes of knowing identified in 6.3 provide certainty and together are exhaustive of the ways certainty can be attained—although he silently drops art from the list. This omission might be attributed to the fact that Aristotle has just acknowledged at 1140b22–23 that in art one can err and even err voluntarily.[24] We might have expected that active wisdom would be dropped from consideration as well, since it pertains to what can be otherwise, while the quest of this chapter seems to have been for "the principle of what is known scientifically [*epistētou*]" (1140b33–34)—but instead Aristotle keeps active wisdom in contention and even makes a point of mentioning the possibility of unerring knowledge regarding things that admit of being otherwise. Adding to our perplexity, as Sparshott observes, *nous* in the *Metaphysics* refers especially to god, and in *On the Soul* to intellect altogether: perhaps, as Sparshott suggests, a god and only a god would grasp all truth immediately, intuitively, and with certainty.[25]

What are we left with, then, if we set aside all that is merely affirmed as an assumption or characterized as a supposition in this chapter? Despite the soothing reassurances that Aristotle's most gentlemanly readers will be inclined to trust, Aristotle leaves us doubting whether human beings have an unerring grasp of any first principles, even the most basic principles of thought. If not, the function given to *nous*, in the precise and strong sense here claimed for it, would disappear, and we would be left only with our human art, science, active wisdom, and wisdom to give us such truth as we can attain. If art is really applied science, it does not provide independent access to the starting points of thought, but perhaps all three of the others do, with a degree but never a perfect degree of certainty. Science does so in the function that was mentioned in 6.3 but omitted here, the induction that is the "source [*archē*] of the universals" (1139b28–29) from which conclusions may be deduced.[26] Wisdom does so in its capacity to just "see" certain things that present themselves to us as necessary truths, together with its capacity to reflect on the character of these apparent necessities, as Aristotle does in the *Metaphysics*. And as Aristotle will soon suggest (in a most controversial passage), active wisdom as ordinary moral insight perhaps provides starting points of another kind. Indeed, the most complete active wisdom, as the comprehensive wisdom about the human good and the human condition possessed by Aristotle, may even have some part to play in helping us know where we stand in the cosmos, and in that way rendering more solid the foundations of the other sciences.

WISDOM (6.7)

Aristotle approaches the theme of wisdom (*sophia*) from a surprising direction, by reminding his readers of a common usage of the word *sophia* to mean precision or excellence (*aretē*) in any of the arts. At 1140b21–22 he used the fact that there is excellence in the arts but not in active wisdom as grounds for distinguishing those, but now he suggests that wisdom in one sense is just excellence in art. But, he adds, speaking more generally, "we suppose some people to be wise as a whole and not partially or in some other respect, just as Homer says in the *Margites*: 'But him gods made neither digger nor ploughman, Nor wise in anything else'" (1141a12–16). In none of his extant works does Homer attribute to any of his characters such a comprehensive wisdom as the author of the *Margites* here denies to this one, but he arguably displays it himself through his own shadowy presence in his *Iliad* and *Odyssey*. Was Homer, who with Hesiod gave the Greek gods their names, genealogies, and powers[27] and who in the lines quoted attributes to the gods the making of human beings, wise with the same wisdom as the philosophers, or with a rival wisdom? This Aristotle does not say, but he does put Homer's great theme, the relation between the divine and the human, quietly on the table in opening this most important chapter on wisdom.

With this allusion to a master poet, Aristotle reminds us that art can be high indeed, and in opening his discussion of wisdom with art after elevating both art and wisdom since his initial catalogue of modes of knowing at the start of 6.3, he reinforces our hunch that art and wisdom are in his account somehow a pair. Just as art proves both higher and more comprehensive than it at first seemed, inspiring and deploying all the sciences that provide knowledge of the beings around us and perhaps culminating in an architectonic art of living or in poetic wisdom, so wisdom now comes to sight as more comprehensive than it did at first. In one sense it embodies the perfection of the arts or even the unity of all of them, and in a different sense, which Aristotle takes up now, both knowledge of the sciences and the knowledge of first principles that in 6.6 he attributed only to intellect. Is there a single wisdom, then, that comprises knowledge of all things high and low and good and bad? This is certainly the suggestion of *Metaphysics* 1.1, where Aristotle attributes to wisdom knowledge of all things, including of the good, with the consequence that "the wise should give orders and not be given them" (982a18–19).[28]

But here in the *Ethics* Aristotle immediately pulls back from such a suggestion. If, as the particular attribution of the word *sophia* to perfection in the arts suggests, wisdom is characterized above all by its precision, it must not pertain to the messy realm of human affairs; it unites intellect and science, but only as regards "the most honorable things." For, Aristotle says now, "it is strange if someone supposes the political art or active wisdom to be the most serious thing, if indeed man is not the best of the things in the cosmos" (1141a16–22).[29] But as Aristotle withdraws his claim for wisdom's comprehensive character, he ceases to speak in his own name. "If indeed health and the good are different for human beings and for fish, but the white and the straight are always the same, all would say that wisdom is also the same but active wisdom is different: they would say that that which theorizes well about the good condition for each sort of thing has active wisdom, and they would entrust such concerns to this" (1141a22–26). In this indirect way Aristotle now suggests that wisdom may extend as far as the white and the straight—which, if they are not exalted, at least have something constant and universal to them—but not to the human or the piscine, or at least not to the human and the piscine good, which immediately becomes his sole focus. But is there not available a science of the nature of each kind of living being and what is best for it, including a science of human nature that would serve as the foundation for active wisdom, and would such knowledge not be the same for any intelligent observer? If Aristotle encourages this thought, he at once pours cold water on it. Such knowledge as he now calls "active wisdom" is so far from being a science, so far even from involving reason and deliberate choice, that it is allegedly available to animals: "Hence they say that certain beasts too have active wisdom, as many as appear to have a capacity for forethought regarding their own lives" (1141a26–28). If active wisdom requires not knowledge of nature but only awareness of what is good for each separate being, is this not substantially available even to crafty foxes? Once again we see erupting in a different form the problem of why the active life needs philosophy at all.

Aristotle then reiterates that human beings are not the highest things that exist; he even alleges that it is "most obvious" that, for example, the component parts of the cosmos are "by nature much more divine" (1141a34–b2). Wisdom has nothing to do with human things only if we assume the existence of a realm of things sublime, eternal, unchanging, and unconcerned with human beings, if we confine wisdom to the understanding of this, and if we assume that knowledge of what is eternal and knowledge of the human good can each be complete in itself, independent of the other. All of this is plausible in turn only if there is no intermediate science of biology, part of wisdom but informing human affairs, and no dialectical study of human nature, part of the study of politics but shedding light on wisdom itself. And on both of these latter points Aristotle's account of human knowledge in book 6 falls quietly into conformity, maintaining almost complete silence on both biology and political philosophy. It is as if, in deference to active wisdom's claim to autonomy, he has carefully made them disappear.

Reinforcing the impression of a deep divide between the domains of wisdom and active wisdom, Aristotle proceeds to depict men of wisdom as utterly, even ridiculously impractical in their devotion to the study of things so divine that they have nothing to do with the human good. "Therefore people deny that Anaxagoras and Thales and such wise men have active wisdom, when they see them ignorant of what is advantageous for themselves, and they say that they know things that are extraordinary, wondrous, difficult, and daimonic, yet useless, because they do not seek out the human good" (1141b3–8).

Yet we notice that in disparaging the knowledge of Anaxagoras and Thales, Aristotle is again reporting common opinion and not his own considered judgment. In book 10 of the *Ethics*, where he makes the case for the life of philosophy as the happy life, he cites Anaxagoras as one who rightly saw that true happiness does not require riches or political power, yet who remarked that "he would not wonder" if one who lacks these things "should appear strange to the many," who "judge by external things, since they perceive only these" (1179a13–16). And in the *Politics* Aristotle tells the story of how Thales, when reproached for his uselessness, responded by cornering the market on olive presses in a year when through his observations he foresaw that the olive harvest would be abundant, proving that "it is easy for philosophers to get rich if they want to, but this is not what they are serious about" (1259a5–17). Thales and Anaxagoras themselves thought not only that they were successfully pursuing their own greatest good by philosophizing but that their investigations had implications for politics. Thales predicted eclipses, showing them to be the result of natural necessities and not divine signs, and Anaxagoras taught Pericles that lightning was merely another natural phenomenon and not to be feared as the sign of Zeus's wrath, a lesson that seems to have had important implications for Pericles' conduct of political affairs.[30] Thus the wisdom of Thales and Anaxagoras appears in one way as an alternative and rival to the active wisdom of Pericles, but in another important way as a foundation for it.

The discussion of the wisdom of the early philosophers also raises critical questions about the character and foundations of that wisdom. Again, how did they know that the regularities they found in the cosmos were unchanging—that at the bottom of things really were natural necessities and not willing, loving, hating, rewarding, and punishing divinities? How could they be certain that they were not being foolishly impious? Why is their theoretical activity honorable, and what is the relation between this and the ways in which other things are honored and honorable? What did they learn about human nature, and what implications do their discoveries have for all aspects of life? All these questions point to our need for a wisdom that is comprehensive.

The impression Aristotle is creating for his gentlemanly readers, however, is that the activity of philosophers is remote and pure and indeed so impractical as to be a bit ridiculous; it certainly does not cast any doubt on the completeness of the sphere of *praxis* and the active wisdom that guides it. This impression recalls the device Socrates introduces in the *Republic*, when he asks Glaucon how they can possibly persuade the city that philosophers should rule. "What if this man gets harsh with us, the one who we say opines but does not know, and disputes that we speak the truth? Will we have some way to soothe and gently persuade him, while hiding from him that he's not healthy?" (476d7–e2). Socrates' answer to this question is the doctrine of the ideas—the doctrine that the realms of knowledge and opinion are wholly separate; that knowledge pertains only to unchanging universals and opinion only to the separate realm of coming to be and passing away; that the philosopher is a noble-minded, harmless dreamer preoccupied with his castles in the sky of another world; and yet that somehow he would also make the perfect ruler if the all-but-impossible conditions should come about to set him on a throne. Failing that, Socrates encourages the gentleman to regard the philosopher and his odd pursuits with a mixture of admiration and bemused tolerance, precisely as Aristotle is doing now.[31]

At the end of 6.7 Aristotle returns to the mundane realm of active wisdom, and now he concedes or almost concedes that it, too, must be grounded in knowledge of universal principles, perhaps of human nature or at least of the human good. Yet he does so in a curious way. What he says is that active wisdom needs knowledge *not only* of universals but also of particulars, indeed above all of particulars; thereupon he almost forces a choice between them, in which knowledge of particulars prevails. "For if someone should know that light meat is easily digested and healthy but should be ignorant of what sort is light, he will not produce health; rather [*mallon*], the one who knows that poultry is light and healthy will produce it. For active wisdom is concerned with action. Thus one ought to have both, or rather the latter [*ē tautēn mallon*]. But here too there would be something architectonic" (1141b18–23). This is a difficult passage. Is knowledge of particulars just *more* necessary while that of universals is *also* necessary, as the general drift of the passage and the use of the word *mallon*, which can mean "more" as well as "rather," reassuringly suggests? Or is knowledge of particulars alone really necessary, as the use of "not" before the first *mallon* and of "or" before the second indicate? Does the second individual Aristotle mentions have knowledge of both the universal principle and the particular application, or just of the particular character of poultry as both light and healthy?[32] And what is the antecedent of "the latter" (feminine singular) in line 22? Is it the implicit noun "knowledge" (*epistēmē* or *gnōsis*) possessed by the second individual? Or is it active wisdom itself, grammatically most natural but semantically surprising?[33] Then there would be a shift from considering the relative importance of universals and particulars to considering the relative importance of knowledge of universals and active wisdom, understood as pertaining only to particulars but still having *something* universal about it—if only that it makes an architectonic claim to rule.[34]

ACTIVE WISDOM AND THE POLITICAL ART (6.8)

It is the character of active wisdom as architectonic and not as grounded in universal principles that comes to the fore in the next chapter. "The art of politics and active wisdom are the same characteristic, but the being of each is not the same," Aristotle begins (1142b32–24), using a dark but characteristic expression. For Aristotle, the being of a thing is especially its way of being active in the world; thus he said in book 5 that virtue and justice are the same but their being is not the same, justice being the exercise of virtue toward another (1130a11–13). The art of politics would seem to be active wisdom when exercised toward others. Now, he continues, "As applied to the city, active wisdom as architectonic art is legislation, while active wisdom as concerned with particulars has the common name, the political art, and this is involved with action and deliberation. For a decree is a matter of action, as it is the ultimate thing. Thus people say that only those [who issue decrees] are engaged in political life, for they alone act [*prattō*], just as craftsmen do" (1141b24–29). Active wisdom in the political sense is the architectonic art, manifesting itself now as virtue, now as productive art, and now as action (*praxis*).[35] But the distinction between art and action has become tangled indeed. We might have expected Aristotle to distinguish here the legislative art that governs the production of a constitution or a law for subsequent use from the political actions that are the real stuff of the active life that is good in itself as an end, and that require flexible, intelligent, experienced judgment in responding to new challenges. But instead Aristotle calls both legislation and politics arts, and even though it is legislation that results in a lasting product, it is political action that he compares to the work of a craftsman. The distinction between art or making and action or doing, which relegated the arts to a low, instrumental plane and elevated action to a high sphere of things choiceworthy in themselves, seems to have broken down completely. Or have art and action, beneath the surface, actually exchanged places? For if anything, it is the productive art of legislation that is most sovereign, inasmuch as it has the power to set down an enduring body of laws that will shape a whole people and way of life. The political action that exercises what in modern political science we call executive power, using judgment to apply established principles to new circumstances and carrying out its trust when it faithfully upholds the established constitution, is properly subordinate to the art of the lawgiver or founder, just as the craftsman is subordinate to the architect. Indeed, at its best politics too is engaged in making things—laws, regulations, treaties, institutions, and programs—for the subsequent use of others. It is a high-level art.

But is the truest expression of active wisdom in fact found in either the architectonic art of the legislator or the flexible art of the skilled executive? Aristotle now brings forward a rival perspective, yielding a similar but not identical taxonomy of forms of active wisdom. "But," he begins again, "active wisdom seems most to be that which concerns oneself individually" (1141b29–30). Now instead of a division of active wisdom into "political" and unspecified "other," with the political divided again into legislation and the active art of politics, we have a division of active wisdom into a primary form directed to one's own good and another form divided three ways between household management, legislation, and politics, the latter being divided again into deliberative and judicial forms. Here legislation and politics are presented as coordinate with and not necessarily higher than household management; legislation is not called architectonic nor is the art of politics characterized as the embodiment of action; and the less exalted activity of judging crimes and adjudicating lawsuits is added. At the beginning of the *Ethics* Aristotle expressed the widely shared intuition that securing one's own good is desirable but that securing the good of a whole city or nation is "nobler and more divine" (1094b10). Now, however, he captures an equally prevalent but opposite sentiment: "the one who knows what concerns himself and spends his time on that is held to have active wisdom, while the politicians are held to be busybodies" (1142a1–2).[36] Again Aristotle quotes lines from a lost work of poetry, this time Euripides' *Philoctetes*, in which Odysseus is questioning his own judgment in choosing a prominent role in the army that has drawn upon him so many troubles. In the lines surrounding the ones Aristotle quotes, Odysseus also places the wise among those who leave such troubles to others and implies that humans are unwise to honor the ambitious, who do not know the proper limits of what is good for them and who seek to lord it over others.[37] Is the active wisdom of those who practice the political art after all defective as wisdom? Might the true masters of the political art be private men, as Socrates claimed (cf. Plato, *Gorgias* 521d–e)? To these sharp doubts about the active political life Aristotle makes a lame reply: "perhaps it is not possible for one's own affairs to go well without household management and a regime. Further, how one ought to manage one's own affairs is unclear and must be examined" (1142a9–11). Indeed the former is not possible, but if the political life is a life of troubles, this is scarcely sufficient reason to take it on oneself. And has the whole treatment of the moral virtues not been an examination of how one ought to live? Or is the fundamental character of the good life somehow still eluding us or only now coming to light?

In the last part of chapter 8 Aristotle offers further evidence for "what he has said" (1142a11)—evidently for the high status and unique sphere he has been giving to active wisdom, but perhaps also for the claim that knowing how to manage one's own affairs takes great thought. This is why young people, he says, can possess expertise in geometry and mathematics but not active wisdom, theoretical wisdom, or knowledge of nature. For "the former subjects exist through abstraction, whereas the principles of the latter come from experience" (1142a18–19). Aristotle thus briefly alludes to the sciences of the natural beings in the world around us that he has been leaving out of view. The principles of at least these sciences, he says now, rest firmly in observation and experience, and mathematics itself is dependent on at least minimal experience of the world.

Much more experience is needed to apply practical rules correctly, such as the rule Aristotle gives that heavy water is bad, requiring a grasp of the rule, a correct perception of the particular before one, and correct syllogistic deduction. But, Aristotle says, "active wisdom is not science" (1142a23–24). It must thus consist not (or not chiefly) in syllogistic reasoning of this kind, which many commentators have attributed to Aristotelian moral thought and several criticize as inadequate to the task.[38] Rather than grasping and working down from universals, the focus of science (*Metaphysics* 1059b26), active wisdom begins from and seems largely to remain on the level of direct perception of particulars. As Aristotle elaborates,

> Active wisdom . . . is of the ultimate thing [or ultimate particular: *eschaton*], just as has been said. And the thing to be done is of this sort. And it lies opposite [or over against: *antikeitai*] intellect. For intellect is of the defining limits [*horoi*], of which there is no rational account, but the other is of the ultimate thing, of which there is not science but perception—not that of the individual senses, but the sort by which we perceive in mathematics that the triangle is the ultimate thing. For here, too, there is a stop. But this is more perception than active wisdom is, though perception of a different form from the other. (1142a24–30)

The beginning of this statement is dark, like all Aristotle's statements on intellect in the *Ethics*, but evidently he is assigning to intellect the grasp of the ultimate unprovable principles of thought, such as the principle of noncontradiction, the postulates in mathematics, or the structure of space and time that limits and defines all experience.[39] Apparently at the opposite pole is a different kind of direct perception of particulars belonging to active wisdom, the perception of a particular moral fact such as "striking this man would be wrong." What the objects of intellect and of active wisdom have in common is that they cannot be proven but must simply be seen. The perception involved in active wisdom is analogous not to the eye's perception of color but to something grasped by multiple senses, or by the mind using multiple senses, in common. In *On the Soul* 2.6 Aristotle assigns to this common perception the grasp of such attributes as motion, rest, number, shape, and size. Equally relevant would be the recognition of an object as a particular of a known kind, such as a bird. But now Aristotle is evidently attributing to this common faculty of perception not the simple recognition of one shape, a triangle, but the grasp of the evident but unprovable fact that the triangle is the simplest polygon.[40] And such a fact would appear to be apprehended in much the same way that the axioms and principles of mathematics are, a function Aristotle seemed to assign to intellect. Does intellect grasp the principles of mathematics, then, while a distinct faculty of perception grasps objects and simple facts in both mathematics and ordinary experience, and still another faculty, active wisdom, grasps the truths of morality? Or might it be better to consider all these functions as activities of a single intellect? But in the last line quoted Aristotle still insists on a certain difference: the grasp that a triangle is the simplest polygon is more truly perception, he says, than the grasp that active wisdom provides. Perhaps this is merely because a triangle has shape that the inner eye can more literally "see," but perhaps it is because active wisdom, at least as usually understood, mixes true perception of what is good with opinions that are so powerful as to seem to be direct insight, yet that are not free of confusion.

ACTIVE WISDOM AND GOOD DELIBERATION (6.9)

At the end of 6.8 Aristotle's account of active wisdom focused on its undeniably important power of grasping particular facts, but does it not belong equally or even more to active wisdom to deliberate well toward the right practical conclusion, especially in complex situations in which the right thing to do is not immediately obvious and more than one moral consideration must be weighed? After all, in 6.5 Aristotle identified active wisdom as the virtue by which one deliberates nobly (*kalōs bouleuomai*) about things good and advantageous for oneself as a whole, and of which there is no art (1140a25–28). He takes up now the question of what good deliberation (*euboulia*) is, but he seems to find it surprisingly difficult, especially given that in 3.3 he already gave an account of it, or at least of deliberation (*boulē*). There he defined deliberation as a process of investigation not into ends, which are given by wish, but into that which is conducive to an end attainable through one's own action. Correct deliberation there turned out to be nothing but clear instrumental thinking, no different in kind from the investigation into the way to construct a geometric figure. But if active wisdom is a virtue, expressed mainly in noble deliberation about the human good, it seems that the good deliberation that belongs to it must be something more than this. Clearly it is not knowledge or opinion but a process of thought by which one investigates what has not yet been determined. But neither can it be mere guesswork, Aristotle says, or shrewdness, for this is nothing but skill in guessing. It is rather a matter of reason (*logos*) and thought (*dianoia*), "a certain correctness in deliberation [*orthotēs boulēs*]" (1142b12–16).

On this basis, Aristotle proposes to examine again what deliberation is. Now that we have seen how critically important active wisdom is, will we get a richer account of the deliberation that the person of active wisdom characteristically performs so well? But no; Aristotle instead proceeds without explanation to investigate the different meanings not of deliberation but of "correctness." If the account of deliberation in 3.3 is to stand, then, as an essentially mechanical process of finding means or constituents to a given end, the burden would seem to fall on this correctness to bring the capacity for good deliberation to the level of a virtue. The correctness at work here cannot be mere accuracy in the process of reasoning from end to means, since wicked people too can deliberate skillfully about the means to achieve their ends. Good deliberation is, to be sure, somehow "apt to hit on what is good" (1142b22; cf. 1141b12–14), but hitting on what is good does not define it, for one can do that accidentally through erroneous reasoning. Nor is slow deliberation as such any better than swift deliberation, if both reach the right conclusion.

The problem seems to be that good deliberation is a combination of two things, correct instrumental thinking and a correct grasp of the proper ends, the first of which is not morally good and the second of which Aristotle is consistently reticent in attributing unambiguously to active wisdom. The closest he comes is in the conclusion to the chapter: "If it belongs to those who have active wisdom to have deliberated well, good deliberation would be correctness about what is advantageous with a view to some end,[41] about which active wisdom is a true supposition [*hupolēpsis*]" (1142b31–33). It is not clear, however, that Aristotle is attributing to active wisdom a grasp of the end, rather than merely of what is advantageous for reaching it.[42] Even if he is, he calls what it has a "supposition," which is troubling inasmuch as he earlier excluded supposition from the modes of grasping truth because of its inherent fallibility. To be sure, we have here a true supposition, but this is still not the same as knowledge, let alone the comprehensive, architectonic, firmly grounded and constantly available knowledge that we would hope to find at the bottom of active wisdom. What Aristotle does not say that we would wish him to say is that active wisdom is the intellectual virtue that consists in a complete grasp of the human good: an understanding of what things are good and why and how they should be ranked; an understanding of all the circumstances that may require trade-offs, either deferrals of higher goods to secure more basic ones, sacrifices of basic goods in order to remain true to the higher ones, or judicious compromises; an ability to keep a clear head in weighing all the competing claims that may be made upon one; an ability to withstand the power of pleasures and pains to distort the judgment; and finally, an ability to stick with a reasonable decision once made unless compelling new reasons arise for changing it. All of this Aristotle might easily have said, but he does not. In his example of an error leading accidentally to the right conclusion, he even gives the impression that correct deliberation proceeds through simple syllogistic reasoning. Some of his most sympathetic modern interpreters have therefore set out to supplement what he says here to give a richer account of moral reasoning along the lines I have just suggested, and their interpretations are attractive indeed.[43] But we would do well to consider whether Aristotle has just somehow fallen strangely inarticulate on this most important theme in his master work on ethics, or whether something else is afoot.

ACTIVE WISDOM AND UNDERSTANDING (6.10)

The general dissatisfaction with Aristotle's account so far of active wisdom comes from the fact that we understand it to entail not just instrumental reasoning but good judgment and a capacious, humane understanding of human beings and human affairs altogether. The fact that Aristotle has been emphasizing active wisdom's dependence on both experience and good character points to a special kind of understanding, uniting factual knowledge with moral insight and both with practical know-how, that gives it its rare and impressive qualities. The paragon of active wisdom must know the human heart; he must know how to read people and what to expect of them; he must be neither naïve nor overly harsh in judging their motives. He must understand when to appeal to them with gentleness and when with threats, when with appeals to honor and when with appeals to interest; he must know how to bring out the best in them and when pretty good is good enough. All this involves a special kind of knowledge, possible only for one with a good character. For one must understand both virtue and vice to understand well the human heart, and one must possess virtue to understand it. Whether such a person has studied in a university or only in the school of the public square, he must be a knower of human nature. Aristotle speaks to the relevance of such understanding for active wisdom in the next two chapters, 6.10 on understanding or *sunesis* and 6.11 on judgment or *gnomē*. But he does so in an incomplete way, and in doing so he continues to point as much to the limitations of active wisdom as to its comprehensiveness.

Chapter 10, on understanding or *sunesis*, describes the knowledge involved in judging well the actions of others—the knowledge, we might say, required of a judicious biographer or historian. Aristotle says that understanding differs from active wisdom in that it judges while active wisdom gives commands. But then should we not say, adopting Aristotle's formula, that these two are the same but that their being is different—that is, that they are the same knowledge exercised in one case in reflection and in the other in action? Perhaps not quite; often the impressive intellectual is less impressive on the campaign trail and still less so in office. This may be because to see what compromise should be struck is not yet to know how to negotiate it, or because the man of action must make decisions rapidly without the scholar's luxury of leisure for reflection, or because public pressure can sap a political man's courage, or power can go to his head: hence he has even more need of good character than the one who sits in his private study and sizes him up. For such reasons, as Aristotle said in book 5, "office will show the man" (1130a1–2): high office tests both character and understanding. It would nonetheless seem to be the same understanding of human nature and human affairs that would inform good critical judgment and active wisdom. But what is strange about 6.10 is that Aristotle does not quite attribute understanding to active wisdom or quite call it a form of knowledge.

He does, however, take an interesting step here toward closing the gulf between science and active wisdom. Earlier he distinguished them on the grounds that science is a knowledge of what exists of necessity and is eternal while active wisdom concerns the realm of things that are to be done and hence can be otherwise, and likewise that involve uncertainty and hence require deliberation. But now, even as he reminds us of these distinctions, he mentions medicine as an example of a science.[44] Science does indeed turn out to include the study of natural beings that live and change and die; it even includes understanding the good of those beings, action aimed at securing that good, and deliberation when there are doubts about how best to do so. Is the understanding that is relevant to active wisdom, we wonder again, not a close cousin to the science of medicine, involving just such knowledge and use of knowledge regarding the human soul? Or does it indeed comprise this and much else, since Aristotle brought up medicine to make the point that understanding is not a particular science like that, as if in preparation for saying that it is much broader?

But rather than identifying the specific or comprehensive knowledge that constitutes understanding and that lies at the heart of active wisdom, Aristotle merely says that understanding is concerned with "the things about which someone might be perplexed and deliberate" and "the same things as active wisdom" (1143a6–7). The perplexity he mentions is surely due in part to the fact that happiness is hard to understand and harder to achieve, and in part to the way practical affairs tend to involve disparate goals and conditions that are imperfectly known and impossible to control. But it may also be related to two other features of active wisdom that Aristotle keeps quietly bringing to the fore. First, it is directed to something that both does and does not seem to be the final end: its goal is not quite happiness or the well-being of the political community but just action itself, or "what one ought or ought not to do" (1143a8–9; cf. 1142b28). Second, active wisdom is uniquely bound up with both opinion and the noble. For, conceding now that understanding in a broader sense does pertain to all the sciences, Aristotle observes, "Just as learning is called understanding when one uses what one knows, so is it when one uses opinion to judge about those things with which active wisdom is concerned when another is speaking, and to judge nobly. For 'well' and 'nobly' are the same" (1143a12–15). While knowledge governs the sciences, it is opinion that governs active wisdom and even understanding insofar as it pertains to the objects of active wisdom, and it is not quite truth but nobility that is its standard. Unlike sciences such as medicine that rest on clear-cut knowledge and that can aim at a good that can be fully and unambiguously articulated, active wisdom and its corresponding understanding seem always to have above them a low ceiling of clouds that prevents them from taking their sights by the fixed stars.

ACTIVE WISDOM AND JUDGMENT (6.11)

Closely related to understanding are judgment and sympathetic judgment (*gnōmē* and *suggnōmē*), the dispositions of mind that underlie the virtue of equity. Equity, or *epieikeia*, which is somehow the same as and somehow higher than justice (1137b10–11) and which also, more broadly, means simply "decency," is the fair-mindedness that does not insist on rigid consistency in applying rules; it is able to see in each particular case what is appropriate, giving all the relevant claims and circumstances their proper weight. Good judgment, Aristotle suggests, leads naturally to sympathetic judgment or compassion when an act that would normally be blamed was done under duress or other extenuating circumstances.[45] This line between moral blame and sympathy or forgiveness (*suggnōmē*) has appeared before in the *Ethics* as both important and difficult to draw correctly. In 3.1 Aristotle brought together the thought that sympathy naturally arises when someone acts improperly under pressures "greater than human nature can bear and that no one could endure" with the thought that "some things it is perhaps not possible to be forced to do" (1110a24–26) without resolving the tension. In the same chapter he said that we generally accord sympathy for involuntary acts due to ignorance, yet also he attributed to the most wicked the deepest kind of ignorance of what is best. In his treatments of the particular virtues, sympathy arose in conjunction with gentleness, a puzzling virtue inasmuch as it shares a name with one of its corresponding extremes. The gentle person, Aristotle said, "seems to err more in the direction of the deficiency" of anger, since he "is given not to revenge but rather to sympathy" (4.5.1126a1–3). In fact, Aristotle never adequately explained why any degree of irascibility is good, or if so, what that degree is. As we saw in book 5 and shall see in book 7, sympathy is sometimes accorded to those overtaken by anger or otherwise lacking self-control when the pressures they face are very great, but only if these are pressures felt by most of us. Behind all these problems in drawing the correct line between blame and sympathy is the question of whether and how people's perceptions of good and bad have compelling power over their actions. Is good judgment as Aristotle now delineates it able to pursue this problem to the bottom so as to assign responsibility in a truly rational and principled way? Or does it, with the eye of experience, merely mix moral rigor with sympathy in a way that generally strikes the decent observer as fair?

Instead of explaining precisely how judgment works, Aristotle stresses its close connection to understanding, active wisdom, and even intellect (*nous*), all of which he now says we attribute to the same people and says are concerned with the same ultimate particulars. But then, in an important statement on what has come to be known as the "moral sense," he gives special attention and a new task to intellect.

> And intellect is concerned with the ultimate things at both ends. For the first definitions and the ultimate things are matters of intellect and not reason, and on one hand intellect pertaining to demonstrations is concerned with the unchangeable definitions and axioms, and on the other, in matters of action, it is concerned with the ultimate thing, that is, the premise that admits of being otherwise. For these are the starting points of that for the sake of which one acts. For the universals come from the particulars, and of these it is necessary to have perception, and this is intellect. (1143a35–b5)

The function of simply grasping what is right in a particular case that Aristotle assigned to active wisdom in 6.8 he now seems to be assigning to intellect. Confirming our hunches about the more expansive meaning of the term, intellect would then be not a distinct faculty of insight into the foundations of the most exalted sciences, but rather the mind's power of direct perception in all spheres.[46] And going along with his attribution of moral perception to the high faculty of intellect, and with his now unambiguous statement that moral reasoning does involve an ascent to universal principles, Aristotle makes a dramatic declaration that all of this takes place, or at least is thought to take place, according to nature:

> Hence these things are also thought to be natural, and though nobody is held to be wise by nature, a person is held to have judgment, understanding, and intellect by nature. A sign of this is that we suppose these accompany the various times of life, and that a given time of life is possessed of

> intellect and judgment, on the grounds that nature is the cause of them. Hence intellect is both starting point and end, for the demonstrations start with these and are concerned with these. As a result, it is necessary to listen to the undemonstrated sayings and opinions of the experienced and elders or of those with active wisdom no less than to what is demonstrated. For by having an eye from experience, they see correctly. (1143b6–14)

This is another important but difficult passage. Several editors have suggested that the third sentence is out of place;[47] another objects that attributing "undemonstrated sayings and opinions" to those with active wisdom is unacceptable, since those with active wisdom have real knowledge.[48] The shifting use of the terms judgment, understanding, and intellect, then intellect and judgment, then intellect alone, then active wisdom is obscure. The whole passage is framed in terms of what is thought and what is supposed to take place; and it is particularly curious that Aristotle argues for the natural basis of judgment, understanding, and intellect on the grounds that we suppose them to come with age. Even when they do emerge in maturity, it is not at all clear that this is a natural process in the way that the emergence of permanent teeth and gray hair is. The characteristic moral outlook of the old seems rather to be in part the product of experience, as Aristotle has himself been saying, and perhaps also in part the deepening effect of society's customs and opinions, especially at that time of life when contrary passions are losing their hold and the fears and hopes for the afterlife are growing, as Cephalus illustrates in book 1 of Plato's *Republic*. Still, if there is direct natural insight into the starting points of ethics, would it not in the best cases expand and deepen with experience into a comprehensive grasp of the human good according to nature? If so, should it not provide the basis for a rigorous moral science, in which particular moral truths grasped by intellect would be united through induction into solid principles from which applications could again be deduced, and affirmed by the good eye of judgment? The passage quoted once again holds out hope that this is so, only to undercut it again in the end: what the experienced and old and even those with active wisdom have to offer is after all only "undemonstrated sayings and opinions," not knowledge. And as if to underscore this discouraging result, Aristotle ends 6.11 by stating that this concludes his discussion of what active wisdom and wisdom each are, and reiterating "that each is the virtue of a different part of the soul" (1143b14–17). Active wisdom is merely the perfection of the "opining part" (1140b25–26), or—if we refuse to accept the strange proposition that we opine and grasp truth with separate parts of the soul—merely the refinement of ineradicably defective opinion.

Or might there be something important at work in the curious way Aristotle assimilates intellect to judgment and understanding and active wisdom and then isolates intellect, and likewise in the way he calls only intellect the source of the perceptions that yield universals and demonstrations at 1143b5 and 1143b10–11, and finally in the way active wisdom, which seemed to be concerned with both universals and particulars or perhaps only particulars at the end of 6.7, and seemed to grasp the starting points of morals in 6.8 but has ceded that role now to intellect, turns out to have only opinion? Perhaps intellect, by contrast, does grasp solid starting points in morals as in other things, and in this is distinct although not generally distinguished from a form of understanding that is impressive but not wholly true and from a judgment that is sympathetic and decent but not wholly rational, both guiding something that is considered active wisdom but that does not rise above the plane of opinion, decent and sensible as that opinion may generally be. If all of this is so, it should be possible to construct on the basis of intellect's true insights a science of ethics as solid as any other, beginning from careful observations of human nature as part of nature simply, a study of human needs and human happiness parallel to medicine's study of bodily health. Aristotle has given repeated hints throughout the *Ethics* and especially throughout book 6 that some such project is both possible and necessary. But perhaps it can never be pursued clearheadedly until we have listened with utmost respect to the opinions of the old and reputedly wise, engaged those opinions dialectically, and brought them into critical conversation with one another and with our own deep hopes and fears and yearnings to which they speak. This would explain why Aristotle still insists that we must listen "no less" to the opinions of the old and reputedly wise (1143b13), and even begin with those, as the things most "known to us" (1095b3–4).

If all of this is on the right track, it seems that Aristotle is in these chapters providing signposts for three distinct paths of moral inquiry. One, which turns out to be a false path, consists in attending to the particular moral judgments of what comes to sight as active wisdom or understanding or judgment or perhaps intellect, judgments such as "killing this man would be wrong"; deriving from them universals such as "killing is always wrong"; and then applying them by means of a practical syllogism to further cases. This path is false because it yields rules that will invariably break down in the complex life of active affairs that Aristotle has already said is not reducible to an art, requiring equity and good judgment to correct them. This is the problem with any rules-based ethics for which Aristotle's virtue ethics offers such a promising solution. Aristotle plants just enough signposts to this path to lend credibility to the thought that active wisdom does work on the basis of solid knowledge applied through practical syllogisms, but he allows the path to remain sketchy and ultimately to peter out. It is much better for the good citizen to think in terms of character than of rules, to admire and defer to good character informed by long experience, and to admire and emulate wise statesmen all the more in recognizing that their wisdom is too subtle and complex a thing to be reducible to rules or even to an art. The second path, which would use induction quite differently to create a science of human nature, Aristotle likewise only leaves occasional signposts for, but it will carry us further if we can find it. The third, dialectical path, essential as preparatory work for the second, has been the main project of the *Ethics*, but that project consists not in the words of the book but in the active, ongoing conversation that those words invite the reader to enter into with our wily philosopher.

THE USES OF WISDOM AND ACTIVE WISDOM (6.12)

In the next chapter Aristotle returns to the surface. He continues to speak of active wisdom as wholly separate in source and subject matter from wisdom and, doubtless not coincidentally, begins wondering of what use either is for happiness. One might well object, he says, that if wisdom is confined to unchanging things, it is impractical and contributes nothing to happiness; if one is already virtuous it is not clear what active wisdom adds; and if one is not virtuous one need not possess active wisdom oneself but need only listen to one who has it. And such compliance, Aristotle or his objector now claims, "would be enough for us, just as it is also with health: although we wish to be healthy, nonetheless we do not learn the art of medicine" (1143b31–33) for "we are not more skilled in the relevant actions by possessing the arts of medicine and gymnastic training" (1143b27–28). This is a strange if by now not altogether surprising objection. Even if we do not all need to know the mechanism of a malaria infection, we do all benefit from learning many things about health, which is why good doctors and trainers teach in addition to giving orders. In the active affairs in which virtues are needed and tested, the challenges are great, little is routine, and knowledge both of one's own soul and of human nature generally would seem essential. Stranger still, this objection echoes but runs counter to the argument in 6.1 that launched the discussion of the intellectual virtues in the first place. There Aristotle said that we need more clarity on the target of virtue and on the defining characteristic of the proper mean, and that it was not enough to say "neither too much nor too little," just as one would not know what the body needs if simply told "so many things as the art of medicine commands" (1138b28, 1138b31), suggesting that moral virtue needs guidance from intellectual virtue that is grounded in thorough knowledge just as the medical art is. Finally, Aristotle poses a related but different objection: if active wisdom is the sovereign, architectonic art, it would seem to exercise greater authority than wisdom, even though it is the virtue of a lower part than wisdom is. While book 6 began with a promise to shed more light on both the target and the nature of correct reason, immediately the discussion of the target was dropped and now the need for correct reason itself is under question.

To begin addressing these objections, Aristotle stresses again his division of the soul into separate parts, which now finally are explicitly four: the contemplating, the calculating, the desiring, and the nutritive (1144a1–2, 1144a9–10). First, he says of active wisdom and wisdom that each is choiceworthy in itself as the virtue of one part of the soul. Furthermore, "they do in fact produce something, not as the art of medicine produces health, but rather just as health [produces health],[49] so wisdom produces happiness. For wisdom, being a part of the whole of virtue, makes one happy by being possessed and by being in action. Further, the work is completed in accord with active wisdom and moral virtue" (1144a3–7). The phrasing leads us to expect Aristotle to say that wisdom and active wisdom, each being a part of virtue, each in its exercise constitutes a part of the happiness of the whole human being. This claim, however, he makes only for wisdom, assigning to active wisdom and moral virtue a ministerial role. Does active wisdom, then, ascertain the goal of happy contemplation and the best means to it, giving orders for its provision, while moral virtue provides the good habits that keep the passions in order and obedient to reason? But as if even this were a bridge too far, Aristotle now in a breathtaking retreat suddenly restricts the scope of active wisdom: "For virtue makes the target correct, and active wisdom finds the things conducive to this" (1144a7–10). After eleven chapters of silence, the target finally reappears in the discussion, the target about which Aristotle launched book 6 seeking clarity, and it turns out that active wisdom does not grasp it at all. This is especially striking because Aristotle's guiding question for book 6, prepared by his outline of the soul in 1.13, seemed to have been this: what is it that the rational part sees and commands to the desiring part that the latter obeys when it is virtuous, and how does the rational part determine the proper orders to give? But now the virtue that perfects the desiring part, and that always seemed to need correct reason to guide it to the right mean, is proclaimed to be the guide for reason itself. Is the semirational desiring part, which in 1.13 Aristotle said is reasonable in the limited sense that it is able to hear and to obey the commands of reason as a child does those of his father, wise after all about the end—and wiser than active wisdom itself? Can it somehow make the target "correct" without understanding it? Or do active wisdom and moral virtue turn out to be like two tipsy fellows strolling cheerfully along arm in arm, each saying of the other, "I'm just following him"?[50]

Perhaps matters are even worse: for with this momentous concession that active wisdom does not grasp the end, active wisdom itself seems to begin evaporating. Aristotle returns to the thought that virtuous action involves doing the right things through choice and for the sake of the actions themselves. It seems as if he is preparing to argue, in reply to the question of why one who has virtue needs active wisdom in addition, that listening to someone else's reasonable command is not enough because one needs to have the right purpose within oneself. The problem with this answer, however, is that the right purpose seems now to be already given by virtue, so that reason would be needed only to find the means. "Virtue makes the choice correct, but to carry out what is by nature for the sake of that belongs not to virtue but to another capacity" (1144a20–22). And that capacity turns out to be not active wisdom but sheer cleverness, which the wicked have just as much as the good, and which can find the means to any proposed target at all. Then Aristotle adds, "Active wisdom is not this capacity, but it does not exist without this capacity. But the characteristic does not arise in this eye of the soul without virtue, as has been said and is clear" (1144a28–31). In the context, the eye of the soul cannot be active wisdom as the previous chapter suggested (1143b13–14), for if it were, what could the "characteristic" be that arises in it? The eye of the soul can only be cleverness, and active wisdom the good condition or "characteristic" that comes about in cleverness when guided by moral virtue.[51] Active wisdom appears to be not an entity in its own right, then, or an integrated whole, but something analogous to the "good condition" of a guided missile when being used in a just war, a fortuitous combination of cleverness with virtue.

Also strange is that Aristotle speaks now of moral choice as if the end were almost arbitrary: "For the syllogisms dealing with matters of action have a principle, 'since the end, that is, what is best, is of such-and-such a character,' whatever it may be (let it be, for the sake of argument, any chance thing), but this end does not appear if someone is not good" (1144a31–35).[52] Perhaps, however, this formulation is not so strange if we consider that the end of virtue is precisely to do whatever it is we do "well" or "correctly," and above all to do just this "doing it well" for its own sake. If virtue consists in action for its own sake and if reason contributes not an independent standard of action but merely cleverness in finding effective means, the true end seems to be lost in the clouds. And thus the chapter that was meant to explain what need there is for active wisdom in addition to virtue shows only the need for virtue in addition to cleverness, leaving not only the contribution but the independent existence of active wisdom increasingly in doubt.

VIRTUE REVISITED (6.13)

"So it is necessary to examine virtue again" (1144b1), Aristotle begins the final chapter of book 6. He does not specify what it is we have uncovered about virtue that requires a reconsideration, but the most troubling question that emerged in the last chapter was that of where it gets its guidance. Up until then that source had seemed to be twofold: the good habituation from childhood that shapes the passions to accord with what reason judges good, and the active wisdom that with growing experience sees increasingly well for itself what is good and thus gives the mature adult wise, autonomous direction. Now if active wisdom after all gets its guidance only from moral virtue or well-habituated passions—if it provides no independent standard by which to judge for oneself what is best so as to correct for an imperfect upbringing, or to improve on one's parents' upbringing in raising one's own children—then moral virtue turns out to be less autonomous and dignified than it at first seemed, and indeed incapable of rising above the plane of convention. This is a most grave problem, and one that the nonintellectualists among current scholars never face.

What has gotten us into this problem is precisely Aristotle's determined project of giving every consideration to and making the best possible defense for the dignity and autonomy of the moral life. If the active wisdom that guides it is distinct from and independent of philosophic wisdom, it is left with no other source of guidance than moral virtue itself. But if in turn moral virtue insists that its own activity is an end in itself, to be judged by its intrinsic nobility and not by its success in securing any extrinsic objective, then reason has nothing to steer by and the "for its own sake" formula has left our ship adrift.[53]

In this *aporia* we are driven to consider again an alternative raised by the "Socratic" objector in 3.5. While Aristotle insisted in 2.2 that correct habituation makes no small difference, indeed a great difference, indeed "all the difference," for moral character (1103b23–25), in 3.5 he gave eloquent expression, albeit without explicit endorsement, to an alternative view that one's natural vision of the good is what makes the whole difference for one's character. These two claims are not ultimately compatible. Might Aristotle have been testing the first up until now and in 6.13 be coming around to conclude that the second is after all correct? He does not explicitly engage in such a radical redirection of his project, but he does raise an intermediate possibility that in fact points far in that direction, the possibility that not habituation but some kind of natural virtue might be the basis for true virtue. Aristotle last mentioned nature in 6.11 where he attributed natural vision to the experienced and old or to those with active wisdom: if nature does not make most people wise with age, might it still give to some a true compass that allows them to see and steer toward what is best? Curiously, as Aristotle considers this question, he begins carrying on two conversations simultaneously, one confirming and even deepening the cul-de-sac that his discussion has already led him into, but the other referring to dialectics and making repeated mention of and a striking concession to the Socratic position that virtue is after all just knowledge. Let us try to disentangle these conversations.

On one hand, taking up the idea of natural virtue, Aristotle now grants natural temperament an importance that his account hitherto has not. Yet it quickly becomes clear that this quality is not the solution to our puzzle. Like animals, children do show natural proclivities, Aristotle says—some to moderation, some to courage, and so on (cf. 1117a4–5). But just as animals cannot have real virtue (1145a25–26), so natural virtue in the absence of intellect, like bodily strength without eyesight, is as liable to do harm as good. If, however, the one who has it "gains intellect, it will alter his actions, and the characteristic that previously resembled it will then become sovereign virtue" (1144b12–14). This statement is as important as it is clear: natural virtue cannot give sufficient guidance, but intellect can;

natural virtue plus intellect yields true or sovereign virtue. But then, as if restating the same thought, Aristotle draws an analogy that drives us back into our cul-de-sac. "Just as there are two forms of that which is opinion-forming, cleverness and active wisdom, so what is moral is also twofold, natural virtue and virtue in the sovereign sense, and of these the sovereign one does not arise without active wisdom" (1144b14–17). Just as cleverness is distinct from active wisdom yet resembles it and will become it with the addition of virtue, as we saw in 6.12, so natural virtue is distinct from virtue in the sovereign sense yet resembles it and will become it with the addition, not after all of intellect, but of active wisdom:

cleverness + virtue = active wisdom;

natural virtue + active wisdom = virtue.

Each term of the analogy is clear, but their relation is obscure, for virtue is both an ingredient and a product of active wisdom, and active wisdom is both an ingredient and a product of virtue. They are always a pair, but how are they related if not in a circle that leaves their ultimate source of guidance forever obscure?

Aristotle seems no closer to resolving this than he was at the beginning of book 6, but in fact there are only two possibilities. Either habit-formed or natural virtue gives guidance to an intellect that merely opines that virtue's ends are right and that provides instrumental reasoning to reach them; or natural or habit-formed virtue is guided by an intellect that can grasp the end, determine the best means to attain it, and direct one's energies and actions accordingly. Quietly underscoring the inadequacy of the first alternative even as he restates it in the passage just quoted and will return to it at the end of the chapter, Aristotle takes up the second. Might Socrates be right after all that the essence of virtue is knowledge, or active wisdom understood in a sovereign and not a merely ministerial sense? Perhaps almost.

Aristotle refuses to concede to Socrates that the various so-called virtues all come down to different expressions of a single true virtue, active wisdom, although he agrees that they each arise "not without active wisdom" (1144b20–21). This much, he says, everyone in fact sees, for all call virtue a characteristic in accord with correct reason. But to this universal opinion one small emendation is needed: "virtue is a characteristic not merely in accordance with correct reason but accompanied by correct reason" (1144b26–27). A person is not virtuous if he is merely following the reasoned directives of another; he must have correct reason himself. Nor was Socrates right to think (if indeed he seriously thought) that the virtues were all just so many sciences;[54] they require a certain foundation in well-ordered passions. On this basis Aristotle reaffirms his oft-stated insistence on the inter-entailment of virtue and active wisdom and seems to conclude the discussion.

Yet with this small emendation Aristotle's disagreement with Socrates begins to close. For now, in taking up the "dialectical" argument that the different virtues can appear separately (1144b33), Aristotle grants that this is true, but only of the natural virtues. If virtue in the sovereign sense requires the possession of active wisdom, active wisdom in turn will assure the presence of all the virtues that order the different passions and govern the different spheres of human activity. Aristotle affirms that active wisdom has this unifying power without explaining how it does. If active wisdom is merely the reasoning power that finds the means to an end supplied by virtue, there would be no reason that the individual virtues should not sometimes and indeed often appear separately. If, however, active wisdom is true insight into what is good and why as well as how it may be achieved, it makes more sense that once fully attained it would inform every aspect of life. And so it seems that Aristotle agrees in substance with Socrates and objects only to his rhetoric: Socrates does not stress sufficiently the importance of either good habituation or a good nature in keeping the passions in order so as to keep the mind clear. Aristotle does not spell any of this out; he instead retreats by reiterating that active wisdom is valuable in itself as the virtue of one part of the soul and that while virtue makes the end right, active wisdom secures what conduces to the end. But in his concession to Socrates, he provides a momentous opening for further thought.

Aristotle closes the chapter and book 6 with a final reply to the objection he stated in the previous chapter that if active wisdom is truly the sovereign, architectonic art, it would seem to exercise greater authority than wisdom, even though it is the virtue of a lower part.

> But indeed it is not sovereign over wisdom or over the better part, just as the medical art is not over health: for it does not use it but sees how it may come into being, and it gives orders for the sake of it but not to it. Furthermore, it would be just as if someone should assert that the political art rules over the gods because it issues commands about all things in the city. (1145a6–11)

While maintaining his official account about the fourfold division of the soul, Aristotle now assigns to active wisdom a task that it can perform only if it is one aspect of a unitary intellect. For, he now indicates, active wisdom is indeed the art and science of tending to souls just as medicine is the art and science of tending to bodies, so that they each require a full and precise knowledge of the nature and good condition of their subject. True active wisdom is nothing but wisdom about the human good, actively deployed to achieve that good. Like doctors and statesmen, it gives orders; like the true art of politics, if such exists, true active wisdom must have knowledge of all that comes within its purview, including even the divine. Like what passes for the political art, what passes for active wisdom may indeed be prone to magnifying the importance of its own activity and claiming all honor and all prerogative for itself, but this is to mistake its proper place. For its truest or highest end, Aristotle says now, is not its own activity or the activity of the moral virtues for its own sake, but happiness, which he now begins to identify with contemplation.[55]

TWO FORMS OF ACTIVE WISDOM

It has by now become clear that book 6 contains a dual account of active wisdom. According to the more prominent or "official" account, active wisdom is the virtue of a distinct, opining part of the rational part of the soul, a virtue that has cognizance over things that change and whose principles change as well, that provides guidance in the realm of *praxis* or moral activity, not by independently ascertaining the proper end of action or by providing an independent standard by which to find the mean, but by affirming the end that moral virtue itself posits—the end of noble activity pursued for its own sake, although also for the sake of the happiness of both oneself and one's community—and by finding the best means to this end or these ends in whatever form they come to sight as most compelling. Conventional active wisdom is the perfection of experienced practical reasoning and of the true opinion that informs it.

That opinion is true because it does secure things that individuals and communities truly need; it does pull individuals into activities that are in all sorts of ways good for them, developing capacities, forging friendships, filling life with engrossing challenges, and fostering a spirit of independence. Nonetheless, the understanding that informs conventional active wisdom is merely opinion and is not well grounded. It is shaped by habituation; it distills respectable opinion without seriously challenging it; it takes its sights by "the undemonstrated sayings and opinions of the experienced and elders" (1143b11–12).

When we look back again at the inquiry that launched the discussion of the virtuous life in the *Ethics*, it is in fact not surprising that the principles of moral virtue should have proven so elusive. In 1.7 Aristotle took up the question of what the final good or end or purpose of human life is, and he suggested two ways of going at the question. One was to try to understand the happiness that we seek, taking guidance from our intuitions about the good that comes to sight as most truly end-like, most self-sufficient, and most complete. The second was to ask what the function or work of a human being is. Through an argument that assumed nature's beneficence, Aristotle located that work in some sort of activity of the soul in accordance with reason. It was in this context of focusing on doing our work that he first introduced the *spoudaios*, the morally serious man. Whatever our function is, Aristotle said, fulfilling it means fulfilling it well, with excellence or virtue. And on that basis he argued that the work of a serious human being is an activity in accordance with excellence or virtue. That thought launched the great arc of the *Ethics*. Leaving the questions of happiness and autonomy aside, without determining what our function is or even whether we have a function, and allowing reason to take a back seat as he brought moral virtue to the fore, Aristotle directed all his attention to the question of *how* we do whatever it is we do, and he defined the end as doing whatever it is well or nobly. In so doing, he adopted precisely the spirit of the *spoudaios*, which is to say: what your job is almost does not matter—there are thousands of jobs that need doing, thousands of ways you can contribute that are worthwhile. The point is to do it well or nobly. The *Ethics* has been an exploration of all that is good and impressive but also all that is obscure or confused in the life lived according to this thought.

For the most part, it is an excellent recipe for happiness. Wherever we look there are needs to be met and tasks worth doing. It makes less difference where we turn our attention than how well we do what we have chosen to do. "For the syllogisms dealing with matters of action have a principle, 'since the end, that is, what is best, is of such-and-such a character,' whatever it may be (let it be, for the sake of argument, any chance thing), but this end does not appear if someone is not good" (1144a31–35). The end is in one sense seen well only by the virtuous—it is to do the right thing well for its own sake—but in another sense it is whatever any sensible person might find that needs to be done. We naturally take satisfaction in meeting even simple needs, for ourselves and for others, and especially when we can do so intelligently and well. We are naturally social; we naturally love a good challenge and feel most alive when we are pushing ourselves to improve and reach some goal; what the goal is almost does not matter. If the task is making dinner, let it be a good dinner. If it is teaching children where to put the commas, let us make them masters of it. If it is enforcing bylaws, let us do it consistently and fairly and reasonably so that the quality of life in the city really improves, if only in small ways. Most of the time, in most respects, it is perfectly clear to a well-raised person with a reasonably healthy soul what doing each thing well consists in. And our spirits are higher when we can see ourselves improving—again at almost anything we set out to do, as long as it holds some interesting challenge and is not overly frustrating, but especially if our improvements make us more proud of the person we are becoming. Even our best efforts will often fall short. It may not be in our power to land the contract, cure the patient, or win the war, but whatever our work is, if we direct our chief attention not to the outcome but to doing our part as skillfully, sensibly, and fairly as we can, we have the basis for a life of dignity and in all likelihood of considerable happiness. Directing attention in this way to doing one's part well fosters independence of spirit and considerable freedom from the vicissitudes of fortune, in something of the same way as a philosopher's independent self-respect and detachment from ordinary concerns does for him.

Moreover, such an outlook is good for civic life as well as for private life, and indeed precisely because it is good for private life. The person who believes that happiness is mainly a matter of virtuous activity and therefore mainly under his own control will welcome public service as an opportunity to exercise and hone his virtues, but with his dignified spirit of independence he will not be inclined to bitter partisanship, vindictiveness, and injustice for the sake of acquiring money or power. And with the elevated place he gives to correct reason, he will be wary of extremism and a friend to learning and to thoughtful deliberation.

Conventional active wisdom is the opinion that the moral life as Aristotle has depicted it is best, without a precise account of why. Such wisdom remains within the realm of mere opinion because it remains perpetually hazy on just what its principles are. The problem has turned out to be not so much that it lacks clear principles as that it has too many principles or ends, and hence they seem to shift about. These include one's individual happiness, the common good, the goods of the body, the goods of the soul, action for the sake of benefiting another, action for its own sake, and action for the sake of the noble. Within the latter we further discern multiple possible meanings: the noble understood as a restraint of desire, in itself bad for oneself and good for another; the noble understood as grounding a claim for honor and recompense; the noble understood as the greatest good of one's own soul; and the noble understood as simply, intrinsically best, sublimely free of all dependence on whether it benefits anyone at all. The controlling opinion that makes conventional active wisdom essentially a matter of opinion and not knowledge is that all these principles amount to *exactly the same thing*. It is especially the untethered nature of the insistence on action "just for itself," this highest expression of human spiritedness, with all the expectation and demands that nonetheless inevitably follow closely in its wake, that makes the principle of moral virtue so hard to pin down.

If active wisdom made it its project to resolve the contradictions between these opinions, to test each against experience, to bring each into dialogue with one's deepest yearnings and most closely held hopes and fears and beliefs, and to put what remained into an ordered hierarchy, it could transform its true opinions into knowledge. Aristotle provides provocative material for such a dialectical inquiry and guides us on the first steps of it, yet he leaves it to us to complete it. By doing so, we would also be prepared to resume the original inquiry of 1.7, the inquiry into what the health of the human soul is and what kind of happiness is possible on that basis. This inquiry would stay focused on what is good for us, bearing in mind Aristotle's argument in 1.6 that there is nothing good in itself, but only things good for the particular living beings that exist and for the particular needs and purposes they turn out to have. It would also take with utmost seriousness Aristotle's thought in 3.2 and 3.4 that wish is what provides the ends that choice then pursues. Wishes can be shallow, fleeting, and ill-informed. But a sustained inquiry into the things that satisfy and the reasons why they do and into the desires and satisfactions that remain strongest when moral confusions have been worked through may lead to a different and clearer version of the thought that the function of a human being is an activity of the soul in accordance with reason and with excellence. This standard would now be clearly defined by the natural needs and natural fulfillment of a healthy soul. And Aristotle's concluding remarks in book 6 about the relative ranking of active wisdom and wisdom suggest what he will reiterate in book 10: that through the critical examination and sifting and purging of all that comes to sight as eligible ends in life, contemplation increasingly comes to the fore as the highest and most finally or intrinsically satisfying. If this is so, active wisdom's highest task will be to support and sustain the pursuit of this end.

In sum, behind and beneath the official account of active wisdom as the perfection of a separate opining part of the soul that lacks knowledge of its own principles or ends we can see the outlines of a truer account of active wisdom as the practical activity of a single, unified intellect, neither divided into parts nor itself radically separate from passion, a wisdom about the heart's deepest desires and about how they might best be met. According to this account, it is the same intellect that is at work in the sciences, covering all branches of knowledge and each including its starting points and methods; in the arts as applied sciences, including all the forms of *poiesis* and *praxis*; in wisdom as the comprehensive science of sciences; and in active wisdom as at once the application of wisdom and the architectonic art of living.[56]

Chapter 6

PROBLEMS OF SELF-CONTROL

SELF-CONTROL AND LACK OF SELF-CONTROL IN CONTEXT (7.1)

At the beginning of book 7 Aristotle calls for a fresh start, laying out a new subject for discussion and even resuming the question of method he seemed to dispose of in book 1.

> After these things it is necessary to say, making a new beginning, that regarding dispositions there are three forms of things to be avoided: vice, lack of self-control [*akrasia*], and brutishness. The contraries to two of these are clear: the one we call virtue and the other self-control [*enkrateia*].[1] As for the contrary to brutishness, it would be most fitting to speak of the virtue that is above us, something heroic and divine. (1145a15–20)

Suddenly the range of good and bad kinds of character opens out far beyond the virtue-vice opposition that we have been considering since book 1. Aristotle does not say why a new beginning is needed now. He leaves it until late in his discussion of the new characteristics to reveal the crucial fact that virtue and vice, understood as the consistent and unconflicted pursuit of good or bad principles, are not even the most common ways in which people go right or wrong: the moral life of most people in fact hovers between self-control and lack of self-control, or successful and unsuccessful efforts to resist the desire to do what is wrong, tending rather more to the latter (1150a15, 1152a25–26). Now we feel the full force of Aristotle's observations in 2.9, which he has not subsequently stressed: the great challenge for most people is not fine-tuning their actions to strike the perfect mean, but beating their unruly passions into submission. At the same time, moral virtue itself now appears less than perfect in the light of what Aristotle enigmatically calls heroic or divine virtue. What is it that we have learned in the treatment of the intellectual virtues that prepares us for this momentous turn?

Active wisdom, it has turned out, is twofold. The form of it that guides ordinary moral life has proved to be unclear on its principles, lacking a clear rationale for the moral virtues on the basis of a clear account of human nature and its natural fulfillment, or happiness. Especially recalcitrant to resolution has been the question of precisely how and for whom virtue is good. A strong element of the pull of virtue remains the thought that it is good in itself because it is noble, and a strong element in the popular concept of the noble is the thought that what is noble is to sacrifice one's own good for that of another, which Aristotle has not actively endorsed but neither has he countered in his surprisingly rare references to happiness since book 1 (1111b24–29, 1117b9–11, 1127b17–18, 1129b17–19, 1143b18–21, 1144a3–5). Because virtue's guiding principles are in most cases never reduced to clarity and consistency and often create inner ambivalence, they *both* retain an almost ineradicable pull on us *and* seriously fail to guide us consistently. At the same time, Aristotle's hints about a higher form of active wisdom invite us to wonder what life on its basis would look like, and whether it refers to something truly beyond the human or merely so unusual as to seem to most people inhuman or even divine.

Of the six qualities Aristotle now lays out, the existence and nature of superhuman virtue is least obvious, and he discusses it first. As his example of this new "heroic and divine" form of virtue, he takes the hero Hector. Yet at least in this instance, Aristotle's only example here for any of the six qualities, we have something divine only by analogy or exaggeration, as Aristotle indicates by quoting Hector's mortal father Priam, in grief over his dead son's mutilated body at the end of the *Iliad*, as the source of the thought that this hero "seemed to be the child not of a mortal man but of a god" (1145a20–22; *Iliad* 24.258–59). Of course this is odd praise coming from Hector's own father, and of course an immortal god would be fearless in quite a different way from that of even the best of humans: the gods presumably possess not the moral virtue of courage but invulnerability. What is it that allows the most divine-seeming human to approach in outward demeanor the calm that comes of having nothing to fear? Aristotle has spoken of Hector before, in his initial discussion of courage in book 3. Yet there Hector exemplified not perfect courage, the steadfastness in battle that the noblest man chooses for its own sake for which Aristotle gave no examples, but only the defective virtue of political courage, rooted in the love of honor and the fear of shame (1116a23–26, quoting *Iliad* 22.100, 8.148–49; cf. 18.249 ff.). Political courage in fact has proved to be a complex phenomenon, but to the extent that it rests on a sense of honor and shame, it seems less a true virtue than an instance of Aristotle's new category of self-control or difficult self-overcoming. In calling the highest virtue divine, Aristotle evokes again the hope that in perfect moral virtue we may find a perfect, sublime, tranquil, self-sufficient, and unassailable happiness, a hope that he earlier evoked in his praise of the life of politics at its highest (1194b7–10). Yet even as Aristotle does this now he reminds us of the earthy nature and struggles at self-overcoming of his exemplar Hector, and of the way in which his father even in grieving him is not fully facing the truth about his mortality and is perhaps dimly hoping that somehow he may still escape the bitter gloom of Hades. In 10.7 and 10.8 Aristotle will say that the gods have no share in moral virtue, and he will hold up the very different life of philosophy as the human life that most truly partakes in divinity. But will this hope prove more solid than Priam's, or is it, like his, a child of the inability to come to terms with the inescapable limits mortality imposes on us?[2]

At the opposite pole from divine virtue Aristotle puts brutishness, which likewise has both literal and metaphorical meanings. The word is used to designate certain natural qualities of animals that cannot properly be called vices but that resemble base qualities of humans; it is also used to describe human perversions that arise through barbaric customs or disease, as well as an extreme degree of ordinary human vice. What seems most brutish in humans is that which accords least with reasoned choice, the drive of blind habits or urges of such destructiveness that they appear monstrous to healthy human beings. Aristotle's examples are people who eat ashes and women who cut out and devour others' unborn children. If any acts are truly devoid of reason, they are these. By showing the horrifying character of such deeds, Aristotle lays the groundwork for his argument that most of what we consider unreasonable behavior is in fact driven not by simply blind impulse but by desires bound up with judgments, however obscure and inadequate, about what is good.

With this sixfold schema Aristotle adopts the traditional image of man as a being between the brutes and the divine, portraying him as one who partakes in a limited way in the nature of both, and yet whose distinctive character is shared by neither, since only man is a moral being in the fullest sense.[3] While beasts have little awareness of death and no share in virtue and vice, being incapable of reasoned choice, divinely perfect beings would have no need for the moral virtues that are called forth by adversities, conflicts, and doubts. As Aristotle puts it, the quality of the gods is something "more worthy" (*timiōteron*) than virtue (1145a26), echoing his statement in 1.12 that while human virtue calls for praise, the highest things, such as happiness and the gods, are beyond praise and are simply blessed (1101b10–27; cf. 1101b28–31 and 1178a1). That reference supports the thought that what is most perfect, even in human life, is beyond moral virtue.

Aristotle's reference to the brutish and the divine also calls to mind a similar passage in *Politics* 1.2, where he lays out his famous thesis that "man is by nature a political animal" and concludes,

> The one who is incapable of participating or who needs nothing because of self-sufficiency has no part in the city, and so is either a beast or a god. By nature, then, there is an inclination in everyone toward such a partnership. And yet the one who first established it is the cause of the greatest of goods. For just as man when completed is better than the animals, so too when separated from law and justice he is the worst of all. . . . He is the most impious and savage without virtue, and the worst with regard to sex and food. But justice belongs to politics. (1253a2–3, 1253a27–33, 1253a35–37)

Here, more explicitly than in most of the *Ethics*, Aristotle acknowledges the dependence of virtue on law and compulsion. The very best citizens, like Hector, may be governed chiefly by shame and honor, but ultimately it is not even these but the awesome power and authority of the law that allow human beings to live together in numbers large enough to sustain civilized life. To the extent that law-bred virtue requires continued social pressures and especially legal sanctions to sustain it, it is not true virtue but mere self-control. Can law do for some more than it does for Hector and his men and set at least a few on the path to loving virtue for its own sake? Or does this passage in the *Politics* taken together with book 10 of the *Ethics* suggest that what we are seeking is in fact an unstable and vanishingly rare middle ground, and that anyone who attains a truly self-sufficient virtue has already left behind the distinctively human horizons of the city and has become in a crucial respect akin to the divinity, living a life devoted not to practical affairs but to an activity more self-sufficient and truly end-like such as philosophy? If so, it would seem that moral virtue hovers uneasily between law-bred civic virtue and philosophic virtue, striving incompletely to transcend the former but falling short of the latter.

Aristotle makes clear that his main interest in the first half of book 7 is in self-control and its failures, and his introduction of sub- and superhuman vice and virtue is meant to put this problem in better perspective. The resulting sixfold hierarchy of characteristics, when arranged from best to worst, shows at each step either a decreasing clarity about what is good or a decreasing capacity of reason to prevail. Aristotle said in book 3 that ignorance of what is good is present in all vice. Now he returns to that thought to explore the question of whether knowledge of the good is sufficient for virtue and what happens when either knowledge or true opinion seems to be ineffective. And immediately he takes up the relation of virtue to an element in morality that he has not yet discussed, especially relevant to self-control but possibly also to much or all of what passes for virtue in real moral life on the ground: strength or steadfastness of soul. He describes these qualities in visceral terms that emphasize their close resemblance to brute strength and bodily frailness. "It is necessary to speak about the lack of self-control and softness and delicacy, and about self-control and steadfastness [*karteria*]," he says (1145a35–36), adding that they are closely related to vice and virtue, respectively, belonging to the same genus if not the same species.

Aristotle also offers a new statement on method as he begins his treatment of self-control and its absence and related characteristics.

> Just as in other cases, after positing the phenomena and first raising perplexities about them, one ought in this way to bring to light especially all the received opinions about these experiences [*pathē*], or if not, the greatest number and most authoritative of them. For if the vexing questions are solved and the received opinions remain standing as well, then the matter would be adequately explained. (1145b2–7)

Curiously, Aristotle calls the phenomena to be studied *pathē*, as if to raise the question of whether lack of self-control and even self-control itself might somehow be less than fully voluntary. As in his investigation of happiness and moral virtue in book 1, so in his investigation of these phenomena he begins with common opinions, which seem to provide the best path of approach to what is good and bad for the human soul. He offers no assurance that any given opinion or group of opinions about the phenomena, however prevalent, will prove true. But his method does imply a confidence that our nature is never wholly obscured from us. Clarity comes by finding the tensions between and within ordinary opinions and developing a comprehensive account that does justice to the insights and concerns at the bottom of each, while showing the confusions that can explain the contradictions.[4] If the result is a comprehensive account of what it means to live well, and if a thorough understanding of such an account results in a life that is happy, we will have a satisfactory moral philosophy, the most satisfactory that is possible for us. If not, there are things that still need to be understood.

However, we note several differences between this statement of method and Aristotle's earlier ones. First, Aristotle no longer stresses the necessary imprecision of moral and political matters, as he repeatedly did in books 1 and 2. Will his account of self-control and its failings be more precise than the one he gave of moral virtue? Second and perhaps related, he never says here as he does in book 2 that we are philosophizing not for the sake of knowledge but in order to be good (1103b27–28)—perhaps only because we should be aiming higher than the mere self-control that is the focus of 7.1–10, but perhaps also because this section will be delving into questions of more fundamental philosophic interest. And related to this last point, we note finally that now some of the opinions to be examined are those of Socrates. We must watch closely to see how many of the non-Socratic opinions will indeed be left standing, for it may well be that the truth about self-control is especially far from common opinion, and even that lack of self-control as ordinarily understood does not exist.

What, then, are the opinions to be examined? Aristotle closes the first chapter with a statement of six of them. First, "self-control and steadfastness seem to be serious and praiseworthy, and the lack of self-control and softness are base and blameworthy" (1145b8–10). Somehow the moral aspect of these qualities is more evident than their precise character, or gives us the first clue to their character: common opinion, at any rate, considers self-control and its failure to be inextricably bound up with moral and immoral actions, and not merely with the successful or unsuccessful adherence to what is advantageous. At the same time, common opinion may well exaggerate the praiseworthiness of self-overcoming and find most moving the moral actions that require the greatest struggle; to many people the calm harmony of true virtue may look tepid and insufficiently heroic. Especially interesting is the moral status of that quality that seems integral to self-control, steadfastness. Is there a difference between the strength or tenacity that lies at the root of self-control when it holds people to a moral course of action and that which holds them to a merely advantageous course—or indeed a foolish one?

Second and third are two closely related opinions. The man of self-control abides by the results of reason or calculation, and the one who lacks self-control fails to do so. And "the person who lacks self-control, knowing that what he does is base, acts on account of passion, but the self-controlled person, knowing that his desires are base, does not follow them on account of reason" (1145b12–14). Common opinion assumes, then, that knowledge is present in both self-control and its opposite. This assumption about knowledge is the most important opinion that Aristotle will query here. Common opinion also assumes both that passion is able to overcome reason and that reason is able to overcome passion, leaving it unclear what gives each this power and what determines which will prevail. Common opinion further assumes that reason takes the noble side whenever one struggles with oneself. But is this always true? Or does reason sometimes counsel what is expedient, while it is the heart that prompts one to make noble sacrifices?[5]

Fourth, it is generally agreed that the moderate person must have self-control and steadfastness, but whether the self-controlled and steadfast person is necessarily moderate is disputed. Yet Aristotle himself concedes neither, for while in his account self-control involves resistance to temptation, moderation involves such a degree of habituation and inner harmony that desire does not oppose what is noble. But then why is this confusion so prevalent? Might there be some important truth glimpsed by the intuition that virtue always requires self-overcoming?[6]

Perhaps the most serious disagreement among the common views of self-control and lack of self-control regards their connection to active wisdom, for in the fifth place, some assert and others deny that a man of active wisdom and cleverness can be uncontrolled. Socrates is the most prominent of those who argue that it is not possible to be wise about what is good and yet fail to do it. If possessing active wisdom necessarily implies doing what is right, does active wisdom consist only in an especially clear insight into what is best, or does it also involve a subrational strength of soul?

Sixth and finally, there is a question about the domain of self-control and lack of self-control, for these characteristics seem both to apply to the same objects as moderation and immoderation and to cover as many spheres of life as virtue and vice themselves. The most salient conflict that shows self-control or its failure is the clash between the noble and the pleasant. Sensual pleasures and comforts are the most obvious enemy of good resolutions because in their vivid immediacy they loom larger than they should, often eclipsing both nobler and more prudent considerations and skewing judgments in favor of present over future goods. It is especially considerations of duty that seem susceptible to the derailing allure of pleasure, but other ends can be subverted by pleasure, and passions other than desire can thwart good resolutions. Hence Aristotle notes that lack of self-control is also thought to exist in regard to anger, honor, and gain. Does this extension to other passions cover all the passions with which virtue and vice are concerned? Will the virtuous man in each case do easily what the self-controlled man will do with a struggle? The most conspicuous absence from the list of relevant passions is fear. This absence accords with our suspicion that courage itself is or always entails self-control; it also points to the question of how completely it is possible to replace self-control with perfect virtue in all spheres of life, and the extent to which something like courageous self-overcoming may always remain necessary.

PROBLEMS AND PUZZLES REGARDING SELF-CONTROL (7.2)

Aristotle turns in the next chapter to the problems that can be raised about self-control, in the process introducing more important opinions about it. First and most fundamentally, he asks, how is it possible for one with a correct assumption (*hupolēpsis*) about what he should do to fail to act upon this assumption? The question as he phrases it at 1145b21–22 covers both knowledge and true opinion under the general class of *hupolēpsis*: it is not only knowledge that presents a difficulty. Aristotle first cites Socrates' argument in the *Protagoras* that when knowledge is present, it must be sovereign and cannot be "dragged around like a slave" by anger, pleasure, pain, eros, and fear (352b–c). But Socrates in the *Protagoras* goes still further, as Aristotle observes, to assert that "no one who either knows or *believes* that other things are better than the ones he does, and possible, proceeds to do these things, since better ones are available" (Plato *Protagoras* 358b–c).[7] This means that one's prevailing judgment about what is good is always sovereign, that every wrong action results from a failure of understanding, and that lack of self-control as we normally think of it does not exist.[8]

It is the chief task of the first half of book 7 to consider the most obvious, massive objection to the Socratic thesis: if people always pursue the good as they understand it, how do we account for the universally familiar moments when we think we know what is best to do, not only most respectable but truly best for ourselves, and yet we do something else, something indisputably more foolish, petty, mean-spirited, lazy, or unhealthy? This exasperatingly common experience seems to prove that it is not insight but some subrational strength of soul that makes most of the difference between better and worse human beings. Thus Aristotle takes up the Socratic thesis in a critical spirit: Socrates claimed that *akrasia* does not even exist, he says, and "that no one acts in the belief that he is acting against what is best, but in ignorance," but this claim "clearly contradicts the phenomena" (1145b26–27).[9] At the least, if failures of self-control are due to ignorance, it is ignorance of a strange kind that needs explaining, for "it is clear that before he is in the grip of passion, the one who acts without self-control does not think [that what he is about to do is good]" (1145b30–31).

Some people agree only in part with Socrates' contention, Aristotle observes. They agree that nothing can vanquish knowledge, but they insist that one can act against one's own opinion of what is best. The position of these semi-Socratics depends on the distinction between knowledge, which is assumed to be invariably held with perfect firmness, and mere opinion, which is considered weak and doubtful and hence open to violation.[10] Aristotle will direct his main fire not against Socrates but against this seemingly sensible qualification of his position. But in fact, his refutation of it will vindicate Socrates' more radical, counterintuitive claim that even our erroneous opinions about what is best always prevail in action.

The initial objection Aristotle mounts against this position is a moral one. If the only thing an uncontrolled man violated were a weak, doubtful opinion, the sort of opinion one holds when one is of two minds about something, we would not blame him as we do for following a strong desire. But we do blame him: this was the first of the "phenomena" Aristotle laid out in 7.1. This blame for lack of self-control always presupposes that the person really "knew better." But to have thorough knowledge of what is good is to have active wisdom, and, Aristotle says, "no one would ever say that it belongs to the person of active wisdom to voluntarily do the basest things" (1146a6–7).[11] If the uncontrolled man is truly culpable, he must violate an understanding of what is good that is somehow both clear and ineffective, and what this knowledge or opinion might be remains a mystery.

With this argument, Aristotle casts doubt on whether the lack of self-control is in fact as bad or as morally blameworthy as people usually think. With the next several arguments, he will go on to raise problems that call into question the merit of self-control. The first of these spells out the error in the common opinion that self-control is identical with or even overlaps with moderation, for self-control implies improper desires. Indeed, continuing to reason from the assumption that self-control is something praiseworthy, Aristotle says it must be the restraint of base and strong desires, since there is nothing impressive about controlling impulses that are either good or weak. He thus brings out the paradox that the more impressive people find an act of self-control, the more baseness of passion and inclination it presupposes.

Aristotle then raises another difficulty about common views of self-control that serves to reinforce the sense that it may be something less impressive than we imagine. "If self-control makes one abide by every opinion, it is base, for example when it makes one abide by even a false one. And if lack of self-control induces one to abandon every opinion, it will sometimes be morally good" (1146a16–19). Aristotle gives the example of Neoptolemus in Sophocles' *Philoctetes*, who is persuaded by Odysseus to try by treachery to deprive the crippled Philoctetes of his bow and then finds that he cannot bear to persist in his deception. While Neoptolemus shows how abandoning a resolution can on occasion actually be praiseworthy, Philoctetes himself is a clear example of unwise steadfastness, in clinging so stubbornly to his bitterness and hatred of Odysseus that it takes the miraculous intervention of Hercules to persuade him to relent, rejoin the Greek forces, and allow his wound to be cured.

Indeed, Aristotle says that the sophists sometimes make the paradoxical argument that folly combined with lack of self-control produces virtue, because folly causes a person to aim at what is bad, but lack of self-control makes him do the opposite of what he thinks he should (1146a21–31). Aristotle implies that the sophists' only motive in making such arguments is a desire to confuse people and show off their cleverness, but we may wonder whether there is not a serious thought here as well: to the extent that ordinary moral scruples are bound up with unreasonable prejudices, like Huck Finn's scruples about helping Jim run away from his master, those who cannot adhere to these opinions may betray a better nature or a greater awareness of what is naturally good than others have. Neoptolemus does something similar when he falls away from his resolve to pursue honor, understood conventionally as mere fame, and follows instead his own deeper sense of honor and his compassion for Philoctetes. The sophists' paradox raises the serious question of whether the self-control that we praise is in itself a unified quality of the soul or just a fortuitous combination of conventionally correct opinion with a steadfastness that is in itself little better than mulish stubbornness.

Yet in another sense steadfastness would seem to be the most important foundation for any character development or correction. A person with bad opinions but great steadfastness in following them is vicious, yet Aristotle observes now that bad opinions may at least be changed, whereas an inability to hold to one's opinions seems beyond the reach of any help that reasoning or persuasion can offer (1146a31–b2).[12] What use is it to persuade someone that he ought to be steadfast if this only adds another item to the list of things he thinks he should do but cannot? This question leads to several further ones. First, is it really impossible to learn steadfastness? Is it a simply intrinsic, simply subrational quality, so that it is a matter of chance whether it arises to support true opinion or even knowledge? Is it even a single thing? For in fact it might be best to distinguish two forms of steadfastness, one a closed stubbornness rooted in an awareness of weakness, and one a proactive and flexible doggedness rooted in an awareness of strength. Persistence in pursuing whatever one judges to be worth pursuing does require a willingness to endure pain and an ability not to be unstrung by it, either innate or acquired by training. But even this ability is perhaps not simply subrational; it seems to involve opinions about what is worth risking for what and about one's own capacity to make the best of whatever fortune or inquiry may turn up. Especially for making progress in philosophy, such opinions seem to be a critical prerequisite.

The last problem Aristotle raises casts further doubt on the idea that steadfastness is a simply fixed, subrational quality. What does it mean, he asks, to call someone unqualifiedly uncontrolled? If people could be shown either to adhere to all of their opinions and resolutions, to abandon all of them, or to abandon one as readily as another, then self-control would seem to be a basic element of temperament, not easily amenable to change. But if, as seems the case, every uncontrolled person has particular weaknesses and remains capable of self-control in other respects, lack of self-control may have more to do with the strength of particular passions or the inadequacy of the reasoning by which one tries to govern them and less to do with a generalized weakness of soul.

These conflicting views, then, are the puzzles that Aristotle sets out to resolve. By disposing of some of these views, he says, he will put others on a sounder footing.

LACK OF SELF-CONTROL AND KNOWLEDGE (7.3)

Aristotle begins to answer these puzzles in the next chapter by identifying the most crucial questions to be addressed in this section of his study.[13]

Does the uncontrolled person act knowing that what he does is wrong, and if so, knowing it in what sense? What is the domain of self-control and lack of self-control? And is self-control the same as steadfastness, or different? He begins with the second, answering that self-control and lack of self-control in the primary sense have the same domain as moderation and immoderation—situations involving pleasure and especially sensual pleasure—but they involve a different way of going right or wrong. The immoderate person "is led by choice, supposing one should always pursue the pleasure of the moment. The other does not suppose so, but pursues it nonetheless" (1146b22–24). Common opinion is correct, Aristotle indicates, in viewing self-control as having an especially close connection to moderation. This suggests that the lack of self-control as Aristotle understands it is not a generalized weakness of soul (much less of "will") but a specific weakness involving pleasure and pain. Since pleasure and pain are important for all of the moral phenomena, however, self-control as regards bodily pleasures will prove to be a focal case of a broader failing that can appear in any aspect of moral life. By seeing more clearly what happens when pleasure overcomes correct reason, we will better understand reason's power and the limits to its power in the soul.

Aristotle now takes up and rebuts the modified Socratic view that passion can override opinion but not knowledge.[14] On one hand, he rejects the view that opinion is easier than knowledge to override because opinion appears more doubtful: false or poorly grounded opinion may be held as firmly as knowledge is. On the other hand, he is unwilling simply to rule out that failures of self-control may involve the violation of knowledge itself as well as opinion. If he agrees with Socrates that knowledge is not precisely "dragged around" by passion, still he observes that knowledge can fall strangely silent and can fail to reach, with any conviction at all, the most obvious applications of its universal premises to specific cases. Since the firmness with which opinions are held does not seem to correlate with their truth or even with the consistency with which they are ultimately followed, Aristotle sharpens the challenge of explaining how *any* violation of one's own convictions is possible and what determines whether they are followed.

To begin to answer this challenge, Aristotle sketches several ways in which the knowledge that one possesses may in fact not be available and usable; all of these will apply as well to opinions. Sometimes one simply fails to consider the relevant principle, or "forgets oneself" in the passion of the moment. "But since we speak of knowing in two senses—for both the one who has and does not use knowledge and the one who is using it is said to know—there is a difference between having but not contemplating what one ought not to do, and having and contemplating it" (1146b31–34).[15] The latter would be strange and in need of explanation, Aristotle says, but not the former.[16] Commentators and translators have shown uneasiness about Aristotle's use of the word *theōreō*, "to contemplate," in such a practical context, and they render it "to exercise."[17] But Aristotle is stressing the connection between theory and practice in this chapter, suggesting both that active effort is essential to clarity of thought and that contemplating what is good and seeing it clearly necessarily sets us in motion.

Perhaps more often, the principle is at least dimly grasped, but it remains unapplied to the case at hand. One may know a universal premise, for instance that dry food (or, we might say, food that is low in trans fats and rich in complex carbohydrates) is good for human beings. One may also know the pertinent minor premises, that a certain kind of food is dry, and of course that one is oneself a human being. But for this knowledge to be efficacious, one must draw the conclusion that this particular food is healthy and use it in making the present choice (1146b35–47a7). One might, in choosing a hamburger and fries over a kale salad, forget what one knows about nutrition, but this is not normally the problem in failures of self-control.[18] Rather, one never bothers to carry through the reasoning process to reach an easily achievable conclusion, or the proper conclusion simply does not seem good to apply in the present case. One deceives oneself; one makes exceptions. "I care about being healthy and I know I must lose weight, but just not right now," one thinks. If there is a cognitive failing here, it is the failure to see that the only meaningful way to uphold a principle is to apply it at *this* moment, and that one's life and character are defined by nothing more than a succession of such moments. Or one treats oneself as a special case: adultery is wrong, but perhaps not quite wrong for those who are truly in love. In Aristotelian terms, the applicable principle remains on the level of universals and is never properly carried down to the level of ultimate particulars. Aristotle concludes that it is not surprising if an uncontrolled man knows in some sense what he should and should not do, but that it would be astonishing if he made the correct application of this knowledge to the present case and understood its significance, and nevertheless acted against it (1147a8–10). In other words, even while an angry man may know that assault is wrong, he does not fully grasp that attacking this infuriating scoundrel right now is wrong as well.

There is a third way in which people can have knowledge that fails to prevail. Not only can they neglect to consider or fail to apply the knowledge they have, but the knowledge itself may be abstract or merely formulaic. Like those who are asleep or mad or drunk, Aristotle says, people may even "state the argument that proceeds from knowledge," but without any more understanding than a sleepwalker repeating verses of Empedocles, or a beginning student reeling off mathematical formulae (1147a10–22; cf. 1142a11–20). In addition to the literal meaning of the three conditions he mentions here, we may consider the way Socrates uses sleep as a metaphor for the dulled perceptions of those who lack self-awareness and fail to face the truth of the human condition, and the way intoxication can come not only from alcohol but from erotic and spirited passions that fire hopes and illusions of self-importance; madness is the end of the road of both conditions. In such states, concerns beyond the present desire may be recognized by the mind, but they lose their force, almost as if they were someone else's concerns. One may even hear oneself saying, "I know I should not be doing this," but these words are only words, devoid of persuasive power, severed from any deeper understanding of the meaning of one's act for one's whole life and character. This cigarette, this piece of cheesecake, this intoxicating evening of love seems to contain happiness itself. "I'll pay for it later," one thinks, meaning perhaps I won't have to pay for it at all. Who knows? Life is uncertain. "I may regret this," one says, but obviously one is not regretting it right now; there is no sense that some alien spirit is moving one's arms and legs toward a goal that is not one's own. Instead, there is a strange dissociation between the "I" that is fully present now and that future person who may regret it, somewhere and someday. In such a state one is not truly awake.

Thus Aristotle delineates a strange and strangely important middle ground between ungrounded true opinion and fully effectual knowledge. Between the carpenter who can apply the Pythagorean theorem to get a right angle without being able to prove the theorem and the geometer who thoroughly understands it is, as it were, a student who can prove the theorem but keeps losing his grip on it just when he most needs to use it. And in moral matters even the most serious people, even serious students of philosophy, can easily remain such beginners. It is simple to grasp in a way the idea that excellence of the soul in accordance with reason is the core of happiness, but it is hard to imbue one's whole soul with that principle. Socrates speaks in the *Theaetetus* of students who seem to make amazing progress in learning, to the point of being able not only to recite conclusions but to reproduce whole arguments and carry out Socratic-sounding refutations of others—but who then forget or reject all that they seemed to learn.[19] Less drastically, many who study Socratic philosophy have had the experience of seeing clearly that anger is irrational, but whenever they really need that insight, it flies out of their hands.

Why does this happen? The problem, Aristotle reveals now, is that where knowledge of good and bad is concerned, grasping with the mind is not enough. Such knowledge "must grow to be a part of one, and this requires time" (1147a22). The error of the partial Socratics is to think that what makes knowledge effective and prevents true opinion from being consistently effective is merely the extent to which one understands the theoretical basis for one's beliefs. Aristotle suggests that such theoretical knowledge is not sufficient: not only must it be integrated into a complete understanding of the world and of oneself, but it must penetrate and transform the passions. New understanding must be brought into dialogue with passions that resist that insight and want to hide from it, and those passions must be given their full weight and not dismissed out of hand. Only when we understand fully the depth of those countervailing passions, only when we see fully the absurdity and weakness inherent in the irrational hopes and wishes that oppose our insights, and only when we practice again and again bringing insights to bear on the passions, do these recalcitrant forces begin to lose their hold on us. Fully assimilating such knowledge can take years, and until that happens the knowledge is always vulnerable, not to being refuted but to appearing simply irrelevant in the heat of the moment. This process is akin to the process Socrates describes in the *Meno* of tying down correct opinion so that it stops running away like the statues of Daedalus and thereby becomes real knowledge.[20] Thus what Socrates refuses to call knowledge at all Aristotle treats as knowledge only in a sense, which one possesses only in a sense. But both see the same need for training or habituation to integrate what the mind somehow grasps. Aristotle has hitherto emphasized the aspect of moral education that begins with the habituation of the passions and later provides a reasoned account for what one has already learned to cherish and despise in childhood; here he hints at the transformative education that can happen at a later stage, which as Socrates shows begins with dialectics and in the best cases proceeds to a conversion of the soul.[21]

Now Aristotle comes to the crux of his argument, as he proceeds to elucidate what he calls the deeper or "more natural" cause of failures of self-control. He argues that when a universal premise—an opinion about what is good to do—is joined with a particular premise of the sort governed by sense perception, and when it is possible to act upon the resulting imperative, the soul is bound "of necessity" to do so (1147a24–28). The soul must follow the logic of its own reasoning; it is not a matter of free will whether we do or refrain from doing what seems best to us if nothing intervenes to stop us. But what is it that can so intervene? To call it desire is correct but insufficient; the key point in Aristotle's analysis of failures of self-control is his insistence that in the end reason is overcome only by other reasons (1147a32–b3). We may seem to observers and to ourselves in retrospect to have acted against reason, but Aristotle says that even as we have a premise about what is good that we are failing to apply, we have another premise that we are indeed following—a "reasoning of a sort" (1147b1)—which at least for a moment seems wholly persuasive. In human beings, there are no desires that do not carry with them the at least implicit judgment "this is good," or fears or hatreds that do not carry with them the opposite, and countervailing judgments must first be vanquished if we are to act against them. In that way judgments and passions are like the concave and convex of a single arc (cf. 1.13), distinguishable in thought but never separable in fact.[22]

Aristotle also shows an interesting kind of substitution that can happen when unwise principles get applied. Beginning with what seems to be a randomly chosen premise—that one ought to taste every sweet thing—Aristotle says that if one holds this premise and perceives something sweet, one necessarily attempts to taste it. But of course the premise is absurd. Aristotle then restates the reasoning in a way that captures more precisely what goes on in actual lapses. The problematic major premise now reappears as the true observation that "everything sweet is pleasant." When one is attending to this fact, aware of the presence of a sweet thing, and experiencing desire for it, then desire, in the absence of compelling countervailing considerations, will set one in motion. But the person who yields to such a desire acts as if he were applying a valid universal rule when in fact he is following just one consideration that ought to be weighed in light of other considerations. The person lacking self-control thus operates thoughtlessly on the basis of a clearly faulty premise that he never allows himself to voice or face.

Considered in itself, however, the particular judgment that is being falsely applied is, Aristotle observes, not intrinsically but only incidentally opposed to "correct reason" (1147a35–b2): sweet things are indeed pleasant. Thus behind every urge that we follow is a thought that is in some sense true, dictating that we pursue what is in some way good, but it is not always the principle that ought to prevail.[23] There is nothing irrational or wrong in the proposition that delicious food ought to be eaten, that men and women with beautiful bodies and souls ought to be loved, that danger ought to be shunned, that harms ought to be punished, that life ought to be full of delights. These principles, when properly brought together and balanced with other sound principles, are in perfect accord with correct reason. Our particular desires, however, often do "oppose correct reason" (1147b2–3), for when one of them is intense it tends to distort our thinking and blind us to other principles that ought to qualify our pursuit of its object. When two different reasonings are present and desire makes one more compelling, the mind is not wholly deprived of the right line of reasoning, but it does become confused. Such confusion is ignorance, and without it failures of self-control do not occur.

Aristotle's great contribution in this chapter is his argument that human passions and opinions are essentially linked, and yet that this linkage is profoundly problematic. Reason is sometimes present even while the desire that should accompany it and at the deepest level does accompany it seems quite eclipsed: one may fail to feel one's desire to be happy tomorrow as well as tonight, and this is a key reason for failures of self-control. Or desires may be keenly felt that are poorly understood, desires for things that are always in some way good, but the reasons we desire them and the implicit ranking of priorities that we are acting upon may not be consciously articulated and may indeed be quite unbearable to articulate. And some of the opinions that we do articulate may amount only to poor excuses. Indeed, probably everyone has had the experience of being more or less aware that what one is about to do is ill-advised and of silencing that recognition with excuses so flimsy that they ought never to convince anyone. Ordinarily this phenomenon is taken as proof that people act *against* their own judgment, but Aristotle suggests something more subtle is at work. The poor excuses we offer are not the reasons we act but only the bones we toss to the watchdogs who get in our way; the reasons for acting are our desires for pleasures and other things that really are good, joined in each case to judgments about the good that, as Aristotle puts it, are not essentially opposed to correct reason, even though they are not wisely applied to the particular case. There is nothing flimsy about the desire for happiness that impels us forward.

But what about those watchdogs and the bones that we toss them? It is a strange thing that so often we need an excuse to do what we want and yet almost any excuse will do. Likely Aristotle would say the root problem in such cases is that one deeply suspects that the good things in life do not go together—that what is pleasant and noble and beneficial are fundamentally at odds—and yet one wishes desperately that it were not so and hides from one's own judgment that it may be. One wishes to act respectably and not to be an unjust scoundrel; one wishes even more to take revenge on the person who has offended one; one fears that one cannot do both; one is too soft to face the hard choices that this would imply and therefore too soft even to investigate whether it is true. Aristotle will argue that lack of self-control always involves a certain softness; perhaps the crucial softness appears in the feeling that it would be unbearable to face the whole truth about the choice before one. Thus the effective opinions at work when one fobs oneself off with a poor excuse would be *not* "acting respectably is important to me, and this really is a respectable act," but rather, "(1) the happiness that comes through satisfying my present desires is important to me; (2) being free of self-reproach is important to me; (3) if I had to choose between pleasure and the dignity of being virtuous, I would probably choose pleasure; (4) it is too painful to confront squarely the probability that I really do face such a choice and really do have these priorities, because then I would have to give up a major source of self-respect and hope; (5) clarity about this matter offers no compensating happiness to make up for the despair I would probably feel at confronting it; therefore (6) doing what I want and silencing my misgivings in whatever way I can really does make the most sense." At the heart of problems with self-control is not raw passion overcoming good reason, but a profound ambivalence within reason itself.

All of this means that even at our most irrational we are still more rational than animals, who hold in their minds not conceptions of what is good but mere images and memories (1147b3–5). Yet our ambivalences drive us into self-induced oblivion, from which we need repeated and concerted efforts to escape. Aristotle compares the recovery of perfect clarity after losing it to the recovery of sobriety after a drinking bout or an awaking from sleep. If most people hover most of the time somewhere between self-control and the absence of self-control, most people are seldom fully awake. It is the most important project of the *Ethics* to help us take the first steps toward a lasting escape from this fog.

Aristotle concludes, then, by agreeing with Socrates about knowledge after all: moral weakness does not occur "in the presence of knowledge in the authoritative sense," knowledge both grounded in reason and thoroughly digested (1147b15–16). It is neither the feeling of certainty with which a proposition is held nor the factual truth of that proposition that makes knowledge invincible, but rather the depth with which the knowledge has been woven into the fabric of one's soul. Knowledge can be forgotten, but Aristotle suggests that crucial knowledge of what we need for happiness can be lost only when it was never fully absorbed. And when the principles we do accept seem to be dragged about by emotion, it is only the applications of knowledge to particular circumstances and not the principles themselves that are shouldered aside as we make exceptions for ourselves. The person who loses control decides not that excessive drinking is after all good, but rather that one's resolution to stop after the second glass of wine was perhaps after all too strict an application of the principle, especially tonight, especially when the wine and the company are so good. If one were to decide that it is best, after all, to eat and drink whatever one wishes, and for this pleasure it is worth paying the price of becoming an overweight alcoholic, one would be not uncontrolled but vicious, a prospect we all recoil from. And so we cling to the belief that the principle of moderation is good, even as we suspect that following it faithfully would be unbearable, and even as we hide from all the consequences of what that "unbearable" really means.

Thus Aristotle shows his agreement with both parts of Socrates' contention, that no one acts either against knowledge in the strict sense or against his particular prevailing opinion about what is best at the moment of acting. Aristotle began by pointing out that Socrates did not believe in lack of self-control at all, at least not in the way that most people conceive of it, as a violation of one's own judgment about what is best, but now it turns out that Aristotle does not believe in such a thing either. His quarrel with Socrates comes down to this: that Socrates moves too quickly to his conclusions, and that he speaks as if knowledge is either present or not present, with no gradations in between and no fantastic hybrids of the two. Thus Socrates does not fully account for what is going on when people appear to act against their own judgment. Aristotle saves the phenomenon of lack of self-control, but he agrees fundamentally with Socrates.

UNQUALIFIED LACK OF SELF-CONTROL (7.4)

Chapter 7.3 has given such a good account of how lapses of self-control occur that Aristotle has in fact made it puzzling how self-control is possible. If one has only a distant, abstract principle pulling one in one direction and a vividly felt desire with its own accompanying judgment pulling in another, how is it ever possible to ignore the strong inclination, overcome the mental distortion that it tends to cause, and follow the weak one? In taking up other problems, 7.4 will indirectly shed light on this one.

Aristotle begins the chapter by asking whether anyone lacks self-control in an unqualified sense, and if so, what such people are concerned with. The question is surprising because he has already spoken of the unqualifiedly uncontrolled at 1146b19–22 as the class of people who are concerned with the same pleasures as the immoderate but in a different way, pursuing them without holding the opinion that it is best to do so. Nothing in the intervening discussion of knowledge has cast doubt on the existence of this phenomenon, yet something about it remains mysterious. Why should it be that failures of self-control seem so intimately bound up with physical pleasures? Why do lapses in that domain receive such blame, while an excessive love of such things as victory, honor, and even wealth appears quite different and receives little censure? And why is it that there does not seem to be such a thing as a general weakness for temptations of all kinds? Aristotle does not directly address the last of these questions, but it is evidently the nature of desire to focus intently on favorite objects that, as he observes, vary dramatically from person to person. Reiterating that self-control and lack of self-control are in every case concerned with pleasures and pains, Aristotle now associates self-control with steadfastness and also lack of self-control with softness (1147b20–23). He then draws a distinction between bodily pleasures, which he calls "necessary," and other pleasures that are "choiceworthy in themselves while admitting of excess" (1147b23–25). A simple reason self-control seems mainly to be about the "necessary" pleasures is that these are the things that are most obviously pleasant. If the desires that overcome people who lack self-control in this respect are not only natural but necessary, if indeed, as Aristotle soon reminds us, they are normally felt strongly by at least the young, is the main problem with people who lack self-control that they feel these desires unusually strongly, or is it that they are too soft to resist temptations that everyone feels? Aristotle soon confirms that softness is indeed involved in all such failings (1148a12). He also adds something curious about choice: the uncontrolled, he says, not only do what they do without choosing it, in contrast to the immoderate, but they actually act "against choice" (1148a9). Choice, it seems, can be either particular or general, and in the latter case it may not be efficacious, ending only in a resolution that is never carried out.[24] What Aristotle strikingly does not say of those who lack control is that they know what is good but choose to act against their knowledge.

The class of pleasures Aristotle calls choiceworthy in themselves while admitting of excess has a shifting membership. In it he first puts victory, honor, and wealth (1147b30). Three lines later he speaks of "these sorts of pleasures" as including those of money, gain, honor, and spiritedness (*thumos*). Then at 1148a11 he mentions lack of self-control regarding anger (*orgē*) as evidently another case of giving way to such pleasures.[25] Sensual pleasures and this second class of pleasures correspond roughly to two of the aims that in 1.5 Aristotle said characterize three types of men: the pleasure-lovers who "choose a life of fatted cattle" (1095b20), the refined who seek honor, and those who philosophize; they also correspond roughly to the first two of the three classes of goods Aristotle categorizes in 1.8 as goods of the body, external goods, and goods of the soul. In each case the highest class of desires and goods seems to be missing from the discussion in 7.4. Might it be that there can be no excess of the pleasures that are best of all?

In a new division at 1148a22 ff., however, Aristotle identifies three groups of desires and pleasures:

> Of desires and pleasures some are for objects that fall into the class of what is noble and serious (for some pleasures are by nature choiceworthy), others are the opposite of these, and others are in between, as was said before, such as money and gain and victory and honor. (1148a22–26)

The most obvious way to read this statement is to interpret the highest class as comprising desires and pleasures that are unqualifiedly choiceworthy and that admit of no excess, such as those associated with virtuous action and philosophy, the intermediate class as comprising those that Aristotle before described as "choiceworthy in themselves but admitting of excess" (1147b23–25), and the third class to comprise the lowest bodily pleasures. But this apparently tidy picture becomes confused as Aristotle continues:

> With respect to all of these, both the pleasures of this sort and the in-between ones, it is not for experiencing them, desiring them, and loving them that people are blamed, but for doing so in a certain way and to excess. Hence all those who, contrary to reason, are overcome by or pursue something by nature noble and good, for example those who are more serious than they should be about honor or children or parents—for these things are good, and those who are serious about them are praised. . . . For by nature each of them is choiceworthy in itself. (1148a26–b2)

By a kind of sleight of hand, and without ever finishing the last sentence, Aristotle has allowed the loves for such things as money, gain, victory, and honor, to which are now added children and parents, to leave the in-between class and instead migrate to the highest class of things by nature noble and choiceworthy. Our three classes have again collapsed into two. What is going on?

Quietly, but not without pointing to what he is leaving out, Aristotle is in this chapter confining himself to the horizon of the conventional gentleman, who scorns sensual indulgence, who seriously loves his estate, his family, honor, and victory, but who does not philosophize. Aristotle blames the same uncontrolled indulgences in coarse sensual pleasures that the gentleman scorns, and all but acquiesces in calling them vices at 1148a2–4, contrary to the careful distinction he has drawn between vice and lack of self-control. At the same time he treats most gently even the extreme love of victory, honor, wealth, and family. Elsewhere he strongly suggests that honor is not good and worth loving in itself (especially in 1.5 and 8.8) and likewise denies that the goods of fortune are good without qualification (especially in 5.1), but here he slips both in the class of things "by nature noble" and "choiceworthy in themselves." Elsewhere he calls the excessive love of at least some of these things vices (consider the treatment of stinginess and excessive ambition in book 4), but now he says that while these excesses are to be avoided, they are not vices, not blameworthy, and not even failures of self-control, except by extension or analogy.[26] Thus, in the chapters that are building toward an acknowledgment of the terrific struggle most people have even to attain self-control, let alone true virtue, Aristotle makes a point of exaggerating the goodness of pleasures that are at least higher than the coarsest ones. Might it not be precisely these less than perfectly noble and less than perfectly clear-sighted concerns that are in most cases the key to self-control? Simple endurance is essential for self-control but by itself cannot provide a motive for resisting the desires that pull us most strongly. When reason's grasp of what is good is weak and prone to distortion, it needs to enlist other desires as allies, and the most eligible are these fundamentally spirited ones, which are most helpful in curbing the appetites, overcoming laziness, and corralling one's energies into something better than sensual indulgence: we recall the psychology of the *Republic* in which *thumos* is needed as the ally of reason to create a simulacrum of virtue. Indeed, we may even wonder whether such concerns as reputation and income do not provide essential "auxiliary troops," to borrow a phrase from Machiavelli, to help even many of those who aspire to a life of philosophy.

If this is right, we have here an important supplement to the pregnant reflections in 7.3 about the way reason is and is not sovereign in the soul. Knowledge of what is good needs to be both understood and felt, both vividly and steadily, in order to sustain virtue. *Sōphrosunē* in the narrow sense of moderate sensual desires is one essential support to the active wisdom that complete virtue requires, but not sufficient: *sōphrosunē* in the broader sense of altogether healthy desires is necessary to keep one's vision clear and to attain a life of genuine flourishing. In the absence of this—when the best desires for a healthy soul, for true understanding, and for the deepest satisfactions life affords are weak and faltering—then other desires for intermediate goods such as honor can be an essential supplement to reason, though one that yields self-control rather than virtue.

In this chapter on unqualified lack of self-control and lack of self-control by extension or analogy, Aristotle has raised the question of how completely self-control and lack of self-control provide analogues to all the virtues and vices. While self-control regarding bodily pleasure, money, honor, and anger correspond respectively to moderation, generosity, greatness of soul, and (in their combination) justice, we note two important omissions. First, we find here no analogue for courage, confirming our suspicion that courage has no shadow among forms of self-control because it is at core a form of self-control, stiffened by anger or hope or the love of victory or the love of those for whom one fights, and cowardice likewise is almost always a failure of self-control and not a wholehearted, unconflicted embrace of safety at all costs. Second, we find here no analogue for wisdom. Wisdom has no shadow-form in the realm of self-control because real wisdom comes only to those who love and seek it. One cannot force oneself into genuine wisdom, and, Aristotle concedes by his silence, one can never love it too much.

LACK OF SELF-CONTROL AND BRUTISHNESS (7.5)

In the next chapter Aristotle moves to the other extreme in the spectrum of character states, from the lack of self-control that is less bad than vice to the brutishness that is worse. He begins by observing that of the natural pleasures some are "pleasant simply" whereas others are so to particular races of men and animals (1148b15–16). By "pleasant simply," he seems to mean things that are pleasant to all healthy beings that can experience them with awareness. These would include, most fundamentally, the pleasure of being alive and awake as well as the "necessary pleasures" of nourishment and sexual need. The specific pleasures of particular kinds of beings might include soaking in the mud for hippopotamuses, soaring for eagles, and all the higher but still natural pleasures of human life at its fullest. In contrast to both of these kinds of pleasures, Aristotle now takes up the class of brutish and morbid pleasures that are not by nature pleasant for any class of creatures but that can become so through defects, habits, and natural vices.

This discussion sheds a helpful light back on Aristotle's threefold division in the previous chapter between desires for things noble and good in themselves, intermediate ones, and ones that are "the opposite." There he left it unspecified what pleasures belong in the third category, inviting the thought that they are the ordinary physical pleasures. Clearly, however, the brutish and morbid pleasures he takes up now are the best candidates, being in every way the opposite of what is noble, serious, and by nature choiceworthy. By contrast, the natural and necessary pleasures of the body fit best into the intermediate category of things choiceworthy in themselves while admitting of excess, along with the pleasures of honor, victory, wealth, and family. Things that to the gentleman seem to differ vastly in rank are not so different to the philosopher.

In considering this new class of pleasures and character states, we enter a different realm of human experience and behavior, which includes such practices as cannibalism, homosexuality, fingernail biting, hair plucking, and the ingestion of ashes. Modern psychiatry has no doubt carried us further in understanding the details and classification of unhealthy—and merely variant—inclinations, but Aristotle makes several interesting observations here that shed light on his concept of nature as well as on our question of the relation between reason and character. As always, nature is Aristotle's standard for what is truly and properly pleasant, yet he acknowledges that especially among humans, nature itself sometimes goes strangely awry. His examples of brutishness or natural depravity, including the once widespread practices of eating raw meat and cannibalism, remind us that Aristotle makes no opposition between nature and civilization. What we call civilization comprises, for Aristotle, both the merely conventional and the realization or fulfillment of natural capacities that cannot be fully achieved among savages. Thus philosophy is natural and cannibalism is not, inasmuch as philosophy fulfills important capacities in human nature and cannibalism fails to respect the difference between the human and the nonhuman, even though cannibalism has occurred independently in many human societies and philosophy in only one.

With his accounts of such unnatural human impulses as ripping open pregnant women and eating their fetuses, eating another person's liver, eating ashes, biting off fingernails, and plucking out one's own hair, Aristotle illustrates what it means to be at the opposite end of the spectrum from complete virtue. It is sometimes possible to control such urges, Aristotle says, but this is different from the mastery of natural desires that constitutes ordinary self-control. Likewise, these brutish and morbid conditions lie "outside the limits of vice" (1148b34–49a1). Acts of virtue are chosen out of self-understanding and clear knowledge of what is good; acts of self-control and failures of self-control both arise from opinions that reflect an incomplete, confused, or intermittent understanding of what is good; acts of vice are chosen out of steady opinions that involve improper rankings of things that are nonetheless in some way good; but the acts that Aristotle calls brutish seem to come out of compulsions that are not accompanied by any sane and natural thoughts—and perhaps not by any thoughts at all—about what is good. Ordinary failures of self-control may look like the simple defeat of reason by desire, but they are really the defeat of better reasons together with their corresponding desires by worse ones. If human beings are ever driven by urges that their minds do not in any way recognize as good, what Aristotle calls brutishness is what it would look like. He will underscore this thought at the end of 7.6 with the observation that while vice involves a corruption of intellect, which is a "starting point" (*archē*), brutishness in the animals is its absence: thus what he calls brutishness in humans would involve at least the partial absence or silence of intellect.

So far, then, Aristotle suggests that brutish and morbid tendencies are altogether different in kind from vice. He narrows the gap between them, however, in the second half of the chapter. "All excessive folly, cowardice, immoderation, and harshness or anger [*chalepotēs*] are either brutish or morbid" (1149a4–7). The idea of excessive vice is odd, since vice itself is an excess or extreme. Is this really a cogent category? Equally curious is the list of four vices, which are almost but not quite the opposites of the four cardinal virtues, the only change being that harshness or anger is substituted for injustice. We pity a coward so craven that he fears the rustling of a mouse, considering it unfortunate to be so utterly irrational. Likewise we pity those who are utterly foolish, and even (if also with revulsion) those so uncontrolled that they grow too obese to leave their homes. We are much less able to pity the unjust who harm us all, but we are at least able to see that a chronically harsh temper is unenviable. Common opinion insists that there is a fundamental difference between ordinary vice, springing from the normal selfishness we all feel, and excessive vice, which can only be attributed to a deranged nature. But does Aristotle agree? Of course no one would choose to be afflicted by a terror of mice. But is ordinary cowardice or foolishness or enslavement to one's stomach or a raging temper any more choiceworthy or chosen? Is injustice really any different in kind from these disorders of the soul, or any less repugnant to one who sees clearly? Aristotle insists here on what we all somehow know, that the most heinous crimes are sick, but are any crimes healthy? If ordinary vice, taken to an extreme, drives one to acts that no one in his right mind would do, does not every moral failing involve a small degree of insanity—which is to say a more or less distorted perception of reality? Although myopia is different in kind from outright hallucination, both are diseases, congenital or acquired. Perhaps, from the Olympian heights of perfect virtue and clarity, the lack of self-control, vice, and brutishness are only different degrees of unhealthiness, and in the end all vice is a disease.

SELF-CONTROL AND ANGER (7.6)

Whereas brutishness shows man at his least rational and least human, the loss of self-control through anger is one of the failings that Aristotle treats as most bound up with reason, most characteristically human, and most deserving of forgiveness. Aristotle has already included anger together with honor, victory, and wealth as causes of failures of self-control that are less shameful than those occasioned by physical pleasure, but anger is complex and important enough to justify a separate treatment.[27] As we have seen, anger has a puzzling place in the *Ethics*. It seems to be an important support to both courage and justice, and yet it naturally carries people to rash and unjust extremes. Recognizing that anger can be a great source of civic courage, Aristotle denies that it is courage itself. The virtue that governs anger, gentleness, is supposed to be a mean between extremes, but we were forced to wonder whether it is not in fact freedom from anger. Righteous indignation, which often fuels a passion for justice, is first included in and then silently demoted from Aristotle's catalogue of virtues. Here in book 7 Aristotle defends the gentlemanly notion that being overcome by anger is less shameful than being overcome by desire, and likewise the common judgment that wrongs committed in anger are less blameworthy than those done out of cold calculation. In this way he continues his pattern of treating with particular gentleness the characteristic failings of the noble-minded citizen whose love of honor and justice is needed to hold the political community together.

On the other hand, now in 7.6 Aristotle explicitly questions the rationality of anger even as he continues to make a place for it. Speaking not about "excessive" anger but about anger or spiritedness (*thumos*) altogether, he says,

> Anger seems to listen in some way to reason, but to hear amiss, just like hasty servants, who run off before hearing all that is said and so err in doing what was ordered, and like dogs, who bark as soon as there is a knock, without seeing whether it is a friend. So anger, through the heat and swiftness of its nature, hearing but not hearing what is ordered, rushes off to take revenge. For when reason or imagination says that an outrage or a slight has been given, anger, just as if it were reasoning that it is necessary to fight against such a thing, flares up at once. (1149a25–34)

Like a guard dog, anger has the task of protecting its owner and his loved ones against enemies. The slights that it perceives may be real or imagined, but it *always* fails to hear reason correctly. It is too vehement; it loses sight of its proper end; it takes on a life and purpose of its own and "rushes off to take revenge."[28] Compared with desire, anger is more bound up with and more dependent upon reasoning of a sort: it involves implicit judgments that a harm or affront has been given, that it was given intentionally, that it was given without justification, that all such acts deserve retaliation, and hence that one must retaliate at once. Depending as it does on such implicit judgments, anger can be dispelled by reasoning that refutes any of these steps. When one discovers that the stranger on the bus who seemed to have shoved one rudely aside has in fact just lost his balance, anger immediately dissipates. More profoundly, when one comes to understand the irrationality of the premises that make anger always hear reason incorrectly—the premises that slights and harms deserve retaliation, that wicked people are enjoying an undeserved happiness, and that one's own dignity and happiness cannot be made whole until one has gotten even by "taking away the gain" from the offender—anger dissipates in time then as well.

The desire for pleasure, by contrast, is less bound up with reason: it is both less rational and less irrational. The knowledge that one risks developing diabetes if one does not lose weight does not dispel the desire for a doughnut when it arises, for desires are more simple than anger and unmediated by assumptions that are subject to refutation. The doughnut truly would be very pleasant, regardless of what other considerations weigh against it. But Aristotle makes this point in a way that is not quite fair to desire: "Spiritedness follows reason in a way, but desire does not. Desire, then, is more shameful. For someone who lacks self-restraint with respect to spiritedness is in a way conquered by reason, but the other is conquered by desire and not by reason" (1149b1–3). As commentators have observed, the force of this consideration is blunted by the argument Aristotle has already made that in every failure of self-control there is reasoning of a sort at work.[29]

Aristotle's second argument for the greater dignity of failures of self-control in anger than in desire is linked to the first in stressing what is uniquely and essentially human: it is more excusable to follow passions that are common to everyone than those that are beyond the normal pale, he says, and for human beings anger "is more natural than excessive desires for unnecessary things" (1149b4–8). Susceptibility to anger and belief in the principles that anger assumes are part of the fabric of human nature, for while there are simple peoples who know no luxury, there are none who know no anger. This, however, is not quite Aristotle's last word on the relation of anger to nature, for he does not even end the sentence we have just cited before he casts anger's naturalness into an odd and comical light. As an example of our tendency to forgive as only natural what is common, Aristotle cites the man whose defense when tried for father-beating was that it ran in his family.[30] Perhaps anger is congenital among human beings in the same way that father-beating is congenital in this family, as an irrational but deep-seated disorder in our habitual ways of thinking and acting. It is not just a learned habit; the proclivity to it is inborn; yet as a proclivity that can be overcome and that is in tension with the rationality that is highest and best in our natures, we can say that it is not part of our nature in its perfection, the primary meaning of nature for Aristotle. Among our congenital but ultimately unnatural habitual judgments may be our sense of what constitutes a reasonable limit to anger in each case. We consider it reasonable to hurl an angry retort at someone who has insulted us but not to burn down his house. But perhaps such distinctions are ultimately no more sensible than the argument of the father-beater who considers it reasonable for him to drag his father (and his son him) to the threshold, but no further (1149b11–12).

Third, Aristotle says, those who act out of anger are less unjust than those who plot and scheme. "The spirited man, then, is not a plotter, nor is spiritedness, but rather open; whereas desire is just as they assert of

Aphrodite: a weaver of wiles" (1149b14–16). There is something to this, but Aristotle again seems to be excusing anger and denigrating desire more than is rational and against his own prior analysis. For in the chapter on gentleness he observed that while there is an irascible form of anger that discharges itself at once, there is also a bitter kind that smolders until it gets revenge—precisely the source of the worst kind of plotting. And once again Aristotle's illustration undercuts his contention. In the passage cited we find Hera using Aphrodite's gifts to seduce Zeus and lull him to sleep—not, however, for the end of enjoying sensual pleasure, but to get free rein for her ambition to help her favored side in the Trojan War, a side that she ultimately favors out of anger that she lost the famous beauty contest, the judgment of Paris, to Aphrodite (Homer *Iliad* 14.214, 14.217, 24.25–30). To be sure, when we think of losing control of anger, we think especially of the hot, open anger of one who is stung by pain to lash out at once, but the tendency to be open rather than deceitful and calculating is less characteristic of anger per se than of lack of self-control: as Aristotle will say at 1152a18, the person who lacks self-control is "not a plotter" because his intentions are too inconsistent.

Aristotle's fourth argument pursues the thought that pain is an extenuating factor in failures of self-control due to anger. "Further, no one acts hubristically while feeling pain, but everyone who acts in anger acts while feeling pain, whereas the hubristic person acts with pleasure" (1149b20–21).[31] As Aristotle says elsewhere in the *Nicomachean Ethics*, things done out of pain are less fully voluntary than those done out of desire for pleasure (1119a21–27; cf. 1135b19–27). This intuition is reflected in legal codes everywhere, which often punish acts done in the heat of anger less severely than coolly premeditated ones, allowing no such extenuation for intense desire. Yet even if Aristotle is right that the pain of anger should mitigate our blame for actions it provokes, this is not yet to show that all or most of what anger perceives as wanton, gratuitous outrage really is that, rather than a lashing out due to pain of its own. Nor is it to disprove that acts of anger are in their own way driven by desire. To the contrary, Aristotle in the *Rhetoric* calls anger the desire for revenge (1378a31), and in *Ethics* 4.6 he observes that "revenge makes anger cease, producing pleasure in place of pain" (1126a21–22). Without this desire for revenge, would real anger remain at all, or merely a calm, vigilant opposition to what is harmful, which the most thoroughgoing Socratic would share? It is in this context that we should consider one other statement about anger in the *Ethics*, which runs in the opposite direction from the surface of the present chapter—a line Aristotle attributes to Heraclitus that "It is more difficult to fight against pleasure than anger" (1105a7–8).[32] Even if the reverse is true for most people most of the time, we may with effort purge ourselves of the desire for vengeance, but not the desire for pleasure.

In sum, we are left with this paradox. Human anger is so universal as to seem natural; it is rooted in our animal natures; yet it is not truly natural in the highest sense. Unlike the instinctive anger seen in animals, human anger involves irrational judgments. Yet if anger is especially felt by those who care about justice and is needed by many in order to be courageous and to overcome their own worst inclinations, Aristotle is right to mute his critique of it. More than that, if the confusions involved in anger are the same ones that are invariably present in a youthful, unexamined yearning to live the noblest life possible, and if such yearnings are a necessary precursor to the philosophic and happiest life, then anger would be natural in the limited sense of being a necessary stage on the way to the life that best satisfies our natural potential.

SELF-CONTROL, STEADFASTNESS, AND SOFTNESS (7.7)

In order to begin to address more deeply the phenomena of self-control and its failures, Aristotle in 7.7 delves into two other characteristics that are closely related and perhaps even more fundamental: steadfastness and softness. Returning again to the primary pleasures and pains of the body, he says of these,

> It is possible to be in such a condition that one is defeated by those which most people overcome, and it is possible to overcome even those by which most people are defeated. With regard to pleasures, the first one is lacking self-control and the second is self-controlled; with regard to pains, the first one is soft and the second is steadfast. But the characteristic belonging to most people is in between these, even if people incline more toward the worse. (1150a11–16)

In introducing this new distinction between characteristics defined by people's responses to pleasure and pain, Aristotle is separating two related pairs of phenomena, the first seen most vividly in the headlong pursuit of or resistance to such pleasures as intoxication, music, thrill-seeking, and love that so strongly attract those who are young and full of life, the second seen most vividly in an invalid's unwillingness to make any exertion on one hand and a peasant's stolid endurance of suffering on the other. But since all self-control involves withstanding the pain of denied gratification, and since succumbing to the pain of denied gratification would seem to be the same as or very close to succumbing to the desire for pleasure—"for desire is accompanied by pain" (1119a4)—it is clear that these phenomena are deeply intertwined. Softness likely underlies at least some and possibly all failures of self-control. The present chapter will show more about the relation between them.

Aristotle also makes an important statement in the passage quoted above about the domain of ordinary moral life and moral struggles. Most people are neither virtuous nor wicked, nor even altogether self-controlled and steadfast or wholly without self-control and soft, but in between in a realm characterized by continual temptations met with uneven success. Indeed, the four characteristics of self-control, lack of self-control, steadfastness, and softness that circumscribe most moral overcoming and failure at first come to sight as simply those responses to pleasures or pains that either exceed or fall short of what an ordinary person can manage, in the simply relative way that we define strong and weak bodies. But then Aristotle says that most people incline to the deficiencies. If softness and steadfastness are relative, how can most people be soft? Aristotle is now shifting to another standard, measured not by what is average but by what is rational: most people pursue pleasures and flee pains more than each is really worth, on balance and in the long run. Most people are bad to a degree, but much more out of weakness than wickedness.[33]

Reiterating now that the immoderate are those who pursue pleasure for itself, by choice, and without regrets, with the result that they are incurable, Aristotle says that there is a similar and parallel group who habitually, deliberately, and without regrets avoid all pain. Likewise, among those who lack self-control or "who do not choose," he says, "one of these is led by pleasure, and another by fleeing the pain that comes from desire, so that these differ from one another" (1150a25–27). But in fact both impetuous desire and intense pain now turn out to provide a certain extenuation for wrongdoing, inasmuch as giving way to them comes to sight as less corrupt than acting basely without being driven by any strong passion at all. "Hence," Aristotle concludes, "the immoderate person is worse than the one who lacks self-control" (1150a30–31), evidently because the former is not defeated by strong passion of any kind. Aristotle then sums up, "For of those mentioned the one is rather a form of softness; the other person is immoderate" (1150a31–32). Aristotle seemed to be drawing a three-way comparison between lack of self-control due to desire for pleasure, lack of self-control due to the pain of deprivation, and immoderation, but now he contrasts only softness with immoderation. Could all of the uncontrolled really be soft? At the same time, if the immoderate are not those who feel impetuous desire or painful deprivation, if they act *only* "by choice," their motivations have become quite mysterious.

Aristotle next compares steadfastness with self-control. Steadfastness involves withstanding what one is contending against, but self-control involves defeating it, "and enduring and overpowering are different, just as are not being defeated and being victorious. Hence self-control is also more choiceworthy than steadfastness" (1150a35–b1). Evidently steadfastness undergirds self-control, but self-control needs in addition to this elemental toughness a positive reason, such as love of the noble or of honor, to make one muster the strength one has. With his martial language Aristotle reminds us of the close kinship between self-control and the courage that requires both toughness and a noble, patriotic, or other such motive.[34]

If steadfastness is an essential component of self-control, that would be another reason to suspect that softness is an essential component of all failures of self-control. Aristotle seems to say again that it is not, however, at least not when we take softness in its primary sense as "falling short of what the majority withstand and are capable of" (1150b1–2). Ordinary people blame as soft those who cannot bear discomforts and deprivations that they themselves could bear, but they sympathize with those who fight vehement passions, even if they fail to defeat them: from the ordinary perspective such people do not seem soft at all. Aristotle does nevertheless add two groups to the soft that may not obviously belong: the delicate or lazy and those who are fond of amusement. Especially interesting are the latter, inasmuch as they can be full of energy. "And someone fond of amusement is held to be immoderate but is actually soft, for play is relaxation" (1150b16–17). That is to say, behind a veneer of pursuing endless amusement wholeheartedly and by deliberate choice, the playboy is really running away from something painful. What might this be? No doubt it is in part the effort of hard work and concerted thought; perhaps it is also the possible disappointment of aiming high and striving and failing, or even of succeeding and finding that life still does not add up to what one hoped. The libertine appears to choose low pleasures without any struggle because the struggle with his faintly felt better inclinations would be too painful to face: we must wonder whether he is not the softest of all.

But if softness really underlies the excessive pursuit of amusement, why would it not be equally involved in the excessive pursuit of bodily pleasures? When we return to the discussion of moderation and immoderation in book 3 with this question in mind, we discover that Aristotle does in fact make an observation there about pleasure and pain, the full importance of which we are only now prepared to understand:

> Concerning pains, it is not the case as it is with courage that one is called moderate for enduring them or immoderate for not doing so, but a person is called immoderate for being pained more than he should because he does not attain his pleasures (and for him, pleasure produces pain), whereas one is called moderate for not being pained by the absence of and by abstaining from pleasure. The immoderate person, then, desires all the pleasures or the especially pleasant ones, and he is led by his desire so that he chooses these instead of other things. Hence he is pained both by failing to obtain his desire and by desiring itself. For desire is accompanied by pain, although it seems strange to be pained on account of pleasure. (1118b28–19a5)

Immoderation turns out not to be quite the calm, deliberate choice of bad pleasures that one could easily refrain from choosing that Aristotle's discussion on the surface suggests. The immoderate are both pulled by pleasure and driven by pain that they are ill equipped to resist. True, we do not see them fighting with themselves as we do the uncontrolled. They seem wholehearted in their pursuit of pleasure, but perhaps this is because they are too soft to fight its pull at all, or to push themselves toward anything higher, or even to bear the pain of self-reproach for failing to resist and failing to push themselves. To be soft is to be unable to endure the exertions and deprivations that are necessary to get any of the greatest satisfactions in life, and this is a condition no one would choose. Hence we may wonder whether anyone can consistently hold to a policy of following the path of least resistance, and whether the immoderate really are immune to regret, a question Aristotle will ultimately answer in the negative at 1166a34–b25. No one chooses to fritter away one's life. The class of the truly, calmly, wholeheartedly, deliberately immoderate thus begins to look like a null set.

But we may also well ask where the moderate themselves stand with respect to pain. For if the immoderate are pained "more than they should be" by the absence of pleasures, are the moderate not pained at all when they are deprived of the "necessary" pleasures or exposed to unusual hardships, or are they free of pain only at the absence of excessive or base pleasures? For as Aristotle says, "desire is accompanied by pain." These considerations lead us to see that even the most moderate will not enjoy the perfect inner harmony that a cursory reading of Aristotle's discussion of moderation might suggest: even the best will need at times a more forceful self-control to withstand the deprivations and temptations that life invariably brings. The difference between the moderate and the merely self-controlled is that the latter's passions are unhealthy and so cause more trouble, not that the former's passions always accord perfectly with what is best.

This thought is underscored by Aristotle's suggestion in 5.11 that the rule of reason over the passions is despotic and his call in 10.7 to try as much as possible to leave one's lower nature behind, as if it were an impediment. Perhaps, even for the wisest, continuing vigilance is necessary to keep in check the unruly inclinations of our composite natures. But the habit of vigilant wakefulness, so strange at first, can take on pleasures of its own that create a new and better order in the soul. With such clarity to support healthy passions, we would have the closest approach to perfect moderation that is available to us.

CURABLE AND INCURABLE (7.8)

In 7.8 Aristotle returns to the puzzle he stated at the beginning of book 7 as to whether the immoderate or the uncontrolled person is more curable. His resolution to this problem sheds more light on the relation between steadfastness, habituation, good nature, and insight in producing good character. As he said in 7.2, it might seem that the immoderate are more curable because they at least have the strength to abide by their convictions, whereas trying to persuade the uncontrolled of the error of their ways seems futile because they already know that what they are doing is bad. But now he indicates that even the most irresolute of those who lack self-control have something essential that the immoderate do not have: awareness of what is best. "For vice escapes the notice of the one who has it, but lack of self-control does not" (1150b36). Whether this lack of awareness is ultimately due simply to the coarseness of their souls or to an even deeper softness that we have been suspecting causes at least many of these people to hide from themselves, their lack of clarity is critical and is what makes them incurable. To be wholly immoderate would be to lack even flickering insight into how it is best to live, and hence to lack the scruples that give the claims of virtue a foothold. Strength of soul is important, but without insight into what is good, decent character is impossible.

Yet there is a curious kind of awareness of what is good that is more defective precisely in being more often present. This is the awareness of people who make good resolutions and fail to abide by them, not under the influence of impetuous desire but simply because they are too weak, "like those who get drunk quickly and on little wine" (1151a3–5). Theirs is the softness of feeling too strongly the pain of effort and deprivation. But they seem at the same time to suffer from a lack of clarity or of imagination: they somehow see what is best but they do not see it vividly enough and feel its pull powerfully enough to pursue it with determined energy.

While Aristotle began 7.8 by drawing a stark contrast between vice and lack of self-control, he soon begins closing the gap between them by conceding that in fact vice and lack of self-control differ little in their effects. He quotes the jibe of Demodicus that "the Milesians are no fools, only they do just what fools would do," adding that in the same way the uncontrolled are not truly unjust, yet they do unjust things. Thus lack of self-control is vice "in a way" (1151a6–10). What is more, Aristotle indicates, in a chapter that increasingly replaces judicial language with medical terminology and analogies, both are unhealthy. To the extent that it makes sense to judge the vicious and the uncontrolled differently, he suggests, it is mainly because of their different prospects for reform or cure. Worst are those with no sense of the noble, no inclination to dedicate themselves to others, and no fellow feeling. Such people we call psychopaths, and modern medicine concurs with Aristotle that their prospects for cure are dim indeed.

Compared with the truly vicious, those who lack self-control are not only less bad but also more curable, Aristotle continues, since they are more easily persuaded to change.

> For virtue preserves and vice destroys the first principle, and in matters of action the end is the first principle, just as the hypotheses are in mathematics. And neither in the one case nor in the other can reason teach the first principles, but virtue, whether natural or habituated, is the source of correct opinion about the first principles. (1151a15–19)

If the principles of virtue could be taught by reasoned argument alone, a robust scoundrel would just need to be persuaded to adopt them and he would become good—a laughable proposition that makes Socrates' "virtue is knowledge" claim look so naïve. Scoundrels know what society considers virtuous, but they lack the crucial foundation on which all moral reasoning must be built. One must simply see—and likewise feel—that courage is admirable, that the pleasures of the mind are higher than those of the body, that generosity is a fine thing, and that the beautiful differs from the gaudy and tasteless; indeed, the value of everything worth having and worth pursuing in life as an end and not merely an instrument, everything both moral and nonmoral, must be grasped by something more basic than reasoning.

This is Aristotle's final statement on the starting points of moral reasoning. Does it shed any more light on just what those starting points are? Read in one way, this statement merely reproduces the cul-de-sac Aristotle fell into in 6.12, where the virtue that was supposed to consist in passion's habituation to follow correct reason turned out to be the only source of guidance that reason has. That this is the suggestion here is consistent with Aristotle's formulation now that virtue gives only "correct opinion" about first principles. Read in another way, however, this statement, with its reminder of the phenomenon of natural virtue, points to the possibility that the ultimate source of guidance is not habituation but naturally healthy desires, discovered to be healthy because of the rich satisfactions that they make possible. To be sure, by themselves even the healthiest desires yield only true opinions about what is best, but through dialectical interrogation they provide the foundation for real knowledge and for the active wisdom that can weave the desires into a comprehensive and stable whole. Is this suggestion in tension with the claim of Aristotle or his Socratic interlocutor in 3.5 that it is insight or naturally good vision that is of fundamental importance? No. Aristotle has appeared to waver between treating virtue and treating intellect as most fundamental, but now in book 7 it has become clear that in the realm of choice and action they come down to the same thing. To see fully the goodness of clarity *is* to desire it; to pursue even the most foolish pleasure is to imagine, for so long as one is in desire's grip, that that pleasure is good. Desire and judgment about the good are but two aspects of the same thing, as inseparable as are the concave and convex of a single arc.

SELF-CONTROL, STEADFASTNESS, AND OBSTINACY (7.9)

Aristotle concludes 7.8 by confirming the common opinion stated in 7.1 that self-control is a quality of significant moral worth: it is not possible without both some grasp of true principles and some considerable strength. Yet as soon as Aristotle establishes the moral worth of self-control, he again calls it into question. Returning to a problem he first raised in 7.2, he asks, "Is one who abides by any reason and any sort of choice self-controlled, or the one who abides by correct reason, and is the one who fails to abide by any sort of choice and any sort of reason uncontrolled, or the one who fails to abide by reason that is not false and choice that is right?" (1151a29–32).[35] If self-control rests only on true opinion, bolstered either by other considerations that are less than rational or by a simple constitutional disinclination to change one's mind, is it really admirable—or is it just a fortuitous combination of qualities, none of which is intrinsically good? If a self-controlled person happens to have been raised with particularly defective moral opinions, it seems he might be better served by a smaller degree of steadfastness. More seriously, a general tendency to hold fast to one's opinions would seem to be a weakness from the highest perspective of discovering the truth. Aristotle's response to this challenge is to say that what a thing is essentially must be understood with reference to its end, for it is the end that is sought "for itself," so that while self-control may incidentally follow the wrong opinion, "in an unqualified sense" it is true opinion that it follows (1151a33–b4). The goal of self-control is to hold fast not just to any opinion but to true opinion about what is good, in the face of countervailing pleasures and pains: it is essentially groping for what is best, even when it is deceived.

Aristotle continues to explore the same question as he ostensibly turns to a different group of people who also hold fast to their opinions but are not admirable. These are the obstinate, who resemble the self-controlled in the way that the extravagant resemble the generous or the rash the courageous, but who are steadfast in the wrong way and for the wrong reason. As Aristotle puts it, the difference is that the self-controlled refuse to be swayed by passion and desire but "may on occasion be readily persuadable" (1151b8–10), whereas the obstinate cannot be swayed even by arguments and are often led by pleasure. Framing the distinction this way, however, Aristotle leaves it a question how far habitual self-control is really open to reason and whether at least some of the obstinate are not governed by an attachment to what they understand as noble. Certainly the person who has been raised according to Aristotle's complete account of moral virtue will be at least somewhat open-minded: he will have been taught to respect reason as the measure of virtue, to eschew excessive pride, and to embrace the graceful, friendly, truthful habits of cultivated society, which include listening respectfully to the opinions of others; he will not have been schooled in religious or political fanaticism. Nonetheless, it may not be easy to draw a perfectly clear distinction between the obstinate man and the patriot who upholds all the laws and customs of his country with passionate dedication. Perhaps everyone who steadfastly upholds the opinions he has been taught about right and wrong is fundamentally obstinate in comparison with the philosopher, who inquires into everything.[36]

Aristotle's implicit answer is that of course we can draw a distinction, clear enough for all practical purposes, between the good, self-controlled citizen who will listen to reasoned arguments and the obstinate boor who will not. Here as everywhere Aristotle is alive to even small shades of difference when those shades matter in the real world of moral and political life. But still he prompts us to move our gaze to a higher perspective, from which these distinctions matter less. He begins to do this with his next observation about why people hold as stubbornly as they do to their opinions. Here he focuses on the most revealing form of obstinacy, that which is not due to mere ignorance or lack of cultivation but which is especially characteristic precisely of people who consider themselves thoughtful. These are the opinionated, whose failing Aristotle attributes to an excessive pleasure in the apparent victory of holding fast to their own opinions and an excessive pain in having those opinions overturned, "like decrees" (1151b14–16). They are impeded by too much love of their own. This passage reminds us of the rareness of the opposite perspective, that of Socrates, who professes to prefer losing an argument to winning one, since when he loses he learns more (*Gorgias* 458a–b). Aristotle concludes, then, that the opinionated in fact resemble the uncontrolled more than the self-controlled. They are soft in their inability to withstand pain, and perhaps few pains are greater for most of us than that of having our most cherished opinions overturned. To be genuinely open to reason takes unusual strength of soul.

In 7.4 Aristotle argued that an excessive pursuit of such noble objects as honor and victory is lack of self-control in a certain sense but not really blameworthy. Now with his comments on the opinionated he casts a darker shadow over the love of victory: even such a seemingly fierce passion as this may be rooted in a certain softness. And on the other hand, even one who seems on the surface irresolute may be moved by something noble, as Aristotle illustrates now by returning to the example of Sophocles' Neoptolemus. He cited Neoptolemus earlier, at 1146a18–21, when he raised the problem of whether a lack of self-control may not sometimes be morally serious if it causes one to depart from a bad resolution. Now, however, Aristotle refuses to call Neoptolemus's abandoning his resolution to lie to Philoctetes a lapse of self-control at all. True, he acted on account of pleasure, but it was the noble pleasure of telling the truth. "For not everyone who acts on account of pleasure is either immoderate or base or uncontrolled, but rather the one who does so on account of a shameful pleasure" (1151b21–22). Perhaps there is still something soft in Neoptolemus, whose love is for the noble pleasure of truthfulness rather than for the truth itself, whatever it may turn out to be. In discussing Neoptolemus's love of truthfulness Aristotle comes as close as he ever does in his treatment of the moral things to a discussion of the love of truth, which can also make one appear irresolute, so strong a resolution does it inspire to put all received opinions to the test and to be deceived by no counterfeit.

SELF-CONTROL AND ACTIVE WISDOM (7.10)

In 7.10 Aristotle returns to the question, first posed at 1145b17–19, of whether the uncontrolled can ever have active wisdom. Of course his answer is that they cannot, but what is seldom noticed is that his reasoning shows that the merely self-controlled lack active wisdom as well. For active wisdom is by its nature efficacious in producing good actions and good character. It is precisely the thorough penetration of passion by reason that prevents the serious inner divisions of the merely self-controlled; it is precisely the difficulty of attaining active wisdom that leaves most people tumbling endlessly between self-control and lapses of self-control. People who think it possible to have active wisdom while lacking self-control are confusing active wisdom with cleverness, which finds the best means to a given goal without entailing any preference for good goals over bad (cf. 1144a23–b1). The confusion occurs because active wisdom, too, is concerned with finding the right means to ends, and sometimes in common parlance means nothing more. But active wisdom as Aristotle presents it entails so comprehensive a grasp of the human good that no room is left for doubt as to what ends are worth pursuing. Thus Aristotle says that cleverness and active wisdom are "close with respect to *logos* but differ with respect to choice" (1152a13–14): both share the definition of correct reasoning, but only active wisdom includes the knowledge of the right end and of why it is right that ensures correct choice. Thus, Aristotle says, the person who lacks self-control is *not* one who has the same understanding as the virtuous but simply allows it to remain at the level of theory or abstraction. With moral knowledge this is not possible. Such a person is rather like one who is asleep or drunk: his knowledge of the end is not available to him; he does not fully have it (1152a14–15). Thus when Aristotle says that the "choice" of the uncontrolled person is decent (1152a17), this is choice in a truncated sense, it is a halfhearted or at least unstably motivated intention rather than a fully informed decision. It resembles the resolutions of a disordered polity that fails to carry out its laws: we may question whether its empty pronouncements are laws at all.

After reiterating that most people fall in between the self-controlled and the uncontrolled—and hence fall far short of true virtue and true active wisdom—Aristotle adds that those who are uncontrolled through habit are more curable than those who are so by nature. Nature and the failure of most human beings to reach their natural fulfillment thus become the theme of the end of the discussion of self-control and its failings. Those who lack self-control only by habit would perhaps be those who are gifted with fine natures and a natural capacity to see what is best but who have been neither schooled in good habits nor yet inspired by a cause that seems worth their devotion. When their hearts do catch fire, they are quickly transformed. Those who lack self-control by nature would be the naturally weak and soft. Yet weak bodies can become stronger with exercise and naturally strong bodies do not remain so without it: in both the physical and the moral realm, habits become second nature. This suggests a reason for hope that for many or most people habit can go far in bringing improvement and establishing self-control. But at the same time it suggests a reason for doubt as to whether the particular forms of excellence we have been taught to admire are altogether good by nature, or whether they seem good mainly because of long habituation. Even or precisely because it is so much subject to habit and tradition, the moral life is in need of wise critical scrutiny.

Epilogue

THE PHILOSOPHIC LIFE

With the treatment of self-control and lack of control, Aristotle concludes his discussion of the moral life. He will turn for the remainder of book 7 to an investigation of pleasure and the question of whether by nature pleasure deserves the contempt in which it is traditionally held by moralists, then in books 8 and 9 to friendship, which is not a moral virtue although in the best case it rests on virtue, and then in the first half of book 10 to a reconsideration of pleasure. These rich discussions go in new directions that shed little light on the relation of reason to moral virtue as such. The two treatments of pleasure do, however, return to Aristotle's original question of the end toward which reason should guide all choice and action, or the substance of happiness. This renewed investigation of happiness continues in the latter half of book 10 as Aristotle takes up philosophy and launches a dramatic defense of the philosophic life as the best life of all, in the course of which he revises his assessment of the morally and politically active life. How, then, do these discussions in book 10 bear on our question of the standard by which reason properly guides moral choice? What light do they shed on the never fully answered question from book 1 of whether true happiness should be understood in a broadly inclusive way to comprise pleasures and activities of many kinds, more narrowly to comprise only the activity of virtue both moral and intellectual, or most narrowly to comprise only the activity of the highest virtue, wisdom?

In his treatment of pleasure in 10.1–5 Aristotle again rejects the claim that pleasure itself is the substance of happiness, arguing that pleasure is not a separate good from the good of activity but rather something that completes the activity and that is properly assessed according to the worth of that activity. Thus he turns in 10.6 to a reconsideration of the various kinds of activity and their proper ranking. Beginning by dividing activities into those that are "necessary and choiceworthy for the sake of other things" and those that are "choiceworthy in themselves" (1176b3), he then provisionally divides the latter class again into activities that accord with virtue and the pleasant activities of play. These divisions yield the fruitful threefold classification of activity into work, the pursuits of serious leisure, and play. But immediately Aristotle begins a radical narrowing of the class of activities that are truly ends. He questions whether play can possibly be the proper focus of the best life and argues that in fact it is choiceworthy only for the sake of serious activity, as restorative recreation or relaxation and not for its own sake. This argument has a certain tendentiousness that recalls the claim in 1.5 that a life given over to pleasure is suitable only for fatted cattle. Even if that is so, Aristotle has not proved that the innocent nonserious pleasurable activities are in themselves a dead loss, like sleeping, and should be indulged only so far as is strictly required by the serious activities. If we are essentially composite beings, body as well as soul, not only individual but also sexual, social, and political, then the argument would still need to be considered whether satisfying activities of many kinds do not belong to the best and most complete life.

In 10.7 Aristotle goes much further, to argue that the philosophic life alone of the serious contenders for the good life is truly choiceworthy for itself. "If happiness is activity in accord with virtue," he begins, "it is reasonable that it would accord with the most excellent virtue, and this would be the virtue belonging to what is best" (1177a12–13). Then in a breathtaking ascent, he calls this best thing in us divine, identifies the activity of its virtue as complete happiness, and affirms, "that this activity is contemplative has been said" (1177a17–18). Nowhere, in fact, has this been said in the *Nicomachean Ethics* as we have it. He praises philosophy not only for the excellence of the part of our nature that engages in it but for the continual availability of its activity, for the unrivaled purity and stability of its pleasures, for the self-sufficiency of the life devoted to it, and because, of human activities

> it alone would seem to be loved for its own sake, for nothing comes into being from it beyond the contemplating; but from matters involving action we obtain something, to a greater or lesser degree, beyond the action.

> Happiness also seems to consist in leisure, for we are busy so that we may be at leisure, and we wage war so that we may be at peace. The activity of the virtues involving action, then, consists of matters either of politics or of war, and the actions concerned with these things seem to be without leisure. (1177b1–8)

A person would have to be bloodthirsty to make war for the sake of making war, he continues, and even the peaceful activities of politics, he now concedes, are all aimed either at gaining power for oneself or at securing the happiness of oneself and one's fellow citizens, both being distinct and separate from the political activity as such.

This is a momentous change from the claim that virtuous activity is just for itself, yet we have seen how Aristotle has been laying a certain groundwork for it throughout the *Ethics*. He has been exploring and testing the claims of the active moral and political life to be simply final and choiceworthy for its own sake, showing at every turn how these claims are bound up with the difficulty of articulating a clear standard of reason that might govern that life. Moral life as such, we have seen, moves within the realm of opinion, of habituation that overlays without transforming nature, and of truth partially but most imperfectly grasped. In tracing the function of reason within moral virtue, we have seen that moral virtue necessarily looks to multiple standards, wavers between them, and characteristically fails to distinguish them clearly. A central limitation of the moral perspective is its continual refusal to acknowledge what Aristotle finally makes explicit now: that the active life is after all fundamentally shaped and defined and only pulled into play at all by pressing but mundane needs that are lower than the thoughtfulness and thoughtful activity that we sense ought to be just for itself.

Our study has pointed us to the need for a science of human nature that can elucidate our deepest natural needs and highest natural perfection, thus informing the true form of active wisdom that would take its guidance not from conventional opinion but from nature. But Aristotle has not directly provided such an account. Rather than doing so now he gives a bold and puzzling injunction to turn our attention as exclusively as possible to the pure contemplative activity of the intellect that he again calls divine, and thereby "as much as possible to make ourselves immortal [*athanatizein*]" (1177b33). Now if the extent to which we truly can immortalize ourselves is not at all, we will have to take this injunction with a certain grain of salt. It belongs to a book about the moral life, a book that

Aristotle openly acknowledges cannot treat philosophy with great precision (1178a23). The picture he here paints of the philosophic life is of one so self-sufficient, so tranquil, so free of ignorance and of the gnawing need to answer urgent questions that it seems rather more rhetorical than serious. This picture does not fit the activity of political philosophy Aristotle himself is engaged in throughout this work, inasmuch as this project is not simply its own end but aims to give guidance to lawgivers, statesmen, educators, and potential philosophers. Nor does this picture acknowledge the urgency of settling the questions about nature, necessity, the divine, and our own place in the cosmos that so animated Socrates; answers to the latter of these are now merely affirmed. This picture really does not fit natural philosophy either, since all philosophy, unlike contemplation of what one already knows, is a love or quest for knowledge that one seeks as a goal that is distinct from the activity. Finally, whereas Aristotle at least makes a plausible argument here that contemplation as such meets two of the criteria for happiness he proposed in 1.7, in being especially end-like and especially self-sufficient, he now falls almost entirely silent on the third criterion he laid out there, completeness—and little wonder, for pure intellect and its satisfactions, however important, scarcely compose the whole of what we are and naturally desire.

To be sure, even as Aristotle claims that happiness is contemplation and "coextensive with contemplation" (1178b30), he acknowledges that a life of pure contemplation "would exceed what is human" (1177b26–27), that the exercise of moral virtue in our relations with our fellows is "characteristically human" (1178a10), and that, having bodies, we need some degree of equipment for life. He even concedes that, because of our composite and social nature, the life that accords with moral virtue is "happy in a secondary way" (1178a9). What he does not do is show how to fit all of this together to structure a life that does full justice to everything in us. Is the need to address the demands of body and neighbors and country just a concession to necessity, like filling the car with gas? Or if the active life can still be substantially happy for most people, as we argued at the end of chapter 5 and Aristotle seems here to concede, what would it really be about contemplating the movements of the stars, for example, that would throw the former life so completely into the shade? How do we know we are not made so as to find our happiness in a mix of active and contemplative seriousness and even play, in pursuing intelligently and well the many things that we naturally need or want?

Aristotle does not leave us with tidy answers to these questions; perhaps it is not possible that he ever could. What he has done is to describe at length what is solid and good in the active moral and political life, sketching throughout with a light hand the many problems with that life as generally understood and lived, and painting in brief and with a broad brush at the end the promise of philosophy. He has not laid out a science of human nature because that science has its main substance in active, ongoing, persistent self-examination. He thus leaves it to us to discover what we ultimately find most satisfying in life, once we have followed up his many hints about the problems with our presuppositions and have allowed this new understanding to grow to be a part of us. In almost his last word on the active and contemplative lives in 10.6–8, he concedes,

> Such considerations, then, foster a certain conviction, but the truth in matters of action is judged from deeds and from life, for it is in these that the authoritative criterion resides. One ought, then, to examine what has been stated previously by applying it to deeds and to life; and if it is in harmony with the deeds one should accept it, but if discordant one should take it as mere speeches. (1179a17–22)

The proof of the pudding is in the eating.

Yet in his last word on the philosophic life Aristotle returns to a higher perspective, affirming again in the strongest terms the divinity of philosophy and the gods' care for those who are most akin to them (1179a22–32). As a simple assertion about the existence and disposition of the gods, this statement, too, must be taken with a certain grain of salt. And yet at the deepest level it is perhaps quite as serious as anything else in the *Ethics*. In the ordinary active lives that most of us will always live, as the composite beings that we all are, our actions are defined by mundane needs, yet we are right to divine that what is the very best in us somehow transcends, somehow must transcend this plane. The human being who tries to live well merely on the basis of nature, practically and prosaically understood, is prone to falling below his nature. As much as Aristotle in his sublimely sober *Ethics* teaches us to make our home in this world and make the best of what nature and fortune give us between the limits of birth and death, and as impressive as have been the human beings who have followed his model, human nature yearns for something higher, which Aristotle captures in his image of the philosopher losing himself in the unneedy and unselfish contemplation of timeless truth. We can be true to ourselves only when we strive, in one such way or another, to reach the divine.

ACKNOWLEDGMENTS

This book grows out of a decades-long meditation on the Socratic claim that virtue is knowledge and the Aristotelian response to that claim. For support with this project I am indebted to fellowships from the National Endowment for the Humanities, the Social Sciences and Humanities Research Council of Canada, and the University of Texas at Austin College of Liberal Arts. A version of the first part of the argument of chapter 3 was published as "The Anatomy of Courage in Aristotle's *Nicomachean Ethics*," *Review of Politics* 80, no. 4 (fall 2018): 569–90. For helpful conversations and critical comments on the argument of this book I am indebted to friends, colleagues, and anonymous reviewers by now too many to recount, but especially to the students of several graduate seminars on the *Nicomachean Ethics* I have had the good fortune to lead at the University of Texas, whose painstaking attention to Aristotle's arguments and whose good-natured critiques of my own have been all that a teacher could wish.

NOTES

Introduction

1 · For a good account of the relation of the two treatises, see Vander Waerdt (1985). While Aristotle's *Eudemian Ethics* (*EE*) bears a somewhat closer relation to the *Politics* than does the *Nicomachean Ethics* (*NE*), inasmuch as most references in the *Politics* to the ethical treatises are to the books common to both (*NE* 5–7) or to the *EE*, I agree with most modern commentators in finding the *NE* the more mature and nuanced of the two, and with Vander Waerdt in conjecturing that the final revision of the whole represented by the *NE* was not completely carried forward into the *Politics*.

2 · *Phronēsis* is most commonly rendered into English as "prudence" or "practical wisdom." In current usage, however, the terms "prudence" and "practical" both imply a focus on what is advantageous and especially materially advantageous; they thus have a narrowness that seems to set them in opposition to the concerns with beauty, eros, and nobility. *Phronēsis* for Aristotle is the form of wisdom that guides *all* intelligent choice and action, especially the choice of noble action in the moral and political sphere, but also the choice to pursue theoretical wisdom (*NE* 6.13). To better capture its full scope, I will translate it throughout as "active wisdom."

3 · To this discovery Strauss (1964, 72) attributes Aristotle's status as the founder of political science.

4 · Compare the complex but strongly affirmative account of human nature as political in *Politics* 1.1–2, where Aristotle says that one who has no share in the political community is "either a beast or a god" (1253a28), with the statement in *The History of Animals* 487b33–88a8 that a human being is one of the animals that "dualizes," being partly gregarious and partly solitary.

5 · Interpreters who read the *Ethics* not as a doctrinal work but as a dialectical project, while remaining a distinct minority, have recently become more common, beginning with Tessitore (1996) and including O'Connor (1999), Thomas Smith (2001), Lorraine Pangle (2003), Salkever (2007), Burger (2008), Bartlett (2008), and Bartlett and Collins (2011). For a fuller defense of this approach, see especially Tessitore (1996) and Lorraine Pangle (2003, 8–16).

6 · All translations from the Greek are my own.

7 · Consider, for example, his definition of courage as steadfastness regarding pleasures as well as pains at *Laches* 191c7–e2, or his virtually indistinguishable definitions of justice and moderation as the good order of the soul in book 4 of the *Republic.*

8 · For this formulation and Socratic denial, see esp. *Protagoras* 352a8–c7.

9 · Consider, for example Kleinias's readiness to question the traditional attribution of his country's laws to Minos in book 1 and to accept the Athenian Stranger's nontraditional cosmology in book 10.

10 · This debate began in the nineteenth century with, among others, Trendelenburg (1855) and Zeller (1897) arguing for the primacy of reason and Walter (1874), followed by Burnet (1900), arguing for the primacy of passion and habituation in determining our ends. In an influential article Allan (1977) summarizes and continues this debate in the twentieth century, himself taking up the former, "intellectualist" position, followed perhaps most prominently by Sorabji (1980a). Contemporary proponents of the alternative position are Fortenbaugh (1991), Tuozzo (1991), and Moss (2011).

11 · Leading proponents of an inclusive reading of Aristotle's concept of happiness are Cooper (1975), Ackrill (1999), and Irwin (1999). Leading proponents on the other side, who argue that happiness for Aristotle consists solely in excellent intellectual activity, are Hardie (1965 and 1979), Kraut (1999) with some modifications, and Lear (2009).

Chapter 1

1 · Saint Thomas (1964, para. 11) insists that there is one ultimate end, even if individuals' proximate ends are not all closely tied to it. Other commentators observe the hypothetical character of the argument but still note the unwarranted strong suggestion that if *everything* is not pointless, there must be a *single* end to all that we do (e.g., Ackrill 1999, 67–69; Lear 2009, 391, *pace* Hardie 1965, 277).

2 · The Greek word *politikē* can mean political art or science. Following the translation of Bartlett and Collins (2011), I will translate it as "political art," as the ending *-ikē* is characteristic of terms for the arts.

3 · On the critical importance of the regime see esp. Aristotle *Politics* 1276a6–b14, 1289a11–20, and 1328a33–b2; Thomas Pangle (2013, 107–11).

4 · For a clear statement of the potential competition here and the consequent necessarily political character of Aristotle's project, see Bartlett (2008, 678). Saint Thomas introduces theology as another competitor with the political art (1964, para. 31).

5 · These digressions on method, each marked at the end by a comment that Aristotle is resuming where he left off, are chapter 1.3, the latter parts of chapters 1.4 and 1.7, and the first half of 2.2. Chapter 1.6, while chiefly concerned with the idea of the good, is similarly marked as a digression and contains another statement on the inappropriateness of seeking precision in moral matters.

6 · Cf. Plato *Meno* 88a.

7 · Aulus Gellius *Attic Nights* 20.5; Bodéüs (1993, chap. 4).

8 · Cf. Aristotle *Metaphysics* 994b33 ff.; *Politics* 1337b15–17.

9 · Cooper (1975, 89); Lear (2009, 393); Ackrill (1999, 66); Bartlett (2008, 677n); Ross (1949, 190); Hardie (1979, 35); Kraut (1979); Burnet (1900, 1).

10 · A cognate of the word here translated as "prevalent," *epipolaios*, can also mean and is used in the next chapter to mean "superficial": cf. *NE* 1095a30, 1095b24.

11 · Saint Thomas (1964, para. 52).

12 · Hesiod, *Works and Days*, ll. 293–97.

13 · Bodéüs (1993, esp. chap. 1). Others grant that this is at least his primary audience, Tessitore (1996) stressing the moral seriousness and O'Connor (1999, 109) and T. W. Smith (2001, 6) the ambition of this group.

14 · Thus Tessitore (1996, 15–20) argues for the presence of a second, philosophical part of Aristotle's intended audience, while stressing the importance of moral seriousness for both groups. Burger (2008, 4, 20–21) suggests that the most important segment of the second group is those who are well raised and morally serious but troubled and perplexed; I would add as equally important those who may already think they have broken free of conventional morality altogether. Whereas Burger maintains that Aristotle is trying to educate the most inquiring "while trying as little as possible to disturb those satisfied with the starting point" (21), I see a rather more active education of all his readers at work in the *Ethics*.

15 · Diogenes Laertius 2.40.

16 · As for Socrates' own views on the being of anything good in itself, see Xenophon *Memorabilia* 3.8.1–3.

17 · Grant (1885) observes of this chapter, "The personal feeling expressed by Aristotle towards Plato, here as elsewhere, is in the highest degree cordial. But in the argument used there is something captious" (1: 439).

18 · Grant (1885) comments, "Even of the *prakton agathon* it might be said that according to Aristotle's own account it falls (in all its manifestations, whether as means or ends) under the one supreme science—Politics" (1: 441).

19 · Among contemporary scholars, Ackrill (1999) argues that Aristotle takes the first or second of these positions (it is hard to tell which), and Cooper (1975) the second throughout most of the *NE*; but they agree that he changes to the third in book 10. Kraut (1999) argues that Aristotle maintains the second throughout but in the end reveals the true meaning of happiness to strongly prioritize the activity of intellectual virtue; Gabriel Lear (2009) seems to agree. Nagel (1972) and Price (1986) both argue that Aristotle is "torn" between a "comprehensive" account of happiness as including the full range of human life and action and an "intellectualist" account of happiness that includes only the activity of contemplation. Hardie (1979) likewise finds that Aristotle "hesitates" and "straddles" between different views but is chiefly devoted to the view that true happiness consists in one "dominant" good, philosophy, to which every other good must give way or contribute. Of all these scholars, then, only Kraut vigorously defends Aristotle as perfectly consistent.

20 · Bartlett (2008) is helpful in showing how much of the work of book 1 consists in an elucidation of these hopes.

21 · Burger (2008, 8) dramatically but helpfully compares the unfolding of the ar-

gument of the *Ethics* to the unfolding of the plot of a tragedy, on the basis of initially hidden underlying necessities.

22 · Ackrill (1999, 62–67). see also Price (1986, 343).

23 · As Lear (2009) says, criticizing Ackrill's account of happiness as (evidently) including everything worth having, "a set like this cannot be an end in an Aristotelian sense" (399), for such an aggregate is not a determinate thing. Hardie (1979, 41) makes the same criticism.

24 · Nagel (1972, 253–55) gives a good account of what is problematic with the work argument: since human beings are in fact composite beings, why should Aristotle not include the good functioning of our bodies and of all parts of our souls? Or if he excludes from our unique work whatever functions we share with other beings, why should he not reject the work of reason too, since we share that with the gods? Relatedly, Burger (2008) points out that Aristotle "never states, let alone defends, the premise that there is a whole of 'life' to the good of which the human species makes a unique contribution" (31–32).

25 · Burnet (1900, 35), troubled by the shift here, suggests bracketing the prior sentence in which Aristotle distinguishes the part that obeys from the part that thinks.

26 · See Plato *Euthydemus* 279b, *Philebus* 48e.

27 · Burger (2008, 41) observes that Aristotle here and in 1.13 provisionally adopts moral virtue's assumption of the independence of soul from body, an assumption Aristotle will overturn in book 10 (see 1178a9–22).

28 · As Grant (1885) says, "Both the terms 'action' and 'well' are implied in ἐνέργεια κατ' αὐτὴν. Εὖ πράξει, however, goes off into a different train of associations" (1: 457), implying that one will fare well in every respect.

29 · Consider Plato *Symposium* 206a ff.

30 · Cf. Plato *Meno* 70a, 100b.

31 · Consider esp. *NE* 1109a24–30, 1150a15–16, 1179b10–16, 1179b20–23.

32 · See esp. Homer *Iliad* 4.1–67.

33 · For the story of Solon's exchange with Croesus on human happiness, see Herodotus *Histories* 1.30–32.

34 · Homer *Odyssey* 11.466–540.

35 · See esp. *NE* 1115a26–27; Aristotle, *On the Soul* 408b19–30; Gooch (1983).

36 · Irwin (1999, section V) makes this point nicely. He suggests that in this regard the *NE* represents an improvement over the corresponding arguments in the *Magna Morality* and *EE*, where Aristotle, reasoning that happiness requires a "complete lifetime," gives qualified assent to Solon's dictum.

37 · Saint Thomas (1964, para. 202).

38 · Plato *Symposium* 201d–12c.

39 · The most important exception is Saint Thomas, who insists that Aristotle is addressing not the actual fate of the dead but only their continued existence "as they live in the memory of men" (1964, para. 211), for a good response to which see Jaffa (1952, 146–48).

40 · Burnet (1900, 49–54), Stewart (1892, 1: 149), and Gauthier and Jolif (1958–59, 2: 78–79 and 86) all take this passage as a bow to popular feeling, Burnet evidently

meaning that it is dialectical in merely this sense. Taking up this meaning, Pritzl (1983, 104 ff.) argues that it is not "*just* a dialectical discussion," inasmuch as Aristotle is showing that his argument about the essence of happiness works whether we believe there is any possibility of awareness after death or not.

41 · For a somewhat different analysis of different levels of meaning in *NE* 1.10–11, see Bartlett (2008).

42 · Thus Grant (1885, 470) calls the topic of this chapter "trifling" and suggests that Aristotle wrote it only out of a kind of pedantic insistence on covering every possible angle of his topic.

43 · Saint Thomas (1964, paras. 215 and 219).

44 · Zeller (1897, 163–64).

45 · Bartlett (2008, 685) observes this shift.

46 · Contrast the approach of Socrates in Plato's *Charmides* 156b–57c, who uses the same example of eye doctors to insist that one part of the body cannot be treated without thorough knowledge of the whole and the body itself cannot be treated without knowledge of the whole soul.

47 · In *On the Soul* 1.5, 2.2, 3.4, 3.9, and 3.10, Aristotle considers whether what he calls the parts of the soul are separate in reality or only in speech. He suggests that the latter may be more accurate and generally refers to them not as parts but as capacities. Burnet (1900, 58) roundly affirms that "Aristotle himself did not believe in 'parts of the soul' at all," treating this concept and the "*exoterikoi logoi*" that defend it as belonging to Plato and the Academy.

48 · Aristotle's choice certainly has been influential. As Grant (1885) puts it, this division "may be said to have regulated almost all subsequent human thought on moral subjects" (473).

49 · Thus, as Burnet (1900, 61) stresses, it "has" reason in the curious sense of being able to listen to one who truly has it.

50 · Thus Cooper (1989, 33) argues that reason persuades rather than forcing the "non-rational" desires to obey, for example by showing anger itself that it was wrong to take a seeming slight as it did. Its ability to do so is possible only because the emotions and especially anger do, after all, entail implicit reasonings, as Fortenbaugh (1969) effectively argues. Yet these considerations are not ones that Aristotle makes here in calling the seat of the emotions rational "in a sense," and they ultimately weigh against dividing the soul into separate parts.

51 · Saint Thomas (1964) says that in habituation "the appetite follows a certain tendency in accordance with the mode of nature, as many drops of water falling on a rock hollow it out." Likewise, "when we act repeatedly according to reason, a modification is impressed in the appetite by the power of reason. This impression is nothing else but moral virtue" (para. 249).

52 · But cf. Grant (1885, 1: 484).

53 · Bartlett and Collins (2011, 28n4).

54 · Ackrill (1978, 596) considers Aristotle's statement that a noble act must be done for its own sake "an unhappy formulation," claiming rather implausibly that Aristotle failed to notice that a just act such as mending a neighbor's fence is never done truly

for its own sake but for the sake of justice. This article lays out the tensions in Aristotle's account of virtuous action as an end especially clearly. Two attempts to defend this formulation—neither, I think very successful, but both revealing of the problems with it—are Whiting (2002) and Luthra (2015).

55 · Saint Thomas (1964) writes, "Virtue is better than art because by art a man is capable of doing a good work, but art does not cause him to do the good work" (para. 316).

56 · Burger (2008, 59–60) brings out this important shift, tying it to the disappearance of *phronēsis* from the discussion in book 2.

Chapter 2

1 · There is much important vocabulary in this passage. The word translated as passions, *pathē*, can mean anything that befalls one, including not only passions but all kinds of experiences, misfortunes, and sufferings. The word translated as sympathy, *suggnomē*, is often rendered as forgiveness, but unlike Christians who are taught to forgive deliberate wrongs, the Greeks tended to forgive only where they could excuse wrongs as at least partly involuntary. The word rendered as rewards, *timas*, can refer to rewards of all kinds but means especially honors. Most important are the words I have rendered as voluntary and involuntary, *hekousion* and *akousion*. The correct translation of these words and their cognates *hekōn* and *akōn* has occasioned much debate. Both "voluntary" and "willing" can carry misleading suggestions of the existence of the will as a separate faculty of the soul, and the word "intentional" is too narrowly restricted to what is deliberately chosen to fit all that Aristotle calls voluntary. The distinction between the *hekousion* and the *akousion* covers both the dichotomy between what one wants to do and what one does inadvertently and the dichotomy between what one does gladly and what one does reluctantly, although it is the former pair of meanings that Aristotle emphasizes. Moline (1989, 284–87) provides a helpful discussion of the meanings of the Greek terms and the difficulty of translating them, although I believe he is wrong in saying that Aristotle ever unambiguously calls emotions or passions *hekousion*. Other objections to the customary English translations may be found in Ross (1925), Kenney (1979), Irwin (1985, 431), Urmson (1988), and Hardie (1980). Meyer (1993, 9–14), however, provides a good defense of these translations.

2 · Joachim (1951, 85) attempts to get around the problem by arguing that virtue is concerned only with the attitude we take *toward* our unchosen and indeed involuntary passions, and the acts we perform in response, an interpretation rightly criticized by Kosman (1980, 108–9). The problem that the unchosenness of passions poses to moral responsibility is much less clearly brought out at the beginning of the parallel passage in *EE* 2.6–11, where only actions and not passions are discussed.

3 · Virtually all commentators on these chapters have viewed them as having a single theoretical or practical aim and thus inevitably end up either ignoring or trying to explain away important elements of the argument. Among those who see these chapters as having an essentially practical aim are Grant (1885), Burnet (1900), Curren (1989), and Moline (1989). Grant (1885) stresses Aristotle's reliance on and even adherence to common opinion in this section, and the "political" rather than "theological"

or "theoretical" character of the arguments, claiming in particular that Aristotle's discussion of the "mixed" class in *NE* 3.1 "does not rise to the level of philosophy" (2: 5–7). Likewise, Burnet (1900) writes, "For us the chief interest of the discussion lies in his anticipation of some of the most important distinctions of Roman and later law. This goes far to justify his claim to be regarded as a teacher of lawgivers" (109). Burnet cites as one such contribution to jurisprudence Aristotle's identification of compulsion and ignorance as the two factors that render an act involuntary (111). These scholars may be correct about Aristotle's chief influence on later thought, but this does not settle the question of his own deepest purpose. Burger (2008), one of the few commentators who recognize the full complexity of Aristotle's project, observes a "necessary conflict between the presuppositions of the legislator and those of the doctor of soul, whose concern is not with praise and blame but with knowledge of the causes of the psychic illnesses he seeks to cure" (63).

4 · In *EE* 2.7–8 Aristotle does not define the voluntary negatively but seeks a common basis for all voluntary action. He says that everything voluntary must result from or accord with desire or choice or thought; from the fact that not everything voluntary is desired or chosen, he concludes that it must all accord with thought. There is a strong element of common sense in this definition: what we do voluntarily is what we intend to do, knowing what we are about. He further stresses that what is completely voluntary is what we do through persuasion and so does not include acts done out of a lack of self-control (1224a39–b3). Aristotle thus comes close to the Socratic position here in making thought central to voluntariness and in conceding that extreme pleasure and extreme duress can make actions involuntary (*EE* 1225a18–33). These concessions he retracts in the *NE*. Evidently he has decided that his original characterization of the voluntary was unhelpful in failing to distinguish voluntary acts that may be excused from those that should not be. In the *NE* he pointedly includes under the rubric of the voluntary the acts of small children and even animals, which clearly do not partake of thought and persuasion in the same way that adult acts do: by extension he thereby includes many thoughtless acts of adults. Thus he opts here for a negative (and hence broader) definition of the voluntary, in which the *EE*'s characterization "through thought" is replaced by "not by force or because of ignorance."

5 · As Burnet (1900, 112) reads it, *paschōn* is a kind of correction, and the event is really a *pathos*, not a *praxis*.

6 · Hardie (1980, 155) argues that Aristotle's class of "mixed" actions blurs important distinctions between those at two ends of the spectrum: improper things done under a terrible and perhaps overwhelming pressure, about which the relevant question is whether they were voluntary, and those done under some pressure, such as jettisoning cargo, which are unquestionably voluntary and about which the relevant question is whether they were justified. Somehow, however, Aristotle both is and is not prepared to say that any of the mixed actions are unquestionably voluntary.

7 · Irwin (1980, 136) observes the problem. Chappell (1995, 14–15) may have the same problem in mind when he insists that to be perfectly consistent Aristotle would have to treat all actions done under duress not even as mixed but as wholly voluntary.

8 · Saint Thomas (1964, 180) insists that Aristotle is merely allowing here for rules

of decorum and not moral rules to be broken in a good cause. This distinction does not appear in Aristotle's text, however, and Aristotle seems deliberately vague on the question of when and to what extent base or shameful things are allowable in a good cause.

9 · Aristotle's formulating the exception in terms of what "no one could endure" implicitly rules out granting such forgiveness to those who succumb to pressures that they could not endure but that others could. But cf. *EE* 1225a25–27: "What is up to oneself—and everything hangs on this—is what one's nature is able to bear." Aristotle there goes on to observe, quoting the Pythagorean philosopher Philolaus, that not only some passions but some arguments are "too strong for us" (1225a33–34).

10 · As Kenny (1979, 28, 36) points out, there is an ambiguity in the word *suggnōmē* as in so many things in this chapter; it may mean sympathy *or* recognition of an excuse that absolves one of guilt *or* the pardon that acknowledges guilt but withholds punishment.

11 · As Burger (2008, 64) observes, the word "perhaps" of course signals that Aristotle is open to the possibility that sufficient pressures might make any act pardonable, a possibility that Saint Thomas silently rejects in omitting the word "perhaps" in his summary of this argument; see also Jaffa (1952, 104–9).

12 · Plato *Euthyphro* 3e ff.

13 · "Alcmaeon," in Grimal (1986, 31).

14 · It is above all the presence of this interlocutor with his penetrating questions about responsibility and the resulting dialectical character of the discussion that distinguish these chapters of *NE* 3.1–5 from the parallel discussion in *EE* 2.6–11, which probes less deeply into the problems of responsibility and focuses more on the difficulties of getting an adequate definition of voluntary action. Perhaps because that work was more narrowly directed to students of philosophy, the discussion in the *EE* begins from and has more to say about causation of all sorts, physical as well as human, and less to say about political and politically delicate issues. In keeping with this emphasis, it contains fewer arguments that are merely rhetorical and logically inadequate, but by the same token it shows a less thorough consideration of the ways in which philosophy may both inform and learn from political life.

15 · The noble and the pleasant, together with the advantageous (*sumpheron*), are the three aspects of the good that Aristotle elsewhere characterizes as *the* ends of all human choices (e.g. 1104b31). Why Aristotle here leaves out the advantageous is not clear. Grant (1885, 2: 85) and Sachs (2002, 38) suggest that the advantageous is merely a means to the pleasant or noble. Perhaps better, following *Rhetoric* 1.9.3, the noble should be taken to encompass all that is good for its own sake including such goods as health and knowledge that are not normally considered noble, so that either the pleasant or the noble in this extended sense would constitute the ultimate sources of all action or, according to the interlocutor, of "compulsion."

16 · This exchange alone seems sufficient refutation of Adkins's (1960, 324) claim that there was no theory of determinism available in Aristotle's day and that he therefore cannot be expected to have grappled with it or developed a theory of free will or free choice in response to it.

17 · Joachim (1951) notes that, while disposing of the possibility that we are respon-

sible only for our good acts, Aristotle never answers the question of whether "man is in any sense the ultimate originator of his own actions" (96).

18 · See, for example, Ross (1949, 198).

19 · Burnet (1900, 117).

20 · This distinction constitutes an advance over the analysis in the *EE*, as Irwin observes (1980, 122 and 147n13).

21 · This crucial statement about the ignorance of the wicked, which concedes such important ground to the Socratic interlocutor, has no analogue in the parallel discussion in the *EE*.

22 · Thus Adkins (1960, 328) and Roberts (1989, 24) both complain that Aristotle fails to explain why ignorance of what is good does not make an act involuntary, if other, less disastrous kinds of ignorance do.

23 · Saint Thomas (1964, para. 411).

24 · Chappell (1995, 6, 25–31) argues that Aristotle should and implicitly does include a third criterion of voluntary action: that there must be a rational connection between the act and the relevant thoughts and feelings that might be given to explain the act, or in other words that the agent must not be insane and acting randomly. One may wonder whether Aristotle thought anyone was so insane as to act in a manner wholly uncaused by desires and thoughts of what is good. But Chappell's point, if followed to its ultimate conclusions, brings us to Socrates' point: voluntary actions in the full sense are rational actions, and rational actions in the full sense are only those which aim intelligently at what is good.

25 · See, for example, Burnet (1900, 109); Saint Thomas (1964, 174 ff.); Ross (1949, 199–201). Aristotle is quite ready to divide the soul into parts when it suits his purpose, but he never claims that there is any separate part dedicated to choice.

26 · This is the Aldine Scholiast's interpretation of this line, which seems correct: see Stewart (1892, 1: 245–46).

27 · As Stewart (1892, 1: 248) argues, *boulēsis* is clearly wish and not will or willing as Saint Thomas renders it—perhaps most obviously, because *boulēsis* can have the impossible as its object.

28 · The inadequacy of the customary translation of this phrase as "means" has been demonstrated by Fortenbaugh (1965) and Wiggins (1980, 222–27).

29 · Consider Alfarabi, *Philosophy of Aristotle*, section 3.

30 · The account of responsible choice in the *EE*, beginning with a contrast between the way in which inanimate nature and necessity function as causes and the way in which the human soul is a cause of its own actions and character, makes a similar suggestion that the necessities of the soul are of a different order from the necessities that rule inanimate bodies. Indeed, there may be three distinct kinds of causation: that governing inanimate bodies, the necessity of the mind's affirming what has been adequately demonstrated, and the necessity of the soul's pursuing the good as it grasps the good, none of these three being simply reducible to either of the others. And this may be why, as Huby (1967, 360) says, the physical determinism of Democritus was never accepted by Aristotle. But cf. Cicero *De Fato* 39, where Cicero strikingly calls Aristotle a determinist.

31 · Bolotin (1999, 168) traces this revision.

32 · Ross (1949) objects that Aristotle's definition of choice as deliberate desire "errs by treating it as one kind of desire, which it plainly is not" (200). In fact this protest helps us see that for Aristotle choice *is* closely akin to other forms of desire. Ross wants to understand *proairesis* as equivalent to the will, that which stands above desire and freely chooses whether to follow it. But in passages many of which Ross himself refers to in a note to the same paragraph, Aristotle will in fact later speak of choice as a species of desire that one may even fail to follow when it is opposed by other desires: see 1148a9, 1150b30, 1151a7, 1151a29–b4, and 1152a17.

33 · Anscombe (1965, 61–66); see also Burnyeat (1980, 82).

34 · On this point see esp. Burnyeat (1980, 73–80).

35 · Cooper (1975, 19–22) gives a good discussion of the ways in which choices may conduce to or satisfy or form constituent parts of the end one has in view. Likewise, Reeve (2006, 205–6) argues that not only means but internal constituents of the end may be the subject of deliberation, citing *Metaphysics* 1032b18–29.

36 · Anscombe (1965, 63), for example, observes that Aristotle's model of deliberation seems better to fit technical than moral deliberation, although she goes on to argue that choice in the full sense for Aristotle is always more than merely technical. Grant (1885, 2: 18) notes the omission of any mention of choices between right and wrong. Stewart (1892, 1: 262) focuses on Aristotle's failure to discuss the weighing of ends against the costs of achieving them and the way such evaluations can lead people to decide that particular ends are not worth pursuing. Broadie (1988, 245–47) carries the same complaint to the point of arguing that the treatment of deliberation is "grossly distorted". Wiggins (1980, esp. 228–37) brings out especially well the complexity and murkiness of much actual moral reasoning, as compared with Aristotle's tidy geometrical paradigm, arguing that it is precisely the indeterminate character of our ends or ideals that constitutes human freedom. In light of these problems, some commentators have tried to reinterpret Aristotle's account so as to make room for deliberation about and choice of ends. Thus Ross (1949, 200) claims—I think unpersuasively—that Aristotle's uses of the word *proairesis* outside of this section mostly treat it as referring to ends, citing 1095a14, 1097a21, 1110b31, and 1117a5. In a similar spirit, Urmson (1988, 54–55) argues that when Aristotle denies that we deliberate about ends, he is really talking not about ends at all, but only about "success." Irwin (1980, 117–44, esp. 118, 130, 135, 139–41) more forthrightly tries to improve on Aristotle's account by extending the process of deliberation to ends, so as to provide better support for moral responsibility than he thinks Aristotle does. For a sharp critique of this line of interpretation, see Mele (1981). For two more moderate accounts that give substantial scope to reason in determining, clarifying, and modifying the ends, see Sorabji (1980a), and Cooper (1975, 62–71).

37 · As Sorabji (1980a) says, "we can choose ends, so long as they are related to further ends, and . . . the relationship may be that of instance, manner, or part, as well as means" (204).

38 · Cooper (1975, 71) makes this point, although he argues that our reflections on

ends are conducted not by means of practical intelligence at all but only by philosophical reflection, which seems doubtful.

39 · Cooper (1989, 35).

40 · Grant (1885, 2: 22–23) argues that the technical discussion of choice and deliberation has done nothing to show how human beings can be free and responsible, and that the question now becomes pressing: are we free in our choices of ends? Echeñique (2012) denies that questions of causation or responsibility or just susceptibility to punishment are on the table at all in these chapters, arguing that Aristotle is merely formulating an account of when actions may and may not be ascribed to the agent's moral character.

41 · This, again, is the problem that divides "intellectualists" and "nonintellectualists" in Aristotle scholarship: see introduction, n. 10. Two commentators who argue for the impossibility of reading Aristotle consistently according to either interpretation, but without offering a reason for his inconsistency, are Broadie (1988) and A. D. Smith (1996).

42 · Plato *Protagoras* 152a.

43 · Cf. *EE* 1227a18–32. Saint Thomas (1964, 215) characteristically says that the bad man chooses wrongly because he follows not reason but the senses, suggesting that he has access to correct reason but chooses to follow something else. But Aristotle indicates rather that those who follow pleasure do not see the truth correctly at all.

44 · Joachim (1951, 110–11) wrestles with the question of what Aristotle means when he says that virtue and vice are up to us, professing himself unable to decide whether Aristotle is claiming that choice is radically undetermined or not. Sorabji (1980b) thinks Aristotle does mean to assert a radical freedom in the agent. Chappell (1995) agrees that Aristotle treats human action as undetermined, but he observes that "Aristotle's argument for this conclusion is entertainingly opaque" (43–46). Roberts (1989) argues to the contrary that Aristotle is actively embracing determinism. All these authors assume that moral responsibility requires freedom of the will: they are in contemporary parlance "incompatibilists" inasmuch as they hold that determinism of any sort is incompatible with moral responsibility. On the other side are "compatibilists" such as Meyer (1993, esp. chaps. 2 and 5) and Everson (1990), who maintain that Aristotle understands moral responsibility to be compatible with determinism. Meyer makes an intelligent case for this position, and I believe there is substantial truth in her argument that Aristotle's primary concern in this section is to argue for the appropriateness of praising and blaming those acts that spring from and reveal character. Aristotle clearly goes further, however, to affirm a kind of responsibility for character itself, and it is here that Meyer's very rational account fails to capture the subtle and problematic complexity of Aristotle's discussion.

45 · Cf. *Magna Moralia* 1187a7–13. I accept the prevailing scholarly view that the *Magna Moralia* is likely but not definitely by Aristotle; to me it seems a briefer, more popular, and probably earlier sketch of Aristotle's ethical teachings than the *EE* and especially the *NE*. For a recent discussion of the question of authorship see Simpson (2014).

46 · See Burnet (1900, 134).

47 · Meyer (1993, 128) acknowledges that this passage, as well as 1114a3–5 and 1114b3–4, appears to concede that moral responsibility requires responsibility for character, but she denies that they really do. Although I do not agree with her interpretation, the difficulty that drives her to it is serious, for as she says, if Aristotle means to argue that our states of character depend wholly on us, he fails to prove his case.

48 · As Broadie (1991, 128) puts it, those things for which we hold people responsible are those actions and aspects of character that are "socially accessible" through praise and blame.

49 · Brickhouse (1991, 141–42) observes that in *NE* 3.5 the voluntary seems to carry more weight than it did in earlier chapters, where it did not in itself imply moral responsibility. Nussbaum (1986, 283–89) argues that *NE* 3.5 offers a distinct account of the voluntary as it applies to agents capable of choice.

50 · This objection and Aristotle's response show that Aristotle is indeed arguing against determinism and defending the common intuition that moral responsibility requires the agent's freedom, at least at some point in time, to act upon different principles, contrary to the claims of Roberts (1989) and Everson (1990).

51 · Saint Thomas (1964, para. 512) goes even further and insists that one who wills a specific action does will its foreseeable consequences, so that if he chooses to walk on a hot day, he also chooses to perspire. We may at least ask whether these two things are voluntary to the same degree, if not whether it makes any sense to speak of willing what one has, however carelessly, failed to consider.

52 · Furley (1977) draws the correct conclusion here: "Aristotle does not seek a criterion of what is voluntary in whether or not a man may act otherwise *now*. . . . He does not say or imply that an act is voluntary only because it is 'freely chosen,' or because it is preceded by a 'free act of will'" (51). But he sees the difficulty in Aristotle's claim that the agent was *once* fully free to determine his course, and he charges that Aristotle "never considered" the question of whether the discipline provided by parents and teachers is not a crucial external cause of a man's disposition (53). Without attributing to Aristotle any such absurdities, Hardie (1980, 175) argues along similar lines that by trying to push real freedom back to the point before one's character was formed, "Aristotle skates over some thin ice," and that he ought rather to insist that man is morally free to act well or badly at *every* point in time. Since he does not do so, Hardie argues, he leaves himself open to the criticism that adolescents and even children with unformed characters are in a sense more fully responsible than adults with settled characters, a problem observed also by Curren (1989, 270–73); Roberts (1989, 28 and 30n14); and Irwin (1980, 141).

53 · In particular, some editors and commentators treat the second sentence of the passage as I have translated it to be Aristotle's interjection, others regard it as part of the exposition of the opposing view, and some question whether the words of the interlocutor should be considered to continue to the end of the passage quoted or to end somewhere earlier. Cf. Burnet (1900, 137) with the translations of Ostwald (1962) and Rackham (1975).

54 · Hardie (1980) wonders whether the enigmatic statement that each individual is "somehow" responsible for his character is meant to suggest that the individual is in

part such an uncaused cause, but he rightly observes that if so, "Aristotle has given no explanation of this alternative and no reason for accepting it" (179).

55 · It is this fact that Kosman (1980, 111–13) fails to address squarely in an otherwise helpful attempt to explain how we may be held responsible for our feelings.

56 · The ad hominem character of this argument has been noted by Furley (1977, 52–53), following Gauthier and Jolif (1958–59).

57 · The parallel account in the *EE* supports this same thought in a different way. By defining the voluntary as that which accords with thought (1225a37–b1), Aristotle suggests that what is voluntary in the deepest and fullest sense can only be what accords with complete self-knowledge.

58 · Stewart (1892, 279) thus understands the chapter to end in failure and assumes that Aristotle simply failed to face up to it. For similar charges see Joachim (1951, 96–97), and Williams (1985).

59 · In particular, Roberts (1989) argues that Aristotle agrees wholly with Socrates and is merely presenting a more practically useful account that stresses the role of education and habituation to balance Socrates' stress on knowledge. I believe there is much truth in this argument. The difficulty with her article is that she gives short shrift to Aristotle's argument that rational adults are truly responsible for their actions while animals and children are not, and that the strongest praise, blame, and punishment are called for by actions that reveal the fixed character of the agent and not merely the destructive behavior that a community most wishes to deter. She interprets Aristotle as saying that legal sanctions are meant only to control behavior and not to offer retribution or register the community's condemnation of bad character.

60 · See especially Curren (1989) and Moline (1989). Curren is incorrect, however, in attributing to Aristotle the view that acts of negligence are involuntary and still punishable: Aristotle treats all negligence as voluntary.

61 · It is surely no accident that the *NE*'s new and more socially constructive account of the way in which we are responsible for our characters, which does not appear in the *EE*, should be presented together with the *NE*'s deeper and more revealing account of the significance of unchosen insight for moral virtue.

Chapter 3

1 · Unlike many commentators (e.g., Ross 1949, 209–11) who view the order of the virtues in *NE* 3.6–5 as largely haphazard, Collins (2009) explains both the primacy and the great detail of Aristotle's treatment of courage as reflections of his project of beginning with but also critically revising common opinion. "In the end, his attention to courage turns out to have been in an important respect in the service of its demotion" (50). Salkever (1986) gives a good account of the critique of manliness and demotion of courage that run through Aristotle's political thought. "On the whole," he writes, "the Aristotelian position is that *sophrosune*, like justice, is a higher virtue than courage or virility to the same degree that leisure is of greater worth than business, and peace than war" (243).

2 · Burger (2008, 78) goes so far as to call it a "caricature" but goes on to acknowledge the power of Aristotle's challenge here to Socrates.

3 · Plato *Symposium* 220e–21c; cf. *Laches* 181a–b.

4 · Churchill, speeches in the House of Commons on May 13 and June 18, 1940.

5 · And so Socrates defines it. At *Laches* 191c7–e2, for example, he attributes courage not only to those who are steadfast in the face of dangers other than war but even to those who steadfastly resist pleasures. This extension of courage to pleasures seems very strange until we consider the importance for Socratic courage not only of keeping one's head in the face of evils but of resisting the pull of irrational hopes: see Rabieh (2006, 87–88).

6 · While modern democratic readers almost invariably wish to extend courage beyond the battlefield, Zavily and Aristidou (2014, 174 and 180) and Sanford (2010, 442–45) both argue that if courage is to be preserved as a distinct quality worthy of the deepest respect, its connection with serious risk and with voluntary action must be maintained.

7 · This question has been much discussed by the commentators. Ross (1949, 206) and Joachim (1951, 118) ultimately reduce courage to self-control, and Heil (1996, 65) comes close, calling it a form of endurance or *karteria*. Their case might be strengthened by noting that in *NE* 7.4 where Aristotle discusses forms of self-control that resemble on a lower plane all the other important moral virtues, he gives no such analogue for courage. Duff (1987) and Pears (2004) at the other extreme insist that courage for Aristotle involves a struggle-free harmony, and Brady (2005) denies that the courageous really desire to escape death at all. In between are Hardie (1980, 403), who says that in courage pain and fear must be overcome but not any base desire as in the case of self-control, and Curzer (2012, 55–62), Leighton (1988, 88–92), Pakaluk (2005, 160), and Young (2009), who all offer sensible distinctions between the fear that causes panic and the fear that functions well to rivet one's attention on the danger and make one fight well. It is a question, however, whether any of them quite escapes the problem that fear as such entails a painful expectation of death as the ultimate evil and requires an inner struggle to overcome the powerful natural desire to escape it.

8 · Curzer (2012, 26), Pakaluk (2005, 153), and Young (2009) all observe the problem.

9 · The temptation to read this thought into this section is enormous, especially in light of Aristotle's statement in book 1 that securing the good of the political community is "nobler and more divine" than securing it for one individual (1094b10; cf. Bartlett and Collins 2011, 258), and his statement in book 9 that the noble man will give up many things and even die for his friends and his fatherland (1169a18–20). Likewise at *Rhetoric* 1366b Aristotle writes, "The greatest virtues are necessarily those which are most useful to others, if virtue is the faculty of conferring benefits. For this reason justice and courage are the most esteemed, the latter being useful to others in war, the former in peace as well." And at *Rhetoric* 1366b–67a he lists among noble things "those desirable things which a man does not do for his own sake, and things which are absolutely good, which a man has done for the sake of his country, while neglecting his own interests." But these passages make it all the more significant that, unlike such commentators as Brady (2005, 199–202), Pears (1980), Lear (2004, 147–62), Ross (1949, 207), Saint Thomas (1964, 1: 236 ff.), and Young (2009), Aristotle never speaks of jus-

tice or the common good or the safety of the fatherland as ends in his thematic statement on courage in the *NE*. Contrast Cicero *De Officiis* 1.62–63: "The Stoics correctly define courage as 'that which champions the cause of right.'" Cicero then quotes a saying attributed to Plato, that "even the courage that is prompt to face danger, if it is inspired not by public spirit but by its own selfish purposes, should have the name of effrontery rather than of courage."

10 · Thus Aristotle strikingly refrains from offering the sort of clarification that Rogers (1994) does in writing, "if we determine that a particular campaign will most certainly end in defeat, it is clearly not the 'right time' to forge ahead. This does not imply that our motive in being courageous is to win . . . but rather that courageous people weigh the risks before acting and are not rash fools" (305). Young (2009) and Zavily and Aristidou (2014, 181–87) distinguish courage from recklessness in the same way. This is a test, however, that even Leonidas and the defenders of the Alamo could scarcely be said to pass.

11 · Commentators have complained about Aristotle's lack of specificity both on how confidence differs from the absence of fear and on its grounds. Curzer (2012, 30) suggests that confidence reflects an assessment not just of the threat but of one's own good ability to meet it. This seems sensible, but it may be significant that Aristotle never says this, for it moves far in the direction of reducing courage to knowledge.

12 · The parallel discussion in *EE* 1229a12 ff. speaks of five almost identical things that are courage only "by analogy," but in the *NE*, where Aristotle defers more respectfully to the citizen's perspective, he presents these rather as imperfect forms of courage.

13 · Ward (2001) suggests that "the potential disjunction between the external appearance of an action and the disposition of the actor," common to all the virtues but especially acute in the case of courage, is behind this unique procedure (75).

14 · Charney (1988, 70–71) notes the tactical errors that shame induces both Hector and Diomedes to make in the examples Aristotle gives, observing that Hector in particular is too dependent on both opinions and omens.

15 · Burger (2008, 77) argues that Aristotle's willingness in these chapters and especially at 1116a27 to treat the sense of shame as a virtue is a concession to the civic outlook on courage that is corrected later at 1128b10 ff., but the sense of shame Aristotle there criticizes is not quite the same as the hypothetical shame discussed here—the shame a man who is not defective *would* feel if he *were* to act basely.

16 · Ward (2001, esp. 77–78) and Collins (2009, 55–56) also note the complex character of citizen virtue, if not its essentially shifting character.

17 · But cf. Plato *Laches* 179a and Cicero *De Officiis* 1.50 on the courage of animals.

18 · Focusing on this passage, Heil (1996, 51–52) insists that passion provides none of the motivation for virtuous action. The courageous man while feeling fear resists acting upon that fear, he argues, and likewise his motive to be courageous comes not from *thumos* but only from the noble.

19 · This is essentially the reading of Joachim (1951, 121), who calls *thumos* "the physical basis of true courage."

20 · As Burger (2008) asks, "Is it possible to be driven by the passion of spiritedness and motivated at the same time by either *logos* or the beautiful?" (79).

21 · Cicero observes the terrific pride characteristic of courageous men at *De Officiis* 1.64. Ward (2001) comments on the same pride with its illusory belief that "we are capable of rising above necessity" (78).

22 · Homer *Iliad* 5.330–51, 5.431–46, 5.846–57, 21.211–83, 24.255–59 (cf. *NE* 1145a18–27); consider also the way that the entire involvement of the gods in human affairs in the *Iliad* is precipitated by human *thumos*, in a cascading series of affronts, angry responses, and pleas for divine aid in book 1.

23 · Pulling these threads together, Charney (1988, 69–73) ties Aristotle's critique of the Homeric heroes Hector and Diomedes in this section to his demotion of both spiritedness and piety in their tendency to oppose rational self-reliance.

24 · Young (2009) suggests that a courageous soldier has confidence in the victory of his side even if he himself does not survive, while Heil (1996, 69–71) and Sanford (2010, 440) both identify the soldiers' own virtue as the thing they place their confidence in. Cicero goes further than either: "The soul that is altogether courageous and great . . . cherishes the conviction that nothing but moral goodness and propriety deserves to be either admired or wished for or striven after, and that he ought not to be subject to any man or any passion or any accident of fortune" (*De Officiis* 1.66). But in this he also goes further than Aristotle.

25 · As Saint Thomas (1964, 1: 259–60) points out, Aristotle here opposes the Stoics' claim that there is no human good except virtue and hence that the courageous man loses nothing when he suffers wounds and death.

26 · Collins (2009) makes this point forcefully: "To the courageous man, it is the deed itself . . . that is noble, and those who act for the sake of any other end possess a courage that is a mere appearance of the true thing" (54); cf. Bartlett and Collins (2011, 256–57).

27 · Herodotus *History* 7.207–28. Cooper (1975, 84–88) makes a revealingly unsuccessful attempt to describe an act of courage as complete in itself and choiceworthy wholly for its own sake as a constituent part of the happy virtuous life. He shows how difficult it is even to talk coherently about courage without speaking of such things as the value of what is to be defended and one's chances of success.

28 · It is this whole level of the problem that Ward (2001) misses in his otherwise helpful analysis of *NE* 3.6–9. He sees that the noble "lacks specific content" (79) but does not explore the deepest reasons for its resistance to being pinned down. Bartlett and Collins (2011) present the problem as "a certain circularity: he who acts courageously must forsake his true or greatest good, his virtuous and happy life, and choose instead to do what is noblest in war; but it is in choosing to do this very noble deed that the courageous human being seeks his own true or greatest good" (258.) Rogers (1994, 306–11) tries to resolve the circle by implicitly denying that the act of courage is sought for itself as something splendid and arguing instead that it is merely accepted as necessary by one who sees clearly that acting shamefully would deprive one of the most basic requisite of happiness. In this way she makes Aristotle more consistent, but she fails to do justice to the felt nobility precisely of sacrifice, thereby demoting courage from a great positive good to an unfortunate necessity.

29 · Aspasias (2006, 89 [87.33–88.2]) and Saint Thomas (1964, 1: 234 and 240) iden-

tify the "irrational parts" mentioned here as the *epithumetikos* and the *thumoeidos* or the appetitive and the irascible part, respectively, followed among modern commentators by Brady (2005, 189). But Aristotle never says that courage is the perfection of *thumos* or that moderation in fact governs the whole of human desires.

30 · The only exception comes at 1120b18 where Aristotle says that fortune's apparent arbitrary disfavoring of the most liberal people is "not without reason," given their own failure to husband their resources—thereby indirectly contrasting his own spirit of close examination with liberality's scorn for precision (cf. 1122b8).

31 · Aristotle underscores the difficulty in getting liberality right and not falling into prodigality when he speaks of the pain the liberal person feels when he spends improperly (1121a1–2): perhaps it is impossible to be wholly without error in this virtue.

32 · The question of whether the best individuals may not be barred by fortune from exercising even the lesser virtue of liberality, let alone this very high virtue, was suggested already in the previous chapter and again here at 1122a27, as Aristotle quotes Odysseus, disguised as a beggar, telling the wicked suitor Antinoos, who is consuming his property, that he too once gave handouts to beggars (Homer *Odyssey* 17.420).

33 · It is especially the pregnant references to the gods in *NE* 4.2 that Irwin (2010, 393) misses in his attempt to explain the *kalon* in magnificence simply as a concern for the common good.

34 · Burger (2008, 83) observes this shift.

35 · Howland (2002) assimilates greatness of soul to what Aristotle calls superhuman or divine virtue in *NE* 7.1. Aristotle makes it clear at 7.1 that he is in fact introducing new forms of excellence and weakness and depravity beyond the moral virtues and vices discussed in *NE* 2–5, but I think Howland is right to connect 4.3 with 7.1: greatness of soul at least points upward to and partially claims the territory of what Aristotle will later enigmatically call divine virtue.

36 · Burger (2008, 71); *NE* 1129b30–33, 1130a8–10, 1145a1–2.

37 · For example, Saint Thomas (1964) reads the chapter as wholly laudatory; Burnet (1900), Dirlmeier (1956, 370), and Tessitore (1996, 31), as at least partly ironic; and Jaffa (1952) as deeply if quietly critical. Hardie (1978, esp. 70), Hanley (2002), and Collins (2009, 61–66) see the great-souled man as fundamentally political; Stewart (1892, 1: 34046) and Gauthier and Jolif (1958–59, 2: 272–98) as philosophic; and Jaffa (1952), Tessitore (1996, 28–35), and Burger (2008, 71–78) as ambiguous.

38 · Bartlett and Collins (2011, 264) question whether, for this reason, the great-souled man may not also lack perfect justice.

39 · Gauthier and Jolif (1958–59, 2: 272–98); Plato *Republic* 486a; *Theaetetus* 172c–76a).

40 · Dirlmeier (1967, 370); Hardie (1978).

41 · Hardie (1978, 70); Collins (2009, 64–65). By contrast Hanley (2002) stresses the great-souled man's equanimity in the face of the vicissitudes of fortune, but without explaining it, given the evident desirability of supreme power.

42 · The only other occurrence of *kalon* in this chapter refers to actions that the small-souled person fails to undertake (1125a26).

43 · Burger (2008) observes, "If, as the *Ethics* will finally argue, it is theoretical ac-

tivity pursued as an end in itself that has the greatest claim to self-sufficiency, the great-souled individual, who should be complete in himself, aims, however unwittingly, at something whose fulfillment necessarily lies beyond himself" (85).

44 · Jaffa (1952) brings out this point well.

45 · Consider especially Plato *Laws* 803a–804c and the quiet humor of Xenophon's *Oeconomicus*, his dialogue on Socrates' investigation of perfect gentlemanliness.

46 · But cf. 1132a2–3 and 1134a17–23, where Aristotle concedes that even decent men can and perhaps often do have lapses, as well as 1179b10–13, which connects a sense of shame with gentlemanliness.

Chapter 4

1 · It is this difficulty, among others, that leads Fossheim (2011) to argue that justice is not a moral virtue at all for Aristotle but only a relation between individuals and a characteristic of actions that accord with it. He cites also the problematic way in which justice, if a virtue, seems to give a second cause for every virtuous act, so that it "cuts across all the other virtues while bringing nothing of its own to the table" (258), and the way in which general justice is identified not with a particular disposition but with the requirements of law. By contrast, Polansky (2014b) argues that justice proper is in *NE* 5 *only* a moral virtue, noting, for example, that when Aristotle speaks of just distributions or transactions, he speaks only of "the just" and not "justice."

2 · E.g., Saint Thomas (1964, para. 910); Grant (1885, 2: 102); Burnet (1900, 209).

3 · Tessitore (1996) stresses the political and mundane character of the concerns defining this aspect of justice: "In sharp contrast to his earlier portrait of the magnanimous person, Aristotle's elucidation of particular justice reveals the lowest common denominator for justice in the city. The initial elevation of justice is gradually superseded by a consideration of the nonheroic principles that furnish the rudimentary bonds of the political association" (38).

4 · Burger (2008, 96) notes the negative way in which Aristotle characterizes the law's commandments to exercise the various virtues. Tessitore (1996) observes, "It is the various species of particular justice (distributive, corrective, and reciprocal) that actually prevail in the city, and each of these is animated by a concern for the equal (*to ison*) rather than for 'excellence' (*aretē*)" (39).

5 · Without fully seeing what is at stake in this chapter, Bernard Williams (1980, 197–99) registers a reasonable reluctance to follow Aristotle's suggestion that the vice of particular injustice is characterized by the single character flaw of *pleonexia*. Everyone who wants anything wants more than he has, Williams argues, but wanting more than others or more than one's fair share is not an important part of the desire in the case of most acts of unfairness and is not a consistent character trait. Williams suggests that instead what distinguishes the unjust person is the absence of a disposition to love justice. What he does not do, however, is query Aristotle's silence on what that love of justice per se is grounded in.

6 · Burnet (1900, 218) is uneasy enough about this concession that he insists Aristotle is here merely alluding to proportional taxes on property in wartime as an "illustration" of proportionality.

7 · What is true of ordinary theft may of course not be true of all theft, since dire necessity may give a different meaning to acts that normally arise from vice.

8 · Again, Burnet's (1900) uneasiness is telling as he wrestles with the inadequacy of Aristotle's apparent embrace of "the childish doctrine that a court of law simply awards compensation" (218). He points out that the victim's loss and the offender's gain are not necessarily the same and insists that surely Aristotle saw this, but he produces no evidence that the current chapter is amending the demand for retribution in this way, nor does he recognize how far this step must carry us away from embracing retribution, when thought through.

9 · As Burnet (1900) puts it, "If an officer strikes a private, that is not merely a blow, but may also be an act of discipline; if a private strikes an officer, that is not merely a blow, but also an act of mutiny" (224).

10 · The *Magna Moralia* makes clear, as the *NE* does not, that this desire for proportionality often means inflicting in turn something worse than, although still proportional to, the harm that was done: "It is just, if one man has knocked out another's eye, not merely for his eye to be knocked out in return, but for him to suffer something more, in accordance with proportionality. He started it and did an injustice, so he is unjust in both respects" (*MM* 1194a37–b1).

11 · Saint Thomas (1964, paras. 976 and 980–85) identifies both the quantity of labor that goes into a product and need as the measure of value, without appearing to observe a tension between them. For a contemporary discussion of this chapter and Aristotle's teaching on money and exchange in the *Politics* that interprets these passages more as explorations of problems than as attempted solutions, see Meikle (1995).

12 · The second *kai* is omitted in MS Kb, removing the ambiguity in favor of the second reading.

13 · MS Mb has *nomos* here instead of *logos*, which seems likely to be the editor's interpretation, although a correct one.

14 · Saint Thomas (1964) shows his resistance to this conclusion when he glosses Aristotle's statement "we do not allow a human being to rule but reason" at 1134a35 with the statement "in good government of the multitude we do not permit that men should rule, that is, according to whim and human passion, but that law, which is a dictate of reason, should rule man, *or that man who acts according to reason should rule*" (para. 1009, emphasis added).

15 · Saint Thomas (1964) solves at least the problem of honor's insufficiency with his unaristotelian addition, "Over and above this reward proffered by man, good princes look for a reward from God" (para. 1011).

16 · Saint Thomas (1964) seeks to blunt the force of Aristotle's striking subsumption of natural justice under political justice by saying he is here merely following "the usage the citizens are accustomed to" (para. 1017).

17 · Saint Thomas (1964, paras. 1018, 1023). Polansky (2014b, 171) makes the same argument.

18 · Marsilius of Padua (2005, 2.12.7); Strauss (1953, 158); see also Strauss (1952, 95–98).

19 · While the discussion of natural justice in the *Magna Moralia* contains some in-

teresting and suggestive formulations, it also seems less coherent than that in the *NE*, in keeping with its generally accepted status as either an earlier Aristotelian work or that of a follower.

20 · Marsilius (2005, 2.12.8).

21 · Strauss (1953, 158).

22 · Strauss (1953, 162).

23 · Abraham Lincoln, First Inaugural Address.

24 · Burnet (1900, 235).

25 · Aristotle discusses at length the arguments for and against such total kingship at *Politics* 3.13–17. For a discussion of these chapters that makes a strong case for total kingship, see Thomas Pangle (2013, 155–65).

26 · The phrase is Thomas Jefferson's: see Adams and Jefferson (1959, 2: 387–92).

27 · See Xenophon *Memorabilia* 3.9.10–13.

28 · On the council see Plato *Laws* 908a–9a, 951d–52c, 961a–c, 964d–69d; for a suggestion that the council may in fact have sovereign powers, see 968c.

29 · Burger (2008, 102–3).

30 · On the contest over the noble, see also the important discussion in *NE* 9.8 and L. Pangle (2003, 169–82).

31 · For an argument that Aristotle's account of friendship allows for this possibility, see L. Pangle (2003), esp. chaps. 2, 7, and 8.

32 · Cf. Leviticus 10:1.

Chapter 5

1 · As Grant (1885, 2: 148) justly complains, the question of what precisely the standard of virtue is will, at least explicitly, "get no answer." Urmson (1988, 79) and Ackrill (1999) complain likewise about the false promise held forth here. Natali (2014, 199–200) says that modern readers are disappointed because they expect to find at the bottom of Aristotle's account of moral reasoning the standard of how to deliberate about ends, whereas Aristotle was interested only in describing the process. The slide to the different question of the division of the intellectual faculties is made easier by the ambiguity of the word *horos*. In its extended meaning it is a standard, and as such the equivalent of *skopos* or target, as Burnet (1900, 251) says, but in its original and more fundamental meaning it is a defining limit or boundary marker, and this is the meaning Aristotle now follows as he begins to divide up the rational soul and its different functions.

2 · Zeller (1897, 178n1) argues with particular force for the centrality of *phronēsis* in book 6, tying it to the fundamentally political purpose of the *NE* as a whole. This view is shared by Burnet (1900, 247–48) and Greenwood (1909, 270–71).

3 · Cf. Gauthier and Jolif (1958–59, 2: 440), who suggest that 1138b35–39a3 is the original introduction to book 6 and 38b18–34 a later and not well integrated addition. Sparshott (1994, 196) likewise finds the whole first chapter "disjointed." Natali (2014, 180) attributes this feature to the dual character of book 6 as a completion of the subject of moral virtue and a new treatment of intellectual virtue.

4 · A confirmation that the shift is intentional is that Aristotle reproduces it at

1140a31–b4. Strangely, most commentators (e.g., Burnet 1900, 253; Reeve 2013, 103–4) insist that this distinction makes no difference; but cf. Sparshott (1994, 203).

5 · He considers and criticizes it at *On the Soul* 1.5.

6 · Burnet (1900, 253) notes the surprising substitution, especially as *logistikon* is Plato's typical term for the whole rational part of the soul in the *Republic.*

7 · Saint Thomas (1964, 541–42), in a rare criticism of Aristotle, voices doubt that it can be with different parts of the soul that we contemplate necessary and contingent things, arguing that it is by the same power that we understand both what is perfect and what is imperfect in the genus of truth, by the same sight we see objects that are both corruptible and incorruptible, and by the same power of intellect we grasp both substances and accidents. Likewise, "Natural science is concerned not only with necessary and incorruptible things but with corruptible and contingent things." Saint Thomas tries to help Aristotle out of the difficulty by arguing that the real distinction in play here is between intellect that grasps principles of all kinds and the "sensory power of judgment which collates particular impressions," but this is not the distinction Aristotle purports to be drawing in 6.1.

8 · In the debate between "intellectualists" and "nonintellectualists" in Aristotle scholarship, this is the solution proposed by members of the latter camp such as Fortenbaugh (1969 and 1991) and Moss (2011), both of whom cite good evidence on their side but neither of whom explains what Aristotle means when he speaks of the emotions obeying reason.

9 · Saint Thomas (1964, para. 1131).

10 · This passage is one of the ones that provoke the worst trouble for "intellectualists," who claim that it is not desire but reason that gives the ultimate end for action.

11 · Ackrill (1978, esp. 598) argues that desire or *orexis* is generally oriented toward results that are distinct from the actions that secure them, and charges that Aristotle did not think enough about the relation between motivating desires and the acts that they motivate. Allan (1977, 75–76), by contrast, seems to take the desire to act nobly as the important desire in moral action, but he regards it as merely formal and empty until *phronēsis* grasps what is good and gives commands to it. He argues that "until such a conception is present, desire will have no object." The difficulty he has in pressing Aristotle into this intellectualist mold is seen above all in his strange claim that when Aristotle says that "thought itself moves nothing," he means only that theoretical wisdom alone moves nothing, and that *phronēsis* is quite sufficient alone to bring action about. Against this, nonintellectualists such as Fortenbaugh (1969) maintain that the desire for the noble is *the* source of moral action, to which reason contributes only the means, but this leaves open again the question of how the correct end is given any specificity.

12 · Consider in this connection that at 1094a9–16 Aristotle describes the *praxis* of horsemanship as being for the sake of the end pursued by the architectonic art of generalship.

13 · Ackrill (1978, 595), as he himself notes, is one of the few commentators who face the real difficulty "that actions often or always are productions and productions often or always are actions."

14 · Thus Burnet (1900, 255) equates Aristotle's use of *nous* in 6.2 with *dianoia*, and

Joachim (1951, 173) with both *dianoia* and *logos*. The same two meanings of *nous* may be seen in Aristotle's *Posterior Analytics*.

15 · Cf. *Metaphysics* 1015a20–b16 on different meanings of necessity.

16 · Contrast Aristotle's statement in the first chapter of *On the Soul* that the proper subject of one who studies nature is bodily beings in all that they do and undergo.

17 · Saint Thomas (1964, 555) is troubled by the gap but attributes it to the thought that particulars as such are of interest to us only in practical affairs.

18 · In *Posterior Analytics* 2.19 he also links them by saying that both are grounded in experience.

19 · Aristotle's statement here that active wisdom guides good deliberation about "living well as a whole" is one of the passages that best shows the limitations of the nonintellectualist reading of the *Ethics*, according to which the ends of action are determined solely by moral virtue and reason is solely instrumental. Thus Moss (2011, 225) is forced to interpret this line as saying that active wisdom is skillful at determining means to whatever ends one might desire in any area of life. Her article, with its telling criticisms of the "intellectualist" position and its brave attempt to defend the "nonintellectualist" position consistently, is helpful in demonstrating the impossibility of fitting all the evidence into either paradigm.

20 · I am indebted to Sparshott (1994, 211) for this observation.

21 · Stewart (1892, 2: 48) hastens to assure us that by the "opining" part Aristotle means merely the "calculating" part of 6.1. Rassow (1874, 43–44) and Ebert (2010, 139–40) are both more troubled, observing the very different domains Aristotle gave to opining and choice in 3.2.

22 · This connection of active wisdom to opinion recalls the end of Plato's *Meno*, where Socrates, also citing the example of Pericles, claims that the political virtue of such men cannot be taught—hence Pericles was unable to educate his sons in it—because it is fundamentally a matter of correct opinion and not knowledge.

23 · Consider, by contrast to this breezy affirmation, Aristotle's discussion of the principle of noncontradiction at *Metaphysics Gamma*, which he defends by turning the tables on the skeptic and showing that to make any argument at all, the skeptic must assume that principle to be true. As Burger (2008) observes, "Such a strategy of demonstration by refutation would not have been necessary, it seems, if this first principle of reasoning could have been declared the self-evident object of an intellectual intuition, and if it is not, nothing else would be a more likely candidate" (188).

24 · Stewart (1892, 2.33–34) makes this suggestion. Alternatively, Saint Thomas (1964, para. 1178) attributes the omission to Aristotle's subsuming art under active wisdom and Burnet (1900, 265) to his subsuming it under wisdom, both thereby implicitly acknowledging that the lines Aristotle draws between his five modes of knowing may be much less sharp than they at first appear.

25 · Sparshott (1994, 217).

26 · In his also dark but in many ways more down-to-earth account in *Posterior Analytics* 2.19, Aristotle attributes the grasp of the first principles of the sciences to experience, working on the basis of some kind of innate capacity. However, he also goes on to say that the first principles are grasped by *nous*, which is unerring.

27 · Herodotus *History* 2.53.

28 · Plato in *Republic* 475b–85b gives a similarly universal scope to wisdom.

29 · As Burger (2008) remarks, "We might wonder why the very human issue of honor has slipped into a description of the objects of knowledge that are supposed to transcend human concerns" (119).

30 · See esp. Plutarch *Life of Pericles* 4–6.

31 · This passage may also be compared to the digression in Plato's *Theaetetus*, where Socrates paints for Theodorus an image of the philosopher as sublimely indifferent to and even naïve regarding the affairs of the city, a portrait that, as Burger (2008, 110) observes, is in striking contrast to Socrates himself.

32 · Trendelenburg (1855, 373) deletes the words *koupha kai* in line 20, thus removing the ambiguity and assigning to this person only knowledge of the conclusion that poultry is healthy.

33 · Thus Stewart (1892, 2: 61) reads it, taking *tautēn* as referring to the implied phrase *tēn kath' hekasta phronēsin*.

34 · As Sparshott (1994: 213) puts it, the universal element in moral virtue in Aristotle always appears in connection with law and politics, not with universal principles of morality that can be codified. Natali (2014, 190) also observes Aristotle's avoidance of the term *katholou* in describing the work of *phronēsis*.

35 · Grant (1885, 2: 168) and Ebert (2010, 142) charge that there is a category error here, since active wisdom is a faculty of the mind and *politike* merely one of the divisions of the sciences or arts. The shift they note is, I submit, just one of many indications that Aristotle is not serious about dividing the mind into parts or faculties or even perfectly distinct virtues but is rather describing its many characteristic activities.

36 · Cf. Plato *Republic* 433a; *Gorgias* 526c.

37 · Wagner (1844, 401).

38 · For the former, see Joachim (1951, 208 ff.), Ando (1971), and Mele (1981); for the latter see Anscombe (1957) and Broadie (1988, 245–47). Without attributing this error to Aristotle, McDowell (1999) makes a good argument as to why practical reasoning cannot generally take a syllogistic form. Two recent commentators who share my skepticism that Aristotle seriously intended the practical syllogism as an account of moral reasoning are Segvic (2011, 165–66) and Natali (2014, 190).

39 · Burnet (1900) takes the *horoi* as "the definitions (*horos = horismos*) which are the starting points of every science" (274).

40 · Saint Thomas (1964, 2: 384–85) and Stewart (1892, 2: 75–76) take it in the former sense, which fits better with the passage in *On the Soul* but fails to account for the word *hoti* in 1142a28. Burnet (1900, 272) and most other commentators take it in the latter sense.

41 · Reading τι with the majority of the MSS, instead of Bywater's (1894) τὸ in line 33.

42 · Burnet (1900, 277) and Greenwood (1909, 65) take it in the latter sense, thereby avoiding what I agree is an unnecessary contradiction with 1144a7–9.

43 · See especially Sorabji (1980a) and Russell (2014).

44 · He also refers to medicine as a science at 1094a6–8 and 1094a16–18 and appears to use art and science interchangeably at 1097a4–8.

45 · As Segvic (2011, 175–76) notes, Aristotle treats all of these qualities as fundamentally virtues of understanding that are as such discriminating: he does not praise sympathy or compassion or forgiveness toward everyone under all circumstances.

46 · Grant (1885, 2: 179–80) notes the shift and charges that our philosopher has gotten himself confused.

47 · Rassow (1874, 31) and Bywater (1892) propose placing that sentence after the following one.

48 · Burnet (1900, 281) thus suggests either bracketing the words "or active wisdom" in that sentence or taking the term to be used only "in its popular sense."

49 · Following the suggested reading of Stewart (1892, 98) and Burnet (1900, 283).

50 · Zeller (1897, 187–88) and A. D. Smith (1996), among others, note the seriousness of the circularity Aristotle here involves himself in. Grant (1885, 186) observes the strangeness and apparent "inversion" in assigning to virtue the intellectual function of apprehending the end of action.

51 · Stewart (1892, 2: 102) defends this reading against that of commentators who, influenced by 1143b13–14, take the eye of the soul to be active virtue. Burnet (1900, 284) argues that the eye must be intellect, citing 1096b29, but as Aristotle has not mentioned intellect in the current passage, Burnet's reading makes no sense of the word "this" in 1144a30.

52 · Ramsauer (1878) objects to the words "any chance thing" as inappropriate to a discussion of virtue or what is best.

53 · This problem with moral virtue as a source of guidance is noted by Cooper (1975, 114).

54 · Stewart (1892, 2: 110) and Burger (2008, 127) both note the unfairness.

55 · As Burger (2008) puts it, we see now that the target of action is understood differently by the man of moral virtue and by the philosopher. "Phronēsis, then, must have a double face, turned in one direction towards the ends of ethical virtue and in another towards *sophia* as happiness." If moral virtue makes its own action an end, the lover of wisdom cannot be a *phronimos* in the strict sense. But if *phronēsis* is concerned with the true good of man, and that is the activity of wisdom, then "the philosopher would be the true *phronimos*" (112, 129).

56 · Sorabji (1980a, 211–14) also entertains the possibility that Aristotle may be offering a dual account of virtue, a lower, habit-formed type and a higher one fully guided by true reason. In support of such a division he cites Plato's discussion of merely civic as opposed to true virtue at *Laws* 653a–c, 643b–45c, 659c–e, 951b; *Republic* 402a, 518e, 619c; and *Phaedo* 82a–b; as well as Aristotle's discussion of the inferior virtues of women, slaves, and subjects in *Politics* 1.5, 1.13, and 3.4. I think all of these passages are good support for the idea of a dual account of virtue in both authors, but we must question whether either ultimately places the moral virtue even of most gentlemen on the rational side of the dividing line.

Chapter 6

1 · The traditional translations for *enkrateia* and *akrasia* are continence and incontinence, which have ceased to be used in English in their original broad sense. The other translations that are commonly used are strength of will and weakness of will, which certainly do have currency in modern English, but which presuppose the existence of the will as a separate faculty and to that extent import alien ideas into Aristotle's thought, and moral strength and moral weakness. The latter terms turn out to express rather well Aristotle's theory of *enkrateia* and *akrasia* and their connection with moral opinions, but they do not fit the usage of Socrates in Xenophon's *Memorabilia*, where *enkrateia* is a simpler and not necessarily moral phenomenon. To capture the full meaning of the Greek terms without prejudging the relation of *enkrateia* and *akrasia* to moral opinion, I translate them as "self-control" and "lack of self-control."

2 · Consider also *NE* 1154b20–31, 1177b1–78a8; cf. Aristotle *Metaphysics* 12.7 and 12.9.

3 · See Plutarch's "Life and Poetry of Homer," 133: "Man is between god and beast. Homer considers the peak of virtue to be divinity, the extreme of vice brutishness, as later Aristotle held" (quoted in Stewart 1892, 117).

4 · As Aristotle says in *Metaphysics* 995b2–3, a philosophic inquiry requires that all the various arguments be heard in turn, like contending parties to a lawsuit. *Pace* Stewart (1892, 123–24), there is nothing in any of Aristotle's discussions of method to guarantee that the final truth arrived at will be similar to the stories told by any of the original contestants or popular opinions, even though it must begin from the evidence they present. But Aristotle makes it clear he will depart from the most widely held opinions only when forced to do so by contradictions between them and even within some of them. According to the Aldine Scholiast and the Paraphrist, quoted by Grant (1885, 194), the *duscherē* needing resolution (1145b6) are false opinions; Ramsauer and Grant (1885, 194–95), citing 1146b6–8, argue that they are tensions between opinions that call for further resolution, but again, this may occur by rejecting some opinions altogether.

5 · For an eloquent example of this view see Jefferson (1944, 395–407).

6 · As Burnet (1900, 292) observes, *sōphrōn* and *enkratēs* are often used interchangeably, and he claims that even Plato falls into this carelessness at *Republic* 430e, where he says that "moderation is a certain order and self-control regarding pleasures and desires." This supposed carelessness of Plato's may show instead that Plato would have regarded Aristotle's glowing characterization of moderation in the *NE* as an edifying exaggeration.

7 · Cf. Xenophon *Memorabilia* 3.9.4–5. This paradoxical claim is close to but not quite the same as the claim Aristotle considered in 6.13 that all of the virtues are forms of active wisdom, for if opinion is sovereign, all one would need to be virtuous would be a firm, unwavering grasp on correct opinion.

8 · Plato does in *Definitions* 416a acknowledge the reality of *akrasia*, defining it as a failure to follow correct reason because of desire, without addressing the question of

whether correct reason is present in the form of knowledge or opinion when this occurs, or not present to the mind at all.

9 · Joachim (1951, 221) finds this opening unfair, since as he notes Aristotle will ultimately come around to essentially the Socratic position.

10 · Burnet (1900, 294) identifies those who hold this view with members of Plato's Academy and suggests that their basic error is to equate the degree of truth of a supposition with the degree of conviction with which it will be held. As we shall see, a refined version of this thesis is shared by Socrates, Plato, and Aristotle, but Aristotle evidently judges it to have become formulaic and abstract among Plato's followers.

11 · Compare, however, 1145b17–19: this would seem to be a point of especially strong popular ambivalence.

12 · Following Ramsauer (1878), Bywater (1892), and most editors, I accept MS Kb's omission of μὴ in 1146a35, as necessary to make sense of that line.

13 · Aristotle uses the word *theōria* to refer to his inquiry at 1146b14, a word he otherwise reserves chiefly for philosophical investigation, suggesting again that the study of self-control may be especially conducive to understanding human nature.

14 · He uses the word *epistēmē* for this practical knowledge, confirming our suspicion that *epistēmē* extends far beyond a knowledge of permanent necessities.

15 · I Follow the reading of MSS Mb and Γ here against Burnet.

16 · Burnet (1900, 299) raises the interesting question of whether, if an agent is really unaware of countervailing arguments, his act would not have to be considered involuntary on the grounds of ignorance.

17 · E.g., Burnet (1900) and Ostwald (1962).

18 · Most commentators, fascinated by the subtleties of Aristotle's syllogistic reasoning, seem to see the chief problem of *akrasia* as the purely intellectual one of failing to draw or recognize the correct conclusion, for example that the salad is the healthy lunch. See, e.g., Stewart (1892, 150–51). I believe Aristotle starts with what seems like a simple lapse of syllogistic reasoning only to make more pressing the question of how such elementary errors could ever happen.

19 · Plato *Theaetetus* 150b–51a; cf. 197a–98a. For Aristotle on potential knowledge in general, see *Metaphysics* 1048a32–35; *Physics* 255a33–b5; *On the Soul* 412a22–28, 429b5–9. But moral knowledge is knowledge of a peculiar sort that is especially hard to actualize and keep actualized.

20 · Plato *Meno* 97d–98a.

21 · Mulhern (1974) is right to see, then, that a lack of thorough habituation is key to failings of self-control, and he helpfully characterizes lack of self-control as a disposition that is less well ingrained than the firm habits that characterize virtue and vice. What he does not recognize, however, is the extent to which the crucial habits are habits of thought.

22 · In a spectacular display of scholarly hubris, Cook-Wilson (1879, 48–56) argues that this whole chapter could not have been written by Aristotle or Eudemus or the author of the rest of book 7, because those authors regard *akrasia* as a straightforward conflict between reason and desire, whereas the author of 7.3 blurs the battle lines by speaking of passion as having its own reasons, and furthermore because those au-

thors reject the Socratic thesis, whereas at the end of 7.3 the author seems to concede its truth. Behind the hubris we see, however, a keener appreciation than most scholars have of how much is at stake in this chapter, and how much Aristotle's teaching here is pushing the reader to re-think what has come before.

23 · At the root of lapses of self-control, then, is not just reasoning that is logical but irrelevant, as Rassow (1874, 127–29) would have it, or reasoning that is passion's purely sophistical use of the practical syllogism, as Stewart (1892, 156) puts it, but reasoning about the good that is in some crucial sense correct. Most commentators do not see this.

24 · For other mentions of acting against choice, see 1150b30, 1151a7, 1151a29–b4, and 1152a17, in at least some of which the problem is not failing to implement a choice at all but failing to follow it consistently.

25 · Cook-Wilson (1879, 64–65) notes the problem that anger fits poorly in this list. On the other hand, consider Achilles' statement that anger is "sweeter than honey" (Homer *Iliad* 18.127–28).

26 · Without ever giving a full reason for this retraction of his blame of such things as greed, Aristotle does something similar in the *Politics*. In *Politics* 1.8–11, after endorsing the view that the spirit of moneymaking is ignoble, Aristotle nonetheless argues that a wise statesman (whose life is the acme of the morally active life) must give careful attention to cultivating his country's economy.

27 · Susemihl (1880) brackets this chapter as a mere repetition of material in 7.4.

28 · Saint Thomas (1964, 647) characteristically offers an interpretation that denies that any radical questions or problems are being raised. He says that the angry man makes a faulty application of a correct principle: he knows that injuries done should be punished, but he does not carefully heed reason's dictates about the amount and mode of punishment that are appropriate.

29 · Grant (1885) notes the problem and suggests that what gives anger a higher dignity than desire is the implicit or explicit presence of a principle of justice and the fact that "anger is a less immediately selfish passion than desire" (216). Significantly, however, Aristotle makes no such argument on anger's behalf; he is pressing us to consider whether its principle is not always defective.

30 · According to *Magna Moralia* 1202a23–27 this defense was successful.

31 · Cf. *Rhetoric* 1380a34.

32 · We have no independent evidence of such a statement by Heraclitus. What we do have is this: "To fight against anger is hard; for it buys what it wants at the price of the soul" Diels-Kranz (1951–52, frg. B85). Did Aristotle revise Heraclitus's words in a Socratic direction?

33 · Grant (1885, 219–20) observes that in this judgment Aristotle is expressing a characteristically Greek view against the biblical teaching that humanity is "desperately wicked."

34 · As Cook-Wilson (1879, 33, 73) observes, in both the *Nicomachean* and the *Eudemian* discussions of courage, *malakia* is associated with *deilia*, and *karteria* with *andreia*.

35 · I follow Bywater (1894) in adopting the reading of MS Lb here. For a good com-

ment on the textual difficulty, see Grant (1885, 227–28). Stewart's (1892, 206–7) effort to save the reading of most manuscripts shows the great awkwardness of doing so.

36 · Socrates adumbrates this problem with his ironic statement in Plato's *Republic* that the good guardian of the city must be like a philosophic dog (375d–76b), an oxymoron if ever there was one.

BIBLIOGRAPHY OF MODERN WORKS AND EDITIONS

Ackrill, J. L. 1999. "Aristotle on *Eudaimonia*." In Sherman 1999, 57–77.

———. 1978. "Aristotle on Action." *Mind* 87: 595–601.

Adams, John, and Thomas Jefferson. 1959. *The Adams-Jefferson Letters*. Ed. Lester Cappon. Chapel Hill, NC: University of North Carolina Press.

Adkins, Arthur W. H. 1960. *Merit and Responsibility: A Study in Greek Values*. Oxford: Clarendon Press.

Alfarabi. 2001. *The Philosophy of Plato and Aristotle*. Trans. Muhsin Mahdi. Rev. ed. Ithaca, NY: Cornell University Press.

Allan, Donald James. 1977. "Aristotle's Account of the Origin of Moral Principles." In Barnes et al. 1977, 72–78.

Anagnostopoulos, Georgios, ed. 2009. *A Companion to Aristotle*. Oxford: Blackwell.

Ando, Takaturo. 1971. *Aristotle's Theory of Practical Cognition*. The Hague: Martinus Nijhoff.

Anscombe, G. E. M. 1965. "Thought and Action in Aristotle." In Barnes et al. 1977, 61–71.

———. 1957. *Intention*. Cambridge, MA: Harvard University Press.

Anton, John P., and Anthony Preus, eds. 1991. *Essays in Ancient Greek Philosophy*, vol. 4: *Aristotle's Ethics*. Albany: SUNY Press.

Aspasias. 2006. *On Aristotle's Nicomachean Ethics 1–4, 7–8*. Trans. David Konstan. Ithaca, NY: Cornell University Press.

———. 1998. *The Earliest Extant Commentary on Aristotle's Ethics*. Ed. Antonina Alberti and R. W. Sharples. Berlin: Walter de Gruyter.

Barnes, Jonathan, Malcolm Schofield, and Richard Sorabji, eds. 1977. *Articles on Aristotle*, vol. 2: *Ethics and Politics*. London: Duckworth.

Bartlett, Robert. 2008. "Aristotle's Introduction to the Problem of Happiness: On Book I of the *Nicomachean Ethics*." *American Journal of Political Science* 52: 677–87.

Bartlett, Robert, and Susan Collins, trans. and ed. 2011. *Aristotle's Nicomachean Ethics*. Chicago: University of Chicago Press.

———, eds. 1999. *Action and Contemplation: Studies in the Moral and Political Thought of Aristotle*. Albany: SUNY Press.

Bodéüs, Richard. 1993. *The Political Dimensions of Aristotle's Ethics*. Trans. Jan Edward Garrett. Albany: SUNY Press.

Bolotin, David. 1999. "Aristotle on the Question of Evil." In Bartlett and Collins 1999, 159–70.

Brady, Michelle. 2005. "The Fearlessness of Courage." *Southern Journal of Philosophy* 43 (2): 189–211.

Brickhouse, Thomas C. 1991. "Roberts on Responsibility for Action and Character in the *Nicomachean Ethics*." *Ancient Philosophy* 11: 137–48.

Broadie, Sarah. 1991. *Ethics with Aristotle*. New York: Oxford University Press.

———. 1988. "The Problem of Practical Intellect in Aristotle's Ethics." *Boston Area Colloquium in Ancient Philosophy* 3: 229–52.

Burger, Ronna. 2008. *Aristotle's Dialogue with Socrates: On the Nicomachean Ethics*. Chicago: University of Chicago Press.

Burnet, John. 1900. *The Ethics of Aristotle*. London: Methuen.

———, ed. 1900–1907. *Platonis Opera*. 5 vols. Oxford: Clarendon Press.

Burnyeat, M. F. 1980. "Aristotle on Learning to Be Good." In Rorty 1980, 69–92.

Bywater, Ingram, ed. 1894. *Aristotelis Ethica Nicomachea*. Oxford: Clarendon Press.

———. 1892. *Contributions to the Textual Criticism of Aristotle's Nicomachean Ethics*. Oxford: Oxford University Press. Rpt., New York: Arno Press, 1973.

Chappell, T. D. J. 1995. *Aristotle and Augustine on Freedom: Two Theories of Freedom, Voluntary Action and Akrasia*. New York: St. Martin's Press.

Charney, Ann. 1988. "Spiritedness and Piety in Aristotle." In *Understanding the Political Spirit: Philosophic Investigations from Socrates to Nietzsche*, ed. Catherine Zuckert, 67–87. New Haven: Yale University Press.

Cicero. 1975. *De Officiis*. Trans. Walter Miller. Cambridge, MA: Harvard University Press, Loeb Classical Library.

Collins, Susan. 2009. *Aristotle and the Rediscovery of Citizenship*. Cambridge: Cambridge University Press.

Cook-Wilson, J. 1879. *Aristotelian Studies: On the Structure of the Seventh Book of the Nicomachean Ethics, Chapters I–X*. Oxford: Clarendon Press.

Cooper, John M. 1999. *Reason and Emotion: Essays on Ancient Moral Psychology and Ethical Theory*. Princeton: Princeton University Press.

———. 1989. "Some Remarks on Aristotle's Moral Psychology." *Southern Journal of Philosophy* 27: 25–42.

———. 1975. *Reason and Human Good in Aristotle*. Cambridge, MA: Harvard University Press. Rpt., Indianapolis: Hackett, 1986.

Curren, Randall R. 1989. "The Contribution of *Nicomachean Ethics* 3.5 to Aristotle's Theory of Responsibility." *History of Philosophy Quarterly* 6: 261–77.

Curzer, Howard J. 2012. *Aristotle and the Virtues*. Oxford: Oxford University Press.

Diels, Hermann, and Walter Kranz, eds. 1951–52. *Die Fragmente der Vorsokratiker*. 6th ed. 3 vols. Berlin: Weidmann.

Dirlmeier, Franz. 1956. *Aristoteles Nikomachische Ethik, übersetzt und kommontiert.* Berlin: Akademie-Verlag.

Duff, Antony. 1987. "Aristotelian Courage." *Ratio* 29: 2–15.

Ebert, Theodor. 2010. "*Phronesis.* Notes on a Concept of Aristotle's *Ethics* (Book VI, chapters 5, 8–13)." In *Aristotle's "Nicomachean Ethics,"* ed. Otfried Hoffe, 133–48. Leiden: Brill.

Echeñique, Javier. 2012. *Aristotle's Ethics and Moral Responsibility.* Cambridge: Cambridge University Press.

Everson, Stephen. 1990. "Aristotle's Compatibilism in the *Nicomachean Ethics.*" *Ancient Philosophy* 10: 81–103.

Fortenbaugh, William W. 1991. "Aristotle's Distinction between Moral Virtue and Practical Wisdom." In Anton and Preus 1991, 97–106.

———. 1969. "Aristotle: Emotion and Moral Virtue." *Arethusa* 2: 163–85.

———. 1965. "Τὰ πρὸς τὸ τέλος and Syllogistic Vocabulary in Aristotle's Ethics." *Phronesis* 10: 191–201.

Fossheim, Hallvard. 2011. "Justice in the *Nicomachean Ethics* Book V." In Miller 2011, 254–75.

Furley, David J. 1977. "Aristotle on the Voluntary." In Barnes et al. 1977, 47–60.

Gauthier, R.-A. 1967. "On the Nature of Aristotle's *Ethics.*" In *Aristotle's Ethics: Issues and Interpretations*, ed. James J. Walsh and Henry Shapiro, 10–29. Belmont, CA: Wadsworth.

Gauthier, R.-A., and Jolif, J. Y. 1958–59. *L'Éthique à Nicomaque.* Louvain: Publications Universitaires de Louvain.

Gooch, Paul W. 1983. "Aristotle and the Happy Dead." *Classical Philology* 78: 112–16.

Grant, Sir Alexander. 1885. *The Ethics of Aristotle, Illustrated with Essays and Notes.* 4th ed. 2 vols. London: Longmans, Green.

Greenwood, L. H. G. 1909. *Aristotle Nicomachean Ethics Book Six with Essays, Notes, and Translation.* Cambridge: Cambridge University Press.

Grimal, Pierre, ed. 1986. *The Dictionary of Classical Mythology.* Trans. A. R. Maxwell-Hyslop. Oxford: Basil Blackwell.

Hanley, Ryan Patrick. 2002. "Aristotle on the Greatness of Greatness of Soul." *History of Political Thought* 23: 1–20.

Hardie, W. F. R. 1980. *Aristotle's Ethical Theory.* 2nd ed. Oxford: Clarendon Press.

———. 1979. "Aristotle on the Best Life for a Man." *Philosophy* 54: 35–50.

———. 1978. "Magnanimity in Aristotle's *Ethics.*" *Phronesis* 7: 63–79.

———. 1965. "The Final Good in Aristotle's *Ethics.*" *Philosophy* 40: 277–95.

Heil, John. 1996. "Why Is Aristotle's Brave Man So Frightened? The Paradox of Courage in the *Eudemian Ethics.*" *Apeiron* 29: 47–74.

Howland, Jacob. 2002. "Aristotle's Great-Souled Man." *Review of Politics* 64: 27–56.

Huby, Pamela. 1967. "The First Discovery of the Freewill Problem." *Philosophy* 42: 353–62.

Irwin, Terence H. 2010. "The Sense and Reference of *Kalon* in Aristotle." *Classical Philology* 105: 381–96.

———. 1999. "Permanent Happiness: Aristotle and Solon." In Sherman 1999, 1–34.

———. 1988. *Aristotle's First Principles.* Oxford: Clarendon Press.

———, trans. and ed. 1985. *Nicomachean Ethics.* Indianapolis: Hackett.

———. 1980. "Reason and Responsibility in Aristotle." In Rorty 1980, 117–56.

Jaffa, Harry. 1952. *Thomism and Aristotelianism: A Study of the Commentary by Thomas Aquinas on the "Nicomachean Ethics."* Chicago: University of Chicago Press. Rpt., Westport, CT: Greenwood Press, 1979.

Jefferson, Thomas. 1944. *The Life and Selected Letters of Thomas Jefferson.* Ed. Adrienne Koch and William Peden. New York: Modern Library.

Joachim, Harold Henry. 1951. *Aristotle: The Nicomachean Ethics, a Commentary.* Oxford: Clarendon Press.

Kenny, Anthony. 1979. *Aristotle's Theory of the Will.* New Haven: Yale University Press.

Kosman, L. A. 1980. "Being Properly Affected: Virtues and Feelings in Aristotle's Ethics." In Rorty 1980, 103–16.

Kraut, Richard, ed. 2006. *Blackwell Guide to Aristotle's Nicomachean Ethics.* London: Blackwell.

Kraut, Richard. 1999. *Aristotle on the Human Good: An Overview.* In Sherman 1999, 79–104.

———. 1979. "Two Conceptions of Happiness." *Philosophical Review* 88: 167–97.

Lear, Gabriel Richardson. 2009. "Happiness and the Structure of Ends." In Anagnostopoulos 2009, 387–403.

———. 2004. *Happy Lives and the Highest Good: An Essay on Aristotle's Nicomachean Ethics.* Princeton: Princeton University Press.

Leighton, Stephen R. 1988. "Aristotle's Courageous Passions." *Phronesis* 33: 76–99.

Luthra, Yanning. 2015. "Aristotle on Choosing Virtuous Action for Its Own Sake." *Pacific Philosophical Quarterly* 96: 423–41.

Marsilius of Padua. 2005. *The Defender of the Peace.* Ed. and trans. Annabel Brett. Cambridge: Cambridge University Press.

McDowell, J. 1999. "Virtue and Reason." In Sherman 1999, 121–43.

Meikle, Scott. 1995. *Aristotle's Economic Thought.* Oxford: Clarendon Press.

Mele, Alfred R. 1981. "Choice and Virtue in the *Nicomachean Ethics.*" *Journal of the History of Philosophy* 19: 405–23.

Meyer, Susan Sauvé. 1993. *Aristotle on Moral Responsibility: Character and Cause.* Oxford: Blackwell.

Miller, Jon, ed. 2011. *Aristotle's Nicomachean Ethics: A Critical Guide.* Cambridge: Cambridge University Press.

Moline, Jon N. 1989. "Aristotle on Praise and Blame." *Archiv für Geschichte der Philosophie* 71: 283–302.

Moss, Jessica. 2011. "'Virtue Makes the Goal Right': Virtue and Phronesis in Aristotle's Ethics." *Phronesis* 56: 204–61.

Mulhern, J. J. 1974. "Aristotle and the Socratic Paradoxes." *Journal of the History of Ideas* 35: 293–99.

Nagel, Thomas. 1972. "Aristotle on Eudaimonia." *Phronesis* 17: 252–59.

Natali, Carlo. 2014. "The Book on Wisdom." In Polansky 2014a, 180–202.

Nussbaum, Martha. 1986. *The Fragility of Goodness: Luck and Ethics in Greek Tragedy and Philosophy*. Cambridge: Cambridge University Press.

O'Connor, David K. 1999. "The Ambitions of Aristotle's Audience and the Activist Ideal of Happiness." In Bartlett and Collins 1999, 107–29.

Ostwald, Martin, trans. and ed. 1962. *Nicomachean Ethics*. New York: Macmillan.

Pakaluk, Michael. 2005. *Aristotle's Nicomachean Ethics: An Introduction*. Cambridge: Cambridge University Press.

Pangle, Lorraine. 2014. *Virtue Is Knowledge: The Moral Foundations of Socratic Political Philosophy*. Chicago: University of Chicago Press.

———. 2003. *Aristotle and the Philosophy of Friendship*. Cambridge: Cambridge University Press.

Pangle, Thomas L. 2013. *Aristotle's Teaching in the Politics*. Chicago: University of Chicago Press.

Pears, David. 2004. "The Anatomy of Courage." *Social Research* 71: 1–12.

———. 1980. "Courage as a Mean." In Rorty 1980, 171–87.

Polansky, Ronald, ed. 2014a. *The Cambridge Companion to Aristotle's Nicomachean Ethics*. Cambridge: Cambridge University Press.

———. 2014b. "Giving Justice Its Due." In Polansky 2014a, 151–79.

Price, A. W. 1986. "Aristotle's Ethical Holism." *Mind* 89: 338–52.

Pritzl, Kurt. 1983. "Aristotle and Happiness after Death: *Nicomachean Ethics* 1.10–11." *Classical Philology* 78: 101–11.

Rabieh, Linda. 2006. *Plato and the Virtue of Courage*. Baltimore, MD: Johns Hopkins University Press.

Rackham, H., trans. and ed. 1975. *Nicomachean Ethics*. Cambridge, MA: Harvard University Press, Loeb Classical Library.

———, trans. and ed. 1961. *Eudemian Ethics*. Cambridge, MA: Harvard University Press, Loeb Classical Library.

Ramsauer, Gottfried. 1878. *Aristotelis Ethica Nicomachea*. Leipzig: Teubner.

Rassow, Hermann. 1874. *Forschungen über die Nikomachische Ethik des Aristoteles*. Weimar: Hermann Böhlau.

Reeve, C. D. C. 2013. *Aristotle on Practical Wisdom: Nicomachean Ethics VI, Translated with an Introduction, Analysis, and Commentary*. Cambridge, MA: Harvard University Press.

———. 2006. "Aristotle on the Virtues of Thought." In Kraut 2006, 198–217.

Roberts, Jean. 1989. "Aristotle on Responsibility for Action and Character." *Ancient Philosophy* 9: 23–36.

Rogers, Kelly. 1994. "Aristotle on the Motive of Courage." *Southern Journal of Philosophy* 32: 303–13.

Rorty, Amélie, ed. 1980. *Essays on Aristotle's Ethics*. Berkeley: University of California Press.

Ross, David, ed. 1959. Aristotle. *Ars Rhetorica*. Oxford: Clarendon Press.

———, ed. 1957. Aristotle. *Politica*. Oxford: Clarendon Press.

———. 1949. *Aristotle: A Complete Exposition of His Works and Thought*. 5th ed.. London: Methuen.

———, ed. 1925. Aristotle. *Nicomachean Ethics*. Oxford: Oxford University Press; World's Classic Paperbacks, 1980.

Russell, Daniel. 2014. "Phronesis and the Virtues (*NE* vi 12–13)." In Polansky 2014a, 203–20.

Sachs, Joe, trans and ed. 2002. Aristotle, *Nicomachean Ethics*. Newburyport, MA: Focus.

Salkever, Stephen. 2007. "Teaching the Questions: Aristotle's Philosophical Pedagogy in the *Nicomachean Ethics* and the *Politics*." *Review of Politics* 69: 192–214.

———. 1986. "Women, Soldiers, Citizens: Plato and Aristotle on the Politics of Virility." *Polity* 19: 232–53.

Sanford, J. J. 2010. "Are You Man Enough? Aristotle and Courage." *International Philosophical Quarterly* 50: 431–45.

Segvic, Heda. 2011. "Deliberation and Choice in Aristotle." In Michael Pakaluk and Giles Pearson, eds., *Moral Psychology and Human Action in Aristotle*. Oxford: Oxford University Press.

Sherman, Nancy, ed. 1999. *Aristotle's Ethics: Critical Essays*. Lanham, MD: Rowman and Littlefield.

Simpson, Peter, trans. and ed. 2014. *The Great Ethics of Aristotle*. New Brunswick, NJ: Transaction.

Smith, A. D. 1996. "Character and Intellect in Aristotle's Ethics." *Phronesis* 41: 56–74.

Smith, Thomas W. 2001. *Revaluing Ethics: Aristotle's Dialectical Pedagogy*. Albany: SUNY Press.

Sorabji, Richard. 1980a. "Aristotle on the Role of Intellect in Virtue." In Rorty 1980, 201–19.

———. 1980b. *Necessity, Cause, and Blame*. London: Duckworth.

Sparshott, Francis. 1994. *Taking Life Seriously: A Study of the Argument of the Nicomachean Ethics*. Toronto: University of Toronto Press.

Stewart, John. A. 1892. *Notes on the Nicomachean Ethics of Aristotle*. 2 vols. Oxford: Clarendon Press.

Strauss, Leo. 1964. *The City and Man*. Chicago: Rand McNally.

———. 1953. *Natural Right and History*. Chicago: University of Chicago Press.

———. 1952. *Persecution and the Art of Writing*. Glencoe, IL: Free Press.

Susemihl, Franz. 1880. *Aristotelis Ethica Nicomachea*. Leipzig: Teubner.

Tessitore, Aristide. 1996. *Reading Aristotle's Ethics: Virtue, Rhetoric, and Political Philosophy*. Albany: SUNY Press.

Thomas Aquinas, Saint. 1964. *Commentary on the Nicomachean Ethics*. Tran. C. I. Litzinger. 2 vols. Chicago: Henry Regnery. Online at http://dhspriory.org/thomas/Ethics.htm.

Trendelenburg, Friedrich A. 1855. *Historische Beiträge zur Philosophie*, vol. 2: *Vermischte Abhandlungen*. Berlin: G. Bethge.

Tuozzo, Thomas M. 1991. "Aristotelian Deliberation Is Not of Ends." In Anton and Preus 1991, 193–212.

Urmson, J. O. 1988. *Aristotle's Ethics*. Oxford: Basil Blackwell.

Vander Waerdt, Paul A. 1985. "The Political Intention of Aristotle's Moral Philosophy." *Ancient Philosophy* 5: 77–89.

Wagner, Fridericus G. 1844. *Poetarum Tragicorum Graecorum Fragmenta*. 2 vols. Wrocław: Impensis Trewendti et Granieri.

Walter, J. 1874. *Die Lehre von der praktischen Vernunft in der griechischen Philosophie*. Jena: Mauke's Verlag.

Ward, Lee. 2001. "Nobility and Necessity: The Problem of Courage in Aristotle's *Nicomachean Ethics*." *American Political Science Review* 95: 71–83.

Whiting, Jennifer. 2002. "Eudaimonia, External Results, and Choosing Virtuous Actions for Themselves." *Philosophy and Phenomenological Research* 65: 270–90.

Wiggins, David. 1980. "Deliberation and Practical Reason." In Rorty 1980, 221–40.

Williams, Bernard. 1985. *Ethics and the Limits of Philosophy*. Cambridge, MA: Harvard University Press.

———. 1980. "Justice as a Virtue." In Rorty 1980, 189–99.

Young, Charles. 2009. "Courage." In Anagnostopoulos 2009, 442–56.

Zavily, Andrei, and Michael Aristidou. 2014. "Courage: A Modern Look at an Ancient Virtue." *Journal of Military Ethics* 13: 174–89.

Zeller, Eduard. 1897. *Aristotle and the Earlier Peripatetics*. Trans. B. F. C. Costelloe and J. H. Muirhead. London: Longmans, Green.

INDEX